Practical Artificial Intelligence with Swift

From Fundamental Theory to Development of AI-Driven Apps

Mars Geldard, Jonathon Manning, Paris Buttfield-Addison, and Tim Nugent

Beijing · Boston · Farnham · Sebastopol · Tokyo

Practical Artificial Intelligence with Swift

by Mars Geldard, Jonathon Manning, Paris Buttfield-Addison, and Tim Nugent

Copyright © 2020 Secret Lab. All rights reserved.

Published by O'Reilly Media, Inc., 1005 Gravenstein Highway North, Sebastopol, CA 95472.

O'Reilly books may be purchased for educational, business, or sales promotional use. Online editions are also available for most titles (*http://oreilly.com*). For more information, contact our corporate/institutional sales department: 800-998-9938 or *corporate@oreilly.com* .

Acquisition Editor: Rachel Roumeliotis
Developmental Editor: Michele Cronin
Production Editor: Nan Barber
Copyeditor: Kim Cofer
Proofreader: Octal Publishing, LLC

Indexer: WordCo Indexing Services, Inc.
Interior Designer: David Futato
Cover Designer: Karen Montgomery
Illustrator: Rebecca Demarest

October 2019: First Edition

Revision History for the First Edition
2019-10-18: First Release

See *http://oreilly.com/catalog/errata.csp?isbn=9781492044819* for release details.

The O'Reilly logo is a registered trademark of O'Reilly Media, Inc. *Practical Artificial Intelligence with Swift*, the cover image, and related trade dress are trademarks of O'Reilly Media, Inc.

978-1-492-04481-9

[LSI]

Praise for *Practical Artificial Intelligence with Swift*

In the long run, the vast majority of AI will be consumed not in data centers, but where the data actually are—on billions of real-world devices. With its combination of speed and expressiveness, Swift has emerged as the language of choice to enable this transition. This book provides a fantastic introduction to the tools forming the foundation of the next decade of AI.

—Dr. Jameson Toole, Cofounder and CTO of Fritz AI

The importance of bananas and apples to machine learning developers cannot be overstated. Fortunately this book has a sufficiency of both, or at least, enough to be getting on with. So if, like me, you're starting to suspect that the future of machine learning is on device, this book is a good place to get started.

—Dr. Alasdair Allan, Babilim Light Industries

Over the past several years, AI has transitioned from academia and science fiction to a pragmatic technology for solving real-world problems. This book shows how to bring AI right to the palm of your hand, implementing ML capabilities that are only now becoming possible. I'm incredibly excited to see what readers do with what they learn from this book.

—Chris Devers, Technical Lead of Sustaining Engineering,
EditShare

Table of Contents

Part II.   Tasks

Part III.   Beyond

Preface

Welcome to *Practical Artificial Intelligence with Swift*.

This book takes a task-based approach to practical implementations of artificial intelligence (AI) using Swift. We do this because we think that you shouldn't need to dive deep into complicated mathematics and algorithms in order to have clever AI- and machine learning-driven features in your iOS application. AI shouldn't be a specialist area that's available only to AI experts. AI should be accessible.

We live in a world where these techniques are becoming more than commonplace. They're becoming part of the fabric of how we interact with computers. Because of the incredible power of machine learning, and its ability to impact, benefit, influence, and control human beings, it's as important for people to be able to have knowledge over how to build and understand artificial intelligence as it was to know how to operate a computer.

To that end, this book is designed to give you a practical understanding of common machine learning tasks. With these, you'll be able to build better tools, and understand the behaviour of the tools used by others in the wider world. We're glad you're here. Let's build the machine.

Resources Used in This Book

We recommend following along with the book by writing code yourself as you progress through each chapter. If you become stuck, or just want to archive a copy of the code, you can find what you need via our website (*http://www.aiwithswift.com*).

Audience and Approach

This book is written for people who already know how to program in Swift, and want to learn about the specific features and techniques that power machine learning. This isn't a book that will teach you the basics of programming, which means that the examples will expect a reasonable familiarity with the language.

In addition to using Swift, we'll occasionally dip into Python from time to time. Python is incredibly common in the world of machine learning and artificial intelligence. The meat of the book is in Swift, though, and we explain why whenever we're using Python. We're going to remind you about this a few times.

Finally, we also assume that you're fairly comfortable navigating macOS and iOS as a user, and that you have access to a Mac to develop on, as well as an iOS device to test on, for the tasks that require certain sensors, like motion tracking or analysing the camera.

Organization of This Book

This book is divided into three parts.

In Part I, *Fundamentals and Tools*, we introduce the fundamental ideas behind machine learning and artificial intelligence. We set you up with the languages and tools you'll be using, and get you ready to build useful things.

In Part II, *Tasks*, we visit a wide range of interesting topics, ranging from computer vision, audio, motion, and language. For each topic, we'll present and build an app that highlights various techniques and APIs; at the end of each chapter, you'll have a complete working demo app that shows off a practical task that your code can now accomplish.

In Part III, *Beyond*, we take a look behind the curtain, and examine the techniques that power the apps in Part II in detail. We'll look closely at the theory of machine learning, and provide a deeper understanding of what it is that your device is actually doing.

Using This Book

We want this book to be deeply founded in the *practical*. Because of this, we've structured it around the practical *tasks* that you might want to do when dealing with artificial intelligence and Swift. We've split the book into three parts.

Part I discusses Swift and AI and the task-based approach to AI that we're taking for the book (you're reading a chapter in that part right now), the tools you can use for Swift and AI (that's Chapter 2), and how and why to approach the datasets you use for your *practical* artificial intelligences (that's the third chapter in this part).

Part II, chapter by chapter, explores the different domains for which AI can be integrated into your Swift apps from a thematic point of view: vision-related tasks (Chapter 4), audio tasks (Chapter 5), language and text tasks (Chapter 6), motion and gestural tasks (Chapter 7), augmentation tasks (Chapter 8) for generating and recommending things, and beyond (Chapter 9) to explore the more advanced tools and frameworks we touched on at the end of the first part. We outline what each of the tasks entails in the next section.

Part III explores how the AI *methods* actually work (Chapter 10), how the practical tasks we made in Part II work under the hood (Chapter 11), and finally how you can *implement* simple versions of these things yourself, the hard way (Chapter 12).

Our Tasks

In this book, we cover the following tasks in the following domains:

- **Vision**
  - Face detection
  - Barcode detection
  - Saliency detection
  - Image similarity
  - Image classification
  - Drawing recognition
  - Style classification
- **Audio**
  - Speech recognition
  - Sound classification
- **Text and Language**
  - Language identification
  - Named entity recognition
  - Lemmatization, tagging, tokenization
  - Sentiment analysis
  - Custom text classifiers
- **Motion and gestures**
  - Activity recognition
  - Gesture classification for drawings
  - Activity classification
  - Using augmented reality with AI

- **Augmentation**
  - — Image style transfer
  - — Sentence generation
  - — Image generation
  - — Movie recommendation
  - — Regression
- **Beyond**
  - — Installing Swift for TensorFlow
  - — Using Python with Swift
  - — Training a classifier using Swift for TensorFlow
  - — Using the CoreML Community Tools
  - — On-device model updates
  - — Downloading models on device

The bulk of this book is dedicated to exploring how you can implement AI-driven things in your apps, (mostly) using Swift. Because we take a top-down, task-focused perspective to AI, we decided to front load our discussion of the tools that you might encounter. We do this in Chapter 2.

There, we explore *some* of the tools that you can use to create models for machine learning and AI tasks with Swift as well as some of the tools for manipulating models, working with data, and generally doing practical AI things with Swift.

Conventions Used in This Book

The following typographical conventions are used in this book:

Italic
> Indicates new terms, URLs, email addresses, filenames, and file extensions.

`Constant width`
> Used for program listings, as well as within paragraphs to refer to program elements such as variable or function names, databases, data types, environment variables, statements, and keywords. Also used for commands and command-line output.

This element signifies a tip or suggestion.

 This element signifies a general note.

 This element indicates a warning or caution.

Using Code Examples

Supplemental material (code examples, exercises, errata, etc.) is available for download at our website (*http://www.aiwithswift.com*).

This book is here to help you get your job done. In general, if example code is offered with this book, you may use it in your programs and documentation. You do not need to contact us for permission unless you're reproducing a significant portion of the code. For example, writing a program that uses several chunks of code from this book does not require permission. Selling or distributing examples from O'Reilly books does require permission. Answering a question by citing this book and quoting example code does not require permission. Incorporating a significant amount of example code from this book into your product's documentation does require permission.

We appreciate, but do not require, attribution. An attribution usually includes the title, author, publisher, and ISBN. For example: "*Practical Artificial Intelligence with Swift*, 1st Edition, by Mars Geldard, Jonathon Manning, Paris Buttfield-Addison, and Tim Nugent. Copyright 2020 Secret Lab, 978-1-492-04481-9."

If you feel your use of code examples falls outside fair use or the permission given above, feel free to contact us at *permissions@oreilly.com*.

O'Reilly Online Learning

 For over 40 years, *O'Reilly Media* has provided technology and business training, knowledge, and insight to help companies succeed.

Our unique network of experts and innovators share their knowledge and expertise through books, articles, conferences, and our online learning platform. O'Reilly's online learning platform gives you on-demand access to live training courses, in-depth learning paths, interactive coding environments, and a vast collection of text and video from O'Reilly and 200+ other publishers. For more information, please visit *http://oreilly.com*.

How to Contact Us

Please address comments and questions concerning this book to the publisher:

O'Reilly Media, Inc.
1005 Gravenstein Highway North
Sebastopol, CA 95472
800-998-9938 (in the United States or Canada)
707-829-0515 (international or local)
707-829-0104 (fax)

We have a web page for this book, where we list errata, examples, and any additional information. You can access this page at *https://oreil.ly/practical-ai-swift*.

To comment or ask technical questions about this book, send email to *bookquestions@oreilly.com*.

For more information about our books, courses, conferences, and news, see our website at *http://www.oreilly.com*.

Find us on Facebook: *http://facebook.com/oreilly*

Follow us on Twitter: *http://twitter.com/oreillymedia*

Watch us on YouTube: *http://www.youtube.com/oreillymedia*

Acknowledgments

Mars would like to thank her family and coauthors for being supportive even when/though she's intolerable, and the University of Tasmania for all the opportunities it has afforded her.

She wishes to particularly acknowledge educators Dr. Julian Dermoudy for making her fall in love with programming when she first started only three years ago, and Nicole Herbert for providing—in her role as a highly effective degree coordinator—the support and confidence she needed to do something with this new passion, along with the Australian Apple developer community and the AUC that gifted her their knowledge and interest in Swift, and her parents who continue to be her primary role models of character.

Jon thanks his mother, father, and the rest of his crazily extended family for their tremendous support.

Paris thanks his mother, without whom he wouldn't be doing anything nearly as interesting, let alone writing books, and his partner (and lead author) Mars, as well as all his friends (several of whom he is lucky enough to have written this book with!).

Tim thanks his parents and family for putting up with his rather lackluster approach to life.

We'd all like to thank Michele Cronin and Rachel Roumeliotis, whose skills and advice were invaluable to completing the book. We're really excited to work on more projects with both of you in the future! Likewise, all the O'Reilly Media staff we've interacted with over the course of writing the book have been the absolute gurus of their fields.

A huge thank you to Tony Gray and the Apple University Consortium (AUC) (*http://www.auc.edu.au*) for the monumental boost they gave us and others listed on this page. We wouldn't be writing this book if it weren't for them. And now you're writing books, too, Tony—sorry about that!

Thanks also to Neal Goldstein, who deserves full credit and/or blame for getting us into the whole book-writing racket.

We're thankful for the support of the goons at MacLab (who know who they are and continue to stand watch for Admiral Dolphin's inevitable apotheosis), as well as professor Christopher Lueg, Dr. Leonie Ellis, and the rest of the current and former staff at the University of Tasmania for putting up with us.

Additional thanks to Dave J., Jason I., Nic W., Andrew B., Jess L., and everyone else who inspires us and helps us. And very special thanks to the team of hard-working engineers, writers, artists, and other workers at Apple, without whom this book (and many others like it) would not have reason to exist.

Thanks also to our tech reviewers, with special thanks to Chris Devers, Dominic Monn, and Nik Saers for their thoroughness and professionalism.

Finally, thank *you* very much for buying our book—we appreciate it! And if you have any feedback, please let us know.

## PART I

Fundamentals and Tools

## CHAPTER 1

Artificial Intelligence!?

Much of the literature on artificial intelligence (AI), machine learning, and deep learning is full of horrifyingly complicated-looking mathematics and dense academic jargon. It's a bit scary to dive into if you're a relatively solid software engineering type who wants to get their feet wet in the world of AI and implement some AI-driven features in their apps.

Don't worry. AI is easy now (well, *easier*), and we're here to show you how to *implement* it in your Swift apps.

This book introduce concepts and processes to implement AI in various *practical* ways with Swift.

 Before we get into all that, some groundwork is required: primarily, this book is about AI and *Swift* (hopefully you saw the large friendly letters on the front cover). Swift is an amazing programming language, and is all you need to build iOS, macOS, tvOS, watchOS, or even web apps.

There is a plot twist, though the world of AI has been in a symbiotic relationship with another language for a very long time— Python. So, although this book *focuses* on Swift, it is not the only programming language that we use in it. We wanted to get that out of the way up front: we do use Python, sometimes.

It's impossible to avoid Python when doing machine learning and artificial intelligence. The meat of the book is in Swift, though, and we explain why whenever we're using Python. We're going to remind you about this a few times.

Something that we need to establish right up front (as we said in the preface) is that we expect you to know how to program already.

This book isn't for totally new programmers to get into programming with Swift, and learn to do AI things. We've designed this book for people who know how to program. You don't need to be an expert programmer, but you need to kind of know what's going on.

 Even though the book is called *Practical* Artificial Intelligence with Swift, it's impossible to create effective AI features without understanding some of the theoretical underpinnings of what you're working on. This means that we do go into theory sometimes. It's useful, we promise, and we've mostly restricted it to Part III of the book. You'll want to work through Part II first, though, to get the nuts and bolts of practical implementation.

Practical AI with Swift...and Python?

As the title states, we do indeed perform *most* of the work in this book using Swift. But swift isn't the only way to do machine learning. Python is very popular in the machine-learning community for training models. Lua has also seen a fair amount of use. Overall, the machine-learning tools you choose will guide the language you pick. CoreML and CreateML (more on those later) are the main ways we perform our machine learning, and they both assume Swift.

We are making the assumption here that you are mostly comfortable with programming in Swift and creating basic iOS applications. As AI and machine learning is such a big topic, if we were to also cover Swift and iOS, the book would be so big it would look ridiculous on your shelf. As we go through the book, we still explain what's going on at each step, so don't worry that we are going to be throwing you into the deep end.

 If you are still feeling your way through Swift and iOS, feel you need a refresher, or are just in the mood for another Swift book, check out *Learning Swift* (*http://oreil.ly/DLVGh*), in which we go through Swift and iOS starting from nothing to building an entire app.
We're pretty biased but we think its a really good book. But don't take our word for it, read it and see.

Coming from a practical perspective means that we're trying to be practical (and pragmatic) in all things, including choice of language. If Python can do the job, we show you how to use that, as well.

Practical in the context of this book means: we get down to getting the *feature* that is driven by the AI implemented, and we don't care about *how* it works, *why* it works, or *what makes it work*. We just care about *making it work*. There are enough books on AI, machine learning, deep learning theory, and how things work; we don't need to write another one for you.

Code Examples

As you probably know, Swift tends to use some *very* long method calls. On your super-duper high-resolution screen with its bucket loads of pixels and miraculous ability to scroll horizontally, you will rarely find yourself having to break up method calls and variable declarations across multiple lines.

Sadly, although paper (and its digital cousins) is a very impressive piece of technology, it has some pretty hard limits regarding horizontal space. Because of this, we often break up our example code over multiple lines.

To be clear, this isn't us saying your code needs to be done like this; it is just how we are doing it so that it fits into the book you now hold in your hands. So, if a line of code looks a bit weird and you are wondering why we broke it up over loads of lines, now you know why.

We aren't really going to go into code style in this book. It is a big topic worthy of its own book (such as *Swift Style*, Second Edition (Pragmatic) (*http://bit.ly/33ub91o*)), and it's mostly subjective and a very easy way to start arguments, so we aren't going to bother. Each person has their own approach that works for them, so stick to that and you'll be better than trying to emulate someone else's.

You do you!

If at any point you aren't feeling comfortable with typing in code based on a book, we've put up a repository with all the code examples here on GitHub (*http://bit.ly/ 2IZjW3o*) for you to use at any time. And, we have additional resources on our website (*https://aiwithswift.com*).

Examples shown are written in Swift 5.x and screenshots depict Xcode 11-ish, running on macOS Catalina. They might not behave the same on versions before or much after that. Swift is stable now, though, so things should work even if the user interface on Xcode looks a bit different.

Everything should work for quite a long time, even a while after this book's publication date.

We also extensively use Swift extensions in our code examples. Swift extensions allow you to add new functionality to existing classes and enumerations. It's easier to show than to explain.

 If you're a grizzled Objective-C programmer, you might remember categories. Extensions are kind of like categories, except extensions don't have names.

Let's say we have a class, called Spaceship:

```
class Spaceship
{
    var fuelReserves: Double = 0

    func setFuel(gallons: Double) {
        fuelReserves = gallons
    }
}
```

Hopefully this code is self-explanatory, but just so that we're on the same page, we'll explain it anyway: it defines a class named Spaceship, and the class has one variable called fuelReserves (it's of type Double, but this doesn't really matter right now).

The Spaceship class also has a function called setFuel(), which takes a Double named gallons as a parameter (we're not sure what a gallon is because we're Australian, but our editors tell us this will make sense). The function sets the fuelReserves to gallons. That's it.

Let's say that somewhere else in our code we want to use the Spaceship class, but add a function that lets us print our fuel reserves in a friendly manner. We can use an extension for that:

```
extension Spaceship
{
    func printFuel() {
        print("There are \(fuelReserves) gallons of fuel left.")
    }
}
```

You can now call the printFuel() function on an instance of class Spaceship, as if it were always there:

```
let starbug = Spaceship()
starbug.setFuel(gallons: 100.00)
starbug.printFuel()
```

We also can use extensions to conform to protocols:

```
extension Spaceship: StarshipProtocol {
    // implementation of StarshipProtocol requirements goes here
}
```

In this code example, we make the Spaceship class conform to the StarshipProto
col. We're going to use extensions a lot, so we wanted to make sure it makes sense.

If you need more information on extensions, check out the Swift documentation
(*http://bit.ly/328ovjy*). Likewise, check the documentation if you want a refresher on
Protocols (*http://bit.ly/32ajAi5*).

Why Swift?

When we talk about AI and Swift, we often get people who come up to us and basically say, "Don't you mean Python?" (sometimes they don't actually say it, but you can
see in their eyes that they're wondering it).

We also get people who say, "artificial intelligence? Don't you mean
machine learning?" We're mostly using the terms interchangeably
because it doesn't really matter these days, and it's not an argument
we want to entertain. Call it whatever you like; we're happy with it.
We touch on this discussion in a moment, too.

Here's why we like Swift for AI.

Swift, the Apple-originated open source systems and data science programming language project, was designed to create a powerful, simple, easy-to-learn language that
incorporated best practices from academia and industry into one multiparadigm,
safe, interoperable language that is suitable for anything from low-level programming
to high-level scripting. It succeeded, to varying degrees.

Swift is an in-demand, fast-growing, popular language, with estimates of more than a
million programmers currently using it. The community is diverse and vibrant, and
the tooling is mature. Swift is dominant in the development of Apple's iOS, macOS,
tvOS, and watchOS, but is gaining ground on the server and in the cloud.

Swift has many great attributes. It's a great choice for learning how to develop software and real-world development of all kinds, including the following:

Design
> Swift iterated fast and loose early on, and it made many language-breaking
> changes through its early life. As a result, Swift is now consistent, elegant, and
> fairly stable syntax-wise. Swift is also part of the C-derived and inspired family of
> programming languages.

Teachability

Swift has a shallow learning curve and, for the most part, is built around the design goal of progressive disclosure of complexity and high locality of reasoning. This means that it's easy to teach and can be quick to learn.

Productive

Swift code is clear, easy to write, and has minimal boilerplate. It's designed to be quick to write and, more important, easy to read and debug.

Safety

Swift is safe by default. The design of the language makes it difficult to create memory safety issues, and it's easy to catch and correct logic bugs.

Performance

Swift is fast, and has sensible memory use. This is likely due to its origins as a mobile programming language.

Deployment/Runtime

Swift compiles to native machine code. There's no annoying garbage collector or bloated runtime. A machine-learning model can be compiled to its own object file and a header.

In addition to all this great stuff, beginning around mid-2018 the language team announced and demonstrated a greater focus on language stability: a factor that was a deal-breaker for some earlier in the language's lifetime. This means less refactoring and refamiliarization for everyone involved, which is a good thing.

Our Approach

Despite Swift's history as an Apple-platform language, this book approaches Swift with concepts first, and platform a distant second. Platforms will be pragmatically explored, but it is our intention that the methods laid out in this book be as platform-agnostic as possible.

Swift is a user-friendly language that is easy to learn when compared to other languages typically employed for AI applications. We hope that the activities we provide will help readers develop a general skill set for AI that goes beyond even the language use.

We're focusing on getting things done and implementing features, not on the nitty-gritty of AI.

Why AI?

Although many non-Swift developers regard it as a language that exists solely for the Apple ecosystem, and specifically for application development therein, this is no longer the case. Swift has evolved into a powerful and robust modern language with an extensive feature set that we (the authors) believe is broadly applicable for machine-learning implementation and education.

Apple has released two key tools in recent years to encourage such pursuits on the platforms:

CoreML

A framework and corresponding model format that enables highly portable and performant use of trained models. Now in its second release, its features focus on computer vision and natural language applications, but you can adapt it for others.

CreateML

A framework and an app designed to create and evaluate CoreML models. It makes training machine-learning models a simple and visual process. Released in 2018, and improved in 2019, it presented a new option for those who had previously been adapting models from other formats for use with CoreML.

We look at CoreML and CreateML a whole lot more in Chapter 2.

 The push for smarter applications does not stop there. With recent offerings such as Siri shortcuts—a feature set that exposes the personal assistant's customization abilities to the user—Apple has participated in the broad cultural movement toward personalized and intelligent devices down to a consumer level.

So users want smart things, and we now have a cool language, suitable platforms, and some great tools to make them with. Still, many will not be drawn from camps of other languages they already know on the basis of that alone. Well, what if they could use some of the tools they already know? You can do that, too.

For the Python-inclined, Apple offers Turi Create (*http://bit.ly/2opKB2p*). Turi Create was the go-to before CreateML came onto the scene: the framework for fast and visual training of custom machine-learning models for use with CoreML. Primarily for use with tabular or graph data, you could step into Python, train a model, visualize it to verify its suitability, and then jump right back into your regular development flow.

But we're here to do stuff with Swift, remember?

In comes Swift for TensorFlow (*http://bit.ly/2MNJUbj*). Famously bemusing Python die-hards with a project page that proudly boasts "...machine learning tools are so important that they deserve a first-class language…," the exposure of TensorFlow and related Python libraries to be accessed directly in Swift can be more fairly described as leveraging the best of both languages. Swift provides better usability and type-safety, adding the full power of the Swift compiler without compromising the sheer flexibility of Python's machine learning.

 A recording of Chris Lattner (the original author of the Swift language, among many other things) announcing Swift for TensorFlow at the TensorFlow Dev Summit in 2018 is available on YouTube (*https://youtu.be/Yze693W4MaU*) and covers the reasons behind the project in greater detail.

If you are after even more reasoning, the Swift for TensorFlow GitHub page has a very in-depth great article (*http://bit.ly/2qaz2wB*) explaining why they chose Swift.

Nowadays, the decision of what tools to use for AI with Swift is pretty simple: if the application is images or natural language, or if the purpose is for learning, use CreateML; if the application is raw data (large tables of values, etc.), the input data is significant, or further customization is required, use TensorFlow.

 We cover more about the tools in Chapter 2, and we look very briefly at Swift for TensorFlow in Chapter 9.

On-Device Machine Learning

AI features have historically been a little different on Apple platforms because they heavily encourage machine learning to occur on-device. Where as many other manufacturers or developers will create a product whose smart features will send user data to the cloud for training and send back results over the network, Apple instead proposes that this poses unnecessary risk to the security of a user's data, which might include personal information or habits.

This unsurprisingly came at a cost. The entire Apple machine-learning suite must prioritize performance above all else, to allow single devices—even an iPhone—to handle all the operations required for smart features locally and offline. Even then, some of the more resource-intensive system functions will run only when the device is inactive and suitably charged.

Before we get into the nitty-gritty of implementing AI with Swift, we must diverge from the practical for a moment for those who do not come from an AI background.

What Is AI and What Can It Do?

AI is a field of research and methods attempting to grant technology the *appearance* of intelligence. What is or is not AI is heavily debated because there is a fuzzy line between a system giving an answer it was *told* to and giving an answer it was told *how to figure out*.

AI fundamentals will often include architectures such as *expert systems*: a type of application designed to supplement or replace a domain expert for highly specific information retrieval or decision-making. These can be constructed from specialized languages or frameworks, but at their core, they boil down to something that could be represented by many nested *if* statements. In fact, we would wager there are some out there that are. For example:

```
func queryExpertSystem(_query: String) -> String {
    var response: String

    if query == "Does this patient have a cold or the flu?" {
        response = ask("Do they have a fever? (Y/N)")

        if response == "Y" {
            return "Most likely the flu."
        }

        reponse = ask("Did symptoms come on rapidly? (Y/N)")

        if response == "N" {
            return "Most likely a cold."
        }

        return "Results are inconclusive."
    }

    // ...
}
```

Expert systems have some useful applications, but are time consuming to construct and require objective answers to clear partitioning questions throughout. Although such a system at scale might appear to possess great domain expertise, it is clearly not discovering any knowledge of its own. Codified human knowledge, even though possibly exceeding an individual's capacity for recall and response time, does not in itself make intelligence. It's just saying what it's told to.

So what about a system that is told how to figure out or guess an answer, or how to discover knowledge on its own? That is what most people mean when referring to AI nowadays. Popular approaches such as neural networks are at their core just algorithms that can take in a large amount of data—comprising of clear attributes and outcomes—and identify links at a level of scrutiny and complexity a human could not. Well, maybe if they had a very long time and a lot of paper.

 The point is that everything involved in AI is not magic: it does not comprise individual steps that a person could not do; it is instead doing *simple* things much *faster* than a human is able to do.

"Hang on, why is it useful to identify links in past data, and how does that make a system intelligent?" you might ask. Well, if we know very well what conditions or attributes lead to which outcomes when those conditions or attributes arise again, we can, with some confidence predict which outcome will occur. Basically, it gives us the ability to make a much more informed *guess*.

With this in mind, it becomes clearer what AI isn't and what it cannot do:

- AI is not magic.
- AI does not produce output that should be trusted on sensitive issues.
- AI cannot be used in applications where total accuracy is important.
- AI cannot identify new knowledge where there isn't an existing abundance.

This means that AI can look at a large amount of data and use statistical data analysis to show correlations. *"Most people who bought book X also bought book Y."*

But it can't turn that information into action without external input or design. *"Show people who bought book X (and who have not previously bought book Y) a recommendation for book Y."*

And, it can't extrapolate information to cover new variables without being given more information. *"Who is most likely to purchase new book Z that has not been purchased by anyone yet?"*

AI Versus Machine Learning

Having intelligence does not equal the ability to learn further—in terms of machines, anyway. The distinction between AI and machine learning is different depending on who you ask, but in this book we adhere to the following:

Where AI has some method for feedback that allows its training to grow and refine over time, it is capable of—and falls under the domain of—ML.

On a technical level, machine learning can simply be implemented as AI supported by architecture that retrains at regular intervals. Companies like Apple often refer to the entire domain as machine learning, further confusing the matter. The line between the two terms is not really important; prescribing which is required for a particular technical solution is.

A system capable of predicting the weather outlook based on temperature and humidity can be trained once and used for quite some time, whereas a recommendation system should take new products and user behaviors into account any time they arise.

Deep Learning versus AI?

You might have noticed that, in addition to the terms "machine learning" and "artificial intelligence," sometimes people refer to *deep learning*. Deep learning is a subset of machine learning. It's a bit of a buzzword, but it also—kind of—refers to the kind of machine learning and AI that relies on repetition, over many layers, to perform tasks.

Deep learning is about using more and more complex layers of neural nets to further extract the actual relevant information from a dataset. The goal is to convert the input into an abstract representation that can then be used later on for various purposes such as classification or recommendations. Essentially, deep learning is deep because it does a lot of repeated learning through layered neural nets.

Where Do the Neural Networks Come In?

Depending on your sources, you might be forgiven for assuming that AI and machine learning were *only* about neural networks. That's not true, and has never been true, and will never be true. Neural networks are just the big buzzword and one of the central themes for the *hype* that exists around these topics.

Much later, after all the *practical* tasks in Part II, we look at neural networks in a more theoretical capacity in Chapter 10, but this book is here to look at the practical. The truth is, it doesn't matter whether you don't care about neural networks these days; the tools are good enough that you can build *features* without knowing, or caring, how they work.

Ethical, Effective, and Appropriate Use of AI

AI can be used for evil. No surprise there; arguably everything can. But we humans figured out how to make intelligent technology quite a while ago and it got rather popular before much effort at all was put into making intelligent technology that could *explain itself*. In this area, AI research is in its infancy.

Now, if we had any other type of system and it occasionally got something wrong we would debug it and figure out where and why it's going wrong.

But we can't do that here.

If we had any other type of system for which output was derived from input and we couldn't change the system itself, we might examine and attempt manual analysis of the input that was causing errors.

But we can't do that here.

A fundamental issue with a smart system that has no way to explain itself is often solved only by starting nearly from scratch.

This lack of agency to change a system in deployment leads to a perceived lack of responsibility—people creating systems they claim do not necessarily represent their views and whose mistakes they refuse to be held liable for.

A recent example: a photo-editing app released for mobiles boasted modes that would tweak your photos to a handful of presets. Feed in one selfie and it would return versions of the picture that were gender-swapped, older, younger, and so on. One of the output categories claimed to tweak the photo to make the individual look "hotter," but users with dark skin quickly noticed that this feature unanimously lightened their skin color.

Justifiably, users were hurt by the implication that having lighter skin would make them more attractive. The developers reeled from claims of "racist design," but admitted that the input datasets for their application had been built in-house. In labeling countless photographs of people for their AI to train on, they had imparted their own inherent biases: they personally found people of European descent attractive far more often.

But an algorithm does not know what racism is. It knows nothing of human bias or of beauty or of self-esteem. This system was given a large number of photographs, told which ones were attractive, and asked to replicate whatever common attribute it identified. One was clear.

And when they tested it in-house, with what happened to be a Caucasian populace, this never occurred. So the product shipped.

Countless examples with more far-reaching consequences have suffered similar issues: a car insurance system that decided all women were dangerous, a job search that determined being called Jared is all that matters, a parole system that decided all dark-skinned people would reoffend, and a health insurance system that devalues people who buy food from fresh markets—due to assessing a person's diet and health status based on credit card transactions from grocery stores, defaulting to low.

So, it is important to understand that although AI is a super-cool and interesting new area of technology that we can use for greater advancement and good, it really can only replicate existing conditions in our society. It fails to be *ethical.*

Questions to Ask Yourself: Part One

1. What issues exist in the real-world domain to which this system will be applied?

2. What can be done to ameliorate such issues in the system? For example:

   - Manipulation of input data to better represent the ideal
   - Multiple systems working to correlate or challenge one another's responses
   - Reframing the question the system is to answer to one with more objective responses

3. If every answer this system gave were inaccurate, what is the worst harm it could cause?

4. How can the risk or potential harm be reduced? For example:

   - Ensuring certain accuracy levels before deployment
   - Built-in fail-safes to ignore or alert to potentially harmful responses
   - Human moderation of responses

5. With the remaining risk and potential harm, could you live with it if the worst case occurred?

 That is not to say that the designer/developer does not have this power. Input data can be molded to represent the world we want rather than the world we have, but targeting either will result in inaccuracy for the other. Right now it MIGHT be that the best we can hope for is awareness and acceptance of responsibility.

Do that, at the very least.

Even ethical use of AI is not always effective or appropriate, however. Many get too caught up in making a smart system full of future tech that is all the rage right now; they stop focusing on the problems they are trying to solve or the user experience they are trying to create.

Suppose that you could train a neural net that would tell someone how long they would likely live. It used all historical and current medical research available, hundreds of years of treating and observing billions of humans, and this made it reasonably accurate—barring death by accident or external force. It even accounted for the growing average lifespan—the whole nine yards.

A person opens this application/web page/whatever, enters all their information, submits it, and gets an answer. Just a number, which they could be confident would be true. No explanation. It has none to give that would mean anything to a person anyway.

This would likely cause havoc even with people who received favorable responses.

Because a person does not want a magic answer. Sure, they'd love the answer to a problem that a person could not solve, but a response alone is not a solution. Most humans would like to know about their projected lifespan so that they could extend it or know how to improve their quality of life later on. The real question here is what is likely to go wrong that they could do anything about, and that answer is not present in the system's response.

An expert system could do a better job of it: it might know less, but it can explain itself, give *actionable* answers with *human interpretable* explanations. In most applications, this is what the design of a smart system should strive for beyond all else, at the expense of intelligence or even a bit of accuracy. The neural network solution has failed to be *effective*.

Questions to Ask Yourself: Part Two

1. Given enough time or work, could a "dumb" solution solve this problem?
2. If so, what value does a smart solution offer that this would not?
3. If a person was asked the question the system is answering, what explanation would you expect to accompany their response?
4. Can a smart solution be designed to provide a comparable explanation?
5. What kind of experience are you trying to provide a user of the end product?

A final example: an industry organization struggles to retain members through first-time renewal. The governing board agonizes over how to keep people on board, but notices communications have low subscription, readership, or response rates. It identifies that the majority of new members cannot be contacted even halfway through their first membership term, and canvas widely for solutions. The board wants to know how to get more information about its members so that it can decide what is wrong or contact them some other way.

Solutions proposed include data scraping, engaging data agencies, or hiring management consultant—the organization begins pulling out all the stops. It's data. The organization just needs more customer data and then the computer will tell it what to do. The organization will make a system that will identify members with a high risk of nonrenewal and what methods of retention are most effective. The system will be great, the board tells itself.

But the problem here is not that the organization has too little data about its members. The problem is that it cannot *contact* its members, cannot sufficiently *demonstrate value* to members so that these members stay around, and the organization doesn't *know* its members or industry beyond what little the data reveals them. Maybe the board doesn't even care to know. It has strayed from the question that it was originally asking, and now failed to devise a solution that is *appropriate* for its purpose.

Questions to Ask Yourself: Part Three

1. If AI did not exist, how would people have solved this problem? Consider domains such as the following:

   Social research
   > User analysis methods nowadays often replace rather than supplement old practices of finding out about or even just directly asking the user—market or literature analysis, customer surveys, and more.

   Mathematics/statistics
   > Manual analysis of a large amount of data might not sound so fun to many, but where a computer can identify links between attributes and outcomes, a human with context of the problem domain can identify *significant* and *meaningful* correlations that align with common sense.

   Mechanical Turk (http://bit.ly/2ptZCjJ)
   > This is a phrase coming from a revolutionary chess-playing automaton in the 18th century that turned out to just be a man in a box. Never underestimate the power of just applying humans *en masse* to solving a problem: we have many skills a computer cannot emulate.

2. What was the question originally asked?

   - Does this solution answer that question?
   - If not, can any smart solution answer that specific question?
   - If not, and the design has strayed due to the data or methods available, does this new kind of response actually contribute to solving the problem originally set out?

With these tenets in mind—ethical, effective, and appropriate—go forth now and learn to create AI-powered features for yourself. (That's what the rest of the book is for, so that's where we're hoping that you'll go forth.)

Practical AI Tasks

We wanted to write this book because we were sick of books claiming to teach useful, practical, AI skills that began by exploring the implementation of a fascinating—but ultimately entirely useless without context—set of neural networks. Most of the books we read about AI were actually really good, but they began with a bottom-up approach, going from algorithms and neural networks, through to implementations and practical uses at the very end.

A Typical Task-Based Approach

The typical approach that we are going to take throughout this book will be a top-down approach in which we break up each domain of AI we're looking at into a task to solve.

This is because rarely do you start with,"I want to make a style classifier system," (although if you do, that's also cool) you generally start with, "I want to make an app that tells me if this painting is in the style of *Romanticism* or *Pre-Raphaelite*" (a problem we've all faced at some point in our lives).

Every section in the chapters found in Part II start with the problem we want to solve and end with a *practical* system that solves it. The general process is the same each and every time, with only minor changes:

- A description of the problem we are tackling
- Deciding on a general approach to solve it
- Collecting or creating a dataset to use to solve it
- Working out our tooling
- Creating the machine learning model to solve the problem
- Training the model
- Creating an app or a Playground that uses the model
- Connecting the model into the app or Playground
- Taking it out for a spin

The reason we are taking this approach is simple—this book is called *"Practical" Artifical Intelligence with Swift*, not *"Interesting but Divorced from the Reality of Using Such a System in the Real World" Artificial Intelligence with Swift*. By wrapping our approach into tasks, we are forcing the elements in this book to be those that best solve the problem at hand while also requiring that it can be used in a practical manner.

Almost all of our chapters use CoreML as the framework to run the models we create, so anything we do will need to support that.

 In some respects CoreML is an arbitrary line we've drawn in the sand, but on the other hand, it gives us clear constraints to stick within. We're all for clear constraints.

A great deal of work on AI is done by academics and giant corporations who, despite their intents, have very different goals and restrictions on training, inference, and data resources from those who must then take their work and try to make it usable for themselves and their (generally) smaller needs and resources.

Models and approaches that might be fascinating to build and study but require massively powerful machines to train and run, or those that are interesting to look at but don't solve any specific problem, simply aren't practical. You can run everything in this book on a regular desktop or laptop computer and and then compile and run it on an iPhone. In many ways, we feel this is the essence of practical.

Because we are breaking up this book into tasks, we can't just stop half way; we need to finish each task by creating something usable. Too many AI approaches either handle the creation of the AI models or cover connecting the model to a user-facing system. We are doing both.

## CHAPTER 2

Tools for Artificial Intelligence

This chapter is the first of two that explores the tools that you're likely to encounter when building artificial intelligence (AI) features using Swift. We're taking a *top-down* approach to AI, which means that you're probably going to be picking a tool based on the practical *problem* you want to address, rather than for a more esoteric or academic reason.

 We have nothing against a more esoteric academic approach. All of your authors come from an academic background. And there are plenty of fabulous books and other content out there that explores the theoretical as well as algorithm- and science-focused side of AI. You can find our recommendations on our website (*https://aiwiths wift.com*). As we said earlier, in "A Typical Task-Based Approach" on page 16, the book isn't called *Interesting but Divorced from the Reality of Using Such a System in the Real World AI with Swift*.

Our discussion of the tools for practical AI takes the same perspective: we care about *what* the tool can do more than we care about *how* it works. We also care about *where it fits* into a potential pipeline that you'd be using to perform a given task. In Chapter 3, we look at finding or building a dataset from the same perspective.

Why Top Down?

AI has shifted toward *implementing* rather than exploring the problem. This book is part of that shift. We want to help you build great Swift apps, with deeply practical implementations of AI–powered features. Although it's really interesting how, for example, a convolutional neural network is assembled, layer by layer, it's not necessary to *grok* that to make use of a convolutional neural network.

There are some great posts on O'Reilly Radar about this topic. If you're interested in exploring the shift from bottom-up AI to top-down AI in more detail, see this article on model governance (*http://bit.ly/31aSjug*).

This chapter is not particularly concerned with using and consuming models. That's what...well...the rest of the book is about. We do touch on it at the very end, though.

Later in the book, in Part III, we do look at things from a bottom-up approach by covering the underlying methods for AI, revisiting some of the top-down tasks we explored to see what makes them tick, and making a neural net from scratch.

Great Tools for Great AI

Many experts are acknowledging that we're in the implementation phase for AI technologies. The past decade of consistently applied research, innovation, and development has resulted in a healthy ecosystem of amazing AI tools.

Amazing tools means that we're now in an era in which we can focus on building experiences using AI, instead of nitpicking the details of how it is working. A great bellwether for this is the fact that the technology giants, such as Google, Amazon, and Apple, have all begun putting their might behind polished developer ecosystems for AI.

To complement Swift, Apple has developed a suite of amazing practical, polished, and evolving AI tools such as CoreML, CreateML, and Turi Create. Alongside Apple's AI tools, the community and other interested parties such as Google have developed even more complementary tools for the world of Swift and AI.

In this chapter, we give you the lay of the land and survey the tools that we work with to create AI features in our Swift apps. These are the tools that we use every day to add practical AI features to the software we build for iOS, macOS, watchOS, tvOS, and beyond, using Swift.

Broadly, there are three categories of tools, each of decreasing Swift-connectedness (but they're all pretty important) to our daily work building Swift-powered AI-driven apps:

Tools from Apple
> Tools for doing AI things built by Apple or acquired by Apple (and now built by Apple) and tightly embedded in Apple's ecosystem of Swift and iOS (and macOS and so on).

These tools are the core of our work with practical AI using Swift, and the vast majority of this book will focus on using the output of these tools from Apple in Swift applications.

We explore these tools in "Tools from Apple" on page 22 and use them throughout the book. The centerpiece of these tools is CoreML.

Tools from others

Tools for doing AI things that are built by companies and individuals other than Apple. These are either strongly coupled to Apple's ecosystem of Swift and iOS (and so on) or incredibly useful for building practical artificial intelligence using Swift.

This book touches on using some of these tools and provides you with pointers to others and explains where they fit in. We don't use these tools as often as we use the first category of tools, not because they're not as good, but because in this era of polished AI tools, we often don't need them. Apple's provided tools are pretty incredible on their own.

We explore these tools in "Tools from Others" on page 44 and touch on their use throughout the book.

AI-adjacent tools

By "AI-adjacent tools" we *really* mean Python and the tools surrounding it. Although this book is focused on Swift, and we try to use Swift wherever possible, it's genuinely difficult to avoid Python if you're serious about working with AI and machine learning.

Python is completely dominant as the programming language *du jour* of the AI, machine learning, and data science communities. Python was at the forefront of the advances in tooling that we mentioned earlier in "Great Tools for Great AI" on page 20.

These tools are often not explicitly for AI or are only tangentially related to the world of AI or Apple's Swift ecosystem, and we wouldn't mention them unless we wanted to present a really complete picture of practical AI with Swift. Some of these tools go without saying (for example, it's DIFFICULT to avoid the Python programming language when you're doing AI), and some of them seem to not rate a mention (e.g., a spreadsheet).

We touch on some of these tools in "AI-Adjacent Tools" on page 46 and use them occasionally throughout the book.

The remainder of this chapter looks at each of these categories, and the tools therein.

Tools from Apple

Apple ships a lot of useful tools for AI. The ones that you're likely to encounter and use are CreateML, CoreML, Turi Create, the CoreML Community Tools, and Apple's domain-specific machine-learning frameworks for vision, speech, natural language, and other specific areas. Apple's tools are shown in Figure 2-1.

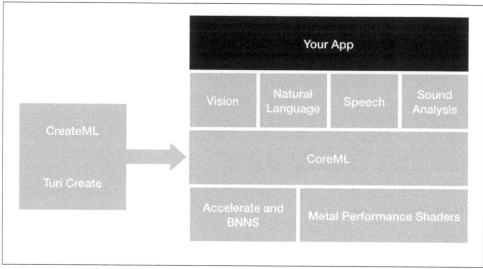

Figure 2-1. Apple's AI tools and how they relate to one another

CoreML and CreateML are both Swift frameworks that allow you to do things with AI. Figure 2-2 shows how CoreML and CreateML relate to each other and your app.

Turi Create is a Python framework for creating models. It's very similar to CreateML, but it lives in the world of Python instead of Swift.

Broadly, CoreML is for *using* models, and CreateML and Turi Create are for *making* models. It's a little bit more nuanced than that, though.

CoreML

CoreML is your framework for using machine-learning models in your apps "Tools from Apple" on page 22, which essentially means asking the model for predictions, but you can also use CoreML to perform on-device training to update the model on the fly. CoreML will be used by your apps, from within your Swift code, to access and use your machine-learning models to provide AI features.

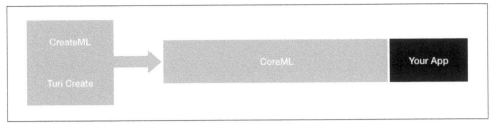

Figure 2-2. What CoreML does

If you come from the world of Android development, you might be familiar with Google's MLKit. CoreML is *kind of* the equivalent to MLKit for iOS. VentureBeat has a good summary of this (*http://bit.ly/2VDqbPw*).

CoreML is also the basis for domain-specific Apple frameworks for working with AI, such as Vision, Natural Language, Speech, and Sound Analysis, as well as the lower-level mathematics- or graphics-related frameworks like Accelerate, BNNS, and Metal. CoreML exists on macOS and on iOS.

In this book, we use CoreML constantly. We also use Vision, Natural Language, Speech, and Sound Analysis throughout the practical tasks that we build in Part II. We also touch on, very briefly, Accelerate and BNNS in Part III.

CoreML does…what?

CoreML is Apple's framework for *running* pretrained machine-learning models on its devices. CoreML handles the loading of a model and creates interfaces to the model, providing you with a standardized way to give the model input and receive output regardless of the model being used in your apps.

Along with being able to use CoreML directly with your own custom models, CoreML is also used in other libraries such as in Apple's Vision framework, where it is used to provide image analysis and detection.

CoreML itself is built upon other Apple technologies such as the Accelerate framework and Metal Performance Shaders. You can use these libraries yourself if you'd like and achieve the same results as CoreML, but you need to do more work to get the same result.

If you are interested in seeing how you can use the underlying technology that makes up CoreML, check out Chapter 12, in Part III, where we build up a neural net one layer at a time.

Rarely will you ever need to dive into the lower-level libraries like Accelerate because CoreML is just the easier way. Likewise, when you can use the more-specific libraries that use CoreML, such as Vision or Natural Language, you will generally be better off doing so rather than trying to put it all together yourself.

There will be plenty of cases, though, for which Apple hasn't provided a library for a specific domain, and that is where CoreML comes in on its own. You're always using CoreML underneath when you use Vision and other Apple frameworks.

 We talk about Apple's other frameworks later in "Apple's Other Frameworks" on page 40.

CoreML presents you with a standard approach to machine learning for Apple's platforms, which means that after you have a grip on CoreML, you can add a huge variety of new functionality into your apps following the same process regardless of the model.

The general approach for any machine learning with CoreML is always the same:

1. Add your model to your project.
2. Load the model file in your app.
3. Provide the necessary input to the model for it to make a prediction.
4. Use the prediction output in your app.

In addition to providing a standard interface, CoreML also handles all the running of the model using device-specific hardware features where possible. This means that you don't need to worry about how the model will run or add in support for device-specific hardware features. CoreML takes care of that for you.

Training a machine-learning model has a well-deserved reputation for taking a lot of time and resources. However, even running machine-learning models can result in quite a performance and battery hit to devices.

In general this means you need to really think about when you need to use machine learning and when you don't. CoreML does its best to use hardware features and run the model as efficently as possible, but you should always make sure you aren't wasting your users' precious device resources unless you have to.

When using CoreML, the machine-learning components of your app shouldn't slow down the rest of the app too much, take up too much memory, or eat up too much of the battery life, although this will fluctuate on a model-by-model basis.

No system is perfect, though, so you will always need to test your apps to make sure they are integrated correctly with the machine-learning aspects and that they aren't taxing too many resources of your devices.

The CoreML model

So far in this chapter, we've been speaking a fair amount about the machine-learning models, but we haven't really spoken about what they are in the context of CoreML, so let's do that now.

At the very high level, the *model* is anything that fully represents the machine-learning approach. It describes everything necessary for reproduction of the machine learning contained within the model.

So, for example, in the case of a neural net (which is just one type of *thing* that a *model* could represent), it would need to describe the different layers, their weights and biases, layer connectivity, and the inputs and outputs.

Although neural nets are definitely the hype of machine learning, CoreML supports much more than just neural nets. We talk more about what a neural net actually is later in "Neural network" on page 422.

At the time of this book's publication, CoreML supports the following:

- Neural nets
- Regressors
- Classifiers
- Feature engineering
- Pipelines
- Custom models for which Apple has specific support

This is true regardless of the machine-learning tools you are using. In the case of CoreML, this all gets neatly packaged up into a single object that then can be easily stored, shared, and integrated into your apps, in an *.mlmodel* file (Figure 2-3).

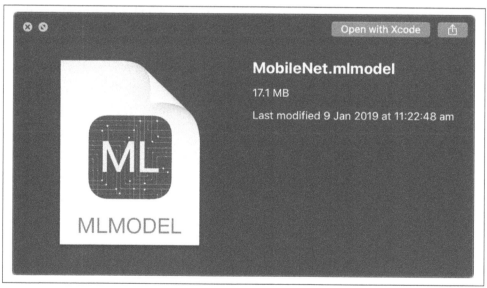

Figure 2-3. The MobileNet image detection CoreML model

Apple has provided a few different popular machine-learning models converted into the CoreML model for you to explore at its Working with Core ML Models (*https://apple.co/2q8EeAY*) page.

The MobileNet *.mlmodel* file shown in Figure 2-3 was downloaded from that site.

CoreML models are supported with Xcode and can be added to any project. After opening an *.mlmodel* file in Xcode, the editor view will change to something like that shown in Figure 2-4. It's magic.

Figure 2-4. The MobileNet .mlmodel inside Xcode

In this case, we've opened the MobileNet model shown earlier inside Xcode so that we can take a look at how Xcode interfaces with this file. The file is broken up into three main sections.

The first is the metadata section, which shows the name, type, and size of the model. In our case, the model is a 17.1 MB Neural Net Classifier called MobileNet. This section also contains any additional metadata inside the model; in this case, we have author, description, and license, but you can put almost anything you like in this section when making a model.

The next section shows any model classes Xcode automatically generated for you. This is one of the strengths of CoreML—after reading through the *.mlmodel* file, Xcode generates any files necessary to interface with it. You shouldn't ever need to touch these files; however, if you are curious, you can inspect the generated file or build your own if you don't trust Xcode or want more direct control.

We go into more detail with these generated files a little bit later, but for now you can think of them as black boxes that give you a class to instantiate that has a `prediction` method that you can call to handle all interfacing with the *.mlmodel* file.

The final section shows the inputs and outputs of the model. In the case of MobileNet it has a single input, a color image that is 224 pixels wide and high; and two outputs, a string called `classLabel` and a dictionary called `classLabelProbs`.

Now in the case of MobileNet, which is designed for object detection, these outputs give you the most likely object and the probability of the other objects. In your own models, the inputs and outputs will be different, but the concept is the same: Xcode is showing you the interface that you'll need to give the model data, and the output you can expect.

The MLModel format

Unless you are building *custom* models, you won't need to worry about exactly what an *.mlmodel* file is, and even then, often the tools Apple has built to help create and convert models will have you covered.

 By *custom* models, we don't mean models that you train yourself; we mean models for which you've defined each component yourself.

There are, however, always going to be times when you need to dive inside and make some changes or custom tools; in that case, you need to know the model format.

The MLmodel format is based on the protocol buffers (*http://bit.ly/2phRylW*) (often called protobufs) serialized data format created by Google. Protobuf is a serialization format like any other (such as JSON or XML), but unlike many serialization formats it is not designed to be human readable and isn't a textual format. However, much like many serialization formats, protobuf is extensible and can store almost any data you need.

Protobuf was designed for efficiency, multiple language support, and forward and backward compatibility. Model formats will need much iteration as they improve and gain new features over time, but they will also be expected to hang around for a long time. Additionally, most training of machine learning currently happens in Python.

All of these reasons and more make protobuf an excellent choice as the format for the MLmodel.

 If you are interested in playing around with protobuf in your apps, Apple has made a Swift library (*http://bit.ly/2Mb5ck7*) available that might be worth checking out.

The MLmodel format comprises various *messages* (protobuf's term for *bundled information*, which can be thought of as similar to classes or structs) that fully describe the information necessary to build any number of different machine-learning models.

The most important message in the specification is the `Model` format, which you can think of as the high-level container that describes every model. This has a version, a description of the model (itself a message), and one `Type`.

The `Type` of the model is another message that contains all the information necessary to describe that model. Each different machine-learning approach CoreML supports has its own custom `Type` message in the file format that encapsulates the data that approach needs.

Going back to the example of a neural net, our `Type` would be `NeuralNetwork`, and within that it has a repeating number of `NeuralNetworkLayer` and `NeuralNetworkPreprocessing` messages. These hold the data necessary for the neural net, with each `NeuralNetworkLayer` having a layer type (such as convolution, pooling, or custom), inputs, outputs, weights, biases, and activation functions.

All of this bundled up becomes an *.mlmodel* file, which CoreML can later read.

If you are after the nitty-gritty details on the CoreML model formats and how you can build and interface with them, Apple has provided a full specification that you can read here (*http://bit.ly/2IMNFfP*).

This information is provided specifically for the creation of custom models and tools and is the best place to go if you are doing so.

Most of the time you can get by thinking of a CoreML model as information that describes the complete model without having to worry about the specifics of how it stores that information.

Why offline?

Apple makes a very big deal about how CoreML is all done *offline*, on-device, with all processing happening locally at all times.

This is quite a bit different than how some other systems approach machine learning, with another popular way being to take the data off the device and upload it to another computer that can crunch through it, and then returning the results to the device.

Apple's decision to make CoreML work this way has some advantages and some disadvantages. Here are the main advantages:

- It's always available. The machine learning and data necessary are on the user's device, so in areas with no signal, it can still perform any machine learning.

- It prevents data use. If it's done locally, there is no need to download or upload anything. This saves precious mobile data.

- It needs no infrastructure. Running models yourself means that you need to provide a machine to do so as well as handle the transference of data.

- It preserves privacy. If everything is done locally, so unless a device is broken into (which is very tricky to achieve), there is no chance for anyone to extract information.

Here are the disadvantages:

- It's more difficult to update models. If you update or make a new model, you either need to send it out to your users or make a new build or use Apple's on-device personalization ("On-Device Model Updates" on page 389), which has a lot of limitations.

- It increases app size. With the models stored on device, your apps are bigger than if they just sent the data over to another computer.

> Depending on what you are doing with machine learning, the models can grow to gigantic proportions.
>
> For this reason, Apple has published some information (*https:// apple.co/33rCIs8*) on how you can shrink down your *.mlmodel* files before deployment.

Apple has taken the view that the advantages to doing everything on-device outweighs the disadvantages, and we tend to agree, especially in the case of privacy. Machine learning has the capability to provide—at times terrifying—insight and functionality, but the potential risks are likewise staggeringly huge.

A computer can't care about privacy, so we have to ensure that we do the thinking for it and keep the privacy of our users in mind at all times.

Understanding the pieces of CoreML

CoreML contains a whole bunch of things, and we're not here to reproduce Apple's API reference for CoreML (*https://developer.apple.com/documentation/coreml/ core_ml_api*).

The central part of CoreML is MLModel. MLModel (*https://apple.co/2MduLkB*) encapsulates and represents a machine-learning model, and provides features to predict from a model and read the metadata of a model.

CoreML also provides MLFeatureProvider, which we talk about more in "A Look Inside CoreML" on page 439. MLFeatureProvider exists as a convenient way to get data into and out of CoreML models. Closely related to this, CoreML provides `MLMul tiArray`. `MLMultiArray` (*https://apple.co/2osAidY*) is is a multidimensional array that can be used as feature input and feature output for a model.

 Multidimensional arrays are common in AI. They're great for representing all sorts of things from images to just plain numbers. CoreML uses `MLMultiArrays` to represent images; the channels, width, and height of the image are each their own dimension of the array.

There are a lot more bits and pieces in CoreML. We recommend working your way through the book and then checking out the documentation from Apple to fill in any gaps that are of interest to you.

Now that we clearly understand everything that there is to know about CoreML (right?), we might as well put our newfound knowledge to the test. That's what Part II of the book is. The next section covers CreateML, the most likely way that you will create CoreML models.

CreateML

CreateML "CreateML" on page 31 is Apple's Swift-based toolkit for creating and training machine-learning models. It has has two primary components: a framework and an app (see "CreateML" on page 31). It primarily exists on macOS, and is designed to be the framework on which to base your workflow.

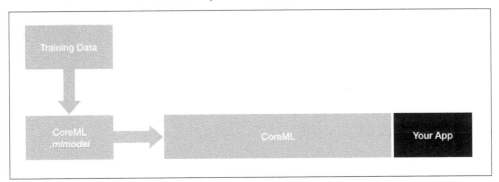

Figure 2-5. CreateML

CreateML is also a macOS app that Apple ships as part of its developer tools, as shown in Figure 2-6. The app lets you create and train machine-learning models in a graphical environment and uses the same underlying machine-learning subsystem that the CreateML framework provides access to, packaged into a user interface.

Figure 2-6. The CreateML app icon

The CreateML framework was the original incarnation of CreateML and was announced by Apple at its WWDC conference in 2018. It was originally designed to allow you to create machine-learning models within Xcode Playgrounds. Since then, it has evolved to be a more general-use machine-learning framework that's not solely designed for building models, but also for working with and manipulating models in general.

 There's nothing magic about CreateML. It's just a framework provided by Apple that has helper functions to create, work with, and manipulate models. It's the manipulation counterpart to CoreML. Other platforms, such as TensorFlow, for example, have bundled this into one framework (e.g., "TensorFlow"). If it helps, you can think of Apple's primary machine-learning stack as *CreateML+CoreML*.

Figure 2-7 shows the template chooser for CreateML.

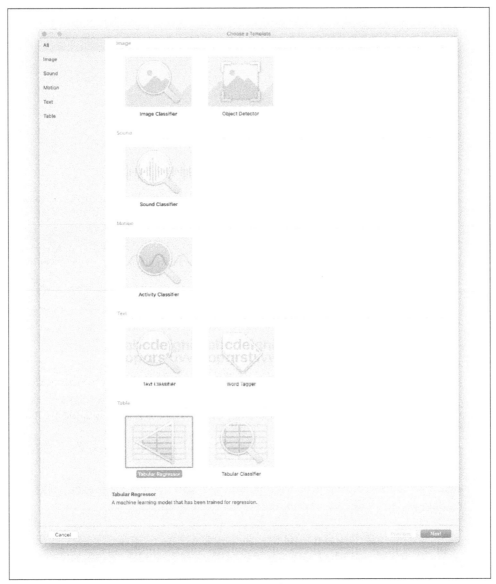

Figure 2-7. The CreateML application's template chooser

When you create a new project in the CreateML appliction, you can supply some metadata that will be visible in Xcode when you use the model you've generated, as shown in Figure 2-8.

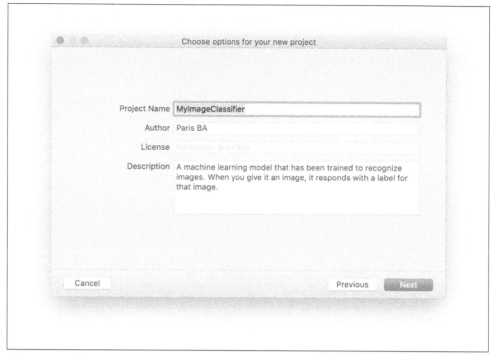

Figure 2-8. The CreateML new project options

 We step through actually using the CreateML application to train a model in Chapter 4, when we build an app that can classify images.

CreateML makes the training process as simple as it can be because it even splits the training data you provide into a training set and a validation set.

 Because CreateML randomly chooses which data goes into a training set and which goes into a validation set, you might get slightly different results if you use the same data to train a model more than once.

Almost everything you can do with the CreateML application you also can do by using the CreateML framework directly, with Swift code. We'll note where this is relevant later, when we're working with CreateML.

At the time of writing, the CreateML application supports training the following types of models:

- image classifier
- sound classifier
- object detector
- activity classifier
- text classifier
- word tagger
- tabular regressor
- tabular classifier

The CreateML framework has the following broad features:

- Image classification
- Object detection within images
- Text classification
- Word tagging models
- Word embedding, for comparing strings
- Sound classification
- Activity classification
- Recommendation systems
- Data structures for storing classified data (`MLClassifier`), continuous values (`MLRegressor`), and tables of data (`MLDataTable`)
- Model accuracy metrics
- Error handling for machine learning
- Metadata storage for machine learning

We touch on many of these CreateML framework features as we work through the examples in Part II.

 Accuracy, evaluation, and validation are a little out of scope for this book, but if you're interested in learning more, Apple's documentation (*https://apple.co/2B37yeq*) is a good starting point.

Understanding the pieces of CreateML

We were going to write a big, long chapter that unpacked every piece of CreateML until we realized that we'd basically be duplicating Apple's CreateML API reference and documentation (*https://apple.co/2B93466*).

Instead of doing that, we're going to summarize the useful bits of CreateML and hope that you explore it yourself as you encounter it through our practical tasks in Part II.

CreateML has a whole bunch of things that will train models, such as these:

- `MLImageClassifier` for classifying images
- `MLObjectDetector` for detecting objects *within* an image
- `MLTextClassifier` for classifying natural language text
- `MLWordTagger` for classifying text at a word level
- `MLSoundClassifier` for classifying audio
- `MLActivityClassifier` for classifying motion data
- `MLClassifier` for classifying tabular data
- `MLRegressor` for estimating (continuous) values using regression (as opposed to classification)
- `MLRecommender` for making recommendations

And a few things to help out when using or training models:

- `MLGazeteer` for defining terms and labels, to augment an `MLWordTagger`
- `MLWordEmbedding` for mapping strings to vectors, so you find neighboring strings
- `MLClassifierMetrics` for metrics on classifier performance
- `MLRegressorMetrics` for metrics on regressor performance
- `MLCreateError` for storing errors that occur when using CreateML

And storing data:

- `MLDataTable` for storing tables of data
- `MLDataValue` for storing a cell of data from an `MLDataTable`
- `MLModelMetadata` for storing metadata about a model (such as creator and licensing information)

You can learn about all of these things in the CreateML documentation (*https://apple.co/2B93466*), but we do touch on almost all of them as part of the practical tasks that we look at throughout the book.

Unless you have a really good reason to go spelunking through Apple's documentation, we recommend that you work through our tasks and then go back and look at the bits of CreateML that interest you. This book really tries its best to stay *practical*, and to that end, we're focused on what you *can do with CreateML*, not the ins-and-outs of CreateML for interest's sake.

Turi Create

Turi Create (*http://bit.ly/2VJaKFC*) is an open source collection of task-based tools for training machine-learning models, manipulating data, and exporting models in the CoreML model format Python library. It runs on anything that supports Python, and is maintained and supported by Apple.

If we were betting types, we'd put money on Apple eventually combining all of the functionality of CreateML and Turi Create into one tool. That day isn't here yet, though.

Apple acquired a startup called Turi in 2016 and open sourced its software a year later (Figure 2-9). Apple's task-focused approach to machine learning and AI is very much rooted in the philosophy espoused by Turi Create, but Turi Create is Python software and doesn't quite fit in, or work the same way, as the rest of Apple's ecosystem.

Turi Create is available on GitHub (*http://bit.ly/2VJaKFC*); however, you probably don't need to download or clone the GitHub repository to work with Turi Create because it's available as a Python package. Later in this chapter, we show you how we set up our preferred Python distribution and environment in "Python" on page 46.

Turi Create is a task-focused ("A Typical Task-Based Approach" on page 16) AI toolkit, with most of its functionality separated into scenarios designed to tackle specific practical tasks. For a refresher on task-focused AI, check back to "Using This Book" on page xii.

Figure 2-9. The Turi Create project on GitHub

At the time of writing, the task-focused toolkits that Turi Create supplies are as follows:

- Recommender systems
- Image classification
- Drawing classification
- Sound classification
- Image similarity
- Object detection
- Style transfer
- Activity classification
- Text classification

We cover the majority of these in the chapters in Part II, so we won't be exploring them in detail here. We also use Turi Create—even though it's Python and not Swift (we have nothing against Python, but this book does say "Swift" on the cover in large, friendly letters)—for the following tasks:

- Image style transfer, in Chapter 8
- Drawing identification, in Chapter 11
- Activity classification, in Chapter 7

Understanding the pieces of Turi Create

As with CreateML (discussed in "Understanding the pieces of CreateML" on page 36), Turi Create comes with a lot of useful bits and pieces separate from the task-focused toolkits we mentioned in "Turi Create" on page 37. The other features provided by Turi Create are broader and not so task focused. Turi Create's manual (*http://bit.ly/ 2VCyyux*) does a good job of covering most of these, but in general Turi Create's less task-focused bits are useful for manipulating data (*http://bit.ly/33uG0un*), including plotting (*http://bit.ly/2OICMzA*) and showing collections of data in an interactive way (*http://bit.ly/2OICMzA*).

The parts of Turi Create that allow you to perform general tabular classification, regression, and clustering are really useful, but we're not going to deep-dive into them right now (we do touch on them throughout the book, though).

We think the most useful bit of Turi Create, other than the task-focused toolkits, are its tools for working with data:

- SArray (*http://bit.ly/35wcMx0*) is an array that can store data that exceeds your machine's main memory capacity. This is really useful when you're working with enormous datasets and need to manipulate them before you can train a model.

- SFrame (*http://bit.ly/31e1eLv*) is a tabular data object (similar to CreateML's MLDataTable) that lets you store enormous amounts of data in columns and rows in a persistent way (on disk, instead of in memory). Each column in an SFrame is an SArray. An SArray can be trivially constructed from a comma-separated values (CSV) file, a text file, a Python dictionary, a DataFrame from the Pandas framework, JSON, or a previously saved SFrame on disk. It's basically magic.

- SGraph (*http://bit.ly/2IJinqj*) is a graph structure with SFrames underneath. It allows you to store complicated networks of relationships and items (vertices and edges) and explore the data.

Additionally (and we think this is probably the most underrated bit), Turi Create comes with a suite of visualization tools:

- SArray and SFrame both have a show method, which displays a plot of the data structure. This is also basically magic. It works using a native GUI, or in a Jupyter Notebook.

- SArray and SFrame both also support an explore method, which opens an *interactive* view of the data structure.

You can learn more about Turi Create's visualization tools in the documentation (*http://bit.ly/2OICMzA*).

Turi Create also comes with a C++ API (*http://bit.ly/2M8ll9R*), which is useful if you want to embed Turi Create features into other applications.

 There are too many third-party frameworks that can be used to supplement Turi Create for us to explore them all here, but one of our favorites is "turi-annotate-od," which allows you to prepare images for use with Turi Create's Object Detection task-focused toolkit. You can learn more about it on the project GitHub (*https://github.com/VolkerBb/turi-annotate-od/blob/master/README.md*).

Apple's Other Frameworks

Apple also supplies a lot of useful frameworks that provide AI features, without any training required. These are part of Apple's collection of libraries that you can use when building for its platforms. There are more frameworks than we have time to cover in this book, but we use some of them quite a bit for our tasks in Part II, specifically:

- Vision (*https://apple.co/2MEeZ11*), for applying computer vision algorithms
- Natural Language (*https://apple.co/2pc5LB9*), for analyzing natural language text
- Sound Analysis (*https://apple.co/2M7WNxD*), for analyzing audio streams and files
- Speech (*https://apple.co/33rwto1*), for recognizing human speech and turning it into text

We're not going to unpack the specifics of these frameworks here, because we look at them in the context of our tasks later in the book. For now, suffice it to say that sometimes you'll make a machine-learning model (say, using CreateML or Turi Create) and access it directly using CoreML, and sometimes you'll access it via (for example) Vision and CoreML (if it was an image-related task). Figure 2-10 shows the tools.

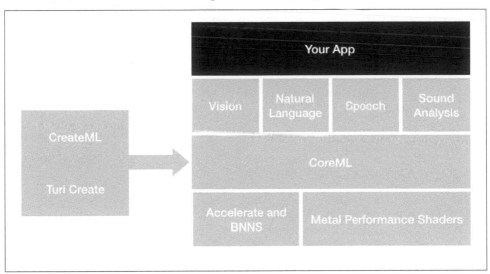

Figure 2-10. Apple's AI tools and how they relate to one another

Sometimes, you won't need to build your own model at all, and you'll be able to implement powerful AI-driven features using Apple's frameworks; for example, if you needed to perform speech recognition in your apps.

This book is broad minded: we discuss what we *think* is the most straightforward way to implement AI features regardless of whether that involves creating and training a model from scratch, using someone else's model, or using one of Apple's frameworks (which, somewhere under the hood, involves using a trained model that Apple made).

You might be wondering where Apple's BNNS and Accelerate frameworks fit in. If you've read through Apple's documentation, you'd be forgiven for assuming that we were trying to pretend these two frameworks didn't exist. We kind of were. However, they're both very useful, and both *very* (in our humble opinions) unrelated to *practical* AI (practical being the operative word here). Chapter 12 looks into this, but please wait until you've read the rest of the book.

CoreML Community Tools

The final tool from Apple that we're going to cover here is the CoreML Community Tools, a suite of Python scripts that allow you to manipulate other machine-learning model formats and convert them to the CoreML format. You can find the CoreML Community Tools on Apple's GitHub (*http://bit.ly/328qggE*), as shown in Figure 2-11.

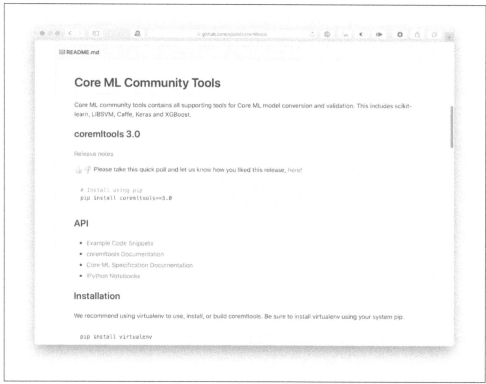

Figure 2-11. CoreML Community Tools

You can use CoreML Community Tools to do the following:

- Convert models from Keras, Caffe, scikit-learn, libsvm, and XGBoost into the CoreML format
- Write the resulting CoreML model out as a file in the *.mlmodel* format following the conversion process
- Perform basic inferences, using a converted model via the CoreML framework, to validate and verify a model conversion
- Build a neural network from scratch, layer by layer
- Create models that an be updated on-device
- Work with TensorFlow models using other packages

 If you're already working with machine-learning tools, you might notice that TensorFlow is a big glaring omission from this list. You'd be right, and we cover what you can do about that in "Tools from Others" on page 44.

CoreML Tools exists so that people who perform significant work using one of the myriad other machine-learning and AI platforms can bring their work into CoreML. It serves to legitimize CoreML, and bring the wider machine-learning ecosystem into the Apple world.

You won't always need to use CoreML Tools—in fact, when you take a predominantly task-based practical approach, as this book does, you'll rarely need them at all—but it's important that we cover them because they're a key part of what makes the Apple- and Swift-based AI ecosystem so powerful.

To install the CoreML Community Tools, use your preferred Python package manager to fetch and install `coremltools`. Later in this chapter, in "Python" on page 46, we discuss our preferred Python distribution and environment setup. If you like to keep your Python installations neat, you can install `coremltools` inside a `virtualenv` or similar. We outline our approach to this in "Python" on page 46.

We're not going to provide a complete guide, or even a full practical example (at this point in the book anyway) on using the CoreML Tools, because the documentation covers that pretty well. We're just here to tell you what CoreML Tools can do and how it fits into the workflow that we're using for the practical examples in this book.

If you'd prefer to manually download, you can grab the CoreML Community Tools from `Apple's GitHub` (*http://bit.ly/328qggE*). After you've downloaded it, you can learn how to build it from source (*http://bit.ly/35pMxbD*). We don't recommend that you do this, because there is no benefit to be gained.

If you're not already doing machine-learning work with another set of tools, the biggest purpose the CoreML Tools serves for you is as a way to get other people's models into a format you can use in your apps.

 Check out the giant list of Caffe models (*http://bit.ly/2B4o9yf*) and the giant list of MXNet models (*http://bit.ly/31gy9zq*) for some food for thought and inspiration on what you might be able to achieve with models from other formats.

We work through some small examples of using CoreML Tools later, in Chapter 9, as part of "Task: Using the CoreML Community Tools" on page 382, and in "Task: Image Generation with a GAN" on page 324.

Tools from Others

The two biggest and most important tools that are of interest for Swift and practical AI that aren't created or distributed by Apple are the TensorFlow to CoreML Model Converter and Swift for TensorFlow, both from Google.

There are also a few useful third-party tools that don't originate with a giant company, which we look at shortly.

Swift for TensorFlow

Swift for TensorFlow is an entirely new suite of machine-learning tools that are designed around Swift. Swift for TensorFlow integrates TensorFlow-inspired features directly into the Swift programming language. It is a very large and complex project, and it takes a different approach than the regular TensorFlow project (which is a Python thing).

 At the time of writing, Swift for TensorFlow's current version is not yet 1.0, and it's under heavy development. It's an early-stage project that isn't feature complete. We'd love to write a book on Swift for TensorFlow, but it's going to change constantly and we'd just have to rewrite it every month, so the best we can offer is a broad, big-picture chapter, exploring what's possible. That's Chapter 9.

You can find Swift for TensorFlow on GitHub (*http://bit.ly/31fhRXz*), as shown in Figure 2-12, but we don't recommend you clone or download the repository just yet.

Figure 2-12. Swift for TensorFlow on GitHub

We look at how you can use Swift for TensorFlow for a practical task-based AI problem in Chapter 9, as part of "Task: Training a Classifier Using Swift for TensorFlow" on page 381.

TensorFlow to CoreML Model Converter

The TensorFlow to CoreML Model Converter does what it says on the box: it lets you convert TensorFlow models to CoreML using Python. It requires that you have the CoreML Tools installed and available from your preferred Python package manager as tfcoreml.

It works much as you'd expect:

```
import tfcoreml as tf_converter

tf_converter.convert(tf_model_path='my_model.pb',
                     mlmodel_path='my_model.mlmodel',
                     output_feature_names=['softmax'],
```

```
input_name_shape_dict={'input': [1, 227, 227, 3]},
use_coreml_3=True)
```

Using the TensorFlow to CoreML Model Converter is outside the scope of this book, but if you're interested, you can learn more on the project's GitHub page (*http://bit.ly/ 2VLRLdD*).

Other Converters

Other converters exist, such as the following:

- MMdnn (*http://bit.ly/2VDhuon*), from Microsoft, which supports a range of conversions to and from CoreML
- torch2coreml (*http://bit.ly/33tjl1w*), which supports converting models from PyTorch to CoreML
- mxnet-to-coreml (*http://bit.ly/2MyWBXq*), which supports converting from MXNet to CoreML

We don't have the space to go into these, but they're all useful. After you've learned how to use one, they're all more or less the same, too!

AI-Adjacent Tools

Python and Swift are actually surprisingly similar languages, but there also are a lot of important differences. As we've mentioned, we use Python a fair bit more than you'd expect in this book, but because this book is about Swift, we gloss over the details of what we're doing in Python more often than not.

We recommend picking up one of the many fabulous Python books that our lovely publisher offers. Our personal favorites are the *Machine Learning with Python Cookbook* (*https://oreil.ly/ CsD2R*) and *Thoughtful Machine Learning with Python* (*https:// oreil.ly/m6As0*).

Python

As we've indicated, it's incredibly out of scope for this book to dive into the depths of Python for practical AI. Not only is it not what this book's about, it's not our area of expertise! That said, you're going to need to use Python occasionally as you work through this book, and we're going to recommend a specific way of getting Python set up on your macOS machine.

We'll remind you about this section later on in the book each time we need you to use a Python environment. Fold a corner of the page back here, if that's your thing (you probably want to avoid doing that if you're reading this as an ebook, but that's just us.)

Python came preinstalled on macOS prior to macOS 10.15 Catalina (which is the version of macOS you'll need to be running to follow along with this book). Older documentation, articles, and books might assume that macOS has Python installed. It doesn't come with it anymore unless you upgraded *to* Catalina from an older version of macOS (in which case any installations of Python you had are likely to be preserved).

To use Python for AI, machine learning, and data science, we recommend using the Anaconda Python Distribution (*http://bit.ly/33u4Yub*). It's an open source package of tools, including a straightforward package manager and all the bits and pieces you need to do AI with Python.

The general steps for setting up Python—which will be useful to you every time we suggest you use Python throughout this book—are as follows:

1. Download the Python 3.7 distribution of Anaconda for macOS.

Anaconda also comes with some graphical tools for managing environments. We prefer to use the command-line tools, and think it's easier to explain and make it part of your workflow, but if you prefer a graphical user interface, it's available for you. Launch "Anaconda Navigator" and explore. You can learn more about Anaconda Navigator at *http://bit.ly/2IIPdrm*.

2. Install Anaconda, as shown in Figure 2-13. The "Preparing Anaconda" stage, as shown in Figure 2-14, might take a little while.

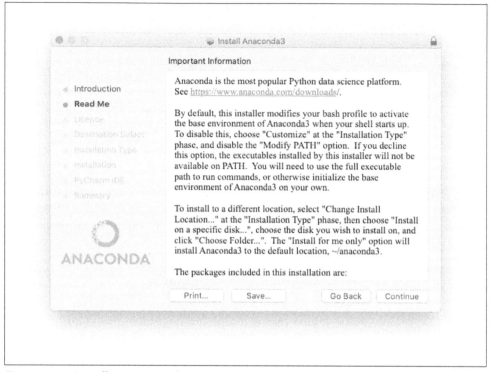

Figure 2-13. Installing Anaconda on macOS

Figure 2-14. Preparing Anaconda might take a while

3. Open a Terminal, and execute the following command:

```
conda create -n MyEnvironment1
```

This creates an empty, new environment for you to work in. You can repeat this command using a different name instead of MyEnvironment1 for each specific set of tasks that you want to do with Python.

4. To activate MyEnvironment1, you can execute the following command:

```
conda activate MyEnvironment1
```

To deactivate (leave the Anaconda environment you're currently in), execute the following:

```
conda deactivate
```

You can see this process in Figure 2-15.

```
bash-3.2$ ./conda create -n "MyPythonEnv1"
Collecting package metadata (current_repodata.json): done
Solving environment: done

## Package Plan ##

  environment location: /Users/parisba/anaconda3/envs/MyPythonEnv1



Proceed ([y]/n)? y

Preparing transaction: done
Verifying transaction: done
Executing transaction: done
#
# To activate this environment, use:
# > conda activate MyPythonEnv1
#
# To deactivate an active environment, use:
# > conda deactivate
#

bash-3.2$ ▉
```

Figure 2-15. Creating a new Anaconda environment

5. Many AI and machine-learning tools require you to use Python 3.6. You can force Anaconda to create a Python 3.6 environment for you by using the following command:

```
conda create -n "MyPythonEnv2" python=3.6
```

6. After you've activated an Anaconda Python environment that you created with a specific Python verison, you can verify you're running the right version of Python by executing the following from within your Anaconda environment:

```
python --version
```

You should see Python print its version number, as shown in Figure 2-16.

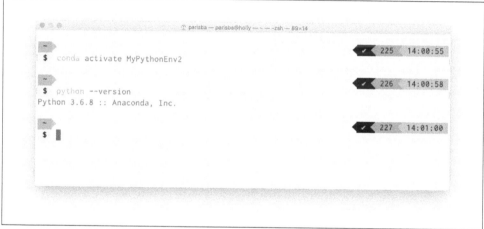

Figure 2-16. Python showing its version

7. You can always check which Anaconda environment you're currently working in, or check on all your environments, by executing the following command:

```
conda info --envs
```

Anaconda will display an asterisk (*) next to the environment in which you're currently working, as shown in Figure 2-17.

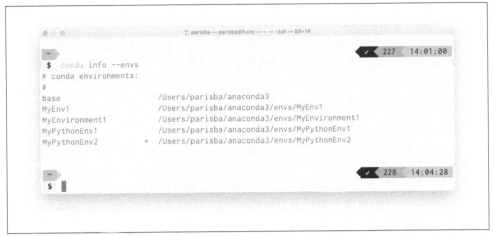

```
                            ⌐ parisba — parisba@holly — ~ — ~ -zah — 89×14
 ~
 $ conda info --envs                                                    ✓   227    14:01:00
 # conda environments:
 #
 base                        /Users/parisba/anaconda3
 MyEnv1                       /Users/parisba/anaconda3/envs/MyEnv1
 MyEnvironment1               /Users/parisba/anaconda3/envs/MyEnvironment1
 MyPythonEnv1                 /Users/parisba/anaconda3/envs/MyPythonEnv1
 MyPythonEnv2              *  /Users/parisba/anaconda3/envs/MyPythonEnv2

 ~                                                                      ✓   228    14:04:28
 $
```

Figure 2-17. Listing your Anaconda environments; the active environment has an asterisk

8. You can duplicate an existing Anaconda environment by executing the following command:

    `conda create --name NewEnvironment --clone OldEnvironment`

    Replace `NewEnvironment` with the name of the new copy that you'd like to create, and `OldEnvironment` with the name of environment you're cloning.

 There are a lot of other environment-managing features available in Anaconda. Check out the Anaconda Documentation (*http:// bit.ly/2VAR32F*) for more information. O'Reilly also has some great books that address the subject, such as *Introducing Python, Second Edition* (*http://bit.ly/2MbxquU*).

9. You can install packages within your Anaconda environment using Anaconda's built-in package manager. To search for packages that are available, you can execute the following command while you're within an environment:

    `conda search scipy`

    This command searches the Anaconda package manager for the `scipy` package.

10. To install a package using the Anaconda package manager, execute the following command:

    `conda install scipy`

The `install` command installs the specified package into the currently active environment. To install a package to a specific environment, use a command like `conda install --name MyEnvironment1 scipy`, instead.

11. You can also install multiple packages at once, as follows:

```
conda install curl scipy
```

12. If the package you need is not available in the Anaconda package manager, you can use `pip` (*http://bit.ly/2nC23QC*) instead. `pip` is the de facto standard package manager for the broader Python community. To install a package using `pip`, activate the environment to which you want to install the package and execute the following command:

```
pip install turicreate
```

Of course, you'll need to replace `turicreate` with the name of the package you want to install.

We strongly recommend installing packages from the Anaconda package manager. Only turn to `pip` if a package is not available via Anaconda.

When we suggest that you make a new Python environment, at various points throughout this book, our recommendation is to make a new Anaconda environment for the specific project or task you're working on, following the process we just outlined.

For each task for which we use Python (and therefore Anaconda), we indicate which packages we recommend installing within the environment you make for that task as we go. We also indicate whether those packags are available in the Anaconda package manager, or in `pip`.

Remember, the Anaconda Python Distribution is designed for data science, machine learning, and AI. If you're more interested in general-purpose programming with Python, you might be better served with an alternative Python setup.

Keras, Pandas, Jupyter, Colaboratory, Docker, Oh My!

Other than Python, the tools you're likely to encounter when working with Swift and AI are diverse and unpredictable. When you're concocting scripts, particularly in

Python, there are all sorts of useful frameworks, ranging from Keras (*http://bit.ly/2OEXtw2*) (a framework that's designed to provide a range of useful functions for machine learning in a human-friendly way, shown in Figure 2-18), to Pandas (*http://bit.ly/2OO86wy*) (a framework for manipulating data, among other things, shown in Figure 2-19).

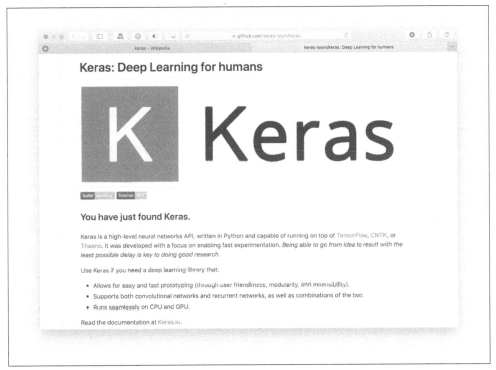

Figure 2-18. Keras GitHub

You can also try the useful Python framework's NumPy and scikit-learn, which allow you to work with and manipulate data in all sorts of useful ways.

We occasionally use these Python frameworks as we work with data to apply it in the book's tasks. We do refrain from going too in depth; they're well covered online and in O'Reilly Online Learning (*https://learning.oreilly.com*).

Figure 2-19. Pandas

We think the final three tools that you're likely to encounter, or want to use, are Jupyter, Google's Colaboratory, and Docker.

Jupyter Notebooks are an online browser-based Python (or any language theoretically, assuming there's a plug-in for it) environment that lets you share, write, and run Python code in a browser.

Jupyter is incredibly popular in the data science world as a great way to share code with integrated explanations, and has been used both as a means of distribution and documentation to explain concepts and ideas. Google's Colaboratory (commonly called just Colab) is a free online hosted and slightly tweaked version of Jupyter Notebooks.

It has all of the same features (and a few more), but you don't need to worry about running Jupyter yourself with Colab; you can let Google run it on its gigantic cloud infrastructure. Figure 2-20 shows Colab, and you can find it online at *https://colab.research.google.com*.

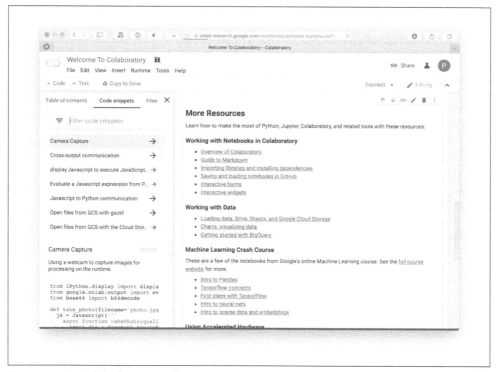

Figure 2-20. Colab, from Google

Colab is a great place to run the Python scripts that you'll inevitably need to write when you're working on AI, especially if you don't want to install Python on your own machine.

Docker is a virtualization system that lets you package up software in a way that allows you distribute it without having to install it all over the underlying host operating system. Docker is a useful way to distribute large, unwieldly installations of things. We use Docker later when we install Swift for TensorFlow in "Task: Installing Swift for TensorFlow" on page 368. You can learn more about Docker here (*https://www.docker.com*).

Other People's Tools

One of our favorite tiny but useful things is Matthijs Hollemans' CoreMLHelpers repository (*http://bit.ly/2phTtqE*). It has a bunch of useful features (and more on the way), including these:

- Convert images to CVPixelBuffer objects and back
- An `MLMultiArray`-to-image conversion
- Useful functions to get top-five predictions, argmax, and so on
- Nonmaximum suppression for bounding boxes
- A more Swift-friendly version of `MLMultiArray`

Many of these things *might not* mean much to you right now, but trust us, they're super useful. And we hope that they'll mean something to you by the end of this book..

 If you want to learn more about these tools, we highly recommend Matthijs Holleman's book *CoreML Survival Guide* (*http://bit.ly/2OHSRVX*).

We're also big fans of Fritz AI and their tutorials, documentation, and projects that make mobile on-device AI a lot easier. Check out their blog (*http://bit.ly/33Ep051*) and Code Examples (*http://bit.ly/2nT0gXy*) particularly.

What's Next?

This chapter is not an exhaustive summary of every conceivable tool you could be using for AI with Swift. There's no such guide that covers that. We've explored the tools that you're most likely to encounter when you're aiming to work with Swift from a top-down, task-focused, deeply practical perspective.

Almost every tool that we mentioned in this chapter is explored further, in some way small or large, in Part II or Part III.

You might be wondering how you use the models that could be created, manipulated, or explored using the tools we've discussed in this chapter. That's a great question, and we're really glad you asked it. We answer that question, chapter by chapter, in Part II.

 We were originally going to write a chapter all about consuming models using CoreML, but then we realized that we were straying from our original goal for this book: a guide to practical AI. The focus is on creating features and experiences using AI, not on exploring tools. This chapter is our only concession, and is by necessity. You can visit our website (*https://www.aiwithswift.com*) for articles, tutorials, and code samples covering this material from other perspectives.

CHAPTER 3

Finding or Building a Dataset

Many introductory exercises on machine learning or artificial intelligence (AI) provide datasets for use, as is done in this book. When faced with your own implementation, this will likely not be the case. Sourcing and transforming input data that can be modeled to solve a specific problem is a challenge in and of itself.

A common colloquialism in data science is *GIGO*, which stands for "garbage in, garbage out," which refers to the fact that a model can be only as good as the data on which it was trained. This chapter covers available options for sourcing premade datasets or designing and building your own.

Be aware that every step in this process is highly subjective to your individual data and solution requirements, so it's a little high-level in places. Many practices in data-wrangling are honed only with experience.

Planning and Identifying Data to Target

Some refer to the dataset planning phase as a design process, and this is no exaggeration. One of the easiest mistakes to make in the machine-learning process is not selecting the appropriate input data for the job—not necessarily data of poor quality or provenance, but even data that does not sufficiently correlate with the outcome the model is looking to predict.

Not all machine-learning problems are solved outside of the technical aspects. Although it might seem intuitive that to predict the weather will require records of historical temperature, humidity, and outlook data at least, other problems might not be so simple.

What if instead a model were needed to predict human behavior? In a local university's AI fundamentals class one of the first problems posed is a discussion on how to design a model that would predict a child prankster's likelihood of acting up on any certain day at school. A purely theoretical exercise, the same ideas usually come up each semester. Along with recording whether they offended on a certain day, we should also record the day of the week, what they had for breakfast, whether they slept enough, whether they were grounded, what the weather was like, whether their best friend was at school that day, and the list goes on.

But where does the list of factors that might affect the moods or movements of a sentient being end? It doesn't, really.

You could easily be sucked down a rabbit hole of trying to model the Butterfly Effect (*http://bit.ly/2OTKQNM*). So, although the data-preparation process leading up to model training can be generalized to something like this:

get data → clean data → transform data → train

The lack of a perfect solution necessitates a more flexible process. Something more like this:

investigate available data sources → get data → *explore data* **→ clean data →** *explore* *data* **→ transform data →** *explore data* **→ train**

In this process, at any point of exploration it is possible to decide to return to the beginning.

It is very common for real-world projects to reach the stage of exploring transformed data multiple times before finally going ahead—using the knowledge gained to try a different approach to transformation or realize some different variable should have been included in the data in each iteration.

There are no clear methods to prescribe here, just a recommendation to generously employ whatever brainstorming techniques you have available to you. However, there are some common mistakes that you need to avoid when it comes to the overall logic applied to the data and problem at hand:

- Negation as failure
- Closed-world assumptions

Let's examine each.

Negation as Failure

This term is used to describe the problems that can arise with defaulting to negative where positive cannot be proven.

For example, the logical difference between using an if/else (defining some catch condition for the positive case, else default to negative) compared to an if/else if (defining two catch cases, else default to no action) might seem minor. But the issues caused if the problem this logic is modeling were not so clearly defined can be extensive. For example:

```
if input == "Y" {
    print("Answer was yes.")
} else {
    print("Answer was no.")
}
```

Although this *might* be safe if input only had two buttons, such code would register *any input* as a no. This means y would be a no, as would yes, or any other character or symbol, likely even just a line break. The answer it is looking for is either Y or N, but the context it exists in is not so neatly partitioned.

Closed-World Assumptions

This term describes inaccurate assumptions that the information possessed about a thing encapsulates or is indicative of the whole. For example, a list that is treated as exhaustive when not in the real world:

```
let yesResponses = ["Y", "y", "yes", "Yes"]
let noResponses = ["N", "n", "no", "No"]

if yesResponses.contains(input) {
    print("Answer was yes.")
} else if noResponses.contains(input) {
    print("Answer was no.")
} else {
    print("Answer was not yes or no.")
}
```

A better approach? Probably. A perfect one? Not by a long shot. An ideal system would be one that could replicate what the human mind goes through when hearing a verbal yes/no response: was the noise within some given threshold of familiarity to any term that individual has heard used for either yes or no before? If yes, assume that's what they meant or that it is unfamiliar slang. Else, clarify because it's almost certain that they meant one of them in response to a yes/no question, right? Easy. For a human, anyway.

Admission of Guilt

One of the authors actually committed an offense in design something like this recently, when quickly hacking together a replacement model for a macOS application she made. A robust image classification model had been trained to classify art styles during the private investigation phase, but had to be extracted before being shown publicly due to being trained on a proprietary and private dataset.

Replacement datasets for this problem are difficult to come by, and a quick piece-together yielded something considerably less accurate than the previous version—it was seeing classes where there were none, because this input data did not cover all the categories the original dataset had.

One quick hack later: if the model was less than $n\%$ certain of its classification, it would instead apply none. But the problem is that now if an image represents multiple classes overtly enough to confuse which it should choose, it still doesn't get classified.

Oh well, good enough for a demo. \cringe

Aside from simple logic errors, errors in reasoning can vary broadly. Most solutions boil down to ensuring that the design and input of a system is as accurate and complete a representation of the phenomena you are trying to model or predict as possible. No easy task, but a worthy one.

Remember, aside from image-based data (photographs, spectrograms, video frames, etc.), the vast majority of datasets you would construct or use are going to be—or need to be transformed into—tables of values. Think to yourself: if all previous observations in your problem space had to fit into a single table, what would be the column headings and types?

Finding a Dataset

It's good to have some idea of how and where to look for a dataset with which to get started. Both of these are very subjective in the broad field of AI and the vast range of problems it can be applied to, but some general truths and recommendations exist.

Where to Look

For the common problems, there are a bunch of places where you can start your search:

Google Dataset Search (*http://bit.ly/2MpUoi0*) is to datasets what Google Scholar is to research papers. Or what Google Search is to, well, everything, everywhere. It's a great first stop to get a feel for what is out there on a particular topic. Google also curates a general public data repository of its own, called Google Public Data (*http://bit.ly/2MmDK2O*), as does Amazon with its AWS Data Registry (*https://registry.open data.aws*).

Kaggle.com (*https://www.kaggle.com/datasets*) is an online community dedicated to data science. It has a large repository of community- and organization-contributed datasets on a huge range of topics to use for whatever you like. This site is also a great resource for learning the minutiae of data analysis by participating in competitions or discussions.

Research organizations will often release scientific data for public use. This is particularly useful if you require sensitive human data that you can be confident has been appropriately anonymized. In Australia we have bodies like the Australian Bureau of Statistics (*http://bit.ly/32pmXlh*), Commonwealth Scientific and Industrial Research Organisation (CSIRO) (*http://bit.ly/2OTi53X*), and even an online portal for all OF our government data called data.gov.au (*https://data.gov.au*).

Elsewhere in the world, notable bodies include NASA (*https://data.nasa.gov*), NOAA (*http://bit.ly/2oSBN57*) NIST (*https://www.nist.gov/data*), the CDC (*https://data.cdc.gov*), WHO (*http://bit.ly/2oPXvH3*), UNICEF (*https://data.unicef.org*), CERN (*http://opendata.cern.ch*), the Max Planck Institute (*http://bit.ly/2VOvV9h*), CNR (*http://bit.ly/2MqZV81*), the EPA (*http://bit.ly/32pCx07*), and many more. So much great science to go around!

Similarly, many countries have a central government data repository such as data.gov (*https://www.data.gov*) (USA), open.canada.ca (*http://bit.ly/2MmWBe7*), data.govt.nz (*https://www.data.govt.nz*), data.europa.eu (*http://bit.ly/2Bnl1xC*), and data.gov.uk (*https://data.gov.uk*), just to name a few.

Some companies with a nonscientific purpose even release data repositories if they reach a size at which they are able or required to conduct research in-house. Some great examples of this are the World Bank (*http://bit.ly/2OX0vvK*) and the International Monetary Fund (IMF) (*http://bit.ly/35HRCMx*), which have grown to become primary sources of open financial and populace data.

Sourcing data from a reputable organization—where permitted—is a great way to ensure quality in both accuracy and coverage as well as value types and formats that are appropriate for use.

Journalism sites such as FiveThirtyEight (*https://53eig.ht/2OWLABL*) and BuzzFeed (*https://github.com/BuzzFeedNews*) make available the data gained from public surveys or that was collected for key articles, representing everything from important social and political data that might concern public well-being—online censorship, government surveillance, firearms, health care, and more—to things like sports scores or opinion polls.

Reddit's /r/datasets (*http://bit.ly/2pA3jEr*) (yes, really) is a great place to look if you've got something in mind but need human help to find it; you can either browse what interesting things people have posted or ask for assistance on a particular problem. There's even great meta-information like the time someone posted an exhaustive list of every open data portal ever (*http://bit.ly/31q2ziH*). While you're there, /r/Machine-Learning (*http://bit.ly/2pwoN56*) is also good.

Random enthusiasts can sometimes also really come through for you, too. A personal favorite website of the authors' is Jonathan's Space Home Page (*http://bit.ly/2IZ5bO4*), wherein an astrophysicist from the Harvard-Smithsonian Center for Astrophysics maintains extensive lists of *everything* launched into space. Just as a side project. It's amazing.

Another great source of slightly unusual data is the Online Encyclopedia of Integer Sequences (OEIS) (*http://oeis.org*) which is a giant collection of various number sequences and additional information about them such as plots, or the formulae used to generate the sequences. So if you were ever curious about the Catalan numbers (*http://oeis.org/A000108*) or want to know about the Busy Beaver Problem (*http://oeis.org/A060843*), OEIS has you sorted.

There are also countless websites dedicated to being a central registry of datasets in areas such as open government, academic data used in key research publications, and all sorts of other things.

This has probably illustrated the point by now: *data is everywhere*. We generate more every moment and a not insignificant number of people and organizations have dedicated themselves to making that useful for all of us. Personal tastes in data sources are established only with time and experience, so explore and experiment widely.

What to Look Out for

Have a clear plan of what you are looking for to model the problem you are solving before you begin your search. In potential data to include, consider the following:

- The values and types of values present in the data.
- The person or organization that collected the data.
- The methods used (if known) to collect the data.
- The time frame during which the data was collected.
- Whether the set alone is sufficient for your problem. If not, how easily could other sources be incorporated?

Preprepared datasets will often need some modification to be appropriate for other uses. In this way, even if it could be assumed that the data is already clean (which should be verified just in case), some data transformation might still need to occur. To ensure quality output, you should observe the usual data preparation steps from this point.

Remember, it might come to a point at which some additional or differently formatted information is required to yield the desired outcome. A prebuilt dataset is a nice starting point, but it should never be exempt from scrutiny: an unsuitable dataset should be modified or replaced even if that will involve significant work in the short term.

Building a Dataset

To make a dataset from scratch, you must obtain raw data from somewhere. These efforts generally fall into three main camps: *recording* data, *collating* data, or *scraping* data.

Disclaimer

Each country has its own laws and regulations with respect to the collection, storage, and maintenance of datasets. Some of the approaches described in this section might be fine in one area but highly illegal in the next. You should never undertake any action to acquire a dataset without first checking the legality of doing so.

In particular, the observation of content online that you do not own, such as through data scraping or tracking methods, can incur significant penalties in some parts of the world, regardless of whether you didn't know or what you were doing it for. It's just not worth it.

Other methods might be unclear in the law, such as the collection of photographs or video recordings from public places or the ownership of data made available for other purposes.

Even if a dataset has a license saying you can use the data however you want, the means to collect it and your responsibilities after you have the data are something you need to carefully consider. Your region's laws *always* override a license giving you permission to data.

As a rule of thumb, if you didn't create the data yourself, you don't own it (and even if you did create it, you still might not own it). So, unless you are given explicit permission, you can't collect it or use it.

Be informed and be careful. We are not lawyers: do your own due diligence.

Data Recording

Data recording is first-class data collection: you are doing the observation of some phenomena and attributes yourself and recording unique data that is all your own. This could be done with physical devices such as sensors or cameras, or with digital observation such as web trackers or crawlers.

You might collect data about actions or environmental conditions occurring in a specific place, record images of different objects you want to recognize, or chronicle the traffic of a web service to predict user behaviors.

You can use these methods to create highly targeted datasets on topics that might not have been observed previously, but this is the most time-consuming path to take. The quality of the data collected is also up to the quality of the devices or methods used to collect it, so some expertise is recommended.

Data Collation

Data collation is the practice of combining multiple sources of information to create new data to analyze. This could be built with methods like extracting figures from reports, merging data from different online sources, or querying APIs. It's taking data that exists in many places and bringing it together in a useful fashion.

Collating data can be almost as time consuming as recording or generating your own in some cases, but it is more likely to enable creation of sets of data about phenomena that occur in difficult-to-reach places such as overseas or within private organizations. A company that does not share its initial dataset for a problem might publish multiple papers with all the figures in them. Or, a site that does not allow you to download a record of *every user that has done Y* might allow countless queries for *has user X done Y?*

The quality of data collated is also only as high as the level of attentiveness taken in combining sources. Traps such as incorporating sources that use different measurement units or simple transcription errors can compromise the entire venture.

Data Scraping

Data scraping is a method of collecting a large amount of *information* that exists but might not be being observed in a way that it is generating *structured data* suitable for use. This is the primary way social media analysis used to be done (particularly by third parties), but many platforms have cracked down on people's ability to scrape data or use data that was scraped from their services.

Scraping is performed with software that loads, observes, and downloads enormous amounts of content—often indiscriminately—from the web target, which then can be adapted for use. You really have to know what you are looking for.

Preparing a Dataset

Raw data is almost never useful on its own. For it to be practically useful, you need to prepare it.

Getting to Know a Dataset

As discussed previously, a key and repeated phase of data preparation is data exploration. A set of data too large to have each value manually read, checked, and edited by a human still needs verification of its quality and suitability before entrusting it to make a model worth the time and computation required.

Methods as simple as dumping a sample of a large dataset into a spreadsheet program and just having a look at what kinds or ranges of values occur in each column can identify errors such as irresponsible default values (say, using zero instead of NULL where no measurement was available) or impossible ranges or incompatible merges (data seemingly grouped from multiple sources for which different units were used in each; e.g., Fahrenheit versus Celsius).

Data analysis tools are available in abundance. Where a dataset is too large to be opened in a spreadsheet program, scripts in Python or applications like RStudio have powerful functionalities capable of visualizing, summarizing, or reporting on data. Using whatever you are comfortable with, aim to at least identify the format and general distributions of values for different attributes.

Tools for Processing Data

Myriad tools are available for cleaning, processing, and gaining insight into a dataset before being able to use it. As we said in Chapter 2, Python is the de facto standard for this: it has *so, so many* tools for understanding and processing data.

Packages like Matplotlib (*https://matplotlib.org*) can be generally very easily used to spit out plots and graphs of your data for visual inspection.

Pillow (*http://bit.ly/2IYOWRa*) provides functionality for all manner of image processing, conversion, and manipulation.

Python has a built-in package for performing statistics (*http://bit.ly/35Jjikk*), as does NumPy (*http://bit.ly/2MOq1AJ*) if you need more.

Python also has a wide range of both built-in and third-party support for handling almost every file format you are going to encounter, from CSV (*http://bit.ly/35Jeb3x*), JSON (*http://bit.ly/2OSbarM*), YAML (*https://pyyaml.org*), XML (*http://bit.ly/31pvgvS*), and HTML (*http://bit.ly/2VP7Pv7*), as well as more esoteric formats like TOML (*http://bit.ly/31q3G1R*) or INI (*http://bit.ly/2VXLxr6*) files.

When none of these work, there is a package indexer (*https://pypi.org*) worth searching through to see whether there is something to solve your problems. Or, just search for "python thing I want to do" and most of the time you'll find that someone has had the same issue and either written a solution for it or at least offers some pointers that you can check out.

If Python isn't your thing, almost any programming language of choice will have similar tools and functionality. The reason we are so fond of Python for this is because the work is already done for you and there are loads of examples out there to use as a starting point. There is nothing magical about Python for this, but it's the most popular choice, so we advocate sticking with the majority on this one.

Another good option for this is spreadsheet programs like Excel, Numbers, or Google Sheets. Even though they tend to cop a lot of flack, you shouldn't discount them. Doing data preparation in them can be clunky, but you can use them to very quickly get a whole bunch of useful insight and preparation before needing to jump into Python (or another tool of your choice). As a bonus you almost certainly already have one of these installed and ready to go on your machine.

Finally, don't be afraid to think outside the box—something as simple as zipping a dataset can give you a rough idea as to how entropic a dataset is without even having to look inside. If one dataset compresses extremely well and another from the same source less so, the second one likely has a higher amount of entropy in the data than the first.

We examine tools in greater detail in Chapter 2, so check there if you're hungry for all the information on practical AI tools.

Image datasets are not so easily observable, but definitely worth the time to at least scroll through them to have a look at the general quality of imagery and what kinds of cropping methods have been used. Tools like Turi Create's visualizations features, which we discussed in "Understanding the pieces of Turi Create" on page 39, are incredibly useful for getting to know your data. Figure 3-1 shows an example.

	row_id	style	stylized_image
0	0	0	
1	0	1	
2	0	2	
3	0	3	
4	0	4	
5	0	5	
6	0	6	
7	0	7	

Figure 3-1. Getting to know your data with Turi Create

Cleaning a Dataset

In getting to know a dataset, it's likely that you will come across something about it that is not right. Recording is an imperfect craft and, like anything humans do, can yield errors. Errors to look for will fall into a few categories:

- Uniform-value error
- Single-value error
- Missing values

Uniform-value error covers circumstances that would cause an entire column or set of values to be inaccurate, such as when an instrument was used to record something that was miscalibrated by a uniform amount, temperature measured from beside something that generates additional heat, weighing using scales that were not zeroed ahead of time, and so on. This also includes when data from various sources was improperly merged without transformation: a simple zip of one set of data from the

United States and one from the United Kingdom and now the system thinks it's totally reasonable to be 100 degrees Celsius.

Single-value error is another term used to describe outliers or inconsistent miscalibration that cause inaccurate or totally illogical values in only a small number of cases. Occurrences such as a sensor that overloaded one day, producing a value 1,000% higher than theoretically possible should be reasonably evident.

Missing values can occur when there were issues in the method used to record data or the dataset had been through some malformed transformation at some point in its lifetime. These might be simply a `nil` or `NULL` value, or something less helpful such as the string `"NONE"` or a default value such as zero. It could even just be nonsense characters. We've seen everything.

Uniform error can usually be remedied by scaling or converting the entire set of values by the uniform error value—if it can be discerned. Single-value errors and missing values require that you either guess the value that needs to be replaced using some viable method, or remove the row/observation entirely to prevent the error.

You can guess the value by getting the mean of all other values in that column, using the value in that column for the observation nearest to that with the missing value, or some application-specific method that uses knowledge of other attributes.

Transforming a Dataset

There are two main reasons to transform data before use: to meet format requirements of the algorithm(s) to be used, and to improve or extend the current data with new inferred attributes. For both of these purposes, there are three transformations that are commonly applied to data:

Normalization
    A method applied to numerical data to bind the upper and lower bounds to a scale that will make them easier to work with.

    An example of this is when observations with numerical data need to be compared with some measure of dissimilarity. If you were trying to assess the health of, say, different fish based on their length, weight, age, and number of missing eyes, presumably anyone would agree that comparing two fish by different metrics (i.e., one eye versus by one year of age or one centimeter in length) would give different results than comparing them by the same metric.

    Normalizing positive-only values is simple:

```
func normalise(_ value: Double, upperBound: Double) -> Double {
    return (value / upperBound) * 1.0
}
```

```
length = normalise(length, upperBound: maxLength)
weight = normalise(weight, upperBound: maxWeight)
age = normalise(age, upperBound: theoreticalAgeLimit)
eyesDifferent = normalise(eyesDifferent, upperBound: 2)
```

Generalization

A method by which specific values will be replaced with higher-level concepts to better group observations.

Examples of this usually occur when the method for recording some attribute was more precise than need be. For example, if you had GPS statistics of a person's movements, you might generalize latitude and longitude to an address, thus preventing a system that regarded every minor movement as a change of location. Or, turning numerical measurements into bands of humans, meaning that instead of individuals' height measurements in millimeters, the relevant factor might be when they are grouped into below-, near-, or above-average height.

Aggregation

A method by which some complex attributes are summarized to allow more efficient analysis.

An example of this is instead of analyzing passages of text as (`Attribute: Text, Classification: Class`), keywords (or even word frequencies) can be extracted from the text to present only the most relevant or unique aspects to link with the classification it was given.

Before, between, or after these steps might come a different type of data transformation, wherein data is not just changed, but expanded or reduced:

Feature construction

A method by which new attributes are created, often through inference or combination of other values already present.

An example of this are things like generalization or aggregation in which the original value is also kept, or, more commonly, when two or more values present can tell you (or enable discovery of a third). For instance, if you have a company's name and country of operation, you can look up its business registry number, or if you have someone's height and weight you can construct their BMI (*http://bit.ly/2IY4Wmc*).

Data reduction

A method by which some attributes are removed, either due to correlating with another attribute or because they're irrelevant to the problem you are trying to solve.

For example, if you have someone's address, postcode, and area code, at least one of those pieces of information is redundant. Maybe—as in the case for feature construction—you have some algorithmic reason for wanting to analyze both, but it's unlikely. High correlation between two or more attributes indicates that they might cause errors in analysis and are candidates for removal.

Verifying the Suitability of a Dataset

After you have reached this point, you should take one more long, hard look at both the problem you are trying to solve and the dataset you propose to use for the job. In the wide world of data analysis that precedes AI applications, there are less strict rules than maybe you would like, but you will often know whether a solution seems off or a dataset doesn't seem to tell the story you want.

Trust that little voice, because the work wasted if you turn back beyond this point becomes much more substantial.

Explore your data again. Skim it, visualize it, test your solution with tiny subsets of the data—do whatever you need to. If it still feels correct, move forward.

Apple's Models

We've mentioned this a few times now, but it always pays to mention it again: Apple provides a website with an entire collection of useful models (*https://apple.co/ 33oLF5p*). If you want to build a feature that can be accomplished with one of Apple's models, it's probably going to be quicker or easier to get it done by using one of those models.

As of this writing, Apple has models available to do the following:

- Predict depth from an image (FCRN-DepthPrediction)
- Classify the dominant object in an image (MobileNetV2, Resnet50, and Squeez-Net)
- Segment pixels in an image into classes (DeeplabV3)
- Detect and classify multiple objects in an image (YOLOv3)
- Generate answers to textual questions based on a supplied piece of text (BERT-SQuAD)

If your *task* can make use of one of these, go nuts! Make it happen, and don't worry about trying to find a dataset and create or train your own model. Just use a premade model and be happy.

We'll be using one or two of the models provided by Apple in some of the tasks that we cover in Part II.

Tasks

CHAPTER 4

Vision

This chapter explores the practical side of implementing *vision*-related artificial intelligence (AI) features in your Swift apps. Taking a top-down approach, we explore seven vision tasks, and how to implement them by using Swift and various AI tools.

Practical AI and Vision

Here are the seven practical AI tasks related to vision that we explore in this chapter:

Face detection
This uses image analysis techniques to count faces in an image and perform various actions with that information, such as applying other images on top of the face, with the correct rotation.

Barcode detection
This uses Apple's frameworks to find barcodes in images.

Saliency detection
This task finds the most salient area of an image using Apple's frameworks.

Image similarity
How similar are two images? We build an app that lets the user pick two images and determine how similar they are.

Image classification
Classification is a classic AI problem. We build a classification app than can tell us what we've taken a photo of.

Drawing recognition

Recognition is basically classification, no matter what you're classifying, but in the interest of exploring a breadth of practical AI topics with you, here we build an app that lets you take a photo of a line-drawing and identify the drawing.

Style classification

We update our Image Classification app to support identifying the style of a supplied image by converting a model built with another set of tools into Apple's CoreML format.

 We've called this chapter "Vision," but it's not solely about the framework that Apple provides for vision-related programming which, helpfully, is also called Vision (*https://apple.co/2MEeZ11*). We do use Vision a fair bit, throughout the book, though! Check the Index for details.

Task: Face Detection

Whether you need to check if there is, in fact, a face present to help a user validate and verify their profile photo, or you want to actually start drawing things on top of a supplied photo SnapChat-style, face detection is a useful feature for lots of apps.

For the first task, we're going to look at how easy it is to add practical face detection features to your Swift iOS apps. We're going to do this without any model training, using Apple's provided AI frameworks ("Apple's Other Frameworks" on page 40).

Because of this, this task is a little different from many of the others in this book in that the toolkit for performing face recognition is largely provided by Apple. We follow a similar process, using Apple's frameworks, in "Task: Image Similarity" on page 109 and "Task: Speech Recognition" on page 173, among others.

You could go and train a model that understands what a face is, but Apple has done the work for you: look no further than the camera app on iOS, and how it can identify a face.

Problem and Approach

Much like many of the practical AI tasks in this book, face detection is everywhere. The authors' collective favorite media depiction of facial detection is in the fabulously forward-looking fictional TV show, *Person of Interest*.

 Seriously, we cannot recommend *Person of Interest* more highly. Stop reading this and go watch it and then come back and continue reading. We'll still be here.

In this task, we're going to explore the practical side of face detection by doing the following:

- Making an app that can detect human faces in images, allowing us to confirm that a user has supplied a useful profile picture
- Using Apple's tools for doing this without training a model
- Exploring the next steps for improved face detection

We're going to build an app that can count the number of faces in a photo chosen by the user. You can see the app in Figure 4-1.

Building the App

We're going to use Apple's newest user interface (UI) framework, SwiftUI, to build the user interface for this app.

We use both SwiftUI and UIKit for different examples in this book to give you a practical grasp of the use of both of Apple's iOS UI frameworks in building AI-driven apps. We often chose which framework to use fairly arbitrarily, just like in the real world (don't tell clients that, though).

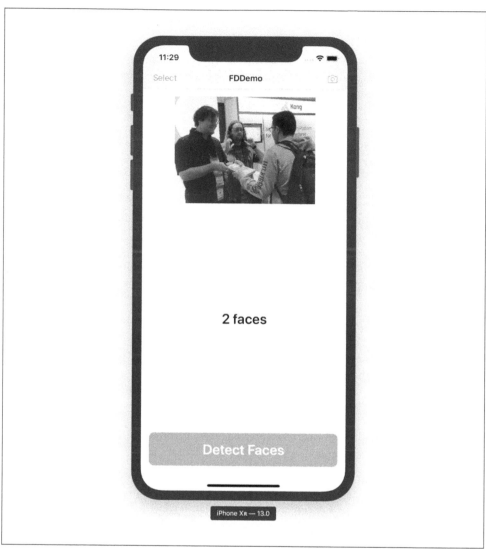

Figure 4-1. *The final version of our face counting app*

The final form of the app in Figure 4-1 consists of the following SwiftUI components:

- A `NavigationView` in which to display the title of the app as well as the button to select a photo
- An `Image` to display the chosen image in which the app will count the faces
- A `Button` to trigger the face counting
- Some `Text` to display the count of faces

If you need a refresher on SwiftUI, check Apple's documentation (*https://apple.co/32eMZYu*) as well as our website (*https://aiwiths wift.com*).

However, we construct this view from multiple subviews, and the way we do this might be a little unfamiliar compared to how we use SwiftUI elsewhere in this book. We've done this to help demonstrate the breadth of approaches that you can take to constructing a UI (for much the same reason as we use SwiftUI and UIKit, for different practical examples, throughout the book). This approach gives you maximum exposure to the real-world ways of doing things.

If you don't want to manually build the face-counting iOS app, you can download the code from our website (*https://aiwithswift.com*); look for the project named `FDDemo-Starter`. After you have that, follow along through the rest of this section (we don't recommend skipping it) and then meet us at "What Just Happened? How Does This Work?" on page 86.

To make the face counting iOS app yourself, you'll need to do the following:

1. Fire up Xcode.
2. Create an iOS app project in Xcode, choosing the "Single View App" template. The project should be Swift and the SwiftUI checkbox should be selected, as shown in Figure 4-2.

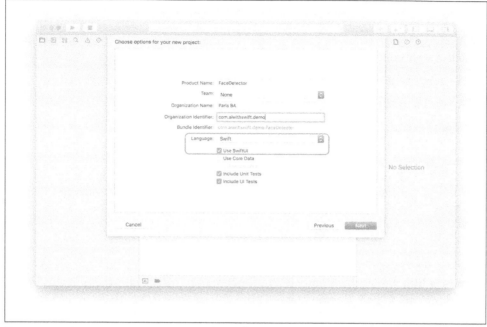

Figure 4-2. Creating a new project with SwiftUI

3. Add a new Swift file called *Faces.swift* to the project (File menu → New → File), and add the following `imports`:

```
import UIKit
import Vision
```

Nothing particularly interesting here: we're importing UIKit because we're using `UIImage`, and it comes with it, and we're importing Vision, because that's the Apple framework that we'll be using to detect faces.

4. Below the `imports`, add the following `extension` on `UIImage`:

```
extension UIImage {
    func detectFaces(completion: @escaping ([VNFaceObservation]?) -> ()) {

        guard let image = self.cgImage else { return completion(nil) }
        let request = VNDetectFaceRectanglesRequest()

        DispatchQueue.global().async {
            let handler = VNImageRequestHandler(
                cgImage: image,
                orientation: self.cgImageOrientation
            )

            try? handler.perform([request])
```

```
            guard let observations =
                request.results as? [VNFaceObservation] else {
                    return completion(nil)
            }

            completion(observations)
        }
      }
   }
```

This extension on UIImage adds a detectFaces function to UIImage, allowing us to ask any UIImage to detect the faces in it. The code within the function creates VNDetectFaceRectanglesRequest and dispatches it on a queue.

What does VNDetectFaceRectanglesRequest do? It returns the bounding box (rectangular box) for any faces detected in the image that it's analyzing. You can learn more about it in Apple's documentation (*https://apple.co/33vHvsC*). We run the VNDetectFaceRectanglesRequest as part of a VNImageRequestHandler, which is an object that allows us to run image analysis requests (*https://apple.co/2OGsGiq*).

 This book isn't here to teach Swift, but just in case you need a reminder: an extension allows you to add new functionality to existing classes, structures, enumerations, or protocols. This new functionality, as you might have guessed, includes functions. You can read more about extensions in Swift in the Swift documentation (*http://blt.ly/328ovjy*).

The call to DispatchQueue.global().async { } allows us to run the call to VNImageRequestHandler (in which we run our VNDetectFaceRectanglesRequest) on a global thread so that our UI is not locked. You can learn more about the Dispatch Queue class in Apple's documentation (*https://apple.co/2IKkxGc*).

Next, create a new file in the project (ours is called *Views.swift*), which we use to define some SwiftUI elements for our app:

1. import SwiftUI and then add a new View struct, called TwoStateButton:

```
struct TwoStateButton: View {
    private let text: String
    private let disabled: Bool
    private let background: Color
    private let action: () -> Void

}
```

The TwoStateButton struct defines a Button that can be enabled or disabled, change color, and otherwise do button-y things. Very useful.

2. The TwoStateButton will also need a body:

```
var body: some View {
    Button(action: action) {
        HStack {
            Spacer()
            Text(text).font(.title).bold().foregroundColor(.white)
            Spacer()
            }.padding().background(background).cornerRadius(10)
        }.disabled(disabled)
}
```

The body handles the drawing of the TwoStateButton (which actually just draws a Button and some Text, based on the values of the variables).

3. It will also need an init() function:

```
init(text: String,
    disabled: Bool,
    background: Color = .blue,
    action: @escaping () -> Void) {

    self.text = text
    self.disabled = disabled
    self.background = disabled ? .gray : background
    self.action = action
}
```

The init() function initializes a new ThreeStateButton to certain parameters (text, whether it's disabled, a background color, and an action when the button is pressed).

4. Next, create another View struct, called MainView:

```
struct Main View: View {
    private let image: UIImage
    private let text: String
    private let button: TwoStateButton
```

This View has some variables to store a UIImage, a String, and a TwoStateButton (which we created a moment ago!).

5. The MainView will need a body:

```
var body: some View {
    VStack {
        Image(uiImage: image)
            .resizable()
            .aspectRatio(contentMode: .fit)
        Spacer()
```

```
        Text(text).font(.title).bold()
        Spacer()
        self.button
    }
}
```

The body draws an Image, some Spacers, some Text, and a TwoStateButton (defined by the variable).

6. The MainView will also need an init():

```
init(image: UIImage, text: String, button: () -> TwoStateButton) {
    self.image = image
    self.text = text
    self.button = button()
}
```

The init() function creates the MainView, setting the value of the image, the text, and the button.

7. We also need to add a rather long struct, inheriting from UIViewControllerRe presentable, in order to be able to summon a UIImagePicker, which is part of the older UIKit framework, from within SwiftUI:

```
struct ImagePicker: UIViewControllerRepresentable {
    typealias UIViewControllerType = UIImagePickerController
    private(set) var selectedImage: UIImage?
    private(set) var cameraSource: Bool
    private let completion: (UIImage?) -> ()

    init(camera: Bool = false, completion: @escaping (UIImage?) -> ()) {
        self.cameraSource = camera
        self.completion = completion
    }

    func makeCoordinator() -> ImagePicker.Coordinator {
        let coordinator = Coordinator(self)
        coordinator.completion = self.completion
        return coordinator
    }

    func makeUIViewController(context: Context)
        -> UIImagePickerController {

        let imagePickerController = UIImagePickerController()
        imagePickerController.delegate = context.coordinator
        imagePickerController.sourceType =
            cameraSource ? .camera : .photoLibrary

        return imagePickerController
    }
```

```
func updateUIViewController(
    _ uiViewController: UIImagePickerController, context: Context) {}

class Coordinator: NSObject, UIImagePickerControllerDelegate,
    UINavigationControllerDelegate {

    var parent: ImagePicker
    var completion: ((UIImage?) -> ())?

    init(_ imagePickerControllerWrapper: ImagePicker) {
        self.parent = imagePickerControllerWrapper
    }

    func imagePickerController(_ picker: UIImagePickerController,
        didFinishPickingMediaWithInfo info:
            [UIImagePickerController.InfoKey: Any]) {

        print("Image picker complete...")

        let selectedImage =
            info[UIImagePickerController.InfoKey.originalImage]
                as? UIImage

        picker.dismiss(animated: true)
        completion?(selectedImage)
    }

    func imagePickerControllerDidCancel(
            _ picker: UIImagePickerController) {

        print("Image picker cancelled...")
        picker.dismiss(animated: true)
        completion?(nil)
    }
}
}
}
```

This is a lot of code that allows SwiftUI to provide enough of UIKit's functionality to summon a `UIImagePicker`.

You can learn more about `UIViewControllerRepresentable` in Apple's documentation (*https://apple.co/2IKkxGc*): you use it to fake the abilities of a UIKit view when you're using SwiftUI. Essentially, it's a way to bridge features of the older UI framework with the new one.

8. Finally, still in *Views.swift*, we need to add an extension to `UIImage` that allows us to manipulate the orientation as needed:

```
extension UIImage {
    func fixOrientation() -> UIImage? {
```

```
            UIGraphicsBeginImageContext(self.size)
            self.draw(at: .zero)
            let newImage = UIGraphicsGetImageFromCurrentImageContext()
            UIGraphicsEndImageContext()
            return newImage
        }

        var cgImageOrientation: CGImagePropertyOrientation {
            switch self.imageOrientation {
                case .up: return .up
                case .down: return .down
                case .left: return .left
                case .right: return .right
                case .upMirrored: return .upMirrored
                case .downMirrored: return .downMirrored
                case .leftMirrored: return .leftMirrored
                case .rightMirrored: return .rightMirrored
            }
        }
    }
}
```

Next, we move over to *ContentView.swift*:

9. First, update the `imports` as follows:

```
import SwiftUI
import Vision
```

 ContentView.swift is, kind of, sort of, the equivalent of a View-Controller in UIKit, but for SwiftUI.

10. Add an extension on `ContentView` to the end of the *ContentView.swift* file:

```
extension ContentView {

}
```

11. Within, add a function to return our main view:

```
private func mainView() -> AnyView {
    return AnyView(NavigationView {
        MainView(
            image: image ?? placeholderImage,
            text: "\(faceCount) face\(faceCount == 1 ? "" : "s")") {
                TwoStateButton(
                    text: "Detect Faces",
                    disabled: !detectionEnabled,
                    action: getFaces
                )
```

```
        }
        .padding()
        .navigationBarTitle(Text("FDDemo"), displayMode: .inline)
        .navigationBarItems(
            leading: Button(action: summonImagePicker) {
                Text("Select")
            },
            trailing: Button(action: summonCamera) {
                Image(systemName: "camera")
            }.disabled(!cameraEnabled)
        )
    })
}
```

This function not only returns our main view, but also creates it. SwiftUI magic!

12. Add a function to return the image picker:

```
private func imagePickerView() -> AnyView {
    return  AnyView(ImagePicker { result in
        self.controlReturned(image: result)
        self.imagePickerOpen = false
    })
}
```

13. And add a function to return a camera view:

```
private func cameraView() -> AnyView {
    return  AnyView(ImagePicker(camera: true) { result in
        self.controlReturned(image: result)
        self.cameraOpen = false
    })
}
```

14. Back near the top, add some @State variables to the ContentView:

```
struct ContentView: View {
    @State private var imagePickerOpen: Bool = false
    @State private var cameraOpen: Bool = false
    @State private var image: UIImage? = nil
    @State private var faces: [VNFaceObservation]? = nil

}
```

These define the things that can change: whether the image picker is open, whether the camera is open, the image itself, and the faces detected.

 You can learn more about States in the SwiftUI documentation (*https://apple.co/2B9OOtA*).

15. Add some `private` variables, too:

```
private var faceCount: Int { return faces?.count ?? 0 }
private let placeholderImage = UIImage(named: "placeholder")!

private var cameraEnabled: Bool {
    UIImagePickerController.isSourceTypeAvailable(.camera)
}

private var detectionEnabled: Bool { image != nil && faces == nil }
```

These store the face count, the placeholder image (displayed until the user chooses an image), the availability of a camera, and whether detection (which is reflected in the availability of the button) is enabled.

16. Update the body to look as follows:

```
var body: some View {
    if imagePickerOpen { return imagePickerView() }
    if cameraOpen { return cameraView() }
    return mainView()
}
```

The body `View` returns the image picker if the image picker should be open, the camera likewise; otherwise, it returns `mainView()`, which is the function that we added to the `ContentView` by way of an extension, earlier.

17. Add a function to `getFaces()`:

```
private func getFaces() {
    print("Getting faces...")
    self.faces = []
    self.image?.detectFaces { result in
        self.faces = result
    }
}
```

This function calls the `detectFaces()` function, which we added earlier, as an extension on `UIImage` in the *Faces.swift* file, calling it on the current image.

18. We also need a function to display the image picker:

```
private func summonImagePicker() {
    print("Summoning ImagePicker...")
    imagePickerOpen = true
}
```

19. As well as the camera:

```
private func summonCamera() {
    print("Summoning camera...")
    cameraOpen = true
}
```

Add a launch screen and icon if you want, and launch your app! You can select a photo from the photo library or take a photo if you're running it on a real device, press the Detect Faces button, and the app will tell you how many faces it finds. You can see it working earlier, in Figure 4-1.

What Just Happened? How Does This Work?

There's not much to say here. We're building an app that can detect faces. For our first pass, we've used SwiftUI to create an iOS app that lets the user select a photo from their library, or take a new photo, and count the faces in it. As we said, not much to say.

We didn't have to train any machine-learning models to do this as we made use of Apple's supplied frameworks. If you're curious about how Apple's frameworks might work, we discuss that later in Chapter 11.

But what if we want to do more?

Improving the App

In this section, we improve our face-counting app to not only count the faces in a chosen image, but draw a box around them, as well, as shown earlier, in Figure 4-1.

You'll need to have completed the app described in "Building the App" on page 75 to follow from here. If you don't want to do that, or need a clean starting point, you can download the resources for this book from our website (*https://aiwithswift.com*) and find the project FDDemo-Starter.

If you don't want to follow the instructions in this section, you can also find the project FDDemo-Completed, which is the end result of this section. If you go down that route, we strongly recommend reading the code as we discuss it in this section and comparing it with the code in FDDemo-Completed so that you understand what we're adding.

There are not too many code changes to make here, so let's get started and get those boxes drawn around some faces:

1. Open the *Faces.swift* file and add the following extension on Collection below the existing extension:

    ```
    extension Collection where Element == VNFaceObservation {

    }
    ```

2. The extension to Collection is valid only where the elements of the Collection are of type VNFaceObservation.

3. Within this extension add the following:

```swift
func drawnOn(_ image: UIImage) -> UIImage? {
    UIGraphicsBeginImageContextWithOptions(image.size, false, 1.0)

    guard let context = UIGraphicsGetCurrentContext() else {
        return nil
    }

    image.draw(in: CGRect(
        x: 0,
        y: 0,
        width: image.size.width,
        height: image.size.height))

    context.setStrokeColor(UIColor.red.cgColor)
    context.setLineWidth(0.01 * image.size.width)

    let transform = CGAffineTransform(scaleX: 1, y: -1)
        .translatedBy(x: 0, y: -image.size.height)

    for observation in self {
        let rect = observation.boundingBox

        let normalizedRect =
            VNImageRectForNormalizedRect(rect,
                Int(image.size.width),
                Int(image.size.height))
            .applying(transform)

        context.stroke(normalizedRect)
    }

    let result = UIGraphicsGetImageFromCurrentImageContext()
    UIGraphicsEndImageContext()

    return result
}
```

4. This extension on `Collection` allows us to work with the `VNFaceObservations` we get back and adds a function called `drawnOn()`, which draws a box around each face in the image.

5. Update the `getFaces()` function in *ContentView.swift* to call the new `drawnOn()` function we added a moment ago:

```swift
private func getFaces() {
    print("Getting faces...")
    self.faces = []
    self.image?.detectFaces { result in
        self.faces = result
```

```
        if let image = self.image,
        let annotatedImage = result?.drawnOn(image) {
            self.image =  annotatedImage
        }
    }
}
```

 You might be wondering why we're using extensions for every-thing. We're doing it for a couple of reasons, but first and fore-most we're doing it to make sure our code is split up into relatively easily digestible pieces. We don't want to overcompli-cate things by having enormous classes. There's enough code to digest already.

You can now run your app, choose an image, tap the button, and observe that any faces in the image have a box around them, as shown in Figure 4-3.

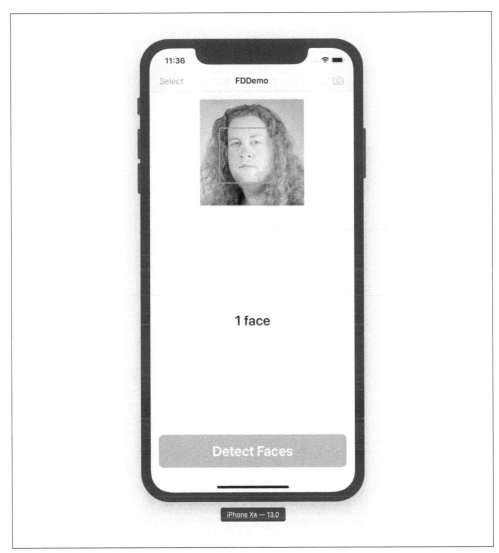

Figure 4-3. The improved face detector

Even More Improvements

We'd normally quit while we we're ahead and talk about how and why everything works at this point, but we're not going to do that here. Face detection is just too much fun. So far in this chapter, we've looked at how you can build an app that counts faces in a supplied image and then modified the app to draw a red box around the faces it detected.

In this section, let's take that a step further, and render an emoji on top of detected faces. You can't get much more practical than that, as shown in Figure 4-4.

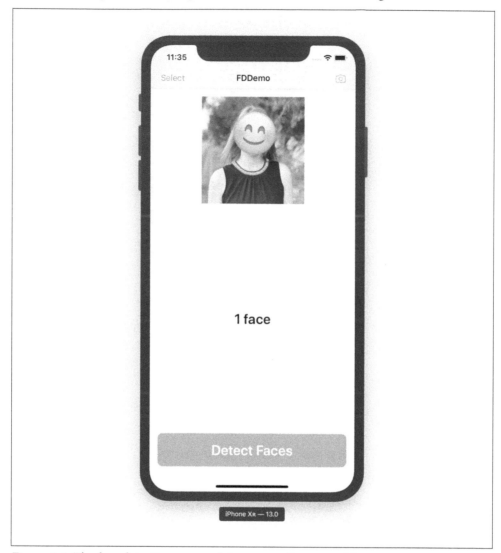

Figure 4-4. The face detection app applying an emoji on top of faces

You'll need to have completed the app described in "Improving the App" on page 86 to follow from here. If you don't want to do that or need a clean starting point, you can download the resources for this book from our website (*https://aiwithswift.com*), and find the project FDDemo-Complete. We build on the app from that point.

If you don't want to follow the instructions in this section, you can also find the project FDDemo-Improved, which is the end result of this section. If you go down that route, we strongly recommend reading the code as we discuss it in this section and comparing it with the code in FDDemo-Improved so that you understand what we're adding.

The only changes we need to make this time occur in *Faces.swift*:

1. Below the detectFaces() function, add a new function named rotatedBy() to the extension we created on UIImage:

```swift
func rotatedBy(degrees: CGFloat, clockwise: Bool = false) -> UIImage? {
    var radians = (degrees) * (.pi / 180)

    if !clockwise {
        radians = -radians
    }

    let transform = CGAffineTransform(rotationAngle: CGFloat(radians))

    let newSize = CGRect(
        origin: CGPoint.zero,
        size: self.size
        ).applying(transform).size

    let roundedSize = CGSize(
        width: floor(newSize.width),
        height: floor(newSize.height))

    let centredRect = CGRect(
        x: -self.size.width / 2,
        y: -self.size.height / 2,
        width: self.size.width,
        height: self.size.height)

    UIGraphicsBeginImageContextWithOptions(
        roundedSize,
        false,
        self.scale)

    guard let context = UIGraphicsGetCurrentContext() else {
        return nil
    }

    context.translateBy(
        x: roundedSize.width / 2,
        y: roundedSize.height / 2
    )
```

```
        context.rotate(by: radians)
        self.draw(in: centredRect)

        let result = UIGraphicsGetImageFromCurrentImageContext()
        UIGraphicsEndImageContext()

        return result
    }
```

This function returns a `UIImage` that's been rotated by the degrees specified as a `CGFloat`, in either a clockwise or counterclockwise direction.

2. Add an extension on `VNFaceLandmarks2D`, which contains a function `anchorPointInImage()` that allows us to center each set of points that may have been detected in a face (representing eyes, eyebrows, lips, and such):

```
extension VNFaceLandmarks2D {
    func anchorPointInImage(_ image: UIImage) ->
        (center: CGPoint?, angle: CGFloat?) {

        // centre each set of points that may have been detected, if
        // present
        let allPoints =
            self.allPoints?.pointsInImage(imageSize: image.size)
            .centerPoint

        let leftPupil =
            self.leftPupil?.pointsInImage(imageSize: image.size)
            .centerPoint

        let leftEye =
            self.leftEye?.pointsInImage(imageSize: image.size)
            .centerPoint

        let leftEyebrow =
            self.leftEyebrow?.pointsInImage(imageSize: image.size)
            .centerPoint

        let rightPupil =
            self.rightPupil?.pointsInImage(imageSize: image.size)
            .centerPoint

        let rightEye =
            self.rightEye?.pointsInImage(imageSize: image.size)
            .centerPoint

        let rightEyebrow =
            self.rightEyebrow?.pointsInImage(imageSize: image.size)
            .centerPoint
```

```
        let outerLips =
            self.outerLips?.pointsInImage(imageSize: image.size)
            .centerPoint

        let innerLips =
            self.innerLips?.pointsInImage(imageSize: image.size)
            .centerPoint

        let leftEyeCenter = leftPupil ?? leftEye ?? leftEyebrow
        let rightEyeCenter = rightPupil ?? rightEye ?? rightEyebrow
        let mouthCenter = innerLips ?? outerLips

        if let leftEyePoint = leftEyeCenter,
            let rightEyePoint = rightEyeCenter,
            let mouthPoint = mouthCenter {

            let triadCenter =
                [leftEyePoint, rightEyePoint, mouthPoint]
                .centerPoint

            let eyesCenter =
                [leftEyePoint, rightEyePoint]
                .centerPoint

            return (eyesCenter, triadCenter.rotationDegreesTo(eyesCenter))
        }

        // else fallback
        return (allPoints, 0.0)
    }
}
```

 VNFaceLandmarks2D represents all of the landmarks that Apple's Vision framework can detect in a face, exposed as properties. You can learn more about it in Apple's documentation (*https://apple.co/2IJ2W1a*).

3. We also need an extension on `CGRect` that returns a `CGRect` centered on a `CGPoint` provided:

```
extension CGRect {
    func centeredOn(_ point: CGPoint) -> CGRect {
        let size = self.size
        let originX = point.x - (self.width / 2.0)
        let originY = point.y - (self.height / 2.0)
        return CGRect(
            x: originX,
            y: originY,
```

```
        width: size.width,
        height: size.height
    )
  }
}
```

4. While we're at it, let's add an extension on `CGPoint`:

```swift
extension CGPoint {
    func rotationDegreesTo(_ otherPoint: CGPoint) -> CGFloat {
        let originX = otherPoint.x - self.x
        let originY = otherPoint.y - self.y

        let degreesFromX = atan2f(
            Float(originY),
            Float(originX)) * (180 / .pi)

        let degreesFromY = degreesFromX - 90.0

        let normalizedDegrees = (degreesFromY + 360.0)
            .truncatingRemainder(dividingBy: 360.0)

        return CGFloat(normalizedDegrees)
    }
}
```

This extension adds a function called `rotationDegreesTo()` that returns some degrees to rotate by, given another point. This helps orient facial features with the emoji we'll be drawing on the face.

5. We also need an extension on `Array`, for arrays of `CGPoints`:

```swift
extension Array where Element == CGPoint {
    var centerPoint: CGPoint {
        let elements = CGFloat(self.count)
        let totalX = self.reduce(0, { $0 + $1.x })
        let totalY = self.reduce(0, { $0 + $1.y })
        return CGPoint(x: totalX / elements, y: totalY / elements)
    }
}
```

This adds a function, `centerPoint()`, which returns a `CGPoint` for an array of points.

6. Because we're working with emojis, which are actually text, we also need an extension on `String`:

```swift
extension String {
    func image(of size: CGSize, scale: CGFloat = 0.94) -> UIImage? {
        UIGraphicsBeginImageContextWithOptions(size, false, 0)
        UIColor.clear.set()
        let rect = CGRect(origin: .zero, size: size)
```

```
            UIRectFill(CGRect(origin: .zero, size: size))
            (self as AnyObject).draw(
                in: rect,
                withAttributes: [
                    .font: UIFont.systemFont(ofSize: size.height * scale)
                ]
            )

            let image = UIGraphicsGetImageFromCurrentImageContext()

            UIGraphicsEndImageContext()

            return image
        }
    }
```

This allows us to get a `UIImage` from a `String`, which is useful because we want to be able to display emojis on top of an image, and we want those emojis to be images.

7. Replace the extension on `Collection` with the following:

```
extension Collection where Element == VNFaceObservation {
    func drawnOn(_ image: UIImage) -> UIImage? {

        UIGraphicsBeginImageContextWithOptions(image.size, false, 1.0)
        guard let _ = UIGraphicsGetCurrentContext() else { return nil }

        image.draw(in: CGRect(
            x: 0,
            y: 0,
            width: image.size.width,
            height: image.size.height)
        )

        let imageSize: (width: Int, height: Int) =
            (Int(image.size.width), Int(image.size.height))

        let transform = CGAffineTransform(scaleX: 1, y: -1)
            .translatedBy(x: 0, y: -image.size.height)

        let padding: CGFloat = 0.3

        for observation in self {
            guard let anchor =
                observation.landmarks?.anchorPointInImage(image) else {
                    continue
            }

            guard let center = anchor.center?.applying(transform) else {
                continue
```

```
        }

        let overlayRect = VNImageRectForNormalizedRect(
            observation.boundingBox,
            imageSize.width,
            imageSize.height
        ).applying(transform).centeredOn(center)

        let insets = (
            x: overlayRect.size.width * padding,
            y: overlayRect.size.height * padding)

        let paddedOverlayRect = overlayRect.insetBy(
            dx: -insets.x,
            dy: -insets.y)

        let randomEmoji = [
            "😀",
            "😁",
            "😂",
            "😃",
            "😄",
            "😅",
            "😆",
            "😉",
            "😊"
        ].randomElement()!

        if var overlayImage = randomEmoji
            .image(of: paddedOverlayRect.size) {

            if let angle = anchor.angle,
                let rotatedImage = overlayImage
                    .rotatedBy(degrees: angle) {

                overlayImage = rotatedImage
            }

            overlayImage.draw(in: paddedOverlayRect)
        }
    }

    let result = UIGraphicsGetImageFromCurrentImageContext()
    UIGraphicsEndImageContext()

    return result
    }
}
```

To cut a long story short, this extension (and its new `drawnOn()` function) draws a random emoji on top of the face.

And with that, we're done. You can launch your app, choose an image, and watch it apply a random emoji to the faces detected in the image. Show your friends and family and annoy them with it; we'll be here when you get back. You can see an example of the final app in Figure 4-5.

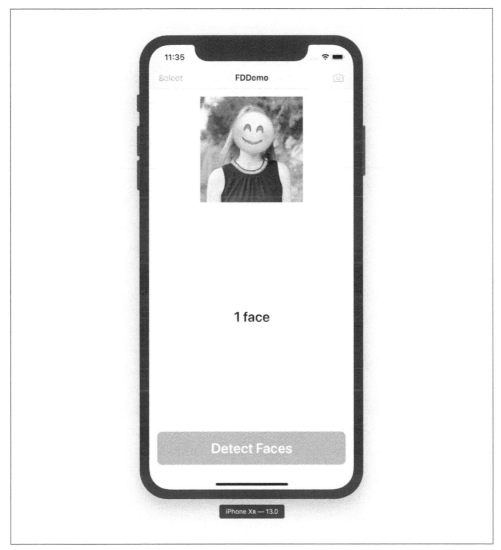

Figure 4-5. Our final face detector, replete with emoji

Task: Barcode Detection

We're not going to unpack this task much, especially not after looking at "Task: Face Detection" on page 74, because it's both similar to face detection and very simple.

We're going to do this one in a Playground because it's so simple to step through. It does require a fair bit of boilerplate code, though:

1. Fire up Xcode and create a new iOS-flavor Playground, as shown in Figure 4-6.

Figure 4-6. Creating a new iOS-flavor Playground in Xcode

2. Add a new source file called *Extensions.swift* to the Playground. In *Extensions.swift*, import the following:

```
import UIKit
```

> To find this code in our resources, head to our website (*https://aiwithswift.com*), download the resources, and find the Playground in the *BarcodeAndSaliencyDetection* folder.

3. Add the following extension on `CGSize`:

```
public extension CGSize {
    func scaleFactor(to size: CGSize) -> CGFloat {
        let horizontalScale = self.width / size.width
        let verticalScale = self.height / size.height

        return max(horizontalScale, verticalScale)
    }
}
```

This extension will allow us to call our function, scaleFactor(), on a CGSize, to return the scaling factor that would make the CGRect fit in a box of the indicated size.

4. Add an extension on CGRect:

```
public extension CGRect {
    func scaled(by scaleFactor: CGFloat) -> CGRect {
        let horizontalInsets =
            (self.width - (self.width * scaleFactor)) / 2.0
        let verticalInsets =
            (self.height - (self.height * scaleFactor)) / 2.0

        let edgeInsets = UIEdgeInsets(
            top: verticalInsets,
            left: horizontalInsets,
            bottom: verticalInsets,
            right: horizontalInsets
        )

        let leftOffset = min(self.origin.x + horizontalInsets, 0)
        let upOffset = min(self.origin.y + verticalInsets, 0)

        return self
            .inset(by: edgeInsets)
            .offsetBy(dx: -leftOffset, dy: -upOffset)
    }

    func cropped(to size: CGSize, centering: Bool = true) -> CGRect {
        if centering {
            let horizontalDifference = self.width - size.width
            let verticalDifference = self.height - size.height
            let newOrigin = CGPoint(
                x: self.origin.x + (horizontalDifference / 2.0),
                y: self.origin.y + (verticalDifference / 2.0)
            )
            return CGRect(
                x: newOrigin.x,
                y: newOrigin.y,
                width: size.width,
                height: size.height
            )
```

```
        }
            return CGRect(x: 0, y: 0, width: size.width, height: size.height)
        }
    }
```

This extension allows us to call `scaled()` on a CGRect to likewise scale it by a size (a scale factor), or call `cropped()` on a CGRect to crop it to a specified CGSize.

5. Create an extension on UIImage:

```
public extension UIImage {
    var width: CGFloat {
        return self.size.width
    }

    var height: CGFloat {
        return self.size.height
    }

    var rect: CGRect {
        return CGRect(x: 0, y: 0, width: self.width, height: self.height)
    }

    var invertTransform: CGAffineTransform {
        return CGAffineTransform(scaleX: 1, y: -1)
            .translatedBy(x: 0, y: -self.height)
    }

}
```

This extension has a few variables to store width and height and the like.

6. Within the UIImage extension, we need to add some code to properly handle the orientation of the image:

```
var cgImageOrientation: CGImagePropertyOrientation {
    switch self.imageOrientation {
        case .up: return .up
        case .down: return .down
        case .left: return .left
        case .right: return .right
        case .upMirrored: return .upMirrored
        case .downMirrored: return .downMirrored
        case .leftMirrored: return .leftMirrored
        case .rightMirrored: return .rightMirrored
    }
}
```

7. Crop the image, based on a CGSize:

```
func cropped(to size: CGSize, centering: Bool = true) -> UIImage? {
    let newRect = self.rect.cropped(to: size, centering: centering)
```

```
        return self.cropped(to: newRect, centering: centering)
    }
```

8. And based on a CGRect:

```
    func cropped(to rect: CGRect, centering: Bool = true) -> UIImage? {
        let newRect = rect.applying(self.invertTransform)
        UIGraphicsBeginImageContextWithOptions(newRect.size, false, 0)

        guard let cgImage = self.cgImage,
            let context = UIGraphicsGetCurrentContext() else { return nil }

        context.translateBy(x: 0.0, y: self.size.height)
        context.scaleBy(x: 1.0, y: -1.0)

        context.draw(
            cgImage,
            in: CGRect(
                x: -newRect.origin.x,
                y: newRect.origin.y,
                width: self.width,
                height: self.height),
            byTiling: false)

        context.clip(to: [newRect])

        let croppedImage = UIGraphicsGetImageFromCurrentImageContext()
        UIGraphicsEndImageContext()

        return croppedImage
    }
```

9. Scale the image by using a CGFloat:

```
    func scaled(by scaleFactor: CGFloat) -> UIImage? {
        if scaleFactor.isZero { return self }

        let newRect = self.rect
            .scaled(by: scaleFactor)
            .applying(self.invertTransform)

        UIGraphicsBeginImageContextWithOptions(newRect.size, false, 0)

        guard let cgImage = self.cgImage,
            let context = UIGraphicsGetCurrentContext() else { return nil }

        context.translateBy(x: 0.0, y: newRect.height)
        context.scaleBy(x: 1.0, y: -1.0)
        context.draw(
            cgImage,
            in: CGRect(
```

```
            x: 0,
            y: 0,
            width: newRect.width,
            height: newRect.height),
        byTiling: false)

    let resizedImage = UIGraphicsGetImageFromCurrentImageContext()
    UIGraphicsEndImageContext()

    return resizedImage
}
```

10. Back in the main body of the Playground, `import` the following:

```
import UIKit
import Vision
```

11. Create an extension on `VNImageRequestHandler` with a convenience initializer:

```
extension VNImageRequestHandler {
    convenience init?(uiImage: UIImage) {
        guard let cgImage = uiImage.cgImage else { return nil }
        let orientation = uiImage.cgImageOrientation

        self.init(cgImage: cgImage, orientation: orientation)
    }
}
```

A `VNImageRequestHandler` is used to work with images in Apple's Vision framework. It acts as a handle for an image that we're working with, so we don't need to mess with the real definitive copy of an image. Our convenience initializer allows us to create one with a `UIImage` because `VNImageRequestHandler` typically requires a `CGImage`, which is a different way of storing an image in Apple's frameworks.

 A `UIImage` is a very high-level way of storing an image, and is easy to create from files, for example. `UIImages` are safe to use in threaded environments, and are immutable. `CGImage`'s are not immutable, and can be used if you need to meddle with the contents of an image. You can learn about `UIImage` (*https://apple.co/35zmoYe*) and `CGImage` (*https://apple.co/2VzRytQ*) in Apple's documentation, if you're curious.

12. Insert an extension on `VNRequest`, adding a `queueFor()` function:

```
extension VNRequest {
    func queueFor(image: UIImage, completion: @escaping ([Any]?) -> ()) {
        DispatchQueue.global().async {
```

```
                    if let handler = VNImageRequestHandler(uiImage: image) {
                        try? handler.perform([self])
                        completion(self.results)
                    } else {
                        return completion(nil)
                    }
                }
            }
        }
```

This queues up requests for the VNImageRequestHandler: it allows us to push things into Vision to be processed.

13. Add an extension on UIImage, and a function to dectect rectangles (just in case we want to look for those) and to detect barcodes:

```
extension UIImage {
    func detectRectangles(
        completion: @escaping ([VNRectangleObservation]) -> ()) {

        let request = VNDetectRectanglesRequest()
        request.minimumConfidence = 0.8
        request.minimumAspectRatio = 0.3
        request.maximumObservations = 3

        request.queueFor(image: self) { result in
            completion(result as? [VNRectangleObservation] ?? [])
        }
    }

    func detectBarcodes(
        types symbologies: [VNBarcodeSymbology] = [.QR],
        completion: @escaping ([VNBarcodeObservation]) ->()) {

        let request = VNDetectBarcodesRequest()
        request.symbologies = symbologies

        request.queueFor(image: self) { result in
            completion(result as? [VNBarcodeObservation] ?? [])
        }
    }

    // can also detect human figures, animals, the horizon, all sorts of
    // things with inbuilt Vision functions
}
```

Both of these functions work the same way: they add a function to UIImage that lets us ask for barcodes or rectangles. When called, the function creates a request with Vision and looks for the type of thing we're asking for.

To test it, drag an image with a barcode (or a QR code) into the *Resources* folder of the Playground, as shown in Figure 4-7 and then add some code to the Playground to call our barcode-finding code:

```
let barcodeTestImage = UIImage(named: "test.jpg")!

barcodeTestImage.detectBarcodes { barcodes in
    for barcode in barcodes {
        print("Barcode data: \(barcode.payloadStringValue ?? "None")")
    }
}
```

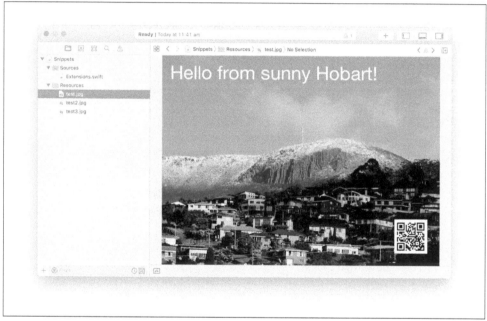

Figure 4-7. Resources for the barcode finder

This code first specifies an image (the one we dragged in, which we know has a barcode in it) and then calls the detectBarcodes() function we created on it. You should see something resembling Figure 4-8 when it works. That's it!

```
123   let barcodeTestImage = UIImage(named: "test.jpg")!
124
125   barcodeTestImage.detectBarcodes { barcodes in
126       for barcode in barcodes {
127           print("Barcode data: \(barcode.payloadStringValue ?? "None")")
```
> Barcode data: https://
> aiwithswift.com...
```
128       }
```
```
Barcode data: https://aiwithswift.com
```

Figure 4-8. Our barcode has been detected

Task: Saliency Detection

Closely related to barcode detection is *saliency detection*: finding the most interesting, or salient, bit of an image. For this task, we take the Playground we wrote for "Task: Barcode Detection" on page 98, and add support for saliency detection.

Confused by what we mean by saliency detection? Check out Figure 4-9 for an example.

Figure 4-9. An example of saliency detection. A box is drawn around the salient bit of this image (Paris with an owl cocktail mug!).

Detecting saliency is, for all intents, generating a heatmap of an image that can be used to highlight areas of interest.

Open the Playground we created in "Task: Barcode Detection" on page 98:

1. Working in the main body of the Playground, we'll need to add an extension on UIImage:

```
extension UIImage {

}
```

2. Within this extension, let's first add an enumeration for the type of saliency we want to look at:

```
enum SaliencyType {
    case objectnessBased, attentionBased

    var request: VNRequest {
        switch self {
        case .objectnessBased:
            return VNGenerateObjectnessBasedSaliencyImageRequest()
        case .attentionBased:
            return VNGenerateAttentionBasedSaliencyImageRequest()
        }
    }
}
```

This gives us a nice shorthand way of accessing either VNGenerateObjectnessBasedSaliencyImageRequest or VNGenerateAttentionBasedSaliencyImageRequest. VNGenerateObjectnessBasedSaliencyImageRequest relates to detecting the parts of an image that are most likely to be objects, whereas VNGenerateAttentionBasedSaliencyImageRequest relates to detecting the parts of an image that are likely to be most interesting.

To find this code in our resources, head to our website (*https://aiwithswift.com*), download the resources, and find the Playground in the *BarcodeAndSaliencyDetection* folder.

3. While still within the UIImage extension, add a function called detectSalientRegions():

```
func detectSalientRegions(
    prioritising saliencyType: SaliencyType = .attentionBased,
    completion: @escaping (VNSaliencyImageObservation?) -> ()) {

    let request = saliencyType.request

    request.queueFor(image: self) { results in
        completion(results?.first as? VNSaliencyImageObservation)
    }
}
```

This function allows us to ask a UIImage to give us its salient regions (this sounds far more exciting than it actually is) based on the type of saliency we want.

4. Add a cropped() function, which crops the image based on the saliency request, cropping to the salient bit:

```
func cropped(
    with saliencyObservation: VNSaliencyImageObservation?,
    to size: CGSize? = nil) -> UIImage? {

    guard let saliencyMap = saliencyObservation,
        let salientObjects = saliencyMap.salientObjects else {
            return nil
    }

    // merge all detected salient objects into one big rect of the
    // overaching 'salient region'
    let salientRect = salientObjects.reduce(into: CGRect.zero) {
        rect, object in
        rect = rect.union(object.boundingBox)
    }
    let normalizedSalientRect =
        VNImageRectForNormalizedRect(
            salientRect, Int(self.width), Int(self.height)
        )

    var finalImage: UIImage?

    // transform normalized salient rect based on larger or smaller
    // than desired size
    if let desiredSize = size {
        if self.width < desiredSize.width ||
            self.height < desiredSize.height { return nil }

        let scaleFactor = desiredSize
            .scaleFactor(to: normalizedSalientRect.size)

        // crop to the interesting bit
        finalImage = self.cropped(to: normalizedSalientRect)
```

```
        // scale the image so that as much of the interesting bit as
        // possible can be kept within desiredSize
        finalImage = finalImage?.scaled(by: -scaleFactor)

        // crop to the final desiredSize aspectRatio
        finalImage = finalImage?.cropped(to: desiredSize)
    } else {
        finalImage = self.cropped(to: normalizedSalientRect)
    }

    return finalImage
}
```

We can test this by dragging some images into the *Resources* folder of the Playground (as we did in "Task: Barcode Detection" on page 98) and then do the following:

1. Define an image (pointing to one of those we dragged to the *Resources* folder) and a size to which to crop it:

   ```
   let saliencyTestImage = UIImage(named: "test3.jpg")!
   let thumbnailSize = CGSize(width: 80, height: 80)
   ```

2. Define some UIImages to store the two different types of saliency crops we want (attention and object):

   ```
   var attentionCrop: UIImage?
   var objectsCrop: UIImage?
   ```

3. Call our detectSalientRegions() function (twice; once for each type of saliency):

   ```
   saliencyTestImage.detectSalientRegions(prioritising: .attentionBased) {
       result in

       if result == nil {
           print("The entire image was found equally interesting!")
       }

       attentionCrop = saliencyTestImage
           .cropped(with: result, to: thumbnailSize)

       print("Image was \(saliencyTestImage.width) * " +
           "\(saliencyTestImage.height), now " +
           "\(attentionCrop?.width ?? 0) * \(attentionCrop?.height ?? 0).")
   }

   saliencyTestImage
       .detectSalientRegions(prioritising: .objectnessBased) { result in
       if result == nil {
           print("The entire image was found equally interesting!")
       }
   ```

```
        objectsCrop = saliencyTestImage
            .cropped(with: result, to: thumbnailSize)

        print("Image was \(saliencyTestImage.width) * " +
        "\(saliencyTestImage.height), now " +
        "\(objectsCrop?.width ?? 0) * \(objectsCrop?.height ?? 0).")
    }
```

You should see something that looks like Figure 4-10. Try it with different images to
see what the app thinks is salient.

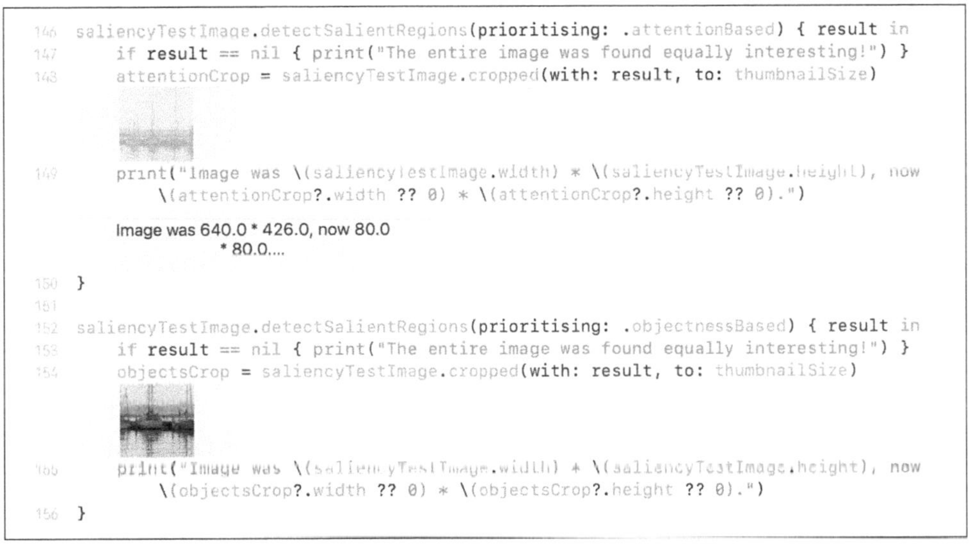

Figure 4-10. The saliency detector is working

Task: Image Similarity

Comparing two images to determine how similar they are is, at its core, a straightforward application of AI. Whether you need this for a game or to see how similar a
user's profile pictures are, there's a variety of uses for checking how similar an image
is.

In this task, we explore how you can quickly and easily compare two images in your
Swift applications and, again, without any model training involved.

This task is similar to the previous ones in that there is a toolkit for checking image
similarity provided by Apple. You could build a machine-learning application that
understands how to inform you of the distance between two images, but Apple has
done the work for you, so why would you? This book is *practical*.

Problem and Approach

Image similarity is one of those subtle practical AI things that's super useful when you need it, but difficult to quantify why you might need it in advance. In this task, we look at the practical side of image similarity by doing the following:

- Building an app that allows the user to select, or take, two pictures, and determine how similar they are (by percentage)
- Using Apple's tools for doing this without training a model
- Exploring the potential next steps for image similarity, and other ways to tackle this and similar problems

To demonstrate how to do this, we're going to build the app shown in Figure 4-11. Let's get started.

Building the App

We're again going to be using Apple's newest UI framework, SwiftUI, to build the app for determining image similarity as a practical AI task.

The final form of the app we're going to build in this task can be seen in (Figure 4-11) and consists of the following SwiftUI components:

- A `NavigationView`, with an app title and some `Buttons` (as `.navigationBarItems`) to allow the user to pick a photo from their library, or take a photo with their camera
- Two `Image` views, which will actually be `OptionalResizableImage` classes (we create these in a moment) to display the two images that we want to get the similarity of
- A `Button` to trigger the comparison of the two images, and another to clear the two images
- Some `Text` to display the similarity percentages

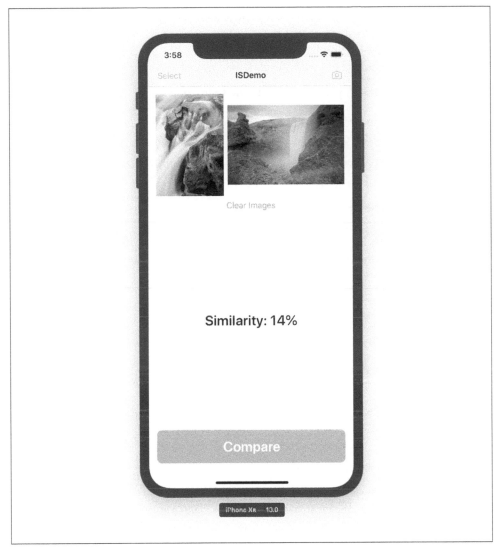

Figure 4-11. The final version of the Image Similarity app

 This book is here to teach you the practical side of using AI and machine-learning features with Swift and on Apple's platforms. Because of this, we don't explain the fine details of how to build apps; we assume that you mostly know that (although if you don't, we think you'll be able to follow along just fine if you pay attention). If you want to learn Swift, we recommend picking up *Learning Swift* (*https://oreil.ly/DLVGh*) (also by us!) from the lovely folks at O'Reilly.

If you don't want to manually build the iOS app, you can download the code from our website (*https://aiwithswift.com*) and then find the project named `ISDemo-Complete`. After you have that, we strongly recommend that you still proceed through this section, comparing the notes here with the code you downloaded.

To create the app yourself, you'll need to do the following:

1. Create an iOS app project in Xcode, choosing the Single View App template, and selecting the SwiftUI checkbox.

2. Add a new filed named *Views.swift* and import the following:

   ```
   import SwiftUI
   ```

3. Create a new `View` for an image that can resize:

   ```
   struct OptionalResizableImage: View {
       let image: UIImage?
       let placeholder: UIImage

       var body: some View {
           if let image = image {
               return Image(uiImage: image)
                   .resizable()
                   .aspectRatio(contentMode: .fit)
           } else {
               return Image(uiImage: placeholder)
                   .resizable()
                   .aspectRatio(contentMode: .fit)
           }
       }
   }
   ```

4. Create a `View` for a `ButtonLabel`:

   ```
   struct ButtonLabel: View {
       private let text: String
       private let background: Color

       var body: some View {
           HStack {
               Spacer()
               Text(text).font(.title).bold().foregroundColor(.white)
               Spacer()
               }.padding().background(background).cornerRadius(10)
       }

       init(_ text: String, background: Color) {
           self.text = text
           self.background = background
       }
   }
   ```

Our ButtonLabel is some text of a certain color.

5. Create a View so that we can work with a UIImagePicker:

```
struct ImagePickerView: View {
    private let completion: (UIImage?) -> ()
    private let camera: Bool

    var body: some View {
        ImagePickerControllerWrapper(
            camera: camera,
            completion: completion
        )
    }

    init(camera: Bool = false, completion: @escaping (UIImage?) -> ()) {
        self.completion = completion
        self.camera = camera
    }
}
```

6. Create a wrapper for UIViewControllerRepresentable so that we can actually use a UIImagePicker:

```
struct ImagePickerControllerWrapper: UIViewControllerRepresentable {
    typealias UIViewControllerType = UIImagePickerController
    private(set) var selectedImage: UIImage?
    private(set) var cameraSource: Bool
    private let completion: (UIImage?) -> ()

    init(camera: Bool, completion: @escaping (UIImage?) -> ()) {
        self.cameraSource = camera
        self.completion = completion
    }

    func makeCoordinator() -> ImagePickerControllerWrapper.Coordinator {
        let coordinator = Coordinator(self)
        coordinator.completion = self.completion
        return coordinator
    }

    func makeUIViewController(context: Context) ->
        UIImagePickerController {

        let imagePickerController = UIImagePickerController()
        imagePickerController.delegate = context.coordinator
        imagePickerController.sourceType =
            cameraSource ? .camera : .photoLibrary
        return imagePickerController
    }
```

```
func updateUIViewController(
    _ uiViewController: UIImagePickerController, context: Context) {
    //uiViewController.setViewControllers(?, animated: true)
}

class Coordinator: NSObject,
    UIImagePickerControllerDelegate, UINavigationControllerDelegate {

    var parent: ImagePickerControllerWrapper
    var completion: ((UIImage?) -> ())?

    init(_ imagePickerControllerWrapper:
        ImagePickerControllerWrapper) {
        self.parent = imagePickerControllerWrapper
    }

    func imagePickerController(_ picker: UIImagePickerController,
        didFinishPickingMediaWithInfo info:
            [UIImagePickerController.InfoKey: Any]) {

        print("Image picker complete...")
        let selectedImage =
            info[UIImagePickerController.InfoKey.originalImage]
            as? UIImage
        picker.dismiss(animated: true)
        completion?(selectedImage)
    }

    func imagePickerControllerDidCancel(
        _ picker: UIImagePickerController) {

        print("Image picker cancelled...")
        picker.dismiss(animated: true)
        completion?(nil)
    }
}
}
```

7. In the *Views.swift* file, add the following extension on UIImage so that we can fix
   an image's orientation:

```
extension UIImage {
    func fixOrientation() -> UIImage? {
        UIGraphicsBeginImageContext(self.size)
        self.draw(at: .zero)
        let newImage = UIGraphicsGetImageFromCurrentImageContext()
        UIGraphicsEndImageContext()
        return newImage
```

```
        }
    }
```

Next, we make a file called *Similarity.swift* in which we perform the actual image similarity test:

1. Add some `imports`:

```
import UIKit
import Vision
```

2. Add an extension on `UIImage`:

```
extension UIImage {

}
```

3. Within the extension, add the following function to compare similarity:

```
func similarity(to image: UIImage) -> Float? {
    var similarity: Float = 0
    guard let firstImageFPO = self.featurePrintObservation(),
        let secondImageFPO = image.featurePrintObservation(),
        let _ = try? secondImageFPO.computeDistance(
            &similarity,
            to: firstImageFPO
        ) else {
            return nil
    }

    return similarity
}
```

The similarity is calculated by computing the distance between the two images in question.

4. Add the following function to generate a feature print observation, which will assist in deriving image similarity:

```
private func featurePrintObservation() -> VNFeaturePrintObservation? {
    guard let cgImage = self.cgImage else { return nil }

    let requestHandler =
        VNImageRequestHandler(cgImage: cgImage,
        orientation: self.cgImageOrientation,
        options: [:]
    )

    let request = VNGenerateImageFeaturePrintRequest()
    if let _ = try? requestHandler.perform([request]),
        let result = request.results?.first
            as? VNFeaturePrintObservation {
        return result
```

```
        }
        return nil
    }
```

Notice that we called the `featurePrintObservation()` function that we wrote here earlier, in the `similarity()` function. The `VNFeaturePrintObservations` are the things that the distance is computed between in `similarity()`.

5. At the end of the *Similarity.swift* file, we need another extension on `UIImage` in order to obtain its orientation:

```
extension UIImage {
    var cgImageOrientation: CGImagePropertyOrientation {
        switch self.imageOrientation {
            case .up: return .up
            case .down: return .down
            case .left: return .left
            case .right: return .right
            case .upMirrored: return .upMirrored
            case .downMirrored: return .downMirrored
            case .leftMirrored: return .leftMirrored
            case .rightMirrored: return .rightMirrored
        }
    }
}
```

Finally, we need to move to the *ContentView.swift* file:

1. Add our `States` to the top of the `ContentView` struct:

```
@State private var imagePickerOpen: Bool = false
@State private var cameraOpen: Bool = false

@State private var firstImage: UIImage? = nil
@State private var secondImage: UIImage? = nil
@State private var similarity: Int = -1
```

2. Below them, add the following attributes:

```
private let placeholderImage = UIImage(named: "placeholder")!

private var cameraEnabled: Bool {
    UIImagePickerController.isSourceTypeAvailable(.camera)
}

private var selectEnabled: Bool {
    secondImage == nil
}

private var comparisonEnabled: Bool {
```

```
        secondImage != nil && similarity < 0
    }
```

3. Within the ContentView struct, but outside of the body View, add a function to clear our images and similarity rating:

```
private func clearImages() {
    firstImage = nil
    secondImage = nil
    similarity = -1
}
```

4. And another to get the similarity:

```
private func getSimilarity() {
    print("Getting similarity...")
    if let firstImage = firstImage, let secondImage = secondImage,
        let similarityMeasure = firstImage.similarity(to: secondImage){
        similarity = Int(similarityMeasure)
    } else {
        similarity = 0
    }
    print("Similarity: \(similarity)%")
}
```

5. And another for when control is returned from getting a similarity:

```
private func controlReturned(image: UIImage?) {
    print("Image return \(image == nil ? "failure" : "success")...")
    if firstImage == nil {
        firstImage = image?.fixOrientation()
    } else {
        secondImage = image?.fixOrientation()
    }
}
```

6. And one more to summon an image picker:

```
private func summonImagePicker() {
    print("Summoning ImagePicker...")
    imagePickerOpen = true
}
```

7. And one to summon a camera view:

```
private func summonCamera() {
    print("Summoning camera...")
    cameraOpen = true
}
```

8. Update your body View as follows:

```
var body: some View {
    if imagePickerOpen {
        return  AnyView(ImagePickerView { result in
```

```
                self.controlReturned(image: result)
                self.imagePickerOpen = false
            })
        } else if cameraOpen {
            return  AnyView(ImagePickerView(camera: true) { result in
                self.controlReturned(image: result)
                self.cameraOpen = false
            })
        } else {
            return AnyView(NavigationView {
                VStack {
                    HStack {
                        OptionalResizableImage(
                            image: firstImage,
                            placeholder: placeholderImage
                        )
                        OptionalResizableImage(
                            image: secondImage,
                            placeholder: placeholderImage
                        )
                    }

                    Button(action: clearImages) { Text("Clear Images") }
                    Spacer()
                    Text(
                        "Similarity: " +
                        "\(similarity > 0 ? String(similarity) : "...")%"
                    ).font(.title).bold()
                    Spacer()

                    if comparisonEnabled {
                        Button(action: getSimilarity) {
                            ButtonLabel("Compare", background: .blue)
                        }.disabled(!comparisonEnabled)
                    } else {
                        Button(action: getSimilarity) {
                            ButtonLabel("Compare", background: .gray)
                        }.disabled(!comparisonEnabled)
                    }
                }
                .padding()
                .navigationBarTitle(Text("ISDemo"), displayMode: .inline)
                .navigationBarItems(
                    leading: Button(action: summonImagePicker) {
                        Text("Select")
                    }.disabled(!selectEnabled),
                    trailing: Button(action: summonCamera) {
                        Image(systemName: "camera")
                    }.disabled(!cameraEnabled))
            })
```

```
        }
    }
```

We don't need to touch the `ContentView_Previews` struct in this case.

You now can run the app, pick two images, take two photos (or some combination thereof), and then tap the button to get a rating of how similar they are. Brilliant.

What Just Happened? How Does This Work?

You might have noticed that we didn't go through the process of finding data to train a model, training a model, and integrating the model into an app. Instead, we just built an app, and it all just worked. (You might also be seeing a theme in our tasks so far...)

Wouldn't it be nice if everything were like this?

So far, we've been using features of Apple's Vision framework, which is a suite of computer vision algorithms, to compare two images. (We introduced Vision back in "Apple's Other Frameworks" on page 40.)

The feature we used to perform the image similarity comparison in this chapter is called `VNFeaturePrintObservation`. Computing a feature print allows two images to have a pair-wise distance computed: this allows us to ask for a similarity (a distance) between images. You can learn more about what might be happening under the hood later, in Chapter 11.

You can learn more about this feature in Apple's documentation (*https://apple.co/2IM0arQ*).

Next Steps

What's next depends on what you want to do next. As mentioned in Chapter 2, Apple's Vision framework has a variety of uses to address practical AI needs in your projects.

As supplied, and without any work from you other than using the appropriate bits of the framework, you can use Vision to detect faces and landmarks in faces such as the nose, mouth, eyes, and similar; text, barcodes, and other types of two-dimensional codes; and track features in video and beyond.

Vision also makes it easier to work with CoreML for image classification and object detection with your own machine-learning models.

You could also do a different kind of image similarity. For example, Apple's Turi Create library adopts an entirely different approach (*http://bit.ly/35xDbuo*).

Task: Image Classification

In this first substantive practical task for which we build our own model, we take a look at an all-time classic practical application of AI: image classification.

Think of an image classifier like a hat that sorts images, as if it were from a certain popular magic-based fictional universe.

A classifier is a machine-learning model that takes input and classifies it into a category based on what it thinks the input is. An image classifier takes this with an image, and informs you as to which label (or class) it thinks the image belongs to, based on however many predefined labels it knows about.

Image classification is typically a deep-learning problem. For a refresher on what deep learning means, check back to Chapter 1.

Deep learning is not the only way in which you can make an image classifier, but it's currently one of the most effective ways.

Problem and Approach

As appropriate as it would be to tackle such a classic AI problem with a classic dataset (classifying whether a picture is of a cat or a dog), we're a little more creative!

We're going to build a binary image classifier that notifies us whether it thinks it sees a banana or an apple (Figure 4-12). Amazing, huh? (We're not much more creative, it would seem.)

The importance of bananas to machine learning researchers cannot be overstated.
—Dr. Alasdair Allan, 2019 (*http://bit.ly/2B6y6ey*)

For this task, we're going to explore the practical side of image classification by doing the following:

- Building an app that allows us to use or take photos and determine whether they contain a banana or an apple
- Selecting a toolkit for creating a machine-learning model and assembling a dataset for the problem
- Building and training an image classification model
- Incorporating the model into our app
- Improving our app

After that, we quickly touch on the theory of how it works, and point you to further resources for improvements and changes that you can make on your own.

We want this book to stay firmly rooted in the practical, task-based side of things that Apple's platforms make so easy, so we're going to approach this top-down. By this we mean that we start with the practical output *we want*: an app that can distinguish between a banana and an apple (Figure 4-12), and work down until we know how *to make that work*. We don't start with an algorithm or a formula; we start with the practical desired result.

Figure 4-12. Our app will be able to identify images of each of these fruits

Figure 4-13 presents some images of what we'd like our resulting app to be. Let's get started.

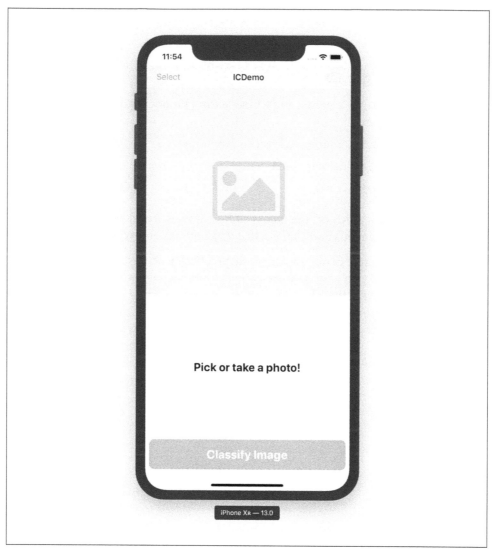

Figure 4-13. Our final app (we'll be ready to win any game of Banana or Apple?!)

Building the App

The hottest, unicorniest startups in the world use machine learning to do things. It is known. We need to get in on this machine-learning action. We obviously need an app.

The starting point iOS app that we're going to build first incorporates the following features:

- Two buttons: one to pick a photo from the user photo library, and one to take a photo with the camera (if a camera is available)
- An image view to display the chosen or taken image
- A label to display some instructions (and eventually display what class it thinks the image chosen is)
- A button to trigger the image classification

Figure 4-14 depicts an image of this first pass of the app. The app is going to be built using Apple's UIKit framework, Apple's older UI framework for iOS. You can learn more about UIKit in Apple's documentation (*https://apple.co/2VASmi4*).

 This book is here to teach you the practical side of using AI and machine-learning features with Swift and on Apple's platforms. Because of this, we don't explain the fine details of how to build apps; we assume that you mostly know that (although if you don't, we think you'll be able to follow along just fine if you pay attention). If you want to learn Swift, we recommend picking up *Learning Swift* (*https://oreil.ly/DLVGh*) (also by us!) from the lovely folks at O'Reilly.

If you don't want to manually build the starting point iOS app, you can download the code from our website (*https://aiwithswift.com*) and find the project named ICDemo-Starter. After you have that, skim through the rest of this section, and then meet us at "AI Toolkit and Dataset" on page 130.

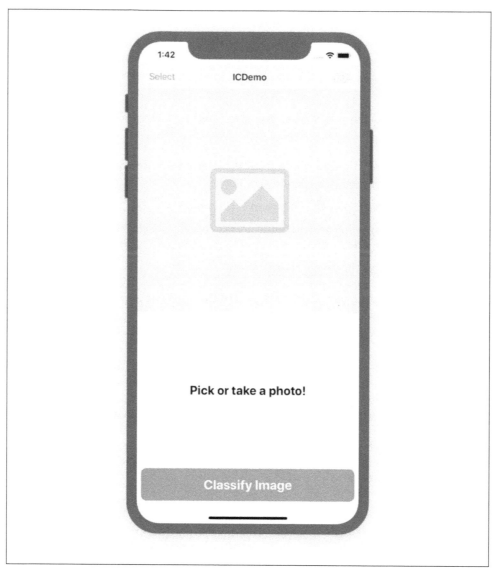

Figure 4-14. The first phase of (what will become) our image classifier app

To make the starting point yourself, you need to do the following:

1. Create an iOS app project in Xcode, choosing the Single View App template. We did not select any of the checkboxes below the Language drop-down (which was, of course, set to "Swift").

2. After you create your project, open the *Main.storyboard* file and create a user interface with the following components:

   - An image view to display the chosen image
   - A label to show both instructions and the classification of an image
   - A button to trigger the image classification
   - buttons to allow the user to pick an image from their photo library and take a photo (we used two navigation bar buttons for this). Figure 4-15 shows an example of our storyboard.

Figure 4-15. Our storyboard

After you've laid out the necessary elements, make sure you add the proper constraints.

3. Connect outlets for the UI objects as follows:

```
@IBOutlet weak var cameraButton: UIBarButtonItem!
@IBOutlet weak var imageView: UIImageView!
@IBOutlet weak var classLabel: UILabel!
@IBOutlet weak var classifyImageButton: UIButton!
```

4. Connect actions for the UI objects as follows:

```
@IBAction func selectButtonPressed(_ sender: Any) {
    getPhoto()
}

@IBAction func cameraButtonPressed(_ sender: Any) {
    getPhoto(cameraSource: true)
}

@IBAction func classifyImageButtonPressed(_ sender: Any) {
    classifyImage()
}
```

5. You also need to declare two variables in the `ViewController` class:

```
private var inputImage: UIImage?
private var classification: String?
```

6. Modify the `viewDidLoad()` function, making it look as follows:

```
override func viewDidLoad() {
    super.viewDidLoad()

    cameraButton.isEnabled =
        UIImagePickerController.isSourceTypeAvailable(.camera)

    imageView.contentMode = .scaleAspectFill

    imageView.image = UIImage.placeholder
}
```

7. Add the following function to enable or disable controls based on the presence of input to classify:

```
private func refresh() {
    if inputImage == nil {
        classLabel.text = "Pick or take a photo!"
        imageView.image = UIImage.placeholder
    } else {
        imageView.image = inputImage

        if classification == nil {
            classLabel.text = "None"
            classifyImageButton.enable()
        } else {
            classLabel.text = classification
            classifyImageButton.disable()
```

```
            }
        }
    }
```

8. Add another function to perform the classification which currently just sets the classification to "FRUIT!" because there's no AI yet):

```
private func classifyImage() {
    classification = "FRUIT!"

    refresh()
}
```

9. Add an extension to the end of the *ViewController.swift* file, as follows (it's a fair chunk of code, which we explain in a moment):

```
extension ViewController: UINavigationControllerDelegate,
    UIPickerViewDelegate, UIImagePickerControllerDelegate {

    private func getPhoto(cameraSource: Bool = false) {
        let photoSource: UIImagePickerController.SourceType
        photoSource = cameraSource ? .camera : .photoLibrary

        let imagePicker = UIImagePickerController()
        imagePicker.delegate = self
        imagePicker.sourceType = photoSource
        imagePicker.mediaTypes = [kUTTypeImage as String]
        present(imagePicker, animated: true)
    }

    @objc func imagePickerController(_ picker: UIImagePickerController,
        didFinishPickingMediaWithInfo info:
            [UIImagePickerController.InfoKey: Any]) {

        inputImage =
            info[UIImagePickerController.InfoKey.originalImage] as? UIImage

        classification = nil

        picker.dismiss(animated: true)
        refresh()

        if inputImage == nil {
            summonAlertView(message: "Image was malformed.")
        }
    }

    private func summonAlertView(message: String? = nil) {
        let alertController = UIAlertController(
            title: "Error",
            message: message ?? "Action could not be completed.",
```

```
            preferredStyle: .alert
        )

        alertController.addAction(
            UIAlertAction(
                title: "OK",
                style: .default
            )
        )
        present(alertController, animated: true)
    }
}
```

This code allows us to summon the camera or the user photo library. After the user has taken a photo or chosen one, the image is returned. If, for some reason, the image chosen is nil, it also provides for the display of an alert view using summonAlertView(), to notify the user what happened.

And finally, code-wise, add a new Swift file to the project and name it *Utils.swift* (or similar):

1. In this new Swift file, add the following:

```
import UIKit

extension UIImage{
    static let placeholder = UIImage(named: "placeholder.png")!
}

extension UIButton {
    func enable() {
        self.isEnabled = true
        self.backgroundColor = UIColor.systemBlue
    }

    func disable() {
        self.isEnabled = false
        self.backgroundColor = UIColor.lightGray
    }
}

extension UIBarButtonItem {
    func enable() { self.isEnabled = true }
    func disable() { self.isEnabled = false }
}
```

This defines an extension on UIImage that allows us to specify a placeholder image. It also defines an extension on UIButton that allows us to enable() or `disable()` the button. We also add the equivalent on `UIBarButtonItem`, which is the navigation bar equivalent of a `UIButton`.

2. Add a launch screen and an icon, if you'd like (our starter project has some), and launch the app in the simulator. You should see something like the image we showed earlier, in Figure 4-14.

You can select an image (or take a photo if you're running it on a real device) and see the image appear in the image view. As Figure 4-16 demonstrates, when you tap the Classify Image button, you should see the label update to say "FRUIT!".

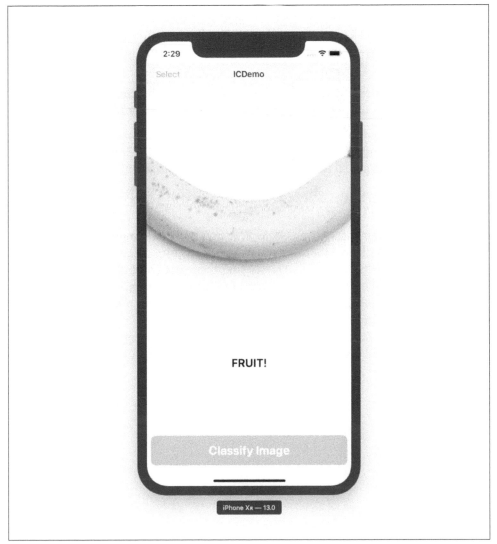

Figure 4-16. Our starter app for the image classifier is ready

You're now ready to get into the AI side of things.

AI Toolkit and Dataset

You'll need to assemble your toolkit for this task. The primary tools we'll be using in this case are the CreateML application and the CoreML and Vision frameworks.

First, we use the CreateML application, Apple's task-based tool for building machine-learning models to assemble, train, and validate a model that can, hopefully, distinguish between bananas and apples.

Then, we use CoreML to work with that model.

At this point you might be thinking, "CoreML? Isn't this entire book about CoreML? Have the authors gone off the rails? Is that why there are four authors? Did they keep replacing one another?"

Well, we can't comment whether we've gone off the rails, but we promise you that even though CoreML is a central component of this book, it's not the only one.

CoreML takes care of the using, reading from, talking to, and otherwise dealing with machine-learning models in your apps. We're going to be using it in this scenario for exactly that: getting a model into our app and communicating with it.

For more details on the nitty-gritty of the tools, check back to Chapter 2, particularly "CreateML" on page 31.

Our final tool for Banana or Apple?! is Vision. Vision is a framework, also from Apple, that provides a whole lot of smarts to help with computer-vision problems. As it turns out, recognizing images and classifying them is a computer-vision problem. We used Vision a lot earlier in this chapter, for Face Detection, Barcode Detection, Saliency Detection, and Image Similarity. For those, we were *directly* using Vision. This time, we use Vision to work with our own model, and with CoreML. We discussed Apple's other frameworks earlier, in "Apple's Other Frameworks" on page 40, and you can see where Vision fits in with the other frameworks in Figure 4-17.

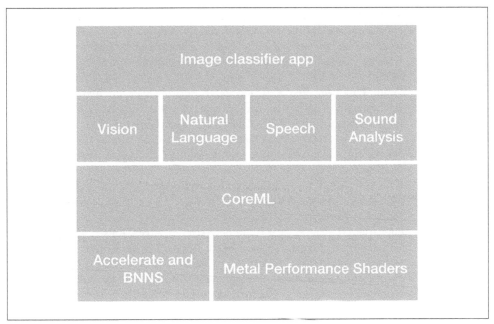

Figure 4-17. Where CoreML fits with our other AI tools

Before we can make an app that can classify different kinds of fruit from a picture, we need some pictures of fruit. Thankfully, as with many things, the boffins from Romania have us covered with the Fruit-360 dataset (*http://bit.ly/2oF5qXt*).

This dataset contains 103 different types of fruit, cleanly separated into training data, test data, as well as images with more than one fruit per image, for audacious multi-fruit classification. Figure 4-18 illustrates an example of the kinds of images that are in the dataset.

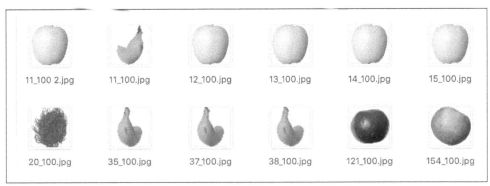

Figure 4-18. Examples of the fruit images

At this point you might have gathered that if we used all of these images for our classification model, the app would not only be able to advise us whether we're looking at a banana or an apple, but whether we're what looking at is one of 103 different fruits: Apples (different varieties: Crimson Snow, Golden, Golden-Red, Granny Smith, Pink Lady, Red, Red Delicious), Apricot, Avocado, Avocado ripe, Banana (Yellow, Red, Lady Finger), Cactus fruit, Cantaloupe (two varieties), Carambula, Cherry (different varieties, Rainier), Cherry Wax (Yellow, Red, Black), Chestnut, Clementine, Cocos, Dates, Granadilla, Grape (Blue, Pink, White (different varieties)), Grapefruit (Pink, White), Guava, Hazelnut, Huckleberry, Kiwi, Kaki, Kohlrabi, Kumsquats, Lemon (normal, Meyer), Lime, Lychee, Mandarine, Mango, Mangostan, Maracuja, Melon Piel de Sapo, Mulberry, Nectarine, Orange, Papaya, Passion fruit, Peach (different varieties), Pepino, Pear (different varieties, Abate, Kaiser, Monster, Red, Williams), Pepper (Red, Green, Yellow), Physalis (normal, with Husk), Pineapple (normal, Mini), Pitahaya Red, Plum (different varieties), Pomegranate, Pomelo Sweetie, Quince, Rambutan, Raspberry, Redcurrant, Salak, Strawberry (normal, Wedge), Tamarillo, Tangelo, Tomato (different varieties, Maroon, Cherry Red, Yellow), Walnut. Truly, we live in an age of marvels. (We're just going to use the apples and bananas right now, though.)

Let's get the dataset ready to train a model. All you'll need to do is head over to the Fruit-360 dataset (*http://bit.ly/2oF5qXt*) and download it by hitting the big green button. After you've extracted it, you should be looking at something that resembles the image shown in Figure 4-19.

Because we only want to look for apples or bananas, you should now copy out the apple and banana folders from the *Training* folder and put them in a new folder somewhere safe, as shown in Figure 4-20.

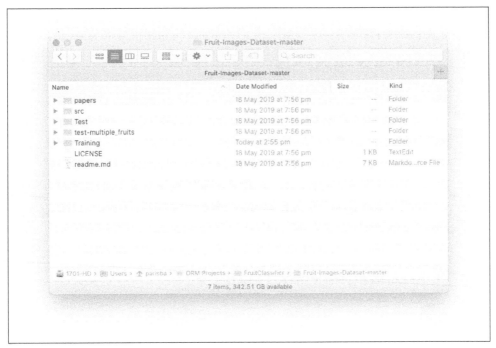

Figure 4-19. The Fruit-360 dataset, extracted and ready to go

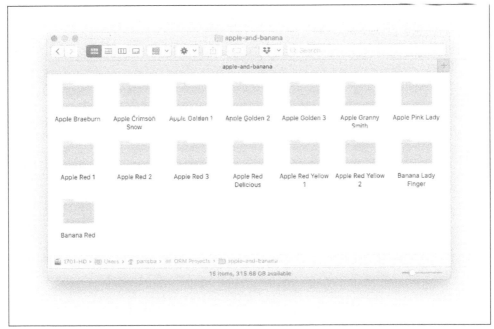

Figure 4-20. The Apple and Banana images, ready to go

Creating a model

With our dataset ready to go, we now turn to Apple's CreateML application to build a model. CreateML has come in a few different iterations over the years, but, here, we use the newest: the application version.

 To learn more about the various incarnations of CreateML, check back to Chapter 2.

Let's build our fruit classifier. Open CreateML: you can find CreateML by firing up Xcode, and then selecting the Xcode menu → Open Developer Tool → CreateML, and then do the following:

 If you like launching macOS apps using Spotlight, you can just summon Spotlight and type **CreateML**. Magic.

1. With CreateML open, select the Image Classifier template, as shown in Figure 4-21, and then click Next.
2. Give your project some details, as shown in Figure 4-22, and again click Next.

Figure 4-21. Selecting the Image Classifier option in the CreateML template picker

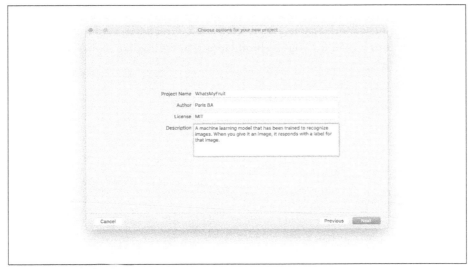

Figure 4-22. Setting the project options for your new CreateML model

You now have an empty CreateML project, ready to train an image classifier. It should look something like Figure 4-23.

Figure 4-23. Your CreateML project is ready to take some images

3. Click the drop-down text box marked Training Data and browse to the folder where you saved the apple and banana images earlier. Select this folder.

4. In the top bar of the CreateML app, click the Play button, and then go watch some TV, play a videogame, or go for a walk. CreateML is going to get to work training your model for you! It should look something like Figure 4-24.

Figure 4-24. CreateML training our fruit classifier

 Don't panic! This might take a while. It took about 47 minutes to train on our 8-core i9 MacBook Pro, but it will go faster with the more CPU cores you have in your machine. However, it will always take a while. On a MacBook Air or MacBook, this could take multiple hours. This is normal.

As training approaches completion, you'll notice the application doing an accuracy and testing pass, showing some charts about how accurate the model is. We talk about these later. The testing phase can take a while, too.

When CreateML is done, you'll be able to drag the model file out from the Output box in the upper-right corner of the window. Drag this file somewhere safe.

 You might notice that the file you dragged out has the extension *.mlmodel*. This is CoreML's native model format, as discussed in "CoreML" on page 22.

Now that we've trained and tested a model that can identify fruit (well, more accurately, CreateML has done it for us), let's put it to work in our app.

 We talk more about what the training, validation, and testing phases of this process are later on in this chapter and throughout the rest of the book. Stay tuned. (The book is called *practical* artificial intelligence, after all!) Also visit our website *https://aiwithswift.com* for articles on the topic.

Incorporating the Model in the App

Now that we have our starting point app and a trained model, we're going to combine them and make an app that can actually perform image classification.

You'll need to have either built the starting point yourself, following the instructions in "Building the App" on page 123, or downloaded the code and the project named `ICDemo-Starter` from our website (*https://aiwithswift.com*). We'll be progressing from that point in this section.

If you don't want to follow along and manually work with the app's code to add the AI features, you can also download the project named `ICDemo-Complete`.

We're going to need to change a few things to get the app working with our model:

1. Add a new variable, `classifier` alongside `inputImage` and `classification`:

    ```
    private let classifier = VisionClassifier(mlmodel: BananaOrApple().model)
    ```

2. Assign the new variable's delegate to `self` at the end of `viewDidLoad()`, and then call `refresh()`:

    ```
    classifier?.delegate = self
    refresh()
    ```

3. At the end of the first `if` statement of the `refresh()` function, add a call to disable the `classifyImageButton` (so that if there's no image present, you can't click the button to ask the model for a classification, which matters now that there will be a model connected):

    ```
    classifyImageButton.disable()
    ```

4. Replace the definition of `classifyImage()` as follows, to actually do something instead of always saying "FRUIT!":

    ```
    private func classifyImage() {
        if let classifier = self.classifier, let image = inputImage {
            classifier.classify(image)
            classifyImageButton.disable()
        }
    }
    ```

Next, add a new Swift file to the project, called *Vision.swift*:

5. Add the following code to it:

```
import UIKit
import CoreML
import Vision

extension VNImageRequestHandler {
    convenience init?(uiImage: UIImage) {
        guard let ciImage = CIImage(image: uiImage) else { return nil }
        let orientation = uiImage.cgImageOrientation

        self.init(ciImage: ciImage, orientation: orientation)
    }
}

class VisionClassifier {

    private let model: VNCoreMLModel
    private lazy var requests: [VNCoreMLRequest] = {
        let request = VNCoreMLRequest(
            model: model,
            completionHandler: {
                [weak self] request, error in
                self?.handleResults(for: request, error: error)
        })

        request.imageCropAndScaleOption = .centerCrop
        return [request]
    }()

    var delegate: ViewController?

    init?(mlmodel: MLModel) {
        if let model = try? VNCoreMLModel(for: mlmodel) {
            self.model = model
        } else {
            return nil
        }
    }

    func classify(_ image: UIImage) {
        DispatchQueue.global(qos: .userInitiated).async {
            guard let handler =
                VNImageRequestHandler(uiImage: image) else {
                    return
            }

            do {
                try handler.perform(self.requests)
```

```
            } catch {
                self.delegate?.summonAlertView(
                    message: error.localizedDescription
                )
            }
        }
    }

    func handleResults(for request: VNRequest, error: Error?) {
        DispatchQueue.main.async {
            guard let results =
                request.results as? [VNClassificationObservation] else {
                    self.delegate?.summonAlertView(
                        message: error?.localizedDescription
                    )
                    return
            }

            if results.isEmpty {
                self.delegate?.classification = "Don't see a thing!"
            } else {
                let result = results[0]

                if result.confidence < 0.6  {
                    self.delegate?.classification = "Not quite sure..."
                } else {
                    self.delegate?.classification =
                        "\(result.identifier) " +
                        "(\(Int(result.confidence * 100))%)"
                }
            }

            self.delegate?.refresh()
        }
    }
}
```

6. Add the following extension to the end of the *Vision.swift* file:

```
extension UIImage {
    var cgImageOrientation: CGImagePropertyOrientation {
        switch self.imageOrientation {
            case .up: return .up
            case .down: return .down
            case .left: return .left
            case .right: return .right
            case .upMirrored: return .upMirrored
            case .downMirrored: return .downMirrored
            case .leftMirrored: return .leftMirrored
            case .rightMirrored: return .rightMirrored
        }
    }
```

```
        }
    }
```

This code comes directly from Apple's documentation on converting between CGImage and UIImage types (*https://apple.co/3189zQZ*). We talked about the difference between CGImage and UIImage earlier in "Task: Barcode Detection" on page 98.

7. Drag the *WhatsMyFruit.mlmodel* file into the root of the projects and allow Xcode to copy it in.

You can now launch the app in the simulator. You should see something that looks like Figure 4-25.

You can select an image (or take a photo if you're running it on a real device), see the image appear in the image view, and then click tap the Classify Image button to ask the model we built for a classification. You should see the label update with the classification (or lack thereof).

Improving the App

You can, of course, make the app able to classify more than just bananas and apples. If you return to the dataset that we prepared earlier in "AI Toolkit and Dataset" on page 130 and look at the complete *Training* folder, with all 103 different fruit classes (labels), you might be able to guess what we suggest trying next.

Train a new image classification model using Apple's CreateML app, following the instructions in "Creating a model" on page 134, but instead, select the entire *Training* folder (giving you 103 different classes) from the Fruit-360 dataset.

Drop this model into your Xcode project, named appropriately, and then update the following line in *ViewController.swift* to point to the new model:

```
    private let classifier = VisionClassifier(mlmodel: BananaOrApple().model)
```

For example, if your new model was called *Fruits360.mlmodel*, you'd update the line to resemble the following:

```
    private let classifier = VisionClassifier(mlmodel: Fruits360().model)
```

You then can launch your app again and detect all 103 different kinds of fruit. Amazing. You're now ready to play app-assisted "What's My Fruit?"

Figure 4-25. Our image classifer works

Task: Drawing Recognition

With the advent of the iPad Pro and the Apple Pencil, drawing on Apple's mobile devices is more popular than ever (check out Procreate (*https://procreate.art*), an app built in the authors' home state of Tasmania).

Classifying a drawing could be useful for all manner of reasons, from making a drawing-based game to figuring out what someone has drawn to turn it into an emoji, and beyond.

Problem and Approach

Drawings are fun, and it's kind of magic to be able to draw something, even if it's all scribbly and weird, and then have a computer tell you what you've drawn. It's a fun feature that could be an app or game all on its own or form the basis of a feature that makes your app a little bit more magic.

In this task, we're going to explore the practical side of drawing detection by the following:

- Building an app that lets users take a photo of a drawing and have the app classify it
- Finding or assembling the data and then training a model that can classify drawings from bitmap images
- Exploring the next steps for better drawing classification

In this task, we build an app that can identify what we've drawn from a photo of a black-and-white scribbly-line drawing. Figure 4-26 illustrates what the final version of the app looks like.

Figure 4-26. The final version of our bitmap drawing detector

AI Toolkit and Dataset

We're going to look at our AI toolkit before we build the app for this task, because there's really only one pass we need to do to build the app. The primary tools we'll be using for this task are Turi Create, CoreML, and Vision. For a reminder on what these tools are, check back to Chapter 2 and "Apple's Other Frameworks" on page 40.

First, let's use Turi Create, Apple's task-based Python toolkit for creating machine-learning models, to train a model that can classify drawings.

Then, we use CoreML and Vision to work with the model, classifying photos of drawings we allow the user to take photos of.

To make an app that can classify drawings, we need a dataset of drawings. We could draw a few million little sketches of different things that we might want the app to be able to identify, but that might take a while.

As you'll find is often the case, the boffins have us covered. This time the boffins are from Google. The Quick Draw Dataset (*http://bit.ly/2Ba4o8M*) is a collection of more than 50 million sketchy drawings, categorized (345 categories), all drawn by users from around the world who were playing Google's Quick, Draw! game (*https://quick draw.withgoogle.com*) online (Google is very good at getting people to contribute data), shown in Figure 4-27.

We've been made aware that those outside the United Kingdom and Australia might not know what a *boffin* is. Please consult this article (*http://bit.ly/2IPqqls*) for more details on boffins. As a wise thought leader (*http://www.vmbrasseur.com*) once said: books are for learning. And now you know!

Figure 4-27. Google's Quick, Draw! game

Because the Quick Draw Dataset has so many categories, and training a classifier with so many samples would take a while (feel free to modify our scripts and give it a go), we're going to limit ourselves to the following 23 categories: apple, banana, bread, broccoli, cake, carrot, coffee cup, cookie, donut, grapes, hot dog, ice cream, lollipop, mushroom, peanut, pear, pineapple, pizza, potato, sandwich, steak, strawberry, and watermelon.

You can see an example of the sorts of drawings the app will be able to classify in Figure 4-28.

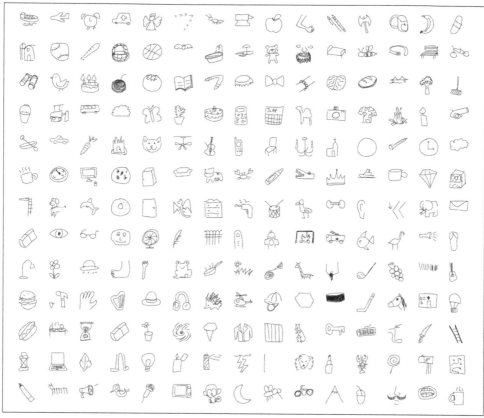

Figure 4-28. Examples of the images our drawing classifier will be able to work with

You don't need to download the Quick Draw Dataset; it's very, *very* large. We download it as part of the script we make to train the model in "Creating a model" on page 146.

Creating a model

We're going to use Apple's Turi Create to train this model. This means that we'll need a Python environment:

1. Set up a Python environment following the process that we outlined in "Python" on page 46, activate the environment, and use `pip` to install Turi Create, as shown in Figure 4-29:

```
conda create -n TuriCreateDrawingClassifierEnvironment python=3.6

conda activate TuriCreateDrawingClassifierEnvironment
```

```
pip install turicreate
```

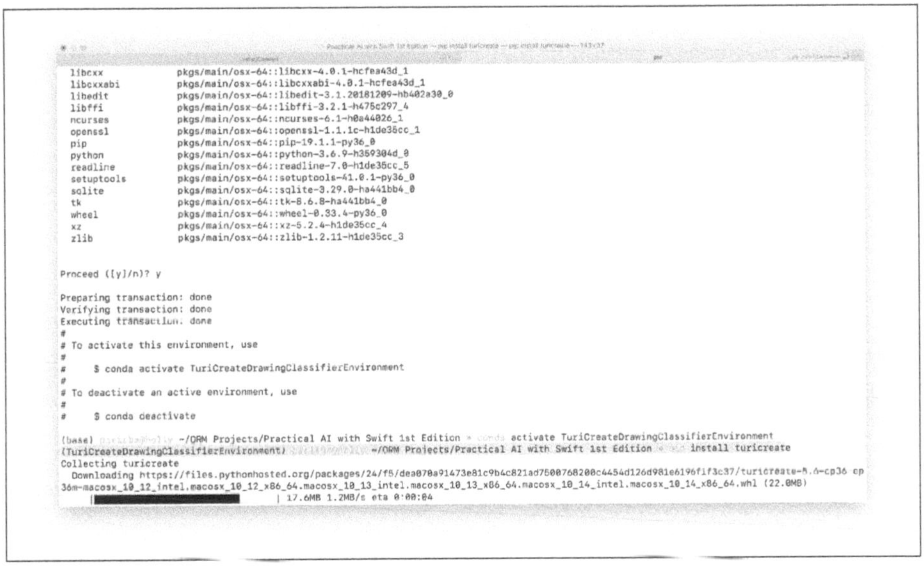

Figure 4-29. Creating our environment

2. Create a new Python script named *train_drawing_classifier.py*, and add the following:

```python
#!/usr/bin/env python

import os
import json
import requests
import numpy as np
import turicreate as tc
```

3. Add some configuration variables, including a list of categories, that we want to train:

```python
# THE CATEGORIES WE WANT TO BE ABLE TO DISTINGUISH
categories = [
    'apple', 'banana', 'bread', 'broccoli', 'cake', 'carrot', 'coffee cup',
    'cookie', 'donut', 'grapes', 'hot dog', 'ice cream', 'lollipop',
    'mushroom', 'peanut', 'pear', 'pineapple', 'pizza', 'potato',
    'sandwich', 'steak', 'strawberry', 'watermelon'
]

# CONFIGURE AS REQUIRED
this_directory = os.path.dirname(os.path.realpath(__file__))
quickdraw_directory = this_directory + '/quickdraw'
bitmap_directory = quickdraw_directory + '/bitmap'
bitmap_sframe_path = quickdraw_directory + '/bitmaps.sframe'
```

```
output_model_filename = this_directory + '/DrawingClassifierModel'
training_samples = 10000
```

4. Add the following function to make directories in which to put the training data:

```
# MAKE SOME FOLDERS TO PUT TRAINING DATA IN
def make_directory(path):
        try:
                os.makedirs(path)
        except OSError:
                if not os.path.isdir(path):
                        raise


make_directory(quickdraw_directory)
make_directory(bitmap_directory)
```

5. Fetch the bitmaps that we're going to use to train:

```
# FETCH SOME DATA
bitmap_url = (
    'https://storage.googleapis.com/quickdraw_dataset/full/numpy_bitmap'
)

total_categories = len(categories)

for index, category in enumerate(categories):
        bitmap_filename = '/' + category + '.npy'

        with open(bitmap_directory + bitmap_filename, 'w+') as bitmap_file:
                bitmap_response = requests.get(bitmap_url + bitmap_filename)
                bitmap_file.write(bitmap_response.content)

        print('Downloaded %s drawings (category %d/%d)' %
        (category, index + 1, total_categories))

random_state = np.random.RandomState(100)
```

6. Add a function to make SFrames from the images:

```
def get_bitmap_sframe():
    labels, drawings = [], []
    for category in categories:
        data = np.load(
            bitmap_directory + '/' + category + '.npy',
            allow_pickle=True
        )
        random_state.shuffle(data)
        sampled_data = data[:training_samples]
        transformed_data = sampled_data.reshape(
            sampled_data.shape[0], 28, 28, 1)

        for pixel_data in transformed_data:
```

```
image = tc.Image(_image_data=np.invert(pixel_data).tobytes(),
    _width=pixel_data.shape[1],
    _height=pixel_data.shape[0],
    _channels=pixel_data.shape[2],
    _format_enum=2,
    _image_data_size=pixel_data.size)
drawings.append(image)
labels.append(category)
print('...%s bitmaps complete' % category)
print('%d bitmaps with %d labels' % (len(drawings), len(labels)))
return tc.SFrame({'drawing': drawings, 'label': labels})
```

7. Add something to save out those `SFrames` to files:

```
# Save intermediate bitmap SFrame to file
bitmap_sframe = get_bitmap_sframe()
bitmap_sframe.save(bitmap_sframe_path)
bitmap_sframe.explore()
```

8. Now, we actually train the drawing classifier:

```
bitmap_model = tc.drawing_classifier.create(
    bitmap_sframe, 'label', max_iterations=1000)
```

9. Export it to CoreML format:

```
bitmap_model.export_coreml(output_model_filename + '.mlmodel')
```

 If you want to make your drawing classifier capable of classifying different drawings than ours, check out the list of categories (*http://bit.ly/31evaaq*) and pick some different ones.

10. Run the script:

```
python train_drawing_classifier.py
```

You should see something that resembles Figure 4-30. As we mentioned earlier,
you don't need to download the Quick Draw Dataset manually, because the script
does this.

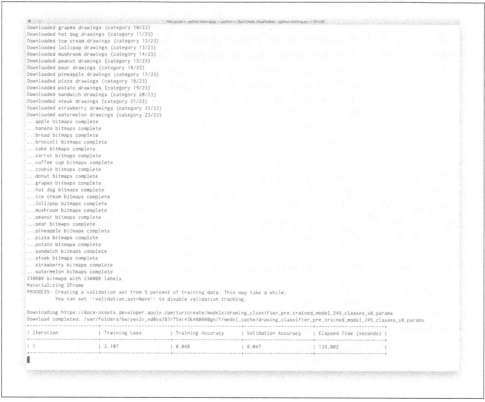

Figure 4-30. Training the drawing classifier

After it's grabbed them and parsed them into the Turi Create internal format, you'll see something like Figure 4-31 pop up for you to browse the images. You can check back to "Turi Create" on page 37 for more information on Turi Create.

Feel free to poke around the visualization while it trains.

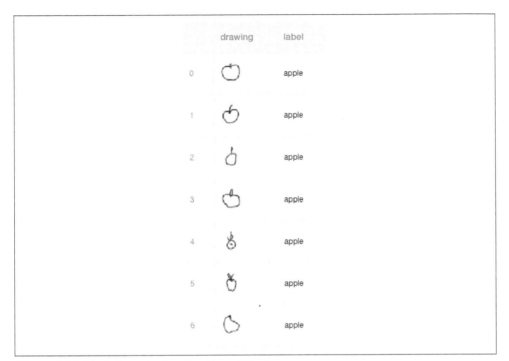

	drawing	label
0		apple
1		apple
2		apple
3		apple
4		apple
5		apple
6		apple

Figure 4-31. Turi Create's visualization of the images

This training might take a while. It took several hours on our modern MacBook Pro. Make a cup of tea, and go watch *Person of Interest*.

When the training is done, you can take a look in the folder where you did this work, and you'll find a brand new *DrawingClassifierModel.mlmodel*, as shown in Figure 4-32. You can use this model just like any other CoreML we've worked with; conincidentally, this is exactly what we'll be doing next, in "Building the App" on page 152.

We mentioned Turi Create's visualization features earlier in "Understanding the pieces of Turi Create" on page 39. We also talked about the broad importance of getting to know your dataset in "Getting to Know a Dataset" on page 65.

Figure 4-32. The final, converted, CoreML model

Building the App

Again, we're going to be using Apple's newest UI framework, SwiftUI, to build the interface for the drawing detection app.

The final form of the app we're going to build to count faces can be seen earlier, in Figure 4-1; it consists of the following SwiftUI components:

- A NavigationView in which to display the title of the app, as well as the button to select a photo
- An Image to display the chosen image (containing a drawing), which the app will attempt to classify
- A Button to trigger the drawing classification
- Some Text to display the count of faces

However, we construct this view out of multiple subviews, as we did for "Building the App" on page 75. If you don't want to manually build the drawing detection iOS app, you can download the code from our website (*https://aiwithswift.com*) and look for the project named DDDemo.

After you have that, follow along through the rest of this section (we don't recommend skipping it) and then meet us at "What's Next?" on page 163.

 You might note that this app is very similar in structure to some of the other SwiftUI apps that we build in the book. We're trying to keep things consistent and as simple as possible. We really hope it helps you learn. Check our website (*https://aiwithswift.com*) for more tips and guides.

To make the drawing-detection iOS app yourself, you'll need to do the following:

1. Fire up Xcode.

2. Create a new iOS app project, choosing the "Single View App" template. We use SwiftUI for this one, as mentioned.

3. Drag in the *.mlmodel* file we created earlier in "AI Toolkit and Dataset" on page 144 and let Xcode copy it over as needed.

4. Add a new Swift file to the project called *Image.swift*. We use this to add an extension on UIImage, so that we can filter it to be more useful for classification.

5. First, we also need an extension on CIFilter:

```
extension CIFilter {
    static let mono = CIFilter(name: "CIPhotoEffectMono")!
    static let noir = CIFilter(name: "CIPhotoEffectNoir")!
    static let tonal = CIFilter(name: "CIPhotoEffectTonal")!
    static let invert = CIFilter(name: "CIColorInvert")!

    static func contrast(amount: Double = 2.0) -> CIFilter {
        let filter = CIFilter(name: "CIColorControls")!
        filter.setValue(amount, forKey: kCIInputContrastKey)
        return filter
    }

    static func brighten(amount: Double = 0.1) -> CIFilter {
        let filter = CIFilter(name: "CIColorControls")!
        filter.setValue(amount, forKey: kCIInputBrightnessKey)
        return filter
    }
}
```

This extension lets us create a CIFilter, which is a Core Image filter that can manipulate an image, and request that it be mono, noir, or tonal. You can learn more about these filters and how to create your own hhttps://apple.co/2otBgGV[in Apple's documentation].

6. The extension on UIImage also:

```
extension UIImage {
    func applying(filter: CIFilter) -> UIImage? {
        filter.setValue(CIImage(image: self), forKey: kCIInputImageKey)

        let context = CIContext(options: nil)
        guard let output = filter.outputImage,
            let cgImage = context.createCGImage(
                output, from: output.extent) else {
            return nil
        }

        return UIImage(
            cgImage: cgImage,
            scale: scale,
            orientation: imageOrientation)
```

```
    }

    func fixOrientation() -> UIImage? {
        UIGraphicsBeginImageContext(self.size)
        self.draw(at: .zero)
        let newImage = UIGraphicsGetImageFromCurrentImageContext()
        UIGraphicsEndImageContext()
        return newImage
    }

    var cgImageOrientation: CGImagePropertyOrientation {
        switch self.imageOrientation {
        case .up: return .up
        case .down: return .down
        case .left: return .left
        case .right: return .right
        case .upMirrored: return .upMirrored
        case .downMirrored: return .downMirrored
        case .leftMirrored: return .leftMirrored
        case .rightMirrored: return .rightMirrored
        }
    }
}
```

This extension adds to two functions: one to apply a `CIFilter`, and one to fix the orientation of an image. We also add the usual orientation fixes.

7. Make another new Swift file called *Drawing.swift* and then add the following imports:

```
import UIKit
import Vision
import Foundation
```

8. Add the following enum:

```
enum Drawing: String, CaseIterable {
    /// These only include those the model was trained on. For others that
    /// can be included in the training phase, see the full list of
    /// categories in the dataset:
    /// https://raw.githubusercontent.com/googlecreativelab/
    ///     quickdraw-dataset/master/categories.txt
    case apple, banana, bread, broccoli, cake, carrot, coffee, cookie
    case donut, grapes, hotdog, icecream, lollipop, mushroom, peanut, pear
    case pineapple, pizza, potato, sandwich, steak, strawberry, watermelon

    init?(rawValue: String) {
        if let match = Drawing.allCases
            .first(where: { $0.rawValue == rawValue }) {
            self = match
        } else {
            switch rawValue {
```

```
                case "coffee cup":  self = .coffee
                case "hot dog":     self = .hotdog
                case "ice cream":   self = .icecream
                default: return nil
            }
        }
    }

    var icon: String {
        switch self {
            case .apple: return "🍎"
            case .banana: return "🍌"
            case .bread: return "🍞"
            case .broccoli: return "🥦"
            case .cake: return "🍰"
            case .carrot: return "🥕"
            case .coffee: return "☕"
            case .cookie: return "🍪"
            case .donut: return "🍩"
            case .grapes: return "🍇"
            case .hotdog: return "🌭"
            case .icecream: return "🍦"
            case .lollipop: return "🍭"
            case .mushroom: return "🍄"
            case .peanut: return "🥜"
            case .pear: return "🍐"
            case .pineapple: return "🍍"
            case .pizza: return "🍕"
            case .potato: return "🥔"
            case .sandwich: return "🥪"
            case .steak: return "🥩"
            case .strawberry: return "🍓"
            case .watermelon: return "🍉"
        }
    }
}

enum Drawing: String, CaseIterable {
    /// These only include those the model was trained on. For others that
    /// can be included in the training phase, see the full list of
    /// categories in the dataset:
    /// https://raw.githubusercontent.com/googlecreativelab/
    ///     quickdraw-dataset/master/categories.txt
    case apple, banana, bread, broccoli, cake, carrot, coffee, cookie
    case donut, grapes, hotdog, icecream, lollipop, mushroom, peanut, pear
    case pineapple, pizza, potato, sandwich, steak, strawberry, watermelon

    init?(rawValue: String) {
        if let match = Drawing.allCases
```

```
            .first(where: { $0.rawValue == rawValue }) {
            self = match
        } else {
            switch rawValue {
                case "coffee cup":  self = .coffee
                case "hot dog":     self = .hotdog
                case "ice cream":   self = .icecream
                default: return nil
            }
        }
    }

    var icon: String {
        switch self {
            case .apple: return "🍎"
            case .banana: return "🍌"
            case .bread: return "🍞"
            case .broccoli: return "🥦"
            case .cake: return "🍰"
            case .carrot: return "🥕"
            case .coffee: return "☕️"
            case .cookie: return "🍪"
            case .donut: return "🍩"
            case .grapes: return "🍇"
            case .hotdog: return "🌭"
            case .icecream: return "🍦"
            case .lollipop: return "🍭"
            case .mushroom: return "🍄"
            case .peanut: return "🥜"
            case .pear: return "🍐"
            case .pineapple: return "🍍"
            case .pizza: return "🍕"
            case .potato: return "🥔"
            case .sandwich: return "🥪"
            case .steak: return "🥩"
            case .strawberry: return "🍓"
            case .watermelon: return "🍉"
        }
    }
}
```

Our enum lets us create a Drawing (which is what the enum is called) from a String (via the init() we created). Each type of the Drawing enum has an icon, which is an emoji, assigned to it.

9. You also need an extension on VNImageRequestHandler:

```
extension VNImageRequestHandler {
    convenience init?(uiImage: UIImage) {
```

```
        guard let ciImage = CIImage(image: uiImage) else { return nil }
        let orientation = uiImage.cgImageOrientation

        self.init(ciImage: ciImage, orientation: orientation)
    }
}
```

This extension extends `VNImageRequestHandler` to add a convenience initializer allowing creation with a `UIImage` instead of a `CIImage`. For a reminder on what `VNImageRequestHandler` does, check Apple's documentation (*https://apple.co/2OGsGiq*).

10. Add another extension on `DrawingClassifierModelBitmap`, which is the name of the model we made earlier (Xcode automatically creates a class from the model we dragged in):

```
extension DrawingClassifierModel {
    func configure(image: UIImage?) -> UIImage? {
        if let rotatedImage = image?.fixOrientation(),
            let grayscaleImage = rotatedImage
                .applying(filter: CIFilter.noir),
            // account for paper photography making everything dark :/
            let brightenedImage = grayscaleImage
                .applying(filter: CIFilter.brighten(amount: 0.4)),
            let contrastedImage = brightenedImage
                .applying(filter: CIFilter.contrast(amount: 10.0)) {

            return contrastedImage
        }

        return nil
    }

    func classify(_ image: UIImage?,
        completion: @escaping (Drawing?) -> ()) {
        guard let image = image,
            let model = try? VNCoreMLModel(for: self.model) else {
                return completion(nil)
        }

        let request = VNCoreMLRequest(model: model)

        DispatchQueue.global(qos: .userInitiated).async {
            if let handler = VNImageRequestHandler(uiImage: image) {
                try? handler.perform([request])

                let results = request.results
                    as? [VNClassificationObservation]

                let highestResult = results?.max {
```

```
                    $0.confidence < $1.confidence
                }

                print(results?.list ?? "")

                completion(
                    Drawing(rawValue: highestResult?.identifier ?? "")
                )
            } else {
                completion(nil)
            }
        }
    }
}
```

This large piece of code extends our model, `DrawingClassifierModel`, adding a `configure()` function that takes a `UIImage` and returns a version of it that's been filtered to grayscale, brightened, and had its contrast increased. It also adds a `classify()` function that runs a `VNCoreMLRequest` on a `DispatchQueue` to attempt to classify the image (drawing) using a `VNImageRequestHandler` and our model (which is `self` in this context, as this is an extension on the model).

11. Add one more extension on `Collection`:

```
extension Collection where Element == VNClassificationObservation {
    var list: String {
        var string = ""
        for element in self {
            string += "\(element.identifier): " +
                "\(element.confidence * 100.0)%\n"
        }
        return string
    }
}
```

This extension on `Collections` of `VNClassificationObservations` (which are what you get back when you perform an image analysis using Apple's Vision framework (*https://apple.co/2IMkSI9*)) adds a `var` called `list`, of type `String`, which allows us to get the identifier and confidence from the `VNClassificatio nObservation`.

12. To add some custom views, add a file called *Views.swift*, import SwiftUI, and then add the following `ImagePicker` struct:

```
struct ImagePicker: UIViewControllerRepresentable {
    typealias UIViewControllerType = UIImagePickerController
    private(set) var selectedImage: UIImage?
    private(set) var cameraSource: Bool
    private let completion: (UIImage?) -> ()
```

```swift
init(camera: Bool = false, completion: @escaping (UIImage?) -> ()) {
    self.cameraSource = camera
    self.completion = completion
}

func makeCoordinator() -> ImagePicker.Coordinator {
    let coordinator = Coordinator(self)
    coordinator.completion = self.completion
    return coordinator
}

func makeUIViewController(context: Context) ->
    UIImagePickerController {

    let imagePickerController = UIImagePickerController()
    imagePickerController.delegate = context.coordinator
    imagePickerController.sourceType =
        cameraSource ? .camera : .photoLibrary
    imagePickerController.allowsEditing = true
    return imagePickerController
}

func updateUIViewController(
    _ uiViewController: UIImagePickerController, context: Context) {}

class Coordinator: NSObject,
    UIImagePickerControllerDelegate, UINavigationControllerDelegate {

    var parent: ImagePicker
    var completion: ((UIImage?) -> ())?

    init(_ imagePickerControllerWrapper: ImagePicker) {
        self.parent = imagePickerControllerWrapper
    }

    func imagePickerController(
        _ picker: UIImagePickerController,
        didFinishPickingMediaWithInfo info:
            [UIImagePickerController.InfoKey: Any]) {

        print("Image picker complete...")

        let selectedImage =
            info[UIImagePickerController.InfoKey.originalImage]
                as? UIImage

        picker.dismiss(animated: true)
        completion?(selectedImage)
    }
```

```
    func imagePickerControllerDidCancel(_ picker:
        UIImagePickerController) {

        print("Image picker cancelled...")
        picker.dismiss(animated: true)
        completion?(nil)
    }
  }
}
```

As we did when we built a face-detection app using SwiftUI in "Building the App" on page 75, this fakes a ViewController in SwiftUI, allowing us to use UIKit features to get an image picker.

13. Add the following TwoStateButton view:

```
struct TwoStateButton: View {
    private let text: String
    private let disabled: Bool
    private let background: Color
    private let action: () -> Void

    var body: some View {
        Button(action: action) {
            HStack {
                Spacer()
                Text(text).font(.title).bold().foregroundColor(.white)
                Spacer()
                }.padding().background(background).cornerRadius(10)
            }.disabled(disabled)
    }

    init(text: String,
        disabled: Bool,
        background: Color = .blue,
        action: @escaping () -> Void) {

        self.text = text
        self.disabled = disabled
        self.background = disabled ? .gray : background
        self.action = action
    }
}
```

This TwoStateButton should look pretty familiar at this point: it defines a SwiftUI view for a Button that can be disabled and have that visually represented.

14. Add the following MainView View:

```
struct MainView: View {
    private let image: UIImage
    private let text: String
```

```
    private let button: TwoStateButton

    var body: some View {
        VStack {
            Image(uiImage: image)
                .resizable()
                .aspectRatio(contentMode: .fit)

            Spacer()
            Text(text).font(.title).bold()
            Spacer()
            self.button
        }
    }

    init(image: UIImage, text: String, button: () -> TwoStateButton) {
        self.image = image
        self.text = text
        self.button = button()
    }
}
```

This MainView defines a VStack with an Image, a Spacer, some Text, and a TwoS
tateButton.

15. Next, open *ContentView.swift*, and then add the following @State variables:

```
@State private var imagePickerOpen: Bool = false
@State private var cameraOpen: Bool = false
@State private var image: UIImage? = nil
@State private var classification: String? = nil
```

16. And the following variables:

```
private let placeholderImage = UIImage(named: "placeholder")!
private let classifier = DrawingClassifierModel()

private var cameraEnabled: Bool {
    UIImagePickerController.isSourceTypeAvailable(.camera)
}

private var classificationEnabled: Bool {
    image != nil && classification == nil
}
```

17. Add a function to perform the classification:

```
private func classify() {
    print("Analysing drawing...")
    classifier.classify(self.image) { result in
        self.classification = result?.icon
    }
}
```

18. Add a function to return control, after classification:

```
private func controlReturned(image: UIImage?) {
    print("Image return \(image == nil ? "failure" : "success")...")

    // turn image right side up, resize it and turn it black-and-white
    self.image = classifier.configure(image: image)
}
```

19. Add a function to summon an image picker:

```
private func summonImagePicker() {
    print("Summoning ImagePicker...")
    imagePickerOpen = true
}
```

20. Add a function to summon the camera:

```
private func summonCamera() {
    print("Summoning camera...")
    cameraOpen = true
}
```

21. Add an extension on ContentView, which returns the right views, as needed:

```
extension ContentView {
    private func mainView() -> AnyView {
        return AnyView(NavigationView {
            MainView(
                image: image ?? placeholderImage,
                text: "\(classification ?? "Nothing detected")") {
                    TwoStateButton(
                        text: "Classify",
                        disabled: !classificationEnabled, action: classify
                    )
            }
            .padding()
            .navigationBarTitle(
                Text("DDDemo"),
                displayMode: .inline)
            .navigationBarItems(
                leading: Button(action: summonImagePicker) {
                    Text("Select")
                    },
                trailing: Button(action: summonCamera) {
                    Image(systemName: "camera")
                    }.disabled(!cameraEnabled)
            )
        })
    }

    private func imagePickerView() -> AnyView {
        return  AnyView(ImagePicker { result in
```

```
            self.classification = nil
            self.controlReturned(image: result)
            self.imagePickerOpen = false
        })
    }

    private func cameraView() -> AnyView {
        return  AnyView(ImagePicker(camera: true) { result in
            self.classification = nil
            self.controlReturned(image: result)
            self.cameraOpen = false
        })
    }
}
```

22. Update the body View to look as follows:

```
var body: some View {
    if imagePickerOpen { return imagePickerView() }
    if cameraOpen { return cameraView() }
    return mainView()
}
```

You can now fire up your drawing classifier app, draw some things on paper, take a photo, and watch your app identify your drawings (well, as long as the drawings match the categories you trained the model with). Figure 4-33 presents some examples of the authors' handiwork.

What's Next?

This is just one way you could make a drawing classification feature. Drawings are often created on iOS devices, which means we're going through some possibly unnecessary steps of taking or selecting a photo. Why not allow the user to draw directly in our app?

Later in Chapter 7, we look at creating a drawing classifier for drawings made on the device "Task: Gestural Classification for Drawing" on page 262.

Figure 4-33. The fabulous artwork of the authors being identified by our app

Task: Style Classification

For our final vision-related task, we modify the app that we built for image classification in "Task: Image Classification" on page 120 to make it capable of identifying the style of a supplied image. We're going to do this quickly, and in the most straightforward and practical way we know how: by converting a preexisting model into Apple's CoreML format.

We need a model that can identify styles. Luckily, the boffins have us covered (*http:// bit.ly/2B77UAP*). The "Finetuning CaffeNet on Flickr Style" is a classifier model that's been trained on many images of different categories and can identify a variety of image styles.

 The styles that the model can identify are Detailed, Pastel, Melancholy, Noir, HDR, Vintage, Long Exposure, Horror, Sunny, Texture, Bright, Hazy, Bokeh, Serene, Ethereal, Macro, Depth of Field, Geometric Composition, Minimal, and Romantic. The model we're using here is based on this research paper (*http://bit.ly/2OEUKTz*).

Converting the Model

We need to use Python to convert the model to something that we can use:

1. Create a new Python environment following the instructions in "Python" on page 46 and then activate it:

   ```
   conda create -n StyleClassifier python=3.6
   ```

   ```
   conda activate StyleClassifier
   ```

2. Install Apple's CoreML Tools (we discussed this earlier, in "CoreML Community Tools" on page 42):

   ```
   pip install coremltools
   ```

3. Create a file called *styles.txt* with the following contents:

   ```
   Detailed
   Pastel
   Melancholy
   Noir
   HDR
   Vintage
   Long Exposure
   Horror
   Sunny
   Bright
   Hazy
   ```

```
Bokeh
Serene
Texture
Ethereal
Macro
Depth of Field
Geometric Composition
Minimal
Romantic
```

4. Download the trained model we're using, in Caffe format, from the Berkeleyvision website (*http://bit.ly/2VC4mji*).

   Save this model file (it's a few hundred megabytes) next to the *styles.txt* file.

5. Download and save this file (*http://bit.ly/2MbuHBx*) next to it. The *deploy.prototxt* file specifies the parameters for the model that we need in order to be able to convert it to the CoreML format.

6. Create a new Python script in the same folder (ours is called *convert_styleclassifier.py*), and then add the following code:

```python
import coremltools

coreml_model = coremltools.converters.caffe.convert(
    ('./finetune_flickr_style.caffemodel', './deploy.prototxt'),
    image_input_names = 'data',
    class_labels = './styles.txt'
)

coreml_model.author = 'Paris BA'

coreml_model.license = 'None'

coreml_model.short_description = 'Flickr Style'

coreml_model.input_description['data'] = 'An image.'

coreml_model.output_description['prob'] = (
    'Probabilities for style type, for a given input.'
)

coreml_model.output_description['classLabel'] = (
    'The most likely style type for the given input.'
)

coreml_model.save('Style.mlmodel')
```

This code imports the CoreML Tools, loads the Caffe converter that is supplied by CoreML Tools, and points to the *finetune_flickr_style.caffemodel* model that we downloaded. It's also where to find the *deploy.prototxt* parameters file, which supplies some metadata and saves out a CoreML format model named *Style.mlmodel*.

Everything should look like Figure 4-34.

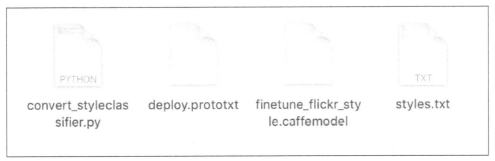

Figure 4-34. The files needed to convert the style classifier

7. Run the Python script:

```
python convert_styleclassifier.py
```

You'll see something that looks like Figure 4-35, and you'll end up with a *Style.mlmodel* file in the folder (Figure 4-36).

Figure 4-35. Converting the style classifier from Caffee to CoreML

convert_styleclas   deploy.prototxt   finetune_flickr_sty   styles.txt   Style.mlmodel
sifier.py   le.caffemodel

Figure 4-36. Our new CoreML style classifier model

Using the Model

First, you'll want to duplicate the final version of the project we created for the classification task in "Task: Image Classification" on page 120. If you don't want to, you can download ours from our website (*https://aiwithswift.com*); look for the project named StyleClassifier.

To use the *Style.mlmodel* file we just converted, do the following:

1. Open the Xcode project that you duplicated (or downloaded from our resources).

2. Drag *Style.mlmodel* into the project, allowing Xcode to copy as needed.

3. In *ViewController.swift*, change the line that references the model from this

```
private let classifier = VisionClassifier(mlmodel: BananaOrApple().model)
```

to this:

```
private let classifier = VisionClassifier(mlmodel: Style().model)
```

Run the app. You can now select an image, tap the button, and receive a classification, as shown in Figure 4-37.

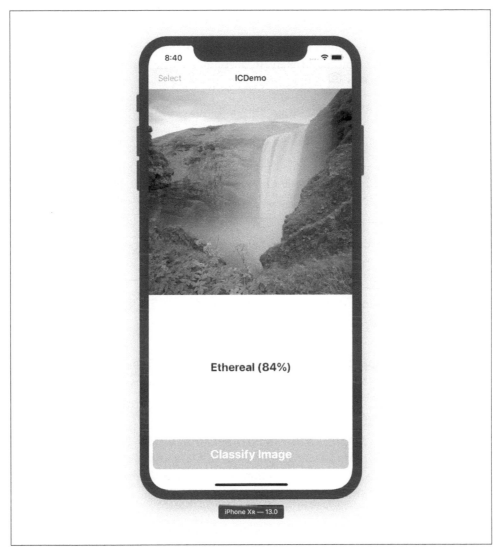

Figure 4-37. Our Style Classifier in action

We look at the use of CoreML Tools ("CoreML Community Tools" on page 42) to convert models more in later activities, such as in "Task: Image Generation with a GAN" on page 324 and "Task: Using the CoreML Community Tools" on page 382.

Next Steps

That's about it for our vision chapter. We've covered some common vision-related practical AI tasks that you might want to accomplish with Swift, and used a fairly wide variety of tools to do so.

We built seven apps and Playgrounds, exploring seven practical AI tasks related to vision:

Face Detection

We used Apple's new SwiftUI for the interface, and Apple's provided framework, Vision, to detect faces and work with that information. We didn't even need to train a model.

Barcode Detection

We used Apple's frameworks to find barcodes in images. Again, we didn't need to train a model.

Saliency Detection

In this task, we found the most salient area of an image using Apple's frameworks. Still no model training!

Image Similarity

We again used Apple's new SwiftUI framework and again used Vision to build an app that lets us see how different (or similar) two images are. And no model training here, either.

Image Classification

This time we used Apple's UIKit framework to build the UI, trained our own image classification model using Apple's CreateML app and an open source dataset of fruit photos, and built an app that can recognize different fruits from photos. Finally, we trained a model!

Drawing Recognition

We again used SwiftUI to build a derivative app of our Face Detection app, creating our own drawing classification model using Apple's Turi Create Python framework to build an app that allows users to identify what they've drawn on paper.

Style Classification

We updated our Image Classification app to support identifying the style of a supplied image by converting a model built with another set of tools into Apple's CoreML format.

As we mentioned in "Apple's Models" on page 70, if you want to solve a practical AI problem regarding vision, you can also check out Apple's Core ML Models (*https://apple.co/33oLF5p*) page and see what it offers in the way of pretrained CoreML models. If you can solve your problem without having to do as much work yourself, it's probably worth it. We also recommend checking out the Awesome CoreML Models list (*http://bit.ly/2OHpDXq*).

In Chapter 11, we look at what might have happened under the hood, algorithm-wise, for each of the tasks we explored in this chapter. Just because that's the end of the chapter named "Vision," it doesn't mean that we won't be working with visual things in other chapters of the book. In Chapter 5, we look at audio, though—also a very exciting topic

For more vision-related practical AI tasks, check out our website (*https://aiwiths wift.com*).

Audio

This chapter explores the practical side of implementing audio-related AI features in your Swift apps. Taking a top-down approach, we explore two audio tasks and how to implement them using Swift and various AI tools.

Audio and Practical AI

Here are the two audio-related practical AI tasks that we explore in this chapter:

Speech Recognition
> Making a computer understand human words is incredibly useful. You can take dictation or order a computer around.

Sound Classification
> Classification is going to crop up repeatedly in this book. We build a sound classifier app that can tell us what animal sound we're listening to.

Images might be the trendy hot topic that triggered an explosion of deep learning, machine learning, and artificial intelligence (AI) features in products, and activity classification might be a novel way of using the myriad sensors in a modern iOS device, but sound is one of the real stars of practical applications of machine learning. Almost everyone has used sound at least once on their mobile device (like the music identification service, Shazam), even before AI was (yet again) a buzzword.

Task: Speech Recognition

Speech recognition is one of those touchpoints of AI that most people have used at some point or another: whether it's on a phone call with an irritating phone robot that's trying to understand your voice, or actively using your computer with assistive and accessibility technologies, speech recognition has been pervasive a lot longer than many other forms of practical AI in consumer applications.

For the first of our two practical AI audio tasks, we're going to explore how you can add speech-recognition capabilities to your Swift applications quickly, easily, and without any model training involved.

As with the face-detection task we covered in "Task: Face Detection" on page 74, speech recognition is a little easier than many of the others in this book in that the toolkit for performing speech recognition is largely provided by Apple ("Apple's Other Frameworks" on page 40).

You could train a model that understands human speech for each of the languages you want to support in your project, but Apple has done the work for you, for lots and lots of languages. So why would you?

This task, therefore, takes a similar approach to "Task: Image Similarity" on page 109, in which we covered checking images for similarity, and "Task: Face Detection" on page 74, in which we looked at face detection.

Problem and Approach

For this task, we're going to explore the practical side of speech recognition by doing the following:

- Making an app that can recognize human speech and display it on screen
- Building an app that allows us to listen to some speech and display it as text
- Using Apple's tools for doing this without training a model
- Exploring the potential next steps for speech recognition

Speech recognition is absolutely everywhere. There's not much more to say. It's pervasive, widely understood, and doesn't require much explanation to users. You can use it for everything from allowing the user to dictate text (although there are other, more appropriate ways to do that), to controlling an app with voice (again, there are other more appropriate ways to do that), to voice-driven features that revolve around understanding what the user is saying.

We're going to build the Speech Recognizer app shown in Figure 5-1.

Figure 5-1. The final look of the Speech Recognizer app

Building the App

As we did in for many of the tasks in Chapter 4, we're going to be using Apple's newest user interface (UI) framework, SwiftUI, to build the app for exploring speech recognition.

The final form of the app we're going to build for this task was shown earlier, in Figure 5-1, and consists the following SwiftUI components:

- A `NavigationView` in which to display the title of the app

- Some `Button` components to start and stop the listening process for speech recognition

- A `Text` component for the result of the speech recognition to be displayed (and for instructions prior to the app being used)

This book is here to teach you the practical side of using AI and machine learning features with Swift and on Apple's platforms. Because of this, we don't explain the fine details of how to build apps; we assume you mostly know that (although if you don't, we think you'll be able to follow along just fine if you pay attention). If you want to learn Swift, we recommend picking up Learning Swift (*http://oreil.ly/DLVGh*) (also by us!) from the lovely folks at O'Reilly Media.

If you don't want to manually build the iOS app, you can download the code from our website (*https://aiwithswift.com*) and find the project named `SRDemo`. After you have that, we strongly recommend that you still proceed through this section, comparing the notes here with the code you downloaded.

To make the app yourself, you'll need to do the following:

1. Create an iOS app project in Xcode, choosing the "Single View App" template, and selecting the SwiftUI checkbox.

2. After your project is created, add a new Swift file called *Speech.swift* to the project. In that file, add a new `class` called `SpeechRecognizer`:

   ```
   class SpeechRecognizer {

   }
   ```

3. Add some attributes, covering all the necessary components you need to recognize speech:

   ```
   private let audioEngine: AVAudioEngine
   private let session: AVAudioSession
   private let recognizer: SFSpeechRecognizer
   private let inputBus: AVAudioNodeBus
   private let inputNode: AVAudioInputNode

   private var request: SFSpeechAudioBufferRecognitionRequest?
   private var task: SFSpeechRecognitionTask?
   private var permissions: Bool = false
   ```

We're creating an AVAudioEngine (*https://apple.co/32nenna*), which is used to perform audio input or output; an AVAudioSession (*https://apple.co/2MsiRDz*), which is used to help you specify to the operating system (OS) what kind of audio you'll be working with; and an AVAudioNodeBus and AVAudioInputNode, which are used to establish connections with the input hardware on an iOS device (i.e., the microphones).

We also create an SFSpeechRecognizer (*https://apple.co/2BktKkr*), which allows us to initiate speech recognition and is part of Apple's provided Speech Framework. We also use SFSpeechAudioBufferRecognitionRequest (*https://apple.co/2oEQAAx*) to capture audio from a live buffer (i.e., a device's microphone) in order to recognize speech.

 An alternative to SFSpeechAudioBufferRecognitionRequest is SFSpeechURLRecognitionRequest (*https://apple.co/35JvrWs*), which allows you to perform speech recognition on a preexisting recorded audio file, instead.

We also create a SFSpeechRecognitionTask, which represents an ongoing speech recognition task. We can use this to see when the task is done or cancel it.

4. Add an initializer:

```
init?(inputBus: AVAudioNodeBus = 0) {
    self.audioEngine = AVAudioEngine()
    self.session = AVAudioSession.sharedInstance()

    guard let recognizer = SFSpeechRecognizer() else { return nil }

    self.recognizer = recognizer
    self.inputBus = inputBus
    self.inputNode = audioEngine.inputNode
}
```

Our initializer creates the necessary audio capture components and assigns the bits and pieces we created a moment ago appropriately.

5. Add a function to check that we have the appropriate permissions to listen on the microphone (in order to do speech recognition):

```
func checkSessionPermissions(_ session: AVAudioSession,
    completion: @escaping (Bool) -> ()) {

    if session.responds(
        to: #selector(AVAudioSession.requestRecordPermission(_:))) {
        session.requestRecordPermission(completion)
    }
}
```

6. Add a function to the start the recording, and some setup at the top:

```
func startRecording(completion: @escaping (String?) -> ()) {
    audioEngine.prepare()
    request = SFSpeechAudioBufferRecognitionRequest()
    request?.shouldReportPartialResults = true

}
```

7. Within this function, below the setup, check for audio and microphone access permissions:

```
// audio/microphone access permissions
checkSessionPermissions(session) {
    success in self.permissions = success
}

guard let _ = try? session.setCategory(
        .record,
        mode: .measurement,
        options: .duckOthers),
    let _ = try? session.setActive(
        true,
        options: .notifyOthersOnDeactivation),
    let _ = try? audioEngine.start(),
    let request = self.request
    else {
        return completion(nil)
    }
```

8. Set the recording format and create the necessary buffer:

```
let recordingFormat = inputNode.outputFormat(forBus: inputBus)
inputNode.installTap(
    onBus: inputBus,
    bufferSize: 1024,
    format: recordingFormat) {
        (buffer: AVAudioPCMBuffer, when: AVAudioTime) in
        self.request?.append(buffer)
    }
```

9. Print out a message (to the console, not visually in the app) that recording (listening) has started:

```
print("Started recording...")
```

You can display the console in Xcode by going to the View menu → Debug Area → Activate Console.

10. Begin the recognition:

```
task = recognizer.recognitionTask(with: request) { result, error in
    if let result = result {
        let transcript = result.bestTranscription.formattedString
        print("Heard: \"\(transcript)\"")
        completion(transcript)
    }

    if error != nil || result?.isFinal == true {
        self.stopRecording()
        completion(nil)
    }
}
```

11. In the *Speech.swift* file, add a function to stop recording:

```
func stopRecording() {
    print("...stopped recording.")
    request?.endAudio()
    audioEngine.stop()
    inputNode.removeTap(onBus: 0)
    request = nil
    task = nil
}
```

Because we're going to access the microphone, you'll need to add the NSMicrophoneUsageDescription (*https://apple.co/2qjePV7*) key to the *Info.plist* file, along with an explanation for why we're using the microphone.

You'll also need to add NSSpeechRecognitionUsageDescription (*https://apple.co/33GmGe2*) for speech recognition. The messages will be be displayed to the user. Figure 5-2 shows our messages.

Figure 5-2. NSMicrophoneUsageDescription in the Info.plist

Next, we need to start working with the view file, *ContentView.swift*:

1. At the top of the file, update the imports:

```
import Speech
import SwiftUI
import AVFoundation
```

In this, we bring in `Speech` for speech recognition, `SwiftUI` for SwiftUI, and `AVFoundation` for audio capabilities.

2. Create a SwiftUI `View` to use within a `Button`, to make it a bit fancier looking. Let's name it `ButtonLabel`:

```
struct ButtonLabel: View {
    private let title: String
    private let background: Color

    var body: some View {
        HStack {
            Spacer()
            Text(title)
                .font(.title)
                .bold()
                .foregroundColor(.white)
            Spacer()
        }.padding().background(background).cornerRadius(10)
    }

    init(_ title: String, background: Color) {
        self.title = title
        self.background = background
    }
}
```

This view basically allows us to style some text in a reusable fashion. It's a `Text` view, wrapped in an `HStack` with an initializer that allows us to provide a title `String` and a `Color`, for convenience.

3. We move now to the bulk of the code in the `View`, the `ContentView`. Much of this came with the project template, but we'll be starting with something that looks like this (it's probably already there):

```
struct ContentView: View {

}
```

4. Into this `View`, we need to add some `@State` variables:

```
@State var recording: Bool = false
@State var speech: String = ""
```

`recording` is a `Bool` that reflects the current state of recording, and `speech` is a `String` that will store the recognized text.

5. Move down below body View (still within the ContentView struct) and add a variable named recognizer to store a SpeechRecognizer:

```
private let recognizer: SpeechRecognizer
```

6. Add an init() to the view:

```
init() {
    guard let recognizer = SpeechRecognizer() else {
        fatalError("Something went wrong...")
    }
    self.recognizer = recognizer
}
```

In this, we initialize a new SpeechRecognizer (the class defined in *Speech.swift*) and store it in recognizer, which we defined a moment ago.

7. Add a function named startRecording(), which will start listening:

```
private func startRecording() {
    self.recording = true
    self.speech = ""

    recognizer.startRecording { result in
        if let text = result {
            self.speech = text
        } else {
            self.stopRecording()
        }
    }
}
```

This function sets the recording state variable to true and the speech state variable to an empty String and then uses our SpeechRecognizer (recognizer) to start recording, storing the result in speech, if there is one.

8. Add a function to stop recording, creatively called stopRecording():

```
private func stopRecording() {
    self.recording = false
    recognizer.stopRecording()
}
```

This function sets the recording state variable to false and instructs the Speech Recognizer in recognizer to stop recording.

We don't need to touch the ContentView_Previews struct in this case.

You can now run the app. Tap the button and speak, and you should see the words you say appear in the Text component.

What Just Happened? How Does This Work?

As we did back in Chapter 4, we used one of Apple's provided frameworks to do literally all the AI work for this practical example. SFSpeechRecognizer is Apple's provided speech recognition framework, and as of macOS Catalina (10.15), it's available to both iOS apps and macOS apps.

 You can also do speech recognition on watchOS and tvOS, but it's a little bit different and beyond the scope of this book. To learn more about speech recognition on Apple platforms in general, head to *https://apple.co/33Hry2t*.

SFSpeechRecognizer supports offline speech recognition for many languages, but also *might* (i.e., does) rely on Apple's server support (which is not something you need to configure), as needed. Apple's documentation (*https://apple.co/2BktKkr*) is vague about which languages support offline recognition, and under what conditions the server is contacted, but it strongly emphasizes that speech recognition via SFSpeechRecognizer should always be assumed to require connectivity.

 It's very important to always follow Apple's guidelines for asking permission. When using SFSpeechRecognizer, Apple requests that you always ask permission from the user to perform speech recognition because it might be cloud-based. Awareness of privacy implications is very important. Do pay attention 007…

There are possibly some limits (e.g., per device, per day, and so on) to how much speech recognition you can perform. Apple isn't clear on this just yet, and implies that it will evolve and crystallize with time.

What's Next?

Answering "What's next?" is a complex question for this topic. If you want to add speech recognition to your iOS or macOS apps, this is everything you need. You're ready to go.

 Because this book is about the *practical* side of AI, and we want to approach things from the top down, we think that this is everything you really need right now.

However, if you're curious, you can go further by exploring how you might train a model to recognize speech. We're not going to step through this, because it's definitely beyond the scope of this book, but the toolkit and data that we'd be exploring for doing this from scratch would resemble the following:

- The Speech Commands Dataset (*http://bit.ly/32rrOSP*), available from Google Brain (this is a very large file!)
- The Common Voice Dataset, available from Mozilla (*https://voice.mozilla.org/en*)
- The Python version of TensorFlow

Alternatively, if you get a copy of the TensorFlow source tree, build anything necessary for you to run TensorFlow, and want to try building your own very small speech recognition model, you could do the following:

1. Execute the Python script *train.py*, located in the *examples/speech_commands* directory of the TensorFlow tree. This downloads the aforementioned Speech Commands Dataset (this might take a while) and begins training.

2. You will see the training occur, step by step, and occasionally a confusion matrix will be displayed that shows you what mistakes the model is making at the time.

3. You will also see some validation measures output, showing the validation accuracy of the model on the validation dataset (which is a 10% split that is done automatically by the *train.py* script).

4. Eventually, after what could be many hours, you will have a model. You will need to freeze the model, which compacts it for use on mobile devices, using the *freeze.py* script located in the same directory.

5. You can use the *label_wav.py* script, also in the same directory, to pass audio files into the model to test it.

There's a full tutorial for a process similar to the one we just outlined available in the TensorFlow documentation (*http://bit.ly/2IZpNWe*).

The simple model that can be trained using TensorFlow that we outline here is based on the paper "Convolutional Neural Networks for Small-footprint Keyword Spotting." (*http://bit.ly/2MNUKy4*) If you're interested in going beyond *practical* AI, it's definitely one of the more readable "proper" AI papers.

You can also use the TensorFlow to CoreML Converter (*http://bit.ly/2VLRLdD*), which is a project from both Apple and Google, to convert the model from TensorFlow's format to an *.mlmodel* file. This would allow you to use it with CoreML and use it in an iOS app.

Check back to Chapter 2 for details on how to use Apple's CoreML-Tools (*http://bit.ly/328qggE*) and the TensorFlow to CoreML Converter (*http://bit.ly/2VLRLdD*). Later in this book, in both Chapter 8 and Chapter 9, we use CoreML Tools to convert models for use with CoreML.

Exploring this in its entirety is beyond the scope of this book, but it is the next step if you're curious. Visit out our website (*https://aiwithswift.com*) for articles and links that explore this sort of thing.

Task: Sound Classification

For our next audio task, we want you to imagine that you're building an app for a zoo. One of the features that you've been asked to create is a system in which users can open up the app when they hear animals in the distance making a noise, and the app can identify and inform the users what kind of animal they're hearing. This is a sound classification problem.

Problem and Approach

Sound classifiers, given a sound, will assign it to one of a predetermined collection of labels. They're classifiers, so they work like any other classifiers. (We discuss how they work under the hood in "Sound Classification" on page 454.)

 None of the sound classification features provided by Apple's machine-learning tools are designed to be used with human speech. You can use them on weird noises that you might want to make, but they're not designed around speech recognition.

In this chapter, we build an app, the final version of which is shown in Figure 5-3, that can assign a sound it hears to one of nine different buckets.

Figure 5-3. The final version of our sound classifier app

For this task, we explore the practical side of sound classification by doing the following:

- Building an app that can record some audio, perform a sound classification on the recording, and inform us as to what animal made the noise
- Selecting a toolkit for creating the sound classification model and assembling a dataset for the problem
- Building and training our sound classification model

- Incorporating the sound classification model into our app

- Improving our app

After that, we'll quickly touch on the theory of how sound classification works and point to some further resources for improvements and changes you can make on your own. Let's get started.

Building the App

Our sound classification app is going to use UIKit, Apple's older UI framework for iOS. This app makes slightly more advanced use of native iOS views, including a `UICollectionView` and a `UIProgressView`, so if you're unfamiliar with those, this app might look a little scary.

Never fear. We explain them as we go in a little more detail than other iOS views that we've been using.

 This book is here to teach you the practical side of using AI and machine learning features with Swift and on Apple's platforms. Because of this, we don't explain the fine details of how to build apps; we assume you mostly know that (although if you don't, we think you'll be able to follow along just fine if you pay attention). If you want to learn Swift, we recommend picking up Learning Swift (*http://oreil.ly/DLVGh*) (also by us!) from the lovely folks at O'Reilly Media:

The general look of the app we're going to build here, even in its starting point form, is shown in Figure 5-3. The starting point will have the following components:

- A `UIButton` to trigger the recording (and later the automatic classification of) a sound

- A `UICollectionView`, showing a collection of different animals (each in a `UICollectionViewCell`) in emoji form, which will light up depending on what type of animal sound is heard

- A `UIProgressView` to indicate how far through its recording (listening) process the app is

- An `AVAudioRecorder` (and its associated `AVAudioRecorderDelegate`) to record audio

If you don't want to manually build the starting point iOS app, you can download the code from our our website (*https://aiwiths wift.com*) and find the project named SCDemo-Starter. After you have that, skim through the rest of this section (don't skip it!) and then meet us at "AI Toolkit and Dataset" on page 196.

To make the sound classification starting point yourself, follow these steps:

1. Create an iOS app project in Xcode, choosing the "Single View App" template. Don't select any of the checkboxes below the Language drop-down (which are, as usual, set to "Swift").

   We're going to start with code instead of the storyboard. That's because we're creating some custom classes that inherit from standard UI objects.

2. Add a new Swift file to the project and name it *Animals.swift*. In that file, add the following enum:

   ```
   enum Animal: String, CaseIterable {

   }
   ```

   We're going to use this enum type to represent the animal sounds that the app can detect. Note that the enum we created, which is called Animal, conforms to both String and CaseIterable. What String means should be obvious: this is an enumeration of Strings, but conforming to CaseIterable allows us to access a collection of all of the cases of Animal by using the .allCases property.

   You can read more about the CaseIteratble protocol in Apple's documentation (*https://apple.co/2Mnwl36*).

3. With our Animal type in place, we need to add some cases. Add the following to the top, within the Animal type:

   ```
   case dog, pig, cow, frog, cat, insects, sheep, crow, chicken
   ```

   These are the nine different animal cases for which we'll be able to classify the sounds.

4. Add an initializer so that the right case can be assigned when an Animal is needed:

```
init?(rawValue: String) {
    if let match = Self.allCases
        .first(where: { $0.rawValue == rawValue }) {
        self = match
    } else if rawValue == "rooster" || rawValue == "hen" {
        self = .chicken
    } else {
        return nil
    }
}
```

This matches the incoming raw value to one of the cases, except in the case of the incoming raw value being either the string "rooster" or the string "hen," which are both also matched to the chicken case because they're varieties of chicken (for the purposes of this app, just in case there are any chickenologists out there who disagree...)

5. We want to return a nice icon (which will just be an emoji) for each case:

```
var icon: String {
    switch self {
        case .dog: "<img src="images/twemoji/dog.svg" />"
        case .pig: return "<img src="images/twemoji/pig.svg" />"
        case .cow: return "<img src="images/twemoji/cow.svg" />"
        case .frog: return "<img src="images/twemoji/frog.svg" />"
        case .cat: return "<img src="images/twemoji/cat.svg" />"
        case .insects: return "<img src="images/twemoji/insects.svg" />"
        case .sheep: return "<img src="images/twemoji/sheep.svg" />"
        case .crow: return "<img src="images/twemoji/crow.svg" />"
        case .chicken: return "<img src="images/twemoji/chicken.svg" />"
    }
}
```

6. Assign a color to each animal so that the views that we ultimately display them in look nice:

```
var color: UIColor {
    switch self {
        case .dog: return .systemRed
        case .pig: return .systemBlue
        case .cow: return .systemOrange
        case .frog: return .systemYellow
        case .cat: return .systemTeal
        case .insects: return .systemPink
        case .sheep: return .systemPurple
        case .crow: return .systemGreen
        case .chicken: return .systemIndigo
    }
}
```

We've just arbitrarily picked some colors here, so go nuts if you have any better ideas than we did. We definitely feel that insects are pink, though.

That's everything we need to do in *Animals.swift*, so make sure that you save the file, and then let's move on to the *ViewController.swift* file. There's a fair bit of work to do there.

The first thing we need to do in *ViewController.swift* is create a button that can move between three different states. We're going to use this button to allow users to record a sound, which will ultimately be classified.

The button needs to be able to switch from being a nice, friendly button inviting users to trigger a recording, to showing that recording is in progress. We also want to set up a state in which it's disabled in case something prevents a recording from being made or the app is busy classifying the recording (which could take some time).

 We could perform all these state changes manually on a standard UIButton, but we want to make sure the code that connects to the AI features later on is as clean and simple as possible, so we're abstracting a few bits and pieces out in ways that make that code more obvious. Also, it's good practice to do it like this!

1. Add a new class to the *ViewController.swift* file:

   ```
   class ThreeStateButton: UIButton {

   }
   ```

   This is just a new class called ThreeStateButton that inherits from UIButton. At this point, we could implement some ThreeStateButtons, and they'd just be UIButtons.

2. Add an enum to represent the different states of the button:

   ```
   enum ButtonState {
       case enabled(title: String, color: UIColor)
       case inProgress(title: String, color: UIColor)
       case disabled(title: String, color: UIColor)
   }
   ```

3. Add a function to change the state of the button:

   ```
   func changeState(to state: ThreeStateButton.ButtonState) {
       switch state {
           case .enabled(let title, let color):
               self.setTitle(title, for: .normal)
               self.backgroundColor = color
               self.isEnabled = true
           case .inProgress(let title, let color):
   ```

```
                self.setTitle(title, for: .disabled)
                self.backgroundColor = color
                self.isEnabled = false
            case .disabled(let title, let color):
                self.setTitle(title, for: .disabled)
                self.backgroundColor = color
                self.isEnabled = false
        }
    }
```

This function takes a state (which is the `ButtonState` enum we created a moment ago) and changes the `ThreeStateButton` to that state. Each state involves a change of title (which is provided when this is called; it is not predefined), a new background color (also provided when this is called), and an actual enabling or disabling of the button.

The time has come to build our UI storyboard, but we need one more thing. Because we're going to use a `UICollectionView`, which is made up of a collection (bet you'd never have guessed!) of cells, we're going to subclass `UICollectionViewCell` and use it to display each of the animal types for which the app can detect the sound.

4. Add the following code to the *ViewController.swift* file, outside of any existing classes or definitions (we recommend adding it to the very bottom):

```
class AnimalCell: UICollectionViewCell {
    static let identifier = "AnimalCollectionViewCell"
}
```

This creates a subclass of `UICollectionViewCell` named `AnimalCell` and provides an identifier by which we can refer to it within our storyboard (which we make next. We promise!)

Now, you can open the *Main.storyboard* file, and create a UI:

5. Add the following components to your storyboard:

   • A `UIButton`, to trigger the sound recording (and show that a recording is in progress)

   • A `UIProgressView`, which shows the length of the recording

   • A `UICollectionView`, which holds cells to show each animal type for which the app can detect the sound

   • Within the `UICollectionView`, a prototype `UICollectionViewCell`, which displays each animal. You can see an image of our storyboard in Figure 5-4. Make sure you add the necessary constraints!

6. We need to change the class of some of these components to the custom types we created in code earlier. Select the `UICollectionViewCell` inside the `UICollec`

`tionView` and then, with the Identity Inspector open, change its class to `Animal Cell` (it should autocomplete for you), as shown in Figure 5-5.

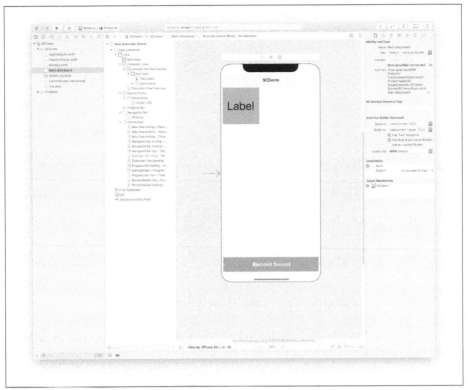

Figure 5-4. Our storyboard for the sound classification app

7. Within the cell's view, in the storyboard, add a large `UILabel` and center it appropriately using constraints.

8. We need to add some outlets for the `AnimalCell`. Add the following outlets within the `AnimalCell` class definition in *ViewController.swift*, connecting them to the "Cell View" (a `UIView`, which came premade in the cell) and the `UILabel` you created, respectively:

```
@IBOutlet weak var cellView: UIView!
@IBOutlet weak var textLabel: UILabel!
```

Figure 5-5. Changing the class of the UICollectionViewCell

9. Select the UIButton you created when we first started working with this Story-board and change its class to ThreeStateButton in its identity inspector (just as we did for the UICollectionViewCell/AnimalCell).

10. Connect some outlets to the ViewController class itself:

```
@IBOutlet weak var collectionView: UICollectionView!
@IBOutlet weak var progressBar: UIProgressView!
@IBOutlet weak var recordButton: ThreeStateButton!
```

These outlets are for the UICollectionView itself, the UIProgressView, and the UIButton for which we just changed the class to ThreeStateButton.

11. Add an action, connected to the ThreeStateButton:

```
@IBAction func recordButtonPressed(_ sender: Any) {
    // start audio recording
    recordAudio()
}
```

12. Add the following attributes to the ViewController class:

```
private var recordingLength: Double = 5.0
private var classification: Animal?

private lazy var audioRecorder: AVAudioRecorder? = {
    return initialiseAudioRecorder()
```

```
    }()

    private lazy var recordedAudioFilename: URL = {
        let directory = FileManager.default.urls(
            for: .documentDirectory,
            in: .userDomainMask)[0]

        return directory.appendingPathComponent("recording.m4a")
    }()
```

These attributes define a recording length, a variable in which to store the ultimate classification of a sound, an AVAudioRecorder, and a filename for the file in which we'll store the recording.

13. Update the viewDidLoad() function to look like the following:

```
override func viewDidLoad() {
    super.viewDidLoad()

    collectionView.dataSource = self
}
```

14. Add a function to start the audio recording, using the attribute we created earlier to access AVAudioRecorder:

```
private func recordAudio() {
    guard let audioRecorder = audioRecorder else { return }

    classification = nil
    collectionView.reloadData()

    recordButton.changeState(
        to: .inProgress(
            title: "Recording...",
            color: .systemRed
        )
    )
    progressBar.isHidden = false

    audioRecorder.record(forDuration: TimeInterval(recordingLength))
    UIView.animate(withDuration: recordingLength) {
        self.progressBar.setProgress(
            Float(self.recordingLength),
            animated: true
        )
    }
}
```

15. You'll also need a function to finish recording, taking a Bool as a parameter to indicate whether the recording was successful, just in case it wasn't (it defaults to true):

```
private func finishRecording(success: Bool = true) {
    progressBar.isHidden = true
    progressBar.progress = 0

    if success, let audioFile = try? AVAudioFile(
        forReading: recordedAudioFilename) {
        recordButton.changeState(
            to: .disabled(
                title: "Record Sound",
                color: .systemGray
            )
        )
        classifySound(file: audioFile)
    } else {
        summonAlertView()
        classify(nil)
    }
}
```

16. Add a method to update the `UICollectionView` to show which animal we think the sound is. This function takes an `Animal` as input:

```
private func classify(_ animal: Animal?) {
    classification = animal
    recordButton.changeState(
        to: .enabled(
            title: "Record Sound",
            color: .systemBlue
        )
    )
    collectionView.reloadData()
}
```

17. In the `ViewController` class (but not in the *ViewController.swift* file), add a function to an `AVAudioFile` (the result of our recording) and do something with it (it will do a lot more after we add the AI features):

```
private func classifySound(file: AVAudioFile) {
    classify(Animal.allCases.randomElement()!)
}
```

We're done with the `ViewController` class for the moment. Now, we need to add an extension or three to the class:

1. Below the end of the `ViewController` class, but still within the *View-Controller.swift* file, add the following extension, which will allow us to present an alert view (a pop up) in case of a problem:

```
extension ViewController {
    private func summonAlertView(message: String? = nil) {
```

```
        let alertController = UIAlertController(
            title: "Error",
            message: message ?? "Action could not be completed.",
            preferredStyle: .alert
        )

        alertController.addAction(
            UIAlertAction(
                title: "OK",
                style: .default
            )
        )

        present(alertController, animated: true)
    }
}
```

2. Below that, add another extension, allowing us to conform to the AVAudioRecor
derDelegate in order to work with the AVAudioRecorder:

```
extension ViewController: AVAudioRecorderDelegate {
    func audioRecorderDidFinishRecording(_ recorder: AVAudioRecorder,
        successfully flag: Bool) {

        finishRecording(success: flag)
    }

    private func initialiseAudioRecorder() -> AVAudioRecorder? {
        let settings = [
            AVFormatIDKey: Int(kAudioFormatMPEG4AAC),
            AVSampleRateKey: 12000,
            AVNumberOfChannelsKey: 1,
            AVEncoderAudioQualityKey: AVAudioQuality.high.rawValue
        ]

        let recorder = try? AVAudioRecorder(
            url: recordedAudioFilename, settings: settings)

        recorder?.delegate = self
        return recorder
    }
}
```

3. Again, below that, add one final extension to allow us to conform to the UICol
lectionViewDataSource, which provides the ability to populate a UICollection
View (we're going to fill it with AnimalCells):

```
extension ViewController: UICollectionViewDataSource {
    func collectionView(_ collectionView: UICollectionView,
        numberOfItemsInSection section: Int) -> Int {
```

```
        return Animal.allCases.count
    }

    func collectionView(_ collectionView: UICollectionView,
        cellForItemAt indexPath: IndexPath) -> UICollectionViewCell {

        guard let cell = collectionView
            .dequeueReusableCell(
                withReuseIdentifier: AnimalCell.identifier,
                for: indexPath) as? AnimalCell else {

                    return UICollectionViewCell()
        }

        let animal = Animal.allCases[indexPath.item]

        cell.textLabel.text = animal.icon
        cell.backgroundColor =
            (animal == self.classification) ? animal.color : .systemGray

        return cell
    }
}
```

4. Add a launch screen and an icon, if you'd like to (as with the previous practical tasks, we've provided some in the downloadable resources), and launch the app in the simulator. You should see something that looks like the figure from earlier, Figure 5-3.

This app actually does record audio, but it doesn't do anything with it. There's no way to play it back, and it's obviously not yet connected to any form of machine-learning model. Back in the `classifySound()` function that we wrote, we just randomly pick one of the animals each time.

Let's keep going and add some AI.

AI Toolkit and Dataset

As usual with our practical AI tasks, we need to assemble a toolkit with which to tackle the problem. The primary tools that we use in this case are Python to prepare the data for training, the CreateML application for training, and CoreML to read the model in our app.

To make a model that will power our app's ability to classify animal sounds, we'll need a dataset full of animal sounds. As is often the case (you might have noticed a pattern) with machine learning and AI datasets, the boffins have us covered.

The Dataset for Environmental Sound Classification (ESC) is a collection of short environmental recordings of a variety of sounds spanning five major categories, as shown in Figure 5-6.

Animals	Natural soundscapes & water sounds	Human, non-speech sounds	Interior/domestic sounds	Exterior/urban noises
Dog	Rain	Crying baby	Door knock	Helicopter
Rooster	Sea waves	Sneezing	Mouse click	Chainsaw
Pig	Crackling fire	Clapping	Keyboard typing	Siren
Cow	Crickets	Breathing	Door, wood creaks	Car horn
Frog	Chirping birds	Coughing	Can opening	Engine
Cat	Water drops	Footsteps	Washing machine	Train
Hen	Wind	Laughing	Vacuum cleaner	Church bells
Insects (flying)	Pouring water	Brushing teeth	Clock alarm	Airplane
Sheep	Toilet flush	Snoring	Clock tick	Fireworks
Crow	Thunderstorm	Drinking, sipping	Glass breaking	Hand saw

Figure 5-6. The major categories of the ESC

Head over to the ESC-50 GitHub repository (*http://bit.ly/2MOC3dw*) and download a copy of the dataset. Save it somewhere safe.

 You could do everything that our Python script does manually by yourself, but it would probably take longer than doing it with a script. It's always good practice to make things repeatable when you're working on machine-learning problems.

Fire up a new Python environment, following the instructions in "Python" on page 46, and then do the following:

1. Create the following Python script (ours is called *preparation.py*) using your favorite text editor (we like Visual Studio Code and BBEdit, but anything works):

```
import os
import shutil
import pandas as pd

# Make output directory
try:
    os.makedirs(output_directory)
except OSError:
    if not os.path.isdir(output_directory):
        raise
```

```
# Make class directories within it
for class_name in classes_to_include:
    class_directory = output_directory + class_name + '/'
    try:
        os.makedirs(class_directory)
    except OSError:
        if not os.path.isdir(class_directory):
            raise

# Go through CSV to sort audio into class directories
classes_file = pd.read_csv(
    input_classes_filename,
    encoding='utf-8',
    header = 'infer'
)

# format: filename, fold, target, category, esc10, src_file, take
for line in classes_file.itertuples(index = False):
    if include_unlicensed or line[4] == True:
        file_class = line[3]

        if file_class in classes_to_include:
            file_name = line[0]
            file_src = sounds_directory + file_name
            file_dst = output_directory + file_class + '/' + file_name
            try:
                shutil.copy2(file_src, file_dst)
            except IOError:
                raise
```

This script imports Pandas (as shown in Figure 2-18), makes an output folder that contains subfolders for each class, and then parses the comma-separated values (CSV) file and writes out files in a new format.

 We use the Pandas framework here to access its CSV-reading capabilities. Very useful stuff.

2. To point the script to the appropriate classes and input files, at the top of your Python script, add the following configuration variables, after the import statements but before the actual script starts:

```
# Configure as required
input_classes_filename = '/Users/mars/Desktop/ESC-50-master/meta/esc50.csv'
sounds_directory = '/Users/mars/Desktop/ESC-50-master/audio/'
output_directory = '/Users/mars/Desktop/ESC-50-master/classes/'
```

```
classes_to_include = [
    'dog', 'rooster', 'pig', 'cow', 'frog', 'cat', 'hen',
    'insects', 'sheep', 'crow'
]

# whether to use whole ESC-50 dataset or lesser-restricted ESC-10 subset
include_unlicensed = False
```

Update each of the paths to point to the proper place on your system: input_classes_filename should point to the *esc50.csv* file that came with your copy of the dataset; sounds_directory to the */audio/* folder; and output_directory to wherever you want the script to place the subset of files it will need for training (we made a folder called */classes/* in the dataset download).

The classes_to_include list includes all of the animals for which we're going to be allowing our app to classify the sound (which is not all of the animal sounds present in the dataset).

Run the preparation Python script by executing it on the command line (python preparation.py). Your data should now be prepared, and you should have it in a folder structure that looks like Figure 5-7.

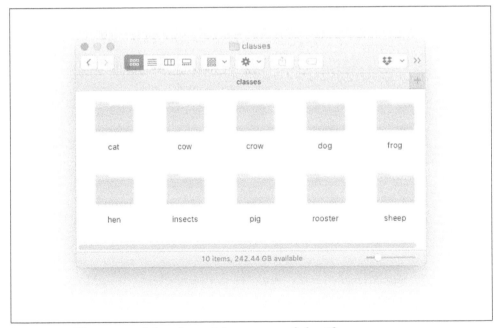

Figure 5-7. The prepared data for training our sound classifier

Creating a Model

With our animal sound dataset ready to go, let's turn to Apple's CreateML application, just as we did in Chapter 4, to build a sound classification model.

 To learn more about the various incarnations of CreateML, check back to "CreateML" on page 31.

Let's build our animal sound classifier model:

1. Fire up CreateML and create a new Sound Classifier project by selecting the appropriate template, as shown in Figure 5-8.

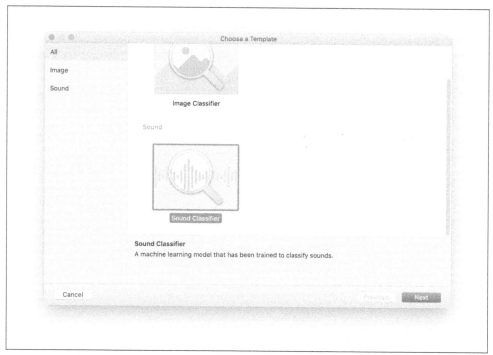

Figure 5-8. The sound classifier in the CreateML template picker

1. After giving your project some details, you'll see a new empty Sound Classifier project, as shown in Figure 5-9.

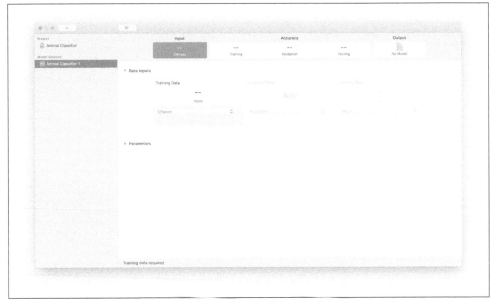

Figure 5-9. Your CreateML project is ready to take some sound

1. In the Training Data section, click the drop-down box and browse to the folder where you put the prepared data earlier (it should have 10 different animal-themed folders in it). Select this folder and then, in the top bar of the CreateML app, click the Play button (the right-facing triangle.)

 Training the sound classifier won't take as long as the image classifier back in "Task: Image Classification" on page 120 did. But it might take a few minutes. (Watch five minutes of an episode of *Person of Interest*.)

When the training is done, you'll see something resembling Figure 5-10. You'll be able to drag the model file out from the Output box in the upper-right corner of the window. Drag this file somewhere safe.

Figure 5-10. The CreateML application after a successful sound classifier training run

With our CoreML model trained by CreateML, we're ready to put it to work in our app.

 You could have also trained the sound classification model using the CreateML framework and the `MLSoundClassifier` structure. You can learn more about it in Apple's documentation (*https://apple.co/2OY02tA*).

Incorporating the Model in the App

At this point, if you've been following along, you have a starter iOS app written in Swift, and a trained sound classifier model built using the CreateML application all ready to go. Let's combine them and make the iOS app capable of sound classification.

 If you didn't build the starting point yourself (following the instructions in "Building the App" on page 186), you can download the code from our website (*https://aiwithswift.com*) and find the project named `SCDemo-Starter`. We'll be progressing from that point in this section.

You'll also find a trained sound classifier model in the same folder as the demo project folder, as shown in Figure 5-11.

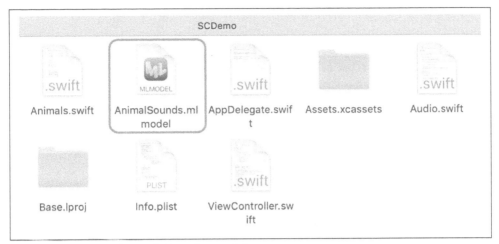

.swift	ML MLMODEL	.swift		.swift
Animals.swift	AnimalSounds.ml model	AppDelegate.swif t	Assets.xcassets	Audio.swift

	PLIST	.swift
Base.lproj	Info.plist	ViewController.sw ift

Figure 5-11. Trained sound classifier model

 If you don't want to follow along and manually work with the iOS app's code to add the AI features via the sound classification model that we trained, you can also download the project named SCDemo-Complete. If you choose to download the SCDemo-Complete project instead of stepping through this section, we still urge you to read this section and look at the relevant bits of the SCDemo-Complete project.

As usual, we're going to need to change quite a few things to get the app working with our sound classification model:

1. Drag the *.mlmodel* file you created earlier into the project's root, allowing Xcode to copy as needed.

2. Add the SoundAnalysis framework to the imports in *ViewController.swift*:

   ```
   import SoundAnalysis
   ```

   SoundAnalysis (*https://apple.co/2M7WNxD*) is a framework provided by Apple that lets you analyze audio and classify it. SoundAnalysis works with a model trained using CreateML's MLSoundClassifier (which is what you end up with whether you used the CreateML app, like we did, or the CreateML framework).

1. Add an attribute for the classifier, pointing to our model file:

   ```
   private let classifier = AudioClassifier(model: AnimalSounds().model)
   ```

   Make sure to change the name from AnimalSounds().model to that of your model if your model is named something else (for example, if your model is named *MyAnimalClassifier.mlmodel*, set this to MyAnimalClassifier().model).

2. Add a new function, refresh(), after the viewDidLoad() function:

```
private func refresh(clear: Bool = false) {
    if clear { classification = nil }
    collectionView.reloadData()
}
```

This function is so that we can ask the UICollectionView to refresh as needed.

3. Change the recordAudio() function to be as follows:

```
private func recordAudio() {
    guard let audioRecorder = audioRecorder else { return }

    refresh(clear: true)

    recordButton.changeState(
        to: .inProgress(
            title: "Recording...",
            color: .systemRed
        )
    )

    progressBar.isHidden = false

    audioRecorder.record(forDuration: TimeInterval(recordingLength))
    UIView.animate(withDuration: recordingLength) {
        self.progressBar.setProgress(
            Float(self.recordingLength),
            animated: true)
    }
}
```

This sets it up so that instead of performing the refresh itself, the function calls our new refresh() function (which we created a moment ago).

4. Update the finishRecording() function to be as follows:

```
private func finishRecording(success: Bool = true) {
    progressBar.isHidden = true
    progressBar.progress = 0

    if success {
        recordButton.changeState(
            to: .disabled(title: "Record Sound", color: .systemGray)
        )
        classifySound(file: recordedAudioFilename)
    } else {
        classify(nil)
    }
}
```

This function is called when recording is finished. If the success Bool is true, it disables the record button and calls classifySound(), passing the recordedAudioFilename.

5. Replace the call to collectionView.reloadData() in the classify() function with the following:

```
refresh()

if classification == nil {
    summonAlertView()
}
```

6. Update the classifySound() function, as follows:

```
private func classifySound(file: URL) {
    classifier?.classify(audioFile: file) { result in
        self.classify(Animal(rawValue: result ?? ""))
    }
}
```

This removes the random animal that we used as a placeholder in the starter app, and actually uses our model to perform a classification. You can now launch the app. You should see something that looks exactly like it always did, as shown in Figure 5-12.

Figure 5-12. The sound classifier

You can now tap the Record Sound, record some noises, and the app should light up the animal relating to the sound that it thinks it heard. Amazing!

 You'll need to add the NSMicrophoneUsageDescription (*https://apple.co/2qjePV7*) key to your *Info.plist* file, as we did for the "Task: Speech Recognition" on page 173, as shown in Figure 5-13.

Figure 5-13. Our Info.plist

Improving the App

At this point, we have an iOS application, written in Swift and using UIKit and integrated with a CoreML model generated using CreateML, that can, with a reasonable degree of reliability, record some audio and then perform a classification on it, using the Sound Analysis framework, and tell us which of nine possible animals the sound in the audio recording might belong to. What's the next step?

In this section, we improve the sound classification app, making it capable of performing real-time sound classification instead of having to record an audio file and then classify it.

You'll need to have completed all the steps presented prior to this section to follow from here.

 If you don't want to do that or you need a clean starting point, you can download the resources for this book from our website (*https://aiwithswift.com*) and find the project SCDemo-Complete. We'll be building on the app from there. If you don't want to follow the instructions in this section, you can also find the project SCDemo-Improved, which is the end result of this section. If you go down that route, we strongly recommend reading the code as we discuss it in this section and comparing it with the code in SCDemo-Improved.

There are a lot of code changes required here, so take your time. To begin, create a new Swift file, named *Audio.swift*, in the project:

1. Add the following imports:

```
import CoreML
import AVFoundation
import SoundAnalysis
```

2. Add the following class to it:

```swift
class ResultsObserver: NSObject, SNResultsObserving {

    private var completion: (String?) -> ()

    init(completion: @escaping (String?) -> ()) {
        self.completion = completion
    }

    func request(_ request: SNRequest, didProduce result: SNResult) {
        guard let results = result as? SNClassificationResult,
            let result = results.classifications.first else { return }
        let label = result.confidence > 0.7 ? result.identifier : nil

        DispatchQueue.main.async {
            self.completion(label)
        }
    }

    func request(_ request: SNRequest, didFailWithError error: Error) {
        completion(nil)
    }
}
```

This class implements the SNResultsObserving protocol, which is part of the
SoundAnalysis framework that we imported. It allows us to create an interface
with which to receive the results of a sound analysis request.

3. Create a class to represent the process of classifying audio. Let's call it AudioClas
sifier (we're incredibly creative). Add the following class to the *Audio.swift* file:

```swift
class AudioClassifier {

}
```

4. Add the following attributes:

```swift
private let model: MLModel
private let request: SNClassifySoundRequest
private let audioEngine = AVAudioEngine()
private let analysisQueue =
    DispatchQueue(label: "com.apple.AnalysisQueue")
private let inputFormat: AVAudioFormat
private let analyzer: SNAudioStreamAnalyzer
private let inputBus: AVAudioNodeBus

private var observer: ResultsObserver?
```

Each of these attributes should be fairly self-explanatory. If you'd like to know more, you can check Apple's documentation (*https://apple.co/32ptxZ9*).

5. Add an initializer:

```
init?(model: MLModel, inputBus: AVAudioNodeBus = 0) {
    guard let request =
        try? SNClassifySoundRequest(mlModel: model) else { return nil }

    self.model = model
    self.request = request
    self.inputBus = inputBus
    self.inputFormat = audioEngine.inputNode.inputFormat(
        forBus: inputBus)
    self.analyzer = SNAudioStreamAnalyzer(format: inputFormat)
}
```

The initializer should also be fairly self-explanatory: it sets the various attributes appropriately.

6. Add a function to begin the analysis to perform a classification:

```
func beginAnalysis(completion: @escaping (String?) -> ()) {
    guard let _ = try? audioEngine.start() else { return }

    print("Begin recording...")
    let observer = ResultsObserver(completion: completion)
    guard let _ = try? analyzer.add(
        request, withObserver: observer) else { return }

    self.observer = observer

    audioEngine.inputNode.installTap(
        onBus: inputBus,
        bufferSize: 8192,
        format: inputFormat) { buffer, time in
            self.analysisQueue.async {
                self.analyzer.analyze(
                    buffer,
                    atAudioFramePosition: time.sampleTime)
            }
        }
}
```

This code starts the analysis. It first attempts to fire up the audio system and then, effectively, just waits for results.

7. Add a function to stop the analysis:

```
func stopAnalysis() {
    print("End recording...")
    analyzer.completeAnalysis()
    analyzer.remove(request)
```

```
        audioEngine.inputNode.removeTap(onBus: inputBus)
        audioEngine.stop()
    }
```

That's it for the *Audio.swift* file. Make sure that you save it and then open *View-Controller.swift*:

1. Replace the entire set of attributes in the ViewController class, as follows:

```
@IBOutlet weak var collectionView: UICollectionView!
@IBOutlet weak var progressBar: UIProgressView!
@IBOutlet weak var recordButton: ThreeStateButton!

@IBAction func recordButtonPressed(_ sender: Any) { toggleRecording() }

private var recording: Bool = false
private var classification: Animal?
private let classifier = AudioClassifier(model: AnimalSounds().model)
```

Because we're doing some of the work in our new AudioClassifier class (which we just created in *Audio.swift*), we no longer need quite so much code here. Make sure the IBOutlet and IBAction attributes are still connected or reconnected to the correct place in the storyboard (which should remain unmodified).

2. Comment out the recordAudio() function and add a new function, toggleRe cording(), as follows:

```
private func toggleRecording() {
    recording = !recording

    if recording {
        refresh(clear: true)
        recordButton.changeState(to:
            .inProgress(
                title: "Stop",
                color: .systemRed
            )
        )
        classifier?.beginAnalysis { result in
            self.classify(Animal(rawValue: result ?? ""))
        }
    } else {
        refresh()
        recordButton.changeState(
            to: .enabled(
                title: "Record Sound",
                color: .systemBlue
            )
        )
        classifier?.stopAnalysis()
```

```
        }
    }
```

3. Comment out the entire classifySound() function, and then update the clas
sify() function to look as follows:

```
private func classify(_ animal: Animal?) {
    classification = animal
    refresh()
}
```

4. You can also comment out the entire extension of ViewController that conforms
to AVAudioRecorderDelegate (we've moved out the audio functionality and
changed how it works).

5. For a cleaner UI, update the .inProgress case of the switch statement in the
changeState() function of the ThreeStateButton class, as follows:

```
case .inProgress(let title, let color):
    self.setTitle(title, for: .normal)
    self.backgroundColor = color
    self.isEnabled = true
```

6. Launch the improved app in the simulator. You should be able to tap the button
and the app will perform live classification on the sounds it hears, lighting up the
associated animal emoji.

Figure 5-14 shows our finished sound classifier.

Next Steps

That's all for the audio chapter. We've covered some common audio-related practical
AI tasks that you might want to accomplish with Swift, and we used a variety of tools
to do so. We built two apps, exploring two practical AI tasks related to audio:

Speech Recognition
Using Apple's new SwiftUI for the interface and Apple's provided speech recognition framework, we built an app that can turn human speech into text. We didn't
need to train our own model.

Sound Classification
We used Apple's UIKit framework for the interface, some Python scripting to
prepare the data (a whole bunch of animal sounds), and Apple's CreateML application to train the model. We also used CoreML in the app, to work with our
trained model.

Later, in Chapter 11, we'll look at what happened under the hood, algorithm-wise, for
each of the tasks we explored in this chapter ("Audio" on page 454). In the next chapter we look at text and language.

For more audio-related practical AI tasks, check out our website (*https://aiwiths wift.com*).

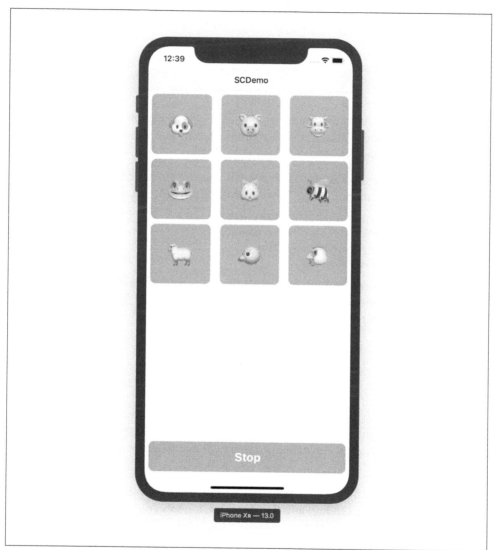

Figure 5-14. Our finished sound classifier

## CHAPTER 6

Text and Language

This chapter explores the practical side of implementing text- and language-related AI features in your Swift apps. Taking a top-down approach, we explore five text and language tasks and how to implement them using a variety of AI tools.

Practical AI, Text, and Language

The five text and language tasks that we explore in this chapter are:

Language Identification
> Determining what language some text might be in.

Named Entity Recognition
> Identifying the elements of text that are people, places, or organizations.

Lemmatization, tagging, tokenization Identifying the lemma of every word in a string, finding the parts of speech (verbs, nouns, and so on), and splitting a string up by words.

Sentiment Analysis
> Determining whether some text has a positive or negative sentiment.

Custom Text Classifiers
> Another way of classifying text for sentiment, extending Apple's tools.

In Chapter 8, we also look at generating text. We put that task there because we think it's more closely related to generating things than it is to text. But really, you're probably reading the whole book, so it doesn't matter where it goes.

Images, human movement, and sound might be flashy, but the majority of apps you'll build in your life will also, or perhaps primarily, deal with text. Humans generate vast amounts of text, and it's often useful to be able to use a clever machine to figure out what's going on with text so that you can make decisions or show the user something contextual relating to it. In this chapter, we tackle the problem of text classification. Specifically, we're going to look at implementing an app that can perform sentiment analysis on some text and determine whether its sentiment is positive or negative.

 You might see other sources mix and match the terms "text classifi-cation," "sentiment analysis," "natural language processing," "opin-ion mining," and many others. The authors of this book are of the opinion that they are quite different things. This chapter explores the specific task of sentiment analysis, which is part of the domain of text classification. In doing so, we use natural language process-ing (NLP) techniques.

Task: Language Identification

Language identification refers to (surprising no one) figuring out what language a string of text might be in. This is actually a very simple practical artificial intelligence (AI) task.

To cut straight to it, we do this task in a Playground:

1. Create a new iOS-flavor Playground in Xcode, as shown in Figure 6-1.

 We're using iOS because we're choosing to use iOS. Everything we're using for this task is available on macOS, too.

Figure 6 1. Creating a new iOS-flavor Playground in Xcode

1. Add the following imports:

```
import NaturalLanguage
import Foundation
import CoreML
```

2. Add the following extension on String:

```
extension String {
    func predictLanguage() -> String {
        let locale = Locale(identifier: "es")
        let recognizer = NLLanguageRecognizer()
        recognizer.processString(self)
        let language = recognizer.dominantLanguage
        return locale.localizedString(
            forLanguageCode: language!.rawValue) ?? "unknown"
    }
}
```

This means that we can ask a String to predictLanguage(), and we'll get its language back. We do this by setting the locale to "en_US" (for US English), creating an NLLanguageRecognizer, processing the String being used, and getting the dominant language for that String.

3. Add a `String` (or in this case, an array of them) for us to identify the languages for the following sentences:

```
let text = ["My hovercraft is full of eels",
            "Mijn hovercraft zit vol palingen",
            "我的氣墊船充滿了鰻魚",
            "Mit luftpudefartøj er fyldt med ål",
            "Το χόβερκραφτ μου είναι γεμάτο χέλια",
            "제 호버크래프트가 장어로 가득해요",
            "Mi aerodeslizador está lleno de anguilas",
            "Mein Luftkissenfahrzeug ist voller Aale"]
```

4. Test it by iterating through the `Strings` in the array and calling `predictLanguage()` on each:

```
for string in text {
    print("\(string) is in \(string.predictLanguage())")
}
```

You will see something like the screenshot in Figure 6-2.

```
My hovercraft is full of eels is in English
Mijn hovercraft zit vol palingen is in Dutch
我的氣墊船充滿了鰻魚 is in Chinese
Mit luftpudefartøj er fyldt med ål is in Danish
Το χόβερκραφτ μου είναι γεμάτο χέλια is in Greek
제 호버크래프트가 장어로 가득해요 is in Korean
Mi aerodeslizador está lleno de anguilas is in Spanish
Mein Luftkissenfahrzeug ist voller Aale is in German
```

Figure 6-2. The language identification for our strings

1. We could change the locale to be somewhere else, for example "es" for Spain, and we'd get back the Spanish names for the various languages instead, as shown in Figure 6-3.

```
My hovercraft is full of eels is in inglés
Mijn hovercraft zit vol palingen is in neerlandés
我的氣墊船充滿了鰻魚 is in chino
Mit luftpudefartøj er fyldt med ål is in danés
Το χόβερκραφτ μου είναι γεμάτο χέλια is in griego
제 호버크래프트가 장어로 가득해요 is in coreano
Mi aerodeslizador está lleno de anguilas is in español
Mein Luftkissenfahrzeug ist voller Aale is in alemán
```

Figure 6-3. The output with our locale set to Spain

Task: Named Entity Recognition

Almost as simple as recognizing language is recognizing the entities in a string. As with language identification, this task relies on using Apple's Natural Language framework (*https://apple.co/2pc5LB9*) to do the work for us. The Natural Language framework works on texts by assigning tag schemes.

Again, let's get straight to it and do our work in a Playground:

1. Create another new iOS-flavor Playground in Xcode.

2. Add the following `import`s:

```
import NaturalLanguage
import Foundation
import CoreML
```

3. Add the following extension on String:

```
extension String {
    func printNamedEntities() {
        let tagger = NSLinguisticTagger(
            tagSchemes: [.nameType],
            options: 0)

        tagger.string = self

        let range = NSRange(location: 0, length: self.utf16.count)

        let options: NSLinguisticTagger.Options = [
            .omitPunctuation, .omitWhitespace, .joinNames
        ]
        let tags: [NSLinguisticTag] = [
            .personalName, .placeName, .organizationName
        ]

        tagger.enumerateTags(in: range,
            unit: .word,
            scheme: .nameType,
            options: options) {
                tag, tokenRange, stop in

                if let tag = tag, tags.contains(tag) {
                    let name = (self as NSString)
                        .substring(with: tokenRange)

                    print("\(name) is a \(tag.rawValue)")
                }
        }
    }
}
```

This means that we can ask a `String` to `printNamedEntities()`, and we'll see it print its name entities.

4. Add a `String` on which we can perform named entity recognition:

```
let sentence = "Marina, Jon, and Tim write books for O'Reilly Media " +
    "and live in Tasmania, Australia."
```

5. Test it by calling `printNamedEntities()` on it:

```
sentence.printNamedEntities()
```

You will see something like the screenshot in Figure 6-4.

```
Jon is a PersonalName
Tim is a PersonalName
O'Reilly Media is a OrganizationName
Tasmania is a PlaceName
Australia is a PlaceName
```

Figure 6-4. The language identification for our strings

Task: Lemmatization, Tagging, and Tokenization

Lemmatization is one of those things that you've probably heard of but aren't quite sure what it is. But it's useful for all manner of things.

Lemmatization is a linguistics term that refers to the process of grouping all the forms of a single word so that they can be identified as a single thing. The single thing that identifies them is the *lemma*.

For example, take the term (a verb) "to walk." "To walk" can appear as "walk," "walked," "walks," "walking." To look up any of those in a dictionary, you'd look up "walk." Not every word has an obvious lemma; for example, the lemma of "better" is "good."

Lemmatization is useful for things like search tools in your apps: if a user searches for "good," you probably want to identify things that are also marked "better," or if your app, for example, deals with photos, and you've performed machine-learning classification to establish what's in each photo, you'd want the search term "mouse" to also present results for "mice," and vice versa.

Again, let's dispense with the usual structure and get straight to it:

1. Create a new iOS-flavor Playground in Xcode.

2. Add the following `imports`:

```
import NaturalLanguage
import Foundation
import CoreML
```

3. Add a sentence on which we can perform lemmatization:

```
let speech = """
Space, the final frontier. These are the voyages of the
Starship Enterprise. Its continuing mission to explore strange new worlds,
to seek out new life and new civilization, to boldly go where no one has
gone before!
"""
```

In this case, we've used the opening monologue to *Star Trek*. The Jean-Luc Picard version, naturally.

4. Add an extension on String:

```
extension String {
    func printLemmas() {
        let tagger = NSLinguisticTagger(tagSchemes:[.lemma], options: 0)
        let options: NSLinguisticTagger.Options = [
            .omitPunctuation, .omitWhitespace, .joinNames
        ]

        tagger.string = self
        let range = NSRange(location: 0, length: self.utf16.count)

        tagger.enumerateTags(
            in: range,
            unit: .word,
            scheme: .lemma,
            options: options) {
                tag, tokenRange, stop in

                if let lemma = tag?.rawValue {
                    print(lemma)
                }
            }
    }
}
```

With this extension, we can ask a String to printLemmas() and get a console output showing the lemmas of the String. Within the printLemmas() function, we create an NSLinguisticTagger, set its scheme to .lemma, and then run it on the String (which is self in this context, because it's an extension on String).

5. To test our extension and printLemmas() function, we can call it on the String speech. See Figure 6-5 for the result:

```
speech.printLemmas()
```

```
### Lemmatization Demo ###
space
the
final
frontier
this
be
the
voyage
of
the
starship
enterprise
it
continue
mission
to
explore
strange
new
world
to
seek
out
new
life
and
new
to
boldly
go
where
no
one
have
go
before
```

Figure 6-5. Lemmatization running on our speech

If you start researching lemmatization—which you should because it's interesting—you might see it referred to as "stemming." They're basically the same thing, as far as their usefulness matters, but in reality, stemming actually just involves stripping plurals and "ings" from words, and lemmatization involves understanding the language in question, and how the vocabulary works.

Parts of Speech

But, what if we want to find the parts of speech in a sentence instead? So instead of finding the lemmas, we identify whether each component of a string is a verb, a noun, or so on.

That's also doable:

1. Add another `func` to our `String` extension:

    ```
    func printPartsOfSpeech() {

    }
    ```

    This function is used, much like we did earlier, to print the parts of speech for the string to which it's attached.

2. First, we need the usual `NSLinguisticTagger`, its options, and a range, so add that in the `printPartsOfSpeech()` function:

    ```
    let tagger = NSLinguisticTagger(
        tagSchemes:[.lexicalClass],
        options: 0)
    let options: NSLinguisticTagger.Options = [
        .omitPunctuation, .omitWhitespace, .joinNames
        ]

    tagger.string = self
    let range = NSRange(location: 0, length: self.utf16.count)
    ```

3. Run the `tagger` and print out each part of speech:

    ```
    tagger.enumerateTags(
        in: range,
        unit: .word,
        scheme: .lexicalClass,
        options: options) {
            tag, tokenRange, _ in

            if let tag = tag {
                let word = (self as NSString)
                    .substring(with: tokenRange)
                print("\(word) is a \(tag.rawValue)")
    ```

```
        }
    }
```

4. Call our new `func` on the speech `String` that we created:

```
speech.printPartsOfSpeech()
```

You will see some output just like the screenshot in Figure 6-6, showing you what part of speech each word in the sentence is.

Tokenizing a Sentence

But what if we just want to split the sentence up by words and don't really care what the lemma of each word is or what part of speech it is? We can do that too:

1. Add another function, `printWords()` to the `String` extension:

```
func printWords() {

    let tagger = NSLinguisticTagger(
        tagSchemes:[.tokenType], options: 0)

    let options: NSLinguisticTagger.Options = [
        .omitPunctuation, .omitWhitespace, .joinNames
    ]

    tagger.string = self
    let range = NSRange(location: 0, length: self.utf16.count)

    tagger.enumerateTags(
        in: range,
        unit: .word,
        scheme: .tokenType,
        options: options) {
            tag, tokenRange, stop in

            let word = (self as NSString).substring(with: tokenRange)
            print(word)
    }
}
```

2. Run it on the monologue:

```
speech.printWords()
```

You'll see something like the screenshot in Figure 6-7.

```
### Parts of Speech Demo ###
Space is a Noun
the is a Determiner
final is a Adjective
frontier is a Noun
These is a Determiner
are is a Verb
the is a Determiner
voyages is a Noun
of is a Preposition
the is a Determiner
Starship is a Noun
Enterprise is a Noun
Its is a Determiner
continuing is a Verb
mission is a Noun
to is a Particle
explore is a Verb
strange is a Adjective
new is a Adjective
worlds is a Noun
to is a Particle
seek is a Verb
out is a Particle
new is a Adjective
life is a Noun
and is a Conjunction
new is a Adjective
civilization is a Noun
to is a Preposition
boldly is a Adverb
go is a Verb
where is a Pronoun
no is a Determiner
one is a Noun
has is a Verb
gone is a Verb
before is a Adverb
```

Figure 6-6. The parts of speech of the Star Trek opening monologue

```
### Tokenization Demo ###
Space
the
final
frontier
These
are
the
voyages
of
the
Starship
Enterprise
Its
continuing
mission
to
explore
strange
new
worlds
to
seek
out
new
life
and
new
civilization
to
boldly
go
where
no
one
has
gone
before
```

Figure 6-7. Printing the words in the Star Trek opening monologue

---

The process of identifying and printing words is called *tokenization*.

You might be wondering why we can't just use a regular expression to split up the sentence by punctuation and spaces. The short answer is that this doesn't guarantee you'll end up with every word, and many languages don't behave the same way that English does in this respect. It's better to rely on the Apple framework's understanding the semantics of the language you want to work with wherever possible.

 In Chapter 8, as part of a Sentence Generation task ("Task: Sentence Generation" on page 315), we manually perform tokenization using regular expressions. We did this to highlight the differences.

Task: Sentiment Analysis

Sometimes, it's really useful to be able to determine whether something your users said is positive or negative, or generally to be able to derive some kind of organized data from unstructured, unorganized information. IBM estimates that 80% of the world's data is unstructured (*https://ibm.co/32pjl2N*) (and you'd expect IBM to know what it's talking about — it has a company song!).

Humans generate vast quantities of unstructured, unorganized text, and our apps and products often need to know what the text is about, what the text means, or the general flavor of the text in order to do something useful with it or provide useful options to the user.

Put simply, performing text classification in order to derive sentiment—*sentiment analysis*—is a way to bring order to the chaos of human-generated text.

For this task, we look at how we might build a model that allows us to determine the sentiment of some text. This isn't something that Apple's provided frameworks can do out of the box, so we'll actually need to train our own model to do it and then build an app around it.

Problem and Approach

For this task, we're going to explore the practical side of text classification to perform sentiment analysis by doing the following:

- Making an app that can inform us as to whether some user input has a positive or negative sentiment

- Laying out our app with a text field, a display for the sentiment, and a way to ask for a sentiment analysis

- Selecting a toolkit for creating the sentiment analysis model and assembling a dataset for the problem

- Building and training our sentiment analysis model

- Incorporating the model into our app

- Improving our app

After that, we'll quickly touch on the theory of how sentiment analysis works, and point to some further resources for improvements and changes that you can make on your own.

Building the App

We're going to start simple here. We need an app that can detect whether what the user has typed in is positive or negative. We all live high-pressure lives, and often act in the spur of the moment. Having an app that lets us check whether that tweet we're about to send is positive enough might be a good idea. ("Computer! Send Tweet!")

The app we're going to build will look something like Figure 6-8 when we're done.

 This book is here to teach you the practical side of using AI and machine-learning features with Swift and on Apple's platforms. Because of this, we don't explain the fine details of how to build apps; we assume that you mostly know that (although if you don't, we think you'll be able to follow along just fine if you pay attention). If you want to learn Swift, we recommend picking up *Learning Swift* (*https://oreil.ly/DLVGh*) (also by us!) from the lovely folks at O'Reilly.

The starting point iOS app that we're going to build, which will ultimately house our sentiment analysis system, has the following components (see Figure 6-9):

- A UITextView, for a user to type text that will be analyzed for sentiment

- A UIButton for the user to press when they want to type text in the aforementioned field to be analyzed for sentiment

- A UIView that will be set to a color that dictates the sentiment we've detected in the text (e.g., red or green, for negative and positive, respectively), two UILabels to display a relevant emoji, and a string describing the sentiment

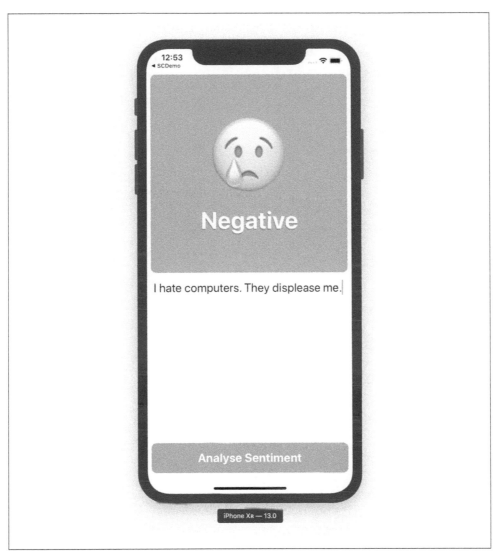

Figure 6-8. Our sentiment classification app, in all its finished glory

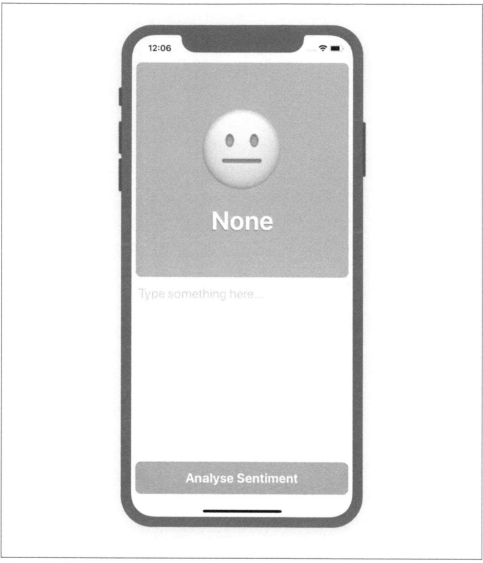

Figure 6-9. The starting point for the sentiment analysing app

 If you don't want to manually build the starting point iOS app, you can download the code from our website (*https://aiwithswift.com*) and find the project named NLPDemo-Starter. After you have that, skim through the rest of this section and then meet us at "AI Toolkit and Dataset" on page 232.

To make the starting point yourself, you'll need to do the following:

1. Create an iOS app project in Xcode, choosing the "Single View App" template. Do not select any of the checkboxes below the Language drop-down (which are, as per usual, set to "Swift").

2. After the project is created, open the *Main.storyboard* file and create a user interface with the following components:

   - A `UIButton` with its title text set to "Analyse Sentiment".

   - A large, editable, scrollable `UITextView`.

   - A generic `UIView` (which will be used to show a color), with two `UILabel` views within it: one with its title set to "None" or similar, and the other with a neutral emoji, such as ▨You can see an example of our storyboard for the app in Figure 6-10.

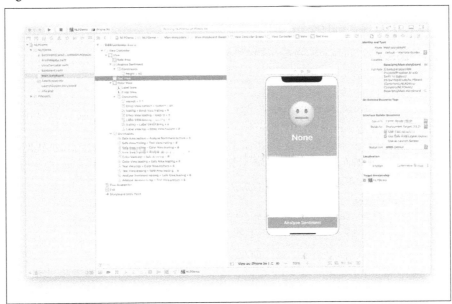

Figure 6-10. Our storyboard for the sentiment classifier

After you have the necessary elements laid out, make sure that you add the proper constraints.

3. Connect the outlets for the user interface (UI) objects, as follows:

```
@IBOutlet weak var emojiView: UILabel!
@IBOutlet weak var labelView: UILabel!
@IBOutlet weak var colorView: UIView!
@IBOutlet weak var textView: UITextView!
```

4. Connect an action for the `UIButton`, as follows:

```
@IBAction func analyseSentimentButtonPressed(_ sender: Any) {
    performSentimentAnalysis()
}
```

5. Declare an attribute for some placeholder text to go in the `UITextView`:

```
private let placeholderText = "Type something here..."
```

6. Modify the `viewDidLoad()` function, making it look as follows:

```
override func viewDidLoad() {
    textView.text = placeholderText
    textView.textColor = UIColor.lightGray
    textView.delegate = self

    super.viewDidLoad()
}
```

7. Add the following function, which is used to actually ask for a sentiment analysis later, after we add the model:

```
private func performSentimentAnalysis() {

    emojiView.text = sentimentClass.icon
    labelView.text = sentimentClass.description
    colorView.backgroundColor = sentimentClass.color
}
```

8. Add an extension to the end of the *ViewController.swift* file, as follows (it's a fairly large block of code, as per our previous examples, but as usual we'll explain it in a moment):

```
extension ViewController: UITextViewDelegate {
    func textViewDidBeginEditing(_ textView: UITextView) {
        if textView.textColor == UIColor.lightGray {
            textView.text = nil
            textView.textColor = UIColor.black
        }
    }

    func textViewDidEndEditing(_ textView: UITextView) {
        if textView.text.isEmpty {
            textView.text = placeholderText
            textView.textColor = UIColor.lightGray
        }
    }
}
```

This extension makes `ViewController` conform to `UITextViewDelegate`, which lets us manage the beginning and ending of someone editing a `UITextView`. We

---

implement two functions that map to that, and change the color of the text when each happens.

9. Add a new Swift file to the project named *Sentiment.swift*, and then place the following code in it:

```swift
import UIKit

extension String {
    func predictSentiment() -> Sentiment {
        return [Sentiment.positive, Sentiment.negative].randomElement()!
    }
}
```

This code adds an extension on the String class (which comes with Swift) to add a function named `predictSentiment()`, so we can just ask any object of type String for its sentiment by calling that function.

At the moment, we just return a random choice between the negative or positive sentiment.

10. Add an enum below this, in the same *Sentiment.swift* file:

```swift
enum Sentiment: String, CustomStringConvertible {
    case positive = "Positive"
    case negative = "Negative"

    var description: String { return self.rawValue }

    var icon: String {
        switch self {
            case .positive: return "🙂"          case .negative: return "🙁"        }
    }

    var color: UIColor {
        switch self {
            case .positive: return UIColor.systemGreen
            case .negative: return UIColor.systemRed
        }
    }
}
```

This enum creates a new type called `Sentiment` that has two cases: Positive and Negative. For each case, we define an icon (which returns an emoji) and a color (which returns a color).

11. Add a launch screen and an icon, if you'd like to (as usual, our starter project has some you can use), and then launch the app in the simulator. You should see something that looks like the image we showed you earlier, in Figure 6-9.

You can type some text into the text field and then tap the button. The color view, emoji, and text label will update with either positive or negative sentiment. Remember that for the moment this is random (because of the code in our extension on the String class, in *Sentiment.swift*).

Let's get moving, and add some AI.

AI Toolkit and Dataset

As usual with our practical AI tasks, we need to assemble a toolkit with which to tackle the problem. The primary tools that we use in this case are CreateML, CoreML, and Xcode's Playgrounds feature.

As we've done before, we use Apple's task-based tool, CreateML, to build a model for our sentiment analysis. Instead of using the CreateML application, we'll be using CreateML from an Xcode Playground, using it as a Swift framework. It's a less visual but more flexible approach to building models.

As with the previous practical AI tasks, we use CoreML to implement the model within our Swift application.

To make an app that can determine whether text is positive or negative, we need a dataset with lots of both sentiments. For that, we turn to internet product reviews. Internet product reviews are a great place to find people being very, very negative, and very, very positive about all manner of things. For this dataset, we turn to the boffins at Carnegie Mellon University, who have done the yeoman's work of acquiring 691 posts that are positive about a certain brand of automobile, and 691 posts that are negative about a certain brand of automobile. You can see some examples of this data in Figure 6-11.

class	text
Neg	drive these cars I don t care how many damn children you have or how many
Pos	A few years ago we bought a Ford Explorer used at the dealership where it ha
Pos	After my daughter was born I just knew that I would have to give up my need
Pos	Are you contemplating the Mustang I know I know it is a Ford But if you car
Pos	As a busy mother with two children and always on the go I live in my car it is
Neg	Could things get any worse I loved how it looked after that it was all down hil
Neg	Driving the Mustang with its hard seats lack of lumbar support and a hard as
Neg	Expedition into vanity selfishness and irresponsibility I realize that this may n
Neg	First of all I have to say that the Ford Contour is a very comfortable vehicle an
Pos	Ford Winstars are the coolest minivans on the market well i guess as cool as
Neg	Four recalls mayor recalls Squeaky wheels from the get go A strange tremor
Pos	I am a recent buyer of the Ford Explorer and out of all the car s and suv s I ve

Figure 6-11. A snapshot of the sentiment data that we use in this task

Head over to Carnegie Mellon's website (*http://bit.ly/2VWt0eD*) and download the *epinions3.zip* file. Unzip the file and then put the output (a file, quite creatively named *epinions3.csv*) in a safe place.

If you open this file, you'll see that it's just a comma-separated list of classes (Neg or Pos) and text (the text of the review of an automobile), as shown in the snapshot in Figure 6-12.

Figure 6-12. Example of the sentiment data

You're not restricted to two categories; you could classify as many categories of text as you want. We're just starting here with two because it makes the app a little simpler to show.

Creating a Model

Now that we have a useful dataset ready to create a model, we turn to Apple's CreateML to perform the training. In Chapter 7 we use Apple's Python library, TuriCreate, to train our model, and in Chapters 4 and 5 we use Apple's CreateML application. But for this task, we use Apple's CreateML framework directly from a Playground in Xcode.

We recommend saving the training Playground alongside the projects you create that will consume the model. This will make it easier to re-create and modify your project in the future or work with a different model.

To do this we need to create a new Xcode Playground:

1. Fire up Xcode and create a new Playground, as shown in Figure 6-13. The Playground needs to be a macOS Playground, not an iOS Playground, because we're using the macOS-only framework, CreateML.

Figure 6-13. Making a new macOS Playground in Xcode

2. Add the following code to the Playground:

```
import CreateML
import Foundation

// Configure as required
let inputFilepath = "/Users/mars/Desktop/"
let inputFilename = "epinions3"
```

```
let outputFilename = "SentimentClassificationModel"

let dataURL = URL(fileURLWithPath: inputFilepath + inputFilename + ".csv")
let data = try MLDataTable(contentsOf: dataURL)
let (trainingData, testingData) = data.randomSplit(by: 0.8, seed: 5)
```

This code imports the CreateML and Foundation frameworks, and sets up some working variables:

- inputFilepath stores the path to the datafile we'll be using. Update this to point to wherever you've saved the dataset we were working with in "AI Toolkit and Dataset" on page 232.

- inputFilename stores the name of the file. If you didn't modify the downloaded file, this should already be correct.

- outputFilename sets a name for the model that we'd like CreateML to output.

- data stores an MLDataTable of the data, based on the inputFilepath and inputFilename. MLDataTable is a type provided by CreateML, which is basically like a spreadsheet for data with which you want to train a model. Each row in an MLDataTable is an entity, and each column is a feature of that entity that your training might be interested in. You can learn more about MLDataTable in Apple's documentation (*https://apple.co/33J4GzJ*), but we unpack it a little more as we work on practical AI tasks throughout this book.

- trainingData and testingData stores a split of the data we've read in, taking 80% of it for training, and 20% of it for testing.

3. In this step, we actually do the training. Add the following code below the variables:

```
print("Begin training...")

do {

    // Final training accuracy as percentages

} catch {
    print("Error: \(error)")
}
```

It's within this do-catch is that we'll actually perform the training.

4. Inside the do-catch, add the following:

```
let sentimentClassifier = try MLTextClassifier(
    trainingData: trainingData,
    textColumn: "text",
    labelColumn: "class")
```

This creates an `MLTextClassifier`, which is a type provided by the CreateML framework.

The `MLTextClassifier` allows us to create a text classifier based on associated labels in the input text. You can learn more about the `MLTextClassifier` in Apple's documentation (*https://apple.co/32njdkk*), but we also explain it a little more, later on in this chapter.

In this case, we're creating an `MLTextClassifier` called `sentimentClassifier`, passing in the `trainingData` (which is 80% of the data we downloaded) in the form of an `MLDataTable`. We instruct the `MLTextClassifier` that we want it to look at the column named "text" for the text source, and the column named "class" for the label source. If you look back to the snapshot of the data we showed in Figure 6-12, you'll notice these column names match the data we imported here.

This line of code actually creates and trains the model. You could, kind of, stop here. But we're not going to.

5. Immediately below this, add the following code:

```
let trainingAccuracy =
    (1.0 - sentimentClassifier.trainingMetrics.classificationError)
        * 100

let validationAccuracy =
    (1.0 - sentimentClassifier.validationMetrics.classificationError)
        * 100

print("Training evaluation: \(trainingAccuracy), " +
    "\(validationAccuracy)")
```

This defines some accuracy variables for us to store some information about the model we just trained in. Specifically, we store both the training accuracy as well as the validation accuracy as percentages and then print them out.

6. Add the following code immediately below this:

```
// Testing accuracy as a percentage

// let evaluationMetrics =
//     sentimentClassifier.evaluation(on: testingData) // Mojave

let evaluationMetrics = sentimentClassifier.evaluation(
    on: testingData,
    textColumn: "text",
    labelColumn: "class") // Catalina

let evaluationAccuracy =
    (1.0 - evaluationMetrics.classificationError) * 100
```

```
    print("Testing evaluation: \(evaluationAccuracy)")

let metadata = MLModelMetadata(
    author: "Mars Geldard",
    shortDescription: "Sentiment analysis model",
    version: "1.0")

try sentimentClassifier.write(
    to: URL(
        fileURLWithPath: inputFilepath + outputFilename + ".mlmodel"),
    metadata: metadata)
```

This evaluates the model, using the 20% segment of the data we separated earlier, stores, and then prints some evaluation metrics. It also sets the model metadata, such as the author, a short description, and version number, and then writes out an *.mlmodel* file for use with CoreML.

This model won't take nearly as long to train as the models in the earlier chapters, because it's a much simpler operation than image classification, sound classification, and the like. It could take a few minutes, but not much longer. No time for *Person of Interest* here, sorry.

If you run the Playground, you should end up with some text output about the model in the console, as well as a new *SentimentClassificationModel.mlmodel* file (if you didn't change our filenames).

Incorporating the Model in the App

As usual, at this juncture we have both a starting point app and a trained model. It's time to combine them to make an app that can actually perform sentiment analysis on text that a user has entered.

You need to either build the starting point yourself, following the instructions in "Building the App" on page 226, or download the code from our website (*https://aiwithswift.com*) finding the project named NLPDemo-Starter. We'll be progressing from that point in this section. If you don't want to follow along and manually work with the app's code to add the sentiment analysis features, you can also work with the project named NLPDemo-Complete.

As usual, we're going to need to change a few things to get the app working with our model.

We recommend working through the next section even if you download our code. Just read along and compare what we did in the code to the book so that you get an understanding of how it's working.

First, let's make some changes to the enum for *Sentiment.swift*s, Sentiment:

1. Add an extra case at the beginning of the Sentiment enum, with the extra line covering a lack of sentiment:

```
case positive = "Positive"
case negative = "Negative"
case neutral = "None"
```

2. Similarly, add a default case to the switch statement in the icon variable, to account for a lack of sentiment:

```
var icon: String {
    switch self {
        case .positive: return "😊"
        case .negative: return "😞"
        default: return "😐"
    }
}
```

3. For the color, return gray if there's no sentiment found:

```
var color: UIColor {
    switch self {
        case .positive: return UIColor.systemGreen
        case .negative: return UIColor.systemRed
        default: return UIColor.systemGray
    }
}
```

4. Add an initializer to the Sentiment enum, where the raw value must precisely match the class labels from the training data (so in this case, "Pos" and "Neg"):

```
init(rawValue: String) {
    // initialising RawValues must match class labels in training files
    switch rawValue {
        case "Pos": self = .positive
        case "Neg": self = .negative
        default: self = .neutral
    }
}
```

Next, we need to update the predictSentiment() function, near the top of the *Sentiment.swift* file, to actually make use of a model.

5. Below the `import` statement, add the following to bring in Apple's natural language framework:

```
import NaturalLanguage
```

6. Change the `predictSentiment()` function to look like the following:

```
func predictSentiment(with nlModel: NLModel) -> Sentiment {
    if self.isEmpty { return .neutral }
    let classString = nlModel.predictedLabel(for: self) ?? ""
    return Sentiment(rawValue: classString)
}
```

This new function takes an `NLModel` as a parameter (we, creatively, call it `nlModel`), returns a `Sentiment` (which is our own `enum` type) and checks whether `nlModel` is empty (returning `Sentiment.neutral` if it is). Otherwise, it asks `nlModel` for a prediction based on its contents (remember the `predictSentiment()` function is an extension of `String`) and returns that prediction as `Sentiment` by initializing a new `Sentiment` using the initializer we just made.

At this point you can drag the *SentimentClassificationModel.mlmodel* file into the project's root, letting Xcode copy it in as needed.

We also need to make some changes to *ViewController.swift* in order to make this work:

1. Add a new import below the existing one, to bring in Apple's language framework (as we did for *Sentiment.swift*):

```
import NaturalLanguage
```

2. Add the following new attribute below `placeholderText`:

```
private lazy var model: NLModel? = {
    return try? NLModel(mlModel: SentimentClassificationModel().model)
}()
```

This attribute, `model`, stores a reference to our actual model. If your model is not called *SentimentClassificationModel.mlmodel*, you'll need to change this as appropriate here.

3. Change the following code in the `performSentimentAnalysis()` function, removing this

```
let text = textView.text ?? ""
let sentimentClass = text.predictSentiment()
```

and replacing it with this:

```
var sentimentClass = Sentiment.neutral

if let text = textView.text, let nlModel = self.model {
    sentimentClass = text.predictSentiment(with: nlModel)
}
```

This code creates a new `Sentiment` (our custom type, from *Sentiment.swift*), setting it to neutral, and then gets the text from our `textView`, uses the `model` attribute we created a moment ago (which is a reference to our model). It then requests a sentiment (using the `predictSentiment()` function with which we've extended `String`, within *Sentiment.swift*) and stores the result in the new `Sentiment` we just created.

The rest of the code, which is unchanged, reads the properties of the `Sentiment` `sentimentClass` we just created (and hopefully stored a predicted sentiment in) and updates the relevant UI elements to match the predicted sentiment.

Everything should be ready to go now. Launch the app in the simulator and try it out. Figure 6-14 shows the results from our app.

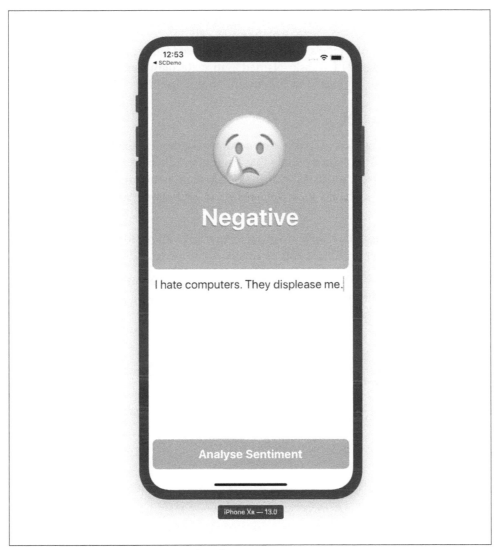

Figure 6-14. The final sentiment classifier

Task: Custom Text Classifiers

In the previous section, we trained our own custom sentiment classifier and implemented it from scratch in an iOS app.

There's another way to do something similar. In this task, we make a custom text classifier that works with the text system we've been using in the earlier tasks. We use CreateML's `MLTextClassifier` to train a model again, as we did in "Task: Sentiment Analysis" on page 225, but, here, we show you a different way to use the model.

Instead of using the trained `MLTextClassifier` model as a more generic CoreML, use it with `NLTagger` and `NLTagScheme`, which lets us call our custom model as if it were one of Apple's provided models (such as those we used earlier for "Task: Language Identification" on page 214, "Task: Named Entity Recognition" on page 217, and "Task: Lemmatization, Tagging, and Tokenization" on page 218).

AI Toolkit and Dataset

As usual with our practical AI tasks, we need to assemble a toolkit with which to tackle the problem. The primary tools that we use in this case are CreateML, CoreML, and Xcode's Playgrounds. As with the "Task: Sentiment Analysis" on page 225, we're using Apple's task-based tool, CreateML, via an Xcode Playground, to train a model.

We use the Kaggle restaurant review dataset (*http://bit.ly/2Bjdi3B*), which is similar to the one we used earlier in "Task: Sentiment Analysis" on page 225.

We've converted it to JSON for ease of parsing, as shown in Figure 6-15. You can find the *Reviews.json* file in the *NaturalLanguage-Demos* folder, which is available in our resource download on our website (*https://aiwithswift.com*).

```json
{
  "label": "POSITIVE",
  "text": "Awesome service and food."
},
{
  "label": "POSITIVE",
  "text": "A fantastic neighborhood gem !!!"
},
{
  "label": "POSITIVE",
  "text": "I can't wait to go back."
},
{
  "label": "NEGATIVE",
  "text": "The plantains were the worst I've ever tasted."
},
{
  "label": "POSITIVE",
  "text": "It's a great place and I highly recommend it."
},
{
  "label": "NEGATIVE",
  "text": "Service was slow and not attentive."
},
{
  "label": "POSITIVE",
  "text": "I gave it 5 stars then, and I'm giving it 5 stars now."
},
{
  "label": "NEGATIVE",
  "text": "Your staff spends more time talking to themselves than me."
},
```

Figure 6-15. A sample of the review data, in JSON

Creating a model

With our dataset chosen, let's fire up CreateML in a Playground to do some training. This process is very similar to the process we used earlier in "Creating a Model" on page 233:

1. Create a new macOS Playground in Xcode named TrainCustomTagger. Ours is shown in Figure 6-16.

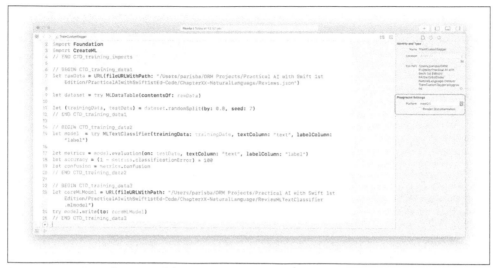

Figure 6-16. Our Playground for training a tagger

1. Add the following `imports`:

```
import Foundation
import CreateML
```

2. Add some code to load the raw data, create an `MLDataTable`, and split the data into training and test sets:

```
let dataPath = "/Users/parisba/ORM Projects/Practical AI with Swift " +
    "1st Edition/PracticalAIwithSwift1stEd-Code/ChapterXX-" +
    "NaturalLanguage/Reviews.json"

let rawData = URL(fileURLWithPath: dataPath)

let dataset = try MLDataTable(contentsOf: rawData)

let (trainingData, testData) = dataset.randomSplit(by: 0.8, seed: 7)
```

3. Create an `MLTextClassifier` model, and set up the evaluations:

```
let model  = try MLTextClassifier(
    trainingData: trainingData,
    textColumn: "text",
    labelColumn: "label")

let metrics = model.evaluation(
    on: testData,
    textColumn: "text",
    labelColumn: "label")
```

```
let accuracy = (1 - metrics.classificationError) * 100
let confusion = metrics.confusion
```

4. Write out the CoreML model:

```
let modelPath = "/Users/parisba/ORM Projects/Practical AI with Swift" +
    "1st Edition/PracticalAIwithSwift1stEd-Code/ChapterXX-" +
    "NaturalLanguage/ReviewMLTextClassifier.mlmodel"

let coreMLModel = URL(fileURLWithPath: modelPath)
try model.write(to: coreMLModel)
```

Run the Playground. The output should show the training progress, the accuracy from testing, and a confirmation that the file was written out successfully, as shown in Figure 6-17.

We recommend saving the training Playground alongside the projects you create that will consume the model. This will make it easier to re-create and modify your project in the future, or work with a different model.

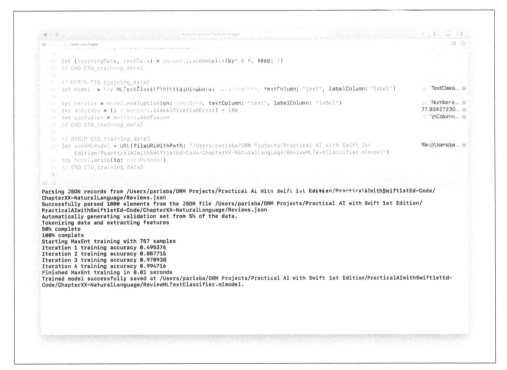

Figure 6-17. The custom tagger training

Using the model

We're not going to step through the creation of a full app for this task, because it's derivative of our sentiment analyzer from "Task: Sentiment Analysis" on page 225.

 We did actually build an app for this, just in case you want to look at it. To see our app for this task, look for `CTDemo` in the resources available on our website (*https://aiwithswift.com*).

To use the custom `NLTagger` model we've trained using `MLTextClassifier`, create a new Swift file in the project you want to use it in (ours is called *ReviewTagger.swift*) and then do the following:

1. `import` the necessary frameworks:

   ```
   import Foundation
   import NaturalLanguage
   import CoreML
   ```

   We're specifically after `NaturalLanguage` and `CoreML`, so we can use `CoreML` to work with models, and `NaturalLanguage` to work with language-specific features.

2. Drag the trained model into the project in question and allow Xcode to copy as necessary.

3. Create a `class` to represent your tagger:

   ```
   final class ReviewTagger {

   }
   ```

4. Add some useful variables:

   ```
   private static let shared = ReviewTagger()

   private let scheme = NLTagScheme("Review")
   private let options: NLTagger.Options = [.omitPunctuation]
   ```

 Make sure the line where you define the `modelFile` points to the name of your classifier model. It might be different from ours (`ReviewMLTextClassifier`).

1. Create an `NLTagger`:

```
private lazy var tagger: NLTagger? = {
    do {
        let modelFile = Bundle.main.url(
            forResource: "ReviewMLTextClassifier",
            withExtension: "mlmodelc")!

        // make the ML model an NL model
        let model = try NLModel(contentsOf: modelFile)

        // connect model to (custom) scheme name
        let tagger = NLTagger(tagSchemes: [scheme])
        tagger.setModels([model], forTagScheme: scheme)

        print("Success loading model")
        return tagger
    } catch {
        return nil
    }
}()
```

2. Stub out the necessary init() function:

```
private init() {}
```

3. Create a function to call for a prediction:

```
static func prediction(for text: String) -> String? {
    guard let tagger = ReviewTagger.shared.tagger else { return nil }
    print("Prediction requested for: \(text)")
    tagger.string = text
    let range = text.startIndex ..< text.endIndex
    tagger.setLanguage(.english, range: range)
    return tagger.tags(in: range,
        unit: .document,
        scheme: ReviewTagger.shared.scheme,
        options: ReviewTagger.shared.options)
    .compactMap { tag, _ -> String? in
        print(tag?.rawValue)
        return tag?.rawValue
    }
    .first
}
```

4. Create an extension on String, allowing you to request a prediction using the ReviewTagger class we just made:

```
extension String {
    func predictSentiment() -> Sentiment {
        if self.isEmpty { return .neutral }
        let classString = ReviewTagger.prediction(for: self) ?? ""
        return Sentiment(rawValue: classString)
    }
}
```

```
        }
    }
```

Here, we use the `Sentiment` enum that we created for "Task: Sentiment Analysis" on page 225 to return an emoji for the sentiment.

5. You could also directly use our `ReviewTagger`:

```
let tagger = ReviewTagger()
let testReviews = [
    "I loved this place and it served amazing food",
    "I did not like this food, and my steak was off",
    "The staff were attentive and the view was lovely.",
    "Everything was great and the service was excellent"
]
testReviews.forEach { review in
    guard let prediction = tagger.prediction(for: review) else { return }
    print("\(review) - \(prediction)")
}
```

Instead of using `MLTextClassifier` to train a model, you could also use `MLWordTagger` to train a model using CreateML. `MLWordTagger` models can be used exactly as we did here (with a custom tag scheme), but they're designed to be used for recognizing words relevant to your app, like product names or unique points of interest.

 You can learn more about `MLWordTagger` in Apple's documentation (*https://apple.co/2oSTp0J*).

For example, using `MLWordTagger`, you could build an AI-powered system that understood which bits of a `String` were, for example, alien races in a sci-fi universe that your app (or perhaps game) was dealing with:

1. If you had a dataset that outlined some example sentences, identifying which bits were aliens, such as this:

```
{
    "tokens": ["The", "Vorlons", "existed",
                "long", "before", "humanity!"],
    "labels": ["other", "alien", "other",
                "other", "other", "other"]
},
{
    "tokens": ["The", "Vorlons", "are", "much",
                "older", "than", "the", "Minbari."],
    "labels": ["other", "alien", "other", "other",
```

```
                      "other", "other", "other", "alien"]
    }
```

 As you might have gathered from our use of it, JSON is an excellent way to work with text in machine learning.

1. You could then load it into an `MLDataTable`, as we did earlier, and train an `MLWordTagger` on it. With the resulting model, you could define a tag scheme:

   ```
   var alienScheme = NLTagScheme("Alien")
   ```

2. And the `NLTag` you want it to look for:

   ```
   var alienTag = NLTag("alien")
   ```

Then, you could run the `MLWordTagger` on sentences, and if you had sufficient training data, it would be able to flag which parts of a sentence were alien races, based on the training.

Next Steps

That's everything for our text and language chapter. We've covered some common text- and language-related practical AI tasks that you might want to accomplish with Swift, and we used a variety of tools to do so.

We performed five practical AI tasks:

Language Identification
Determining what language some text might be in using Apple's Natural Language framework.

Named Entity Recognition
Identifying the elements of text that are people, places, or organizations, again using Apple's Natural Language framework.

Lemmatization, tagging, tokenization
Identifying the lemma of every word in a string, finding the parts of speech (verbs, nouns, and so on), and splitting a string up by words, still using Apple's Natural Language framework.

Sentiment Analysis
Figuring out if some text has a positive or negative sentiment.

Custom Text Classifiers:: Building our own text classifier on top of Apple's Natural Language framework.

In Chapter 11, we look at what happened under the hood, algorithm-wise, for each of the tasks that we explored in this chapter ("Text and Language" on page 459).

If you want to take language and text a step further with practical AI, we recommend taking a look at BERT. BERT stands for Bidirectional Encoder Representations from Transformers, and is the cutting-edge of pretraining languages for NLP AI tasks. BERT is a project of Google Research, and you can learn more about it on the BERT project page (*http://bit.ly/2oHaMSn*). To bring this diversion back to practical AI terms: BERT opens up all sorts of useful, practical NLP tasks, performed in an efficient manner that's doable on a mobile device (e.g., the sort of device for which you might use Swift to write).

The academic paper that introduced BERT to the world, BERT: Pre-training of Deep Bidirectional Transformers for Language Understanding (*http://bit.ly/32qHtlB*), is also a great place to start learning about BERT.

The most accessible, useful, practical NLP task that we recommend starting your exploration of BERT with is question answering. There's a great dataset that you can pair with BERT in order to explore this: the Stanford Question Answering Dataset (SQuAD) (*http://bit.ly/2oQeKbf*). It's full of things like this:

- **TEXT:** Seismologists can use the arrival times of seismic waves in reverse to image the interior of the Earth. Early advances in this field showed the existence of a liquid outer core (where shear waves were not able to propagate) and a dense solid inner core. These advances led to the development of a layered model of the Earth, with a crust and lithosphere on top, the mantle below (separated within itself by seismic discontinuities at 410 and 660 kilometers), and the outer core and inner core below that. More recently, seismologists have been able to create detailed images of wave speeds inside the earth in the same way a doctor images a body in a CT scan. These images have led to a much more detailed view of the interior of the Earth, and have replaced the simplified layered model with a much more dynamic model.

- **QUESTION:** What types of waves do seismologists use to image the interior of the Earth?

- **ANSWER:** Seismic waves.

Apple actually makes BERT available for download as a CoreML model from its models site (*https://apple.co/35LcnqC*). Check it out and see what you can do with it!

Additionally, Apple has released a demo app that makes use of the BERT CoreML model (*https://apple.co/2IYkHcQ*), which you can download the source code to and try out.

A team from a "social artificial intelligence" startup (*https://huggingface.co*) (with which we have zero affiliation) has also done the hard work of making BERT work with iOS and CoreML (and appears to be the source of Apple's provided CoreML version of BERT). You can find their work on GitHub (*http://bit.ly/2VQX8YM*). You can see an example of BERT working in a Swift iOS app using CoreML in Figures 6-18 and 6-19.

You might also be interested in generating text, which we introduce in our "Task: Sentence Generation" on page 315. In the next chapter we'll look at motion.

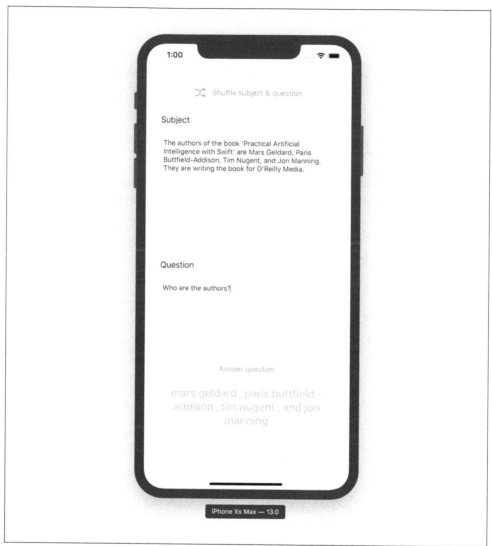

Figure 6-18. BERT, working on iOS, using Swift and CoreML

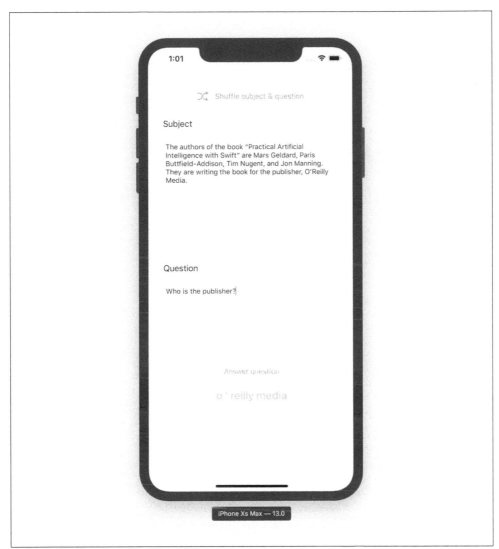

Figure 6-19. BERT, working on iOS, using Swift and CoreML

## CHAPTER 7

Motion and Gestures

This chapter explores the practical side of implementing motion- and gesture-related AI features in your Swift apps. Taking a top-down approach, we explore four tasks, and how to implement them in Swift, using a variety of AI tools.

Practical AI, Motion, and Gestures

Following are the four motion tasks that we explore in this chapter:

Activity recognition
> This uses Apple's built-in frameworks to determine what kind of motion-based activity the user is currently doing.

Gesture classification for drawings
> This task builds on the bitmap drawing detection that we looked at in "Task: Drawing Recognition" on page 142. We build a drawing classifier that classifies drawings made on an iOS device instead of from photos.

Activity classification
> Here we use Turi Create and train our own activity classification model to determine what kind of motion-based activity the user is doing.

Using augmented reality with AI
> We look at using one of Apple's other buzzword-friendly frameworks, ARKit, for combining augmented reality (AR) with AI.

Task: Activity Recognition

Activity classification is really, really, really popular these days, especially with the proliferation or portable activity trackers like the Apple Watch and Fitbit. Activity classification involves determining what physical action(s) the user is doing with their device(s).

It's a useful component of lots of apps, including games like Pokemon Go and all manner of fitness apps.

 Activity classification is just a specific subdomain of a field of machine learning commonly known as *sequence classification*. Activity classification is a practical, task-based application of sequence classification.

Problem and Approach

The Apple Watch can detect when you might be working out and offer to start and track a dedicated workout, in addition to passively tracking everything you're doing. For this task, we explore the practical side of detecting what activity a user might be doing while possessing an iOS device by doing the following:

- Making an app that can recognize what activity the user might be performing
- Building an app that speaks and displays (as text) the physical activity it thinks the user is currently performing
- Using Apple's tools for doing this without training a model
- Exploring the potential next steps for activity recognition

Figure 7-1 shows the final app that we're going to build in this task.

Building the App

To build our activity-recognition app, let's use SwiftUI, Apple's newest user interface framework.

The final form of the app consists of the following SwiftUI components:

- A View
- Some Text

And that's it! Most of the UI of this app is actually a spoken notification when we recognize that there is a different activity happening, which is also what's displayed in the Text of the user interface.

Figure 7-1. Our final activity-recognition app

 This book is here to teach you the practical side of using AI and machine learning features with Swift and on Apple's platforms. Because of this, we don't explain the fine details of how to build apps; we assume that you mostly know that (although if you don't, we think you'll be able to follow along just fine if you pay attention). If you want to learn Swift, we recommend picking up *Learning Swift* (*https://oreil.ly/xP4Tb*) (also by us!) from the lovely folks at O'Reilly Media.

If you don't want to manually build the iOS app, you can download the code from our website (*https://aiwithswift.com*) and find the project named ARDemo. After you have that, we strongly recommend that you still proceed through this section, comparing the notes here with the code you downloaded.

To make the app yourself, you'll need to do the following:

1. Create an iOS app project in Xcode, choosing the Single View App template, and then select the SwiftUI checkbox.

2. Once your project is created, add a new Swift file called *Tracking.swift* to the project, and add the following imports to it:

    ```
    import SwiftUI
    import Combine
    import CoreMotion
    ```

    CoreMotion is Apple's motion framework; we'll be using it in a moment.

3. Create a final class called ActivityTracker, inheriting from BindableObject:

    ```
    final class ActivityTracker: ObservableObject {

    }
    ```

4. Inside ActivityTracker, we need some variables:

    ```
    let willChange = PassthroughSubject<ActivityTracker, Never>()

    private let tracker = CMMotionActivityManager()
    private(set) var currentActivity: String = "None detectable" {
        willSet {
            activityDidChange = (newValue != currentActivity)
        }

        didSet {
            willChange.send(self)
        }
    }
    private(set) var activityDidChange = true
    ```

5. Add an init():

    ```
    init() {}
    ```

6. Add a function to startTracking():

    ```
    func startTracking() {
        do {
            try tracker.startTracking { result in
                self.currentActivity = result?.name ?? "None detectable"
            }
        } catch {
            print("Error: \(error.localizedDescription)")
    ```

```
        stopTracking()
    }
}
```

7. Add a function to `stopTracking()`:

```
func stopTracking() {
    currentActivity = "Not Tracking"
    tracker.stopTracking()
}
```

8. Add a file called *Motion.swift* to the project, and then add the following `import`:

```
import CoreMotion
```

9. Create an extension on `CMMotionActivity`:

```
extension CMMotionActivity {
    var name: String {
        if walking { return "Walking" }
        if running { return "Running" }
        if automotive { return "Driving" }
        if cycling { return "Cycling" }
        if stationary { return "Stationary" }
        return "Unknown"
    }
}
```

10. Add an extension on `CMMotionActivityManager`:

```
extension CMMotionActivityManager {

}
```

11. Within that extension, create an `enum` for `Error`:

```
enum Error: Swift.Error {
    case notAvailable, notAuthorized

    public var localizedDescription: String {
        switch self {
        case .notAvailable: return "Activity Tracking not available"
        case .notAuthorized: return "Activity Tracking not permitted"
        }
    }
}
```

12. Add a function to start tracking:

```
func startTracking(handler: @escaping (CMMotionActivity?) -> Void)
    throws {

    if !CMMotionActivityManager.isActivityAvailable() {
        throw Error.notAvailable
    }
```

```
if CMMotionActivityManager.authorizationStatus() != .authorized {
    throw Error.notAuthorized
}

self.startActivityUpdates(to: .main, withHandler: handler)
}
```

13. Add a function to stop tracking:

```
func stopTracking() {
    self.stopActivityUpdates()
}
```

14. Open *ContentView.swift*, and then add the following imports:

```
import SwiftUI
import AVFoundation
```

15. Add the following extension on AVSpeechSynthesizer:

```
extension AVSpeechSynthesizer {
    func say(_ text: String) {
        self.speak(AVSpeechUtterance(string: text))
    }
}
```

This lets us make the app speak when it detects an activity change.

16. Make your ContentView struct look like this:

```
struct ContentView: View {
    @EnvironmentObject var tracker: ActivityTracker
    private let speechSynthesiser = AVSpeechSynthesizer()

    var body: some View {
        let newActivity = tracker.currentActivity
        if tracker.activityDidChange {
            speechSynthesiser.say(newActivity)
        }

        return Text(newActivity).font(.largeTitle)
    }
}
```

17. Add a key to your *Info.plist* file for Privacy - Motion Usage Description, stating why you want to access the device's motion usage. Ours says "We need this to see what motions the device is doing, so we can speak them!" as shown in Figure 7-2.

Figure 7-2. Our Info.plist for motion usage

Now, if you run the app on a physical iOS device, you'll be able to hear the kind of activity you're doing while moving around with the device. Your app will look something like Figure 7-3.

What Just Happened? How Does This Work?

We just built an app that can detect the physical activity that is currently being performed. We built it by using Apple's CoreMotion framework (*https://apple.co/2Bk7SW2*). CoreMotion provides motion- and environment-related data from the vast array of sensors that exist on a modern iOS device: accelerometers, gyroscopes, pedometers, magnetometers, barometers, and more.

For this activity-recognition app, we used the `CMMotionActivityManager`, which allows us to access the motion data stored by an iOS device, and tracked `CMMotionActivitys`, which represents a single motion update event. Based on the `CMMotionActivity` we get, we returned a string for whether the user is walking, running, driving, cycling, or staying still. Thus, without any need to build a model, we can report back what the user of the device is likely doing.

In Chapter 11, we look at how this Apple-provided motion tracking might work under the hood, and in "Task: Activity Classification" on page 277, we build a similar app from scratch by training our own activity classification model.

Figure 7-3. The activity recognizer working

Task: Gestural Classification for Drawing

Earlier in the book we wrote a drawing-recognition app that allowed the user to take a photo of a drawing and have it classified. In this task, we're going to do something similar, but instead of photos, we classify drawings that are made on the screen of the iOS device.

Problem and Approach

As we said in "Problem and Approach" on page 142, drawings are fun, and it's still kind of magic to be able to draw something and have a computer recognize it.

In this task, we explore the practical side of drawing detection from a slightly different angle than last time, and we build an app that lets a user draw a simple black-and-white image on their iOS device and then have the app classify it.

Figure 7-4 shows our finished app.

Figure 7-4. Our drawing detector

AI Toolkit and Dataset

The AI toolkit that we use for this task is *exactly* the same as the one we used in "AI Toolkit and Dataset" on page 144. In fact, we use the same model (and consequently, the same dataset, as shown in Figure 7-5).

Figure 7-5. Google's Quick, Draw! game

At the end of "Creating a model" on page 146, we ended up with a *DrawingClassifier-Model.mlmodel* model file. We use that model again here.

Building the App

Because we already have our model ready to go from "AI Toolkit and Dataset" on page 264, let's get straight to building the app. Our app consists of the following features and uses UIKit:

- A `UIImageView` to be drawn in
- A `UIButton` to trigger classification of our drawing
- A `UINavigationBar` with some buttons to allow us to clear the drawing, or use undo

 If you don't want to manually build the starting point iOS app, you can download the code from our website (*https://aiwithswift.com*) and find the project named `DDDemo-Drawing`. Once you have that, skim through the rest of this section and then meet us at "AI Toolkit and Dataset" on page 130.

To build the app yourself, you need to do the following:

1. Create an iOS app project in Xcode, choosing the Single View App template.

2. After your project is created, open the *Main.storyboard* file and create a UI with the following components:

   - A `UINavigationBar` containing a `UIBarButtonItem` on the left for clearing the view, and a `UIBarButtonItem` on the right for undoing
   - A `UIImageView`, for the drawing
   - A `UIButton` to perform the classification You can see an example of our storyboard in Figure 7-6.

3. After you have the necessary elements laid out, make sure you add the proper constraints.

4. Connect the outlets for the UI objects in the *ViewController.swift* file, as follows:

   ```
   @IBOutlet weak var clearButton: UIBarButtonItem!
   @IBOutlet weak var undoButton: UIBarButtonItem!
   @IBOutlet weak var imageView: UIImageView!
   @IBOutlet weak var classLabel: UILabel!
   @IBOutlet weak var classifyButton: UIButton!
   ```

5. Connect the actions for the UI objects, as follows:

```
@IBAction func clearButtonPressed(_ sender: Any) { clear() }
@IBAction func undoButtonPressed(_ sender: Any) { undo() }
@IBAction func classifyButtonPressed(_ sender: Any) { classify() }
```

Figure 7-6. Our storyboard for the drawing detector

6. Drag the model file from "AI Toolkit and Dataset" on page 264, *DrawingClassifierModel.mlmodel*, into the project, allowing Xcode to copy as needed, as shown in Figure 7-7.

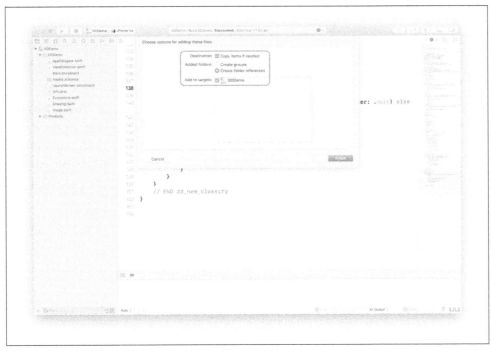

Figure 7-7. Our model being added to the project

Next, we create a new file called *Extensions.swift*, to hold some extensions we need to make things work (we come back to the *ViewController.swift* file later).

1. Add a new Swift file called *Extensions.swift* to the project.

2. Add the following `import`.

   ```
   import UIKit
   ```

3. Add an `extension` on `CGContext`.

   ```swift
   extension CGContext {
       static func create(size: CGSize,
           action: (inout CGContext) -> ()) -> UIImage? {

           UIGraphicsBeginImageContextWithOptions(size, false, 1.0)

           guard var context = UIGraphicsGetCurrentContext() else {
               return nil
           }

           action(&context)

           let result = UIGraphicsGetImageFromCurrentImageContext()
   ```

```
        UIGraphicsEndImageContext()

        return result
    }
}
```

This `extension` extends `CGContext` to add a `create()` function, which takes a `CGSize` and returns a `UIImage`. A `CGContext` is a destination that can be drawn to (not necessarily literally drawn to, just a place that can be used for graphics) in Apple's rendering subsystems. You can read more about `CGContext` in Apple's documentation (*https://apple.co/35HRaht*).

4. Add an extension on `UIButton`:

```
extension UIButton {
    func enable() {
        self.isEnabled = true
        self.backgroundColor = UIColor.systemBlue
    }

    func disable() {
        self.isEnabled = false
        self.backgroundColor = UIColor.lightGray
    }
}
```

This should look relatively familiar if you've worked through some of the other tasks in this book: it lets us call `enable()` or `disable()` on `UIButton`s in order to set their status and colors.

5. In this Swift file, add an extension on `UIBarButtonItem`:

```
extension UIBarButtonItem {
    func enable() { self.isEnabled = true }
    func disable() { self.isEnabled = false }
}
```

This does exactly the same thing as we did for `UIButton`, for the other type of button we'll be using.

Next, add another new file called *Image.swift*, which we'll use for some convenience code to help work with images:

1. Add a new Swift file called *Image.swift* to the project.

2. Add the following `import`:

```
import UIKit
```

3. Add the following extension on `CIFilter`:

```swift
extension CIFilter {
    static let mono = CIFilter(name: "CIPhotoEffectMono")!
    static let noir = CIFilter(name: "CIPhotoEffectNoir")!
    static let tonal = CIFilter(name: "CIPhotoEffectTonal")!
}
```

4. Add an extension on `UIImage`, to which we'll add two functions in a moment:

```swift
extension UIImage {

}
```

5. The first function we need to add to our `UIImage` extension lets us apply a `CIFilter`:

```swift
func applying(filter: CIFilter) -> UIImage? {
    filter.setValue(CIImage(image: self), forKey: kCIInputImageKey)

    let context = CIContext(options: nil)
    guard let output = filter.outputImage,
        let cgImage = context.createCGImage(
                output, from: output.extent
            ) else {
                return nil
    }

    return UIImage(
        cgImage: cgImage,
        scale: scale,
        orientation: imageOrientation)
}
```

6. The second function is our image orientation helper:

```swift
var cgImageOrientation: CGImagePropertyOrientation {
    switch self.imageOrientation {
    case .up: return .up
    case .down: return .down
    case .left: return .left
    case .right: return .right
    case .upMirrored: return .upMirrored
    case .downMirrored: return .downMirrored
    case .leftMirrored: return .leftMirrored
    case .rightMirrored: return .rightMirrored
    }
}
```

In our final new file, *Drawing.swift*, we add some helpers to work with the AI component of things:

1. Add a new Swift file called *Drawing.swift* to the project.

2. Add the following `imports`:

```
import UIKit
import Vision
```

3. Create an `enum` called `Drawing`, implementing the `CaseIterable` protocol and covering cases for all the types of things our drawing classifier knows about:

```
enum Drawing: String, CaseIterable {
    /// These only include those the model was trained on
    /// For others that can be included in the training phase, see the
    /// full list of categories in the dataset:
    /// https://raw.githubusercontent.com/googlecreativelab/
    ///     quickdraw-dataset/master/categories.txt
    case apple, banana, bread, broccoli, cake, carrot, coffee, cookie
    case donut, grapes, hotdog, icecream, lollipop, mushroom, peanut, pear
    case pineapple, pizza, potato, sandwich, steak, strawberry, watermelon

}
```

4. within `Drawing` enum, add an `init()` function:

```
init?(rawValue: String) {
    if let match =
        Drawing.allCases.first(where: { $0.rawValue == rawValue }) {
        self = match
    } else {
        switch rawValue {
            case "coffee cup":  self = .coffee
            case "hot dog":     self = .hotdog
            case "ice cream":   self = .icecream
            default: return nil
        }
    }
}
```

This `init()` function takes a `String` and matches it to one of the cases we implemented a moment ago. We special case a few things, making "coffee cup" match `.coffee`, "hot dog" match `.hotdog`, and "ice cream" match `.icecream`.

5. while still within `Drawing` enum, we set up each case so that it has an emoji icon attached:

```
var icon: String {
    switch self {
```

```
        case .apple: return "🍎"
        case .banana: return "🍌"
        case .bread: return "🍞"
        case .broccoli: return "🥦"
        case .cake: return "🍰"
        case .carrot: return "🥕"
        case .coffee: return "☕"
        case .cookie: return "🍪"
        case .donut: return "🍩"
        case .grapes: return "🍇"
        case .hotdog: return "🌭"
        case .icecream: return "🍦"
        case .lollipop: return "🍭"
        case .mushroom: return "🍄"
        case .peanut: return "🥜"
        case .pear: return "🍐"
        case .pineapple: return "🍍"
        case .pizza: return "🍕"
        case .potato: return "🥔"
        case .sandwich: return "🥪"
        case .steak: return "🥩"
        case .strawberry: return "🍓"
        case .watermelon: return "🍉"
        }
    }
```

6. Add an `extension` on `VNImageRequestHandler`, adding a convenience initializer:

```
extension VNImageRequestHandler {
    convenience init?(uiImage: UIImage) {
        guard let ciImage = CIImage(image: uiImage) else { return nil }
        let orientation = uiImage.cgImageOrientation

        self.init(ciImage: ciImage, orientation: orientation)
    }
}
```

This allows us to create a `VNImageRequestHandler` using a `UIImage`. A `VNImageRequestHandler` is part of Apple's Vision framework; it allows us to request that something happens with an image.

7. Add the following `extension` on our model:

```
extension DrawingClassifierModel {
    func classify(_ image: UIImage?,
        completion: @escaping (Drawing?) -> ()) {

        guard let image = image,
```

```
                let model = try? VNCoreMLModel(for: self.model) else {
                    return completion(nil)
            }

            let request = VNCoreMLRequest(model: model)

            DispatchQueue.global(qos: .userInitiated).async {
                if let handler = VNImageRequestHandler(uiImage: image) {

                    try? handler.perform([request])

                    let results = request.results
                        as? [VNClassificationObservation]

                    let highestResult =
                        results?.max { $0.confidence < $1.confidence }

                    print(results?.list ?? "")

                    completion(
                        Drawing(rawValue: highestResult?.identifier ?? "")
                    )
                } else {
                    completion(nil)
                }
            }
        }
    }
```

This extension on `DrawingClassifierModel` adds a function called `classify()` that
lets us pass in a `UIImage` for classification. This `UIImage` will be the drawing that we
want classified. The `classify()` function checks that it's received an image, then
checks whether it's attached to a CoreML model that can be used to make requests
with Apple's Vision framework (a `VNCoreMLModel`), and then starts a request for a
`VNClassificationObservation` on a queue. We use the `Drawing` enum we created earlier for our result.

If, for some reason, your model file is named something different,
your extension will need to extend that name, instead.

8. Add an extension on `Collections` of `VNClassificationObservations`:

```
extension Collection where Element == VNClassificationObservation {
    var list: String {
        var string = ""
```

```
        for element in self {
            string += "\(element.identifier): " +
                "\(element.confidence * 100.0)%\n"
        }
        return string
    }
}
```

This `extension` adds a `list var`, which allows us to get a `String` that contains the confidence of a classification if we need one.

Now, we can return to *ViewController.swift* and put it all together:

1. Add some useful variables below our outlets and actions:
   ```
   var classification: String? = nil
   private var strokes: [CGMutablePath] = []
   private var currentStroke: CGMutablePath? { return strokes.last }
   private var imageViewSize: CGSize { return imageView.frame.size }
   private let classifier = DrawingClassifierModel()
   ```

   Here, we have somewhere to store a classification, a `CGMutablePath` to store strokes in (a drawing is made up of strokes and a `CGMutablePath` (*https://apple.co/2MSdegG*) is a way to store strokes), a `CGSize` representing the size of the image view, and a handle on our model file.

2. Override `viewDidLoad()`:
   ```
   override func viewDidLoad() {
       super.viewDidLoad()

       undoButton.disable()
       classifyButton.disable()
   }
   ```

   Doing this allows us to disable the buttons in the view given that there's no reason for them to be active immediately after the view has loaded.

3. Now, we get to the actual drawing code. First, override `touchesBegan()`:
   ```
   // new stroke started
   override func touchesBegan(_ touches: Set<UITouch>,
       with event: UIEvent?) {

       guard let touch = touches.first else { return }

       let newStroke = CGMutablePath()
       newStroke.move(to: touch.location(in: imageView))
       strokes.append(newStroke)
   ```

```
        refresh()
    }
```

This allows us to detect when a touch is detected in the view. We take the touch and use it to append to the `CGMutablePath` variable (for strokes) that we created earlier.

4. Similarly, we override touchesMoved():

```
// stroke moved
override func touchesMoved(_ touches: Set<UITouch>,
    with event: UIEvent?) {

    guard let touch = touches.first,
        let currentStroke = self.currentStroke else {
            return
    }

    currentStroke.addLine(to: touch.location(in: imageView))
    refresh()
}
```

This is the same, but when a touch moves instead of starts.

5. In the same vein, override touchesEnded():

```
// stroke ended
override func touchesEnded(_ touches: Set<UITouch>,
    with event: UIEvent?) {

    guard let touch = touches.first,
        let currentStroke = self.currentStroke else {
            return
    }

    currentStroke.addLine(to: touch.location(in: imageView))
    refresh()
}
```

6. Add an undo() function so that we can call it to remove the last stroke if we need to:

```
// undo last stroke
func undo() {
    let _ = strokes.removeLast()
    refresh()
}
```

We're not implementing undo the "correct" way here, because our undoing requirements are so straightforward and this book isn't here to teach you how to use Apple's non-AI frameworks. If you're curious about a more comprehensive way of doing undo in Swift apps, check out UndoManager in Apple's documentation (*https://apple.co/2VOWevQ*).

7. Add a `clear()` function that can be called if we want to remove all the strokes:

```
// clear all strokes
func clear() {
    strokes = []
    classification = nil
    refresh()
}
```

8. Add a `refresh()` function to make the view that's being displayed match the stroke path that we're storing (you might have noticed that we called this as-yet nonexistent function every time we did something with strokes in the last few bits of code):

```
// refresh view to reflect paths
func refresh() {
    if self.strokes.isEmpty { self.imageView.image = nil }

    let drawing = makeImage(from: self.strokes)
    self.imageView.image = drawing

    if classification != nil {
        undoButton.disable()
        clearButton.enable()
        classifyButton.disable()
    } else if !strokes.isEmpty {
        undoButton.enable()
        clearButton.enable()
        classifyButton.enable()
    } else {
        undoButton.disable()
        clearButton.disable()
        classifyButton.disable()
    }

    classLabel.text = classification ?? ""
}
```

9. We also need a function that takes the strokes and generates a bitmap image from them so that we can pass that image into the model for classification:

```
// draw strokes on image
func makeImage(from strokes: [CGMutablePath]) -> UIImage? {
    let image = CGContext.create(size: imageViewSize) { context in
        context.setStrokeColor(UIColor.black.cgColor)
        context.setLineWidth(8.0)
        context.setLineJoin(.round)
        context.setLineCap(.round)

        for stroke in strokes {
            context.beginPath()
            context.addPath(stroke)
            context.strokePath()
        }
    }

    return image
}
```

10. Add a `classify()` function to actually get us a classification:

```
func classify() {
    guard let grayscaleImage =
        imageView.image?.applying(filter: .noir) else {
            return
    }

    classifyButton.disable()
    classifier.classify(grayscaleImage) { result in
        self.classification = result?.icon

        DispatchQueue.main.async {
            self.refresh()
        }
    }
}
```

And that's it. If you run the app, draw a simple version of one of the things that it can detect and then tap the button, you should see a prediction for its classification in the form of an emoji, as demonstrated in Figure 7-8.

Figure 7-8. Our drawing classifier in action

Task: Activity Classification

In "Task: Activity Recognition" on page 255, we built an app that can recognize which activity the user of an app is performing, and we did it using Apple's provided Core-Motion framework. For this task, we're going to further develop that idea and create our own machine-learning model that can classify human movement activities.

Problem and Approach

As we said earlier, activity recognition has become increasingly popular in the era of hardware activity trackers.

For this task, we're going to explore the practical side of activity classification by doing the following:

- Building our own model that can detect the kind of human motion activity being performed by the user of the device
- Selecting a toolkit for creating a machine-learning model and assembling a dataset for the problem
- Building and training an activity classification model
- Looking at how we could incorporate that model into an app

Let's get started.

AI Toolkit and Dataset

We need to assemble our toolkit for this problem. The primary tools we use in this case are Apple's Turi Create Python framework and CoreML.

To give our model the ability to classify movement activity as walking, running, sitting, going upstairs, and so on, we need a dataset with which to train an activity classification model to classify those activities.

We could build one ourselves, but for now we're going to use a dataset created by some clever boffins at UC Irvine: "Smartphone-Based Recognition of Human Activities and Postural Transitions Data Set" (HAPT) (*http://bit.ly/2P3eEI9*), as shown in Figure 7-9.

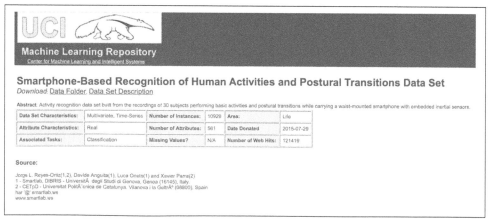

Figure 7-9. The HAPT dataset website

The HAPT dataset contains accelerometer and gyroscope data collected from people who were doing a whole bunch of different human-ish activities (and nonactivities):

- Sitting down
- Standing up
- Lying down
- Walking
- Walking downstairs
- Walking upstairs
- Moving from standing to sitting
- Moving from sitting to standing
- Moving from sitting to lying
- Moving from lying to sitting
- Moving from standing to lying
- Moving from lying to standing

The data was recorded by participants working with the UC Irvine team; each participant wore a Samsung Galaxy smartphone (we won't tell Apple if you won't) on their waist, and accelerometer and gyroscope data was captured at 50 Hz—50 times per second—and was labeled manually by the boffins, who were watching (boffins love to watch).

As a human looking at this sort of data, it's fairly trivial for us to figure out what's going on. Figure 7-10 shows three seconds of walking data, whereas Figure 7-11 shows three seconds of sitting data; can you tell the difference?

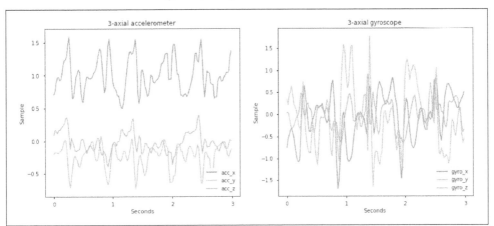

Figure 7-10. Three seconds of APT walking data, graphed

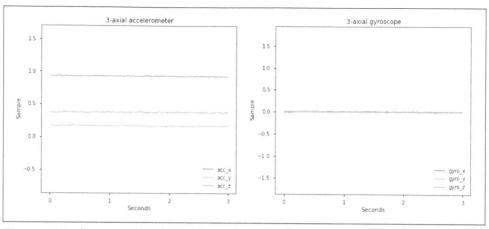

Figure 7-11. Three seconds of APT sitting data, graphed

To grab the dataset, go to the Smartphone-Based Recognition of Human Activities and Postural Transitions Data Set (*http://bit.ly/2P3eEI9*) site and download the HAPT dataset (it's the link that says Data Folder near the top). Save the dataset somewhere safe and unzip it, as shown in Figure 7-12.

Figure 7-12. The HAPT data unzipped

Preparing the data

With our dataset downloaded, we use Apple's Turi Create Python framework to prepare the data so we can build a model with it. Check back to "Turi Create" on page 37 for a reminder on Turi Create's features.

As usual when we work with Python, we recommend that you use Anaconda to manage the situation. Follow the instructions in "Python" on page 46 and then perform the following:

1. Create a new Anaconda environment:

   ```
   conda create -n ActivityClassifierEnv python=3.6
   ```

2. Activate the environment:

   ```
   conda activate ActivityClassifierEnv
   ```

3. Use `pip` to install Turi Create:

```
pip install turicreate
```

4. In the same folder in which you unzipped the data, create a new Python script (ours is called *activity_model_training.py*) using your favorite text editor (we like Visual Studio Code and BBEdit, but anything works) with the following Python imports in it:

```
import turicreate as tc
from glob import glob
```

5. Specify where the data is, from the HAPT dataset:

```
data_dir = 'HAPT/RawData/'
```

6. Define a function to find a label given an index to sample from:

```
def find_label_for_containing_interval(intervals, index):
    containing_interval = intervals[:, 0][
        (intervals[:, 1] <= index) & (index <= intervals[:, 2])
    ]
    if len(containing_interval) == 1:
        return containing_interval[0]
```

7. Read the CSV file, rename the labels appropriately, and print them:

```
labels = tc.SFrame.read_csv(
    data_dir + 'labels.txt',
    delimiter=' ',
    header=False,
    verbose=False)

labels = labels.rename({
    'X1': 'exp_id',
    'X2': 'user_id',
    'X3': 'activity_id',
    'X4': 'start',
    'X5': 'end'
})
print(labels)
```

8. If you run the script at this point (python activity_model_training.py), you'll see something that looks like this:

```
+--------+---------+-------------+-------+------+
| exp_id | user_id | activity_id | start | end  |
+--------+---------+-------------+-------+------+
|   1    |    1    |      5      |  250  | 1232 |
|   1    |    1    |      7      |  1233 | 1392 |
|   1    |    1    |      4      |  1393 | 2194 |
|   1    |    1    |      8      |  2195 | 2359 |
```

```
|   1   |   1   |      5      | 2360 | 3374 |
|   1   |   1   |     11      | 3375 | 3662 |
|   1   |   1   |      6      | 3663 | 4538 |
|   1   |   1   |     10      | 4539 | 4735 |
|   1   |   1   |      4      | 4736 | 5667 |
|   1   |   1   |      9      | 5668 | 5859 |
+--------+--------+--------------+-------+------+
[1214 rows x 5 columns]
```

9. Load the accelerometer and gyroscope data text files from the HAPT dataset:

```
acc_files = glob(data_dir + 'acc_*.txt')
gyro_files = glob(data_dir + 'gyro_*.txt')
```

10. Fet ready to load the data into one SFrame:

```
data = tc.SFrame()
files = zip(sorted(acc_files), sorted(gyro_files))
```

11. Going through every accelerometer and gyroscope file, add to the SFrame:

```
for acc_file, gyro_file in files:
    exp_id = int(acc_file.split('_')[1][-2:])
    user_id = int(acc_file.split('_')[2][4:6])

    # Load accel data
    sf = tc.SFrame.read_csv(
        acc_file,
        delimiter=' ',
        header=False,
        verbose=False)

    sf = sf.rename({'X1': 'acc_x', 'X2': 'acc_y', 'X3': 'acc_z'})
    sf['exp_id'] = exp_id
    sf['user_id'] = user_id

    # Load gyro data
    gyro_sf = tc.SFrame.read_csv(
        gyro_file,
        delimiter=' ',
        header=False,
        verbose=False)

    gyro_sf = gyro_sf.rename({
        'X1': 'gyro_x',
        'X2': 'gyro_y',
        'X3': 'gyro_z'
    })
    sf = sf.add_columns(gyro_sf)
```

```
# Calc labels
exp_labels = labels[labels['exp_id'] == exp_id][
    ['activity_id', 'start', 'end']
].to_numpy()

sf = sf.add_row_number()

sf['activity_id'] = sf['id'].apply(
    lambda x: find_label_for_containing_interval(exp_labels, x)
)

sf = sf.remove_columns(['id'])

data = data.append(sf)
```

12. Define readable labels for each of the labels:

```
target_map = {
    1.: 'walking',
    2.: 'upstairs',
    3.: 'downstairs',
    4.: 'sitting',
    5.: 'standing',
    6.: 'resting'
}
```

13. Using the labels, save the SFrame as a file:

```
data = data.filter_by(target_map.keys(), 'activity_id')
data['activity'] = data['activity_id'].apply(lambda x: target_map[x])
data = data.remove_column('activity_id')

data.save('hapt_data.sframe')
```

This Python script reads the dataset, renames the labels to be more human-readable, and loads both the accelerometer and gyroscope data. The script then puts the data into a Turi Create SFrame object, loading both the accelerometer and gyroscope data, maps the types of activity we're interested in (walking, going upstairs, going downstairs, sitting, standing, and resting), and finally saves the SFrame object as a file.

Creating a model

Next, let's add the code to perform the training. In the same file, at the end, do the following:

1. Split the data into training and test sets:

```
train, test = tc.activity_classifier.util.random_split_by_session(
    data, session_id='exp_id', fraction=0.8)
```

2. Create an activity classifier:

```
model = tc.activity_classifier.create(
    train,
    session_id='exp_id',
    target='activity',
    prediction_window=50)
```

3. Evaluate the model using the test data, and then print out its accuracy:

```
metrics = model.evaluate(test)
print(metrics['accuracy'])
```

4. Save the model in Turi Create's format, in case we need to mess with it later:

```
model.save('ActivityClassifier.model')
```

5. Export the model into CoreML's *.mlmodel* format:

```
model.export_coreml('ActivityClassifier.mlmodel')
```

This script splits the data by training and testing (80% to training, 20% to testing), trains a classifier, evaluates it, and then saves the model as a Turi Create model and as a CoreML model.

6. Run the script:

```
python activity_model_training.py
```

You should see something that looks like Figure 7-13, and your model will be trained.

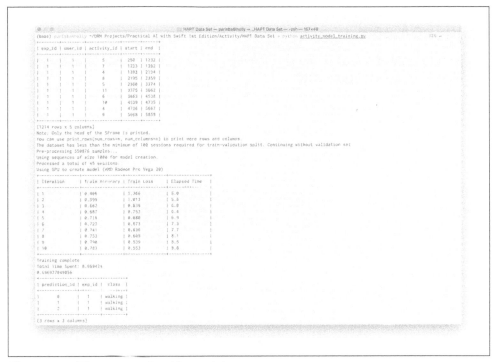

Figure 7-13. The activity classifier training

You'll find the two model files (one .model in Turi Create's format and one .mlmodel in CoreML's format) in the folder with the script, as shown in Figure 7-14.

ActivityClassifier.
model

ActivityClassifier.
mlmodel

Figure 7-14. The output of the activity classifier model creation script

Using the Model

Let's put our trained model to the test. Remember the three seconds of walking data we looked at earlier in Figure 7-15?

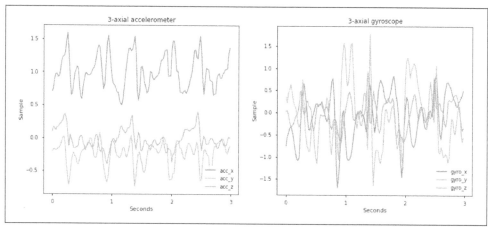

Figure 7-15. Three seconds of APT walking data, graphed

If we make a new Python script (ours is called *test_ac.py*, saved to the same folder as the training script), we can test it:

1. import Turi Create:

   ```
   import turicreate as tc
   ```

2. Load the SFrame we saved:

   ```
   loaded_sframe = tc.load_sframe(`hapt_data.sframe`)
   ```

3. Load the Turi Create model we saved:

   ```
   loaded_model = tc.load_model('ActivityClassifier.model')
   ```

4. Load the three seconds of walking data (shown in Figure 7-15), and then ask for a prediction:

   ```
   walking_3_sec = loaded_sframe[
       (loaded_sframe['activity'] == 'walking') &
           (loaded_sframe['exp_id'] == 1)
   ][1000:1150]

   print(loaded_model.predict(walking_3_sec, output_frequency='per_window'))
   ```

5. Running the script (`python test_ac.py`) will give you a prediction, and you should see something like the following:

```
+----------------+---------+----------+
| prediction_id  | exp_id  |  class   |
+----------------+---------+----------+
|       0        |    1    | walking  |
|       1        |    1    | walking  |
|       2        |    1    | walking  |
+----------------+---------+----------+
[3 rows x 3 columns]
```

You can learn more about how to use the CoreML model in a Swift app for iOS in the Turi Create documentation (*http://bit.ly/2puCkKy*).

Task: Using Augmented Reality with AI

This book is primarily about AI, not augmented reality (AR), but we would be remiss not to at least *mention* the powerful combination of buzzwords that is AR plus AI! This isn't going to be a full task, because we would need an entire book on its own to cover AR in any reasonable detail.

Basically, we implement an image classification system ("Task: Image Classification" on page 120), and then follow these steps:

1. As part of your ARKit implementation, call into your classifier (in this example, that's `classifyCurrentImage()`) every frame:

```swift
func session(_ session: ARSession, didUpdate frame: ARFrame) {
    guard currentBuffer == nil, case .normal = frame.camera.trackingState else {
        return
    }

    self.currentBuffer = frame.capturedImage
    classifyCurrentImage()
}
```

2. In your implementation of `classifyCurrentImage()`, get the `currentBuffer` from the `ViewController`, and do your machine learning:

```swift
let requestHandler = VNImageRequestHandler(cvPixelBuffer: currentBuffer!,
                                           orientation: orientation)
visionQueue.async {
    do {
        defer { self.currentBuffer = nil }
        try requestHandler.perform([self.classificationRequest])
    } catch {
        print("Error: ML request failed: \"\(error)\"")
```

```
        }
    }
```

You can visualize those results in AR however you like.

Apple has an acceptable sample project that goes through this; you can find it in its documentation (*https://apple.co/2Mom0E1*).

Next Steps

That's all for our Motion chapter. We've covered some common motion-related practical AI tasks that you might want to accomplish with Swift, and we used a variety of tools to do so.

We looked at four tasks:

Activity recognition
> We used Apple's built-in frameworks to determine what kind of motion-based activity the user is currently doing. We didn't need to train a model.

Gesture classification for drawings
> Building on the "Task: Drawing Recognition" on page 142, we built a drawing classifier that classifies drawings made on an iOS device instead of from photos.

Activity classification
> We used Turi Create to train our own activity classification model, which allowed us to query a model that can determine what kind of motion-based activity the user is doing based on a sample of accelerometer and gyroscope data.

Using Augmented reality with AI
> We looked at the combination of ARKit, for AR and AI. More magic.

In Chapter 11, we look at what happened under the hood algorithm-wise for each of the tasks we explored in this chapter.

## CHAPTER 8

Augmentation

This chapter explores the practical side of implementing generative- and recommendation-related AI features in your Swift apps: we've collectively called the domain *Augmentation*. Taking a top-down approach, we explore five augmentation tasks, and how to implement them using a variety of AI tools.

Practical AI and Augmentation

We examine augmentation across two subdomains: *generation* and *recommendation*. Here are the five practical augmentation tasks that we explore in this chapter:

Image style transfer
   Transferring style between images

Text generation
   Using a Markov chain to generate sentences.

Image generation
   Creating our own generative adversarial network (GAN) to create images on iOS.

Movie recommendation
   Recommending movies to a user, based on their previous movie reviews.

Regression
   Predicting numeric values using regression.

We've called this chapter "Augmentation" because we've included tasks related to generating things with AI together with our task for recommending things using AI. These things aren't necessarily technically related in a way that makes sense beyond that, and we've chosen to combine them for convenience more than any other reason. "Augmentation" made sense to us as a title.

Task: Image Style Transfer

We've done quite a few practical AI tasks that involve detecting something, or classifying something. Neural Style Transfer (NST, or just style transfer) is a machine-learning technique that, most traditionally, involves two images: a *style image* and a *content image*.

The style image is used as a source of style, and that style is then copied to the content image. You've probably seen this, repeatedly, in popular social media applications: it's a great way of making your mundane, ordinary breakfast look like it was painted by Van Gogh.

Style transfer doesn't just have to apply to images. It's possible to do style transfer with sound, text, and all sorts of other things. These domains are a little beyond the scope of this book, but we touch on them at the end of the chapter.

Problem and Approach

We want to make an app that lets users perform a style transfer on their own images, as shown in Figure 8-1.

In this task, we explore the practical side of style transfer, focusing on images by doing the following:

- Making an app that lets users perform a style transfer on their own images
- Building an app that allows us to use or take photos, select from a predefined choice of style images, and then transfer that style to their chosen image
- Selecting a toolkit for creating a style transfer model and assembling a dataset (style images) for the problem
- Building and training the style transfer model
- Incorporating the style transfer model in our app
- Improving our app

After that, we quickly touch on the theory of style transfer and point you to further resources for improvements and that changes you can make on your own. Let's get started!

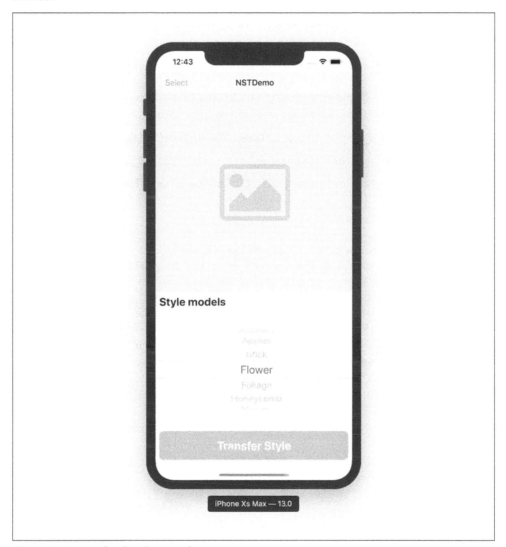

Figure 8-1. Our final style transfer app

Building the App

We obviously need an app. As the previous chapters have no doubt taught you, everything is an app. Let's build an app for this. Before we begin, as usual we're going to build a reasonably simple starting point.

The starting point iOS app that we're going to build has the following features:

- A `UIImageView` to display the image to which the user wants the style transferred, and also to display the same image after the style has been transferred

- A `UIPickerView` to display all the possible styles that can be transferred

- A `UIButton` to trigger the style transfer

- A `UINavigationBar` and some `UIBarButtonItems` to allow an image to be selected

 This book is here to teach you the practical side of using AI and machine-learning features with Swift and on Apple's platforms. Because of this, we don't explain the fine details of how to build apps; we assume you mostly know that (although if you don't, we think you'll be able to follow along just fine if you pay attention). If you want to learn Swift, we recommend picking up *Learning Swift* (*https://oreil.ly/DLVGh*) (also by us) from the lovely folks at O'Reilly Media.

Figure 8-2 presents. Notice that it looks pretty similar to the final version.

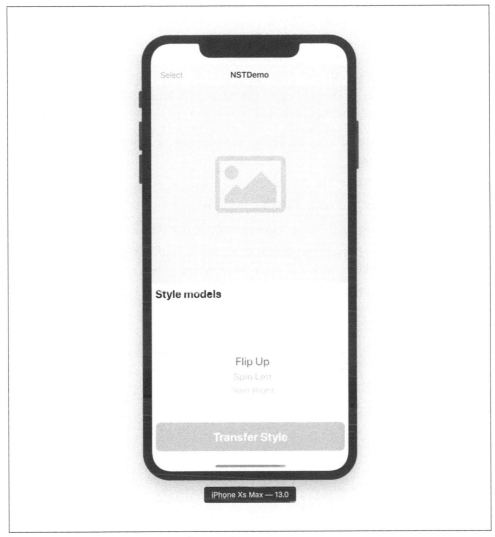

Figure 8-2. The starting point style transfer app

 If you don't want to manually build the starting point iOS app, you can download the code from our website (*https://aiwithswift.com*). and find the project named NSTDemo-Starter. After you have that, read through the rest of this section and then meet us at "AI Toolkit and Dataset" on page 307, where we explore the tools used for creating a style transfer model. We strongly recommend that you read the rest of this section carefully and closely, even if you use our starter project and don't code it yourself. It will be helpful, we promise.

To make the starting point yourself, you'll need to do the following:

1. Create an iOS app project in Xcode, choosing the Single View App template, as usual. We use UIKit for this practical example, so don't select the SwiftUI checkbox.

2. After your project is created, open the *Main.storyboard* file and create a user interface with the following components:

   - A UIImageView to display the image the user selects as well as the final style-transferred image

   - A UIButton to trigger the style transfer

   - A UIPickerView to display a list of possible styles

   - A UILabel above the UIPickerView to indicate that it's a list of styles

   - A UINavigationBar and a UIBarButtonItem on either side of it to allow the user to select/take a photo and share the resulting photo, respectively

     <<nststoryboard>> shows our storyboard.

Figure 8-3. Our storyboard

3. After you have the necessary elements laid out, make sure you add the proper constraints.

First, we need to add a new file called *StyleModel.swift*, which we'll use to work with the style transfer model that we create later on. For now, the "styles" we'll support will just rotate or flip the image. Create a new file, *StyleModel.swift*, and add the following to it:

```swift
import UIKit
import CoreML

enum StyleModel: String, CaseIterable {
    case upsideDown = "Flip Up"
    case left = "Spin Left"
    case right = "Spin RIght"

    var isActive: Bool { return true }
    // Make this a conditional to enable only certain models

    init(index: Int) { self = StyleModel.styles[index] }
    static var styles: [StyleModel] { return self.allCases.filter
    { style in style.isActive }
    }

    var name: String { return self.rawValue }
    var styleIndex: Int { return StyleModel.styles.firstIndex(of: self)! }
}
```

This defines a new enum, called `StyleModel`, that adheres to both `String` and `CaseIterable`, defines some cases for the styles (which, as we mentioned, simply involve flipping and rotating the image) and some variables for the name, an index of the style in the enumeration, and the like.

Next, we create a rather large `UIImage` extension, which will help us work with and manipulate the `UIImage` objects that we need to use to perform a style transfer. Create a new file called *Image.swift*:

4. Add to the file the following extension to `UIImage`:

```swift
import UIKit

// MARK: UIImage Extensions

extension UIImage{

    static let placeholder = UIImage(named: "placeholder.png")!

    /// Attempts Neural Style Transfer upon UIImage with given .mlmodel and
    /// input options
```

```
/// - parameter modelSelection: StyleModel enum case selected to pass
///   as .mlmodel option

/// Returns copy of image .aspectFill-ed to given size with excess
/// cropped, which maintains as much of original image as possible
/// - parameter size: Size to fit new image into

/// Returns copy of image resized to given size
/// - parameter size: Size to fit new image into

/// Returns copy of image cropped to given size
/// - parameter size: Size to fit new image into

/// Creates and returns CVPixelBuffer for given image, size and
/// attributes
}
```

You'll notice that we also define a placeholder UIImage, which points to a place-holder image file. You can find this file in the asset catalog that we provided in the downloadable assets.

5. Add a styled() function:

```
func styled(with modelSelection: StyleModel) -> UIImage? {
    guard let cgImage = self.cgImage else { return nil }

    let orientation: UIImage.Orientation

    switch modelSelection {
        case .upsideDown: orientation = .downMirrored
        case .left: orientation = .left
        case.right: orientation = .right
    }

    return UIImage(
        cgImage: cgImage,
        scale: self.scale,
        orientation: orientation
    )
}
```

This function takes a StyleModel, returns a UIImage, and performs the style transfer (which, in this starting point app, involves selecting one of the orientations from StyleModel).

6. Add a function called aspectFilled():

```
func aspectFilled(to size: CGSize) -> UIImage? {
    if self.size == size { return self }
```

```
    let (width, height) = (Int(size.width), Int(size.height))
    let aspectRatio: CGFloat = self.size.width / self.size.height
    let intermediateSize: CGSize

    if aspectRatio > 0 {
        intermediateSize = CGSize(
            width: Int(aspectRatio * size.height),
            height: height
        )
    } else {
        intermediateSize = CGSize(
            width: width,
            height: Int(aspectRatio * size.width)
        )
    }

    return self.resized(to: intermediateSize)?.cropped(to: size)
}
```

This function returns a copy of the image (`self`, in this case, as this is all in an extension on `UIImage`), filled to a given size with the excess cropped.

7. And the following function to resize the image to a given size:

```
func resized(to size: CGSize) -> UIImage? {
    let newRect = CGRect(origin: CGPoint.zero, size: size)

    UIGraphicsBeginImageContextWithOptions(size, false, 0.0)
    self.draw(in: newRect)
    let newImage = UIGraphicsGetImageFromCurrentImageContext()
    UIGraphicsEndImageContext()

    return newImage
}
```

8. Similarly, add a function to crop the image to a given size:

```
func cropped(to size: CGSize) -> UIImage? {
    guard let cgImage = self.cgImage else { return nil }

    let widthDifference = self.size.width - size.width
    let heightDifference = self.size.height - size.height

    if widthDifference + heightDifference == 0 { return self }
    if min(widthDifference, heightDifference) < 0 { return nil }

    let newRect = CGRect(
        x: widthDifference / 2.0,
        y: heightDifference / 2.0,
        width: size.width,
        height: size.height
```

```
    )

    UIGraphicsBeginImageContextWithOptions(newRect.size, false, 0)

    let context = UIGraphicsGetCurrentContext()

    context?.translateBy(x: 0.0, y: self.size.height)
    context?.scaleBy(x: 1.0, y: -1.0)
    context?.draw(cgImage,
        in: CGRect(
            x:0,
            y:0,
            width: self.size.width,
            height: self.size.height
        ),
        byTiling: false)

    context?.clip(to: [newRect])

    let croppedImage = UIGraphicsGetImageFromCurrentImageContext()

    UIGraphicsEndImageContext()

    return croppedImage
}
```

9. Finally for our `UIImage` extension in this file, add a function to create and return a `CVPixelBuffer`:

```
func pixelBuffer() -> CVPixelBuffer? {

    guard let image = self.cgImage else { return nil }

    let dimensions: (height: Int, width: Int) =
        (Int(self.size.width), Int(self.size.height))

    var pixelBuffer: CVPixelBuffer?
    let status = CVPixelBufferCreate(
        kCFAllocatorDefault,
        dimensions.width,
        dimensions.height,
        kCVPixelFormatType_32BGRA,
        [kCVPixelBufferCGImageCompatibilityKey: kCFBooleanTrue,
         kCVPixelBufferCGBitmapContextCompatibilityKey: kCFBooleanTrue]
            as CFDictionary,
        &pixelBuffer
    )

    guard let createdPixelBuffer = pixelBuffer,
        status == kCVReturnSuccess else {
```

```
                    return nil
        }

    let populatedPixelBuffer =
        createdPixelBuffer.perform(permission: .readAndWrite) {
            guard let graphicsContext =
                CGContext.createContext(for: createdPixelBuffer) else {
                    return nil
            }

            graphicsContext.draw(image,
                in: CGRect(
                    x: 0,
                    y: 0,
                    width: dimensions.width,
                    height: dimensions.height)
            )
            return createdPixelBuffer
        } as CVPixelBuffer?

    return populatedPixelBuffer
}
```

A `CVPixelBuffer` is a pixel buffer object defined by Apple's Core Video frame-work. It allows us to work directly with the contents of an image, in memory. We'll come back to why we need this shortly.

Next, we're going to make a file called *Utils.swift*, in which we add some helper exten-sions and bits and pieces that we need throughout the style transfer app to make things work.

Create a new file in the project named *Utils.swift*, and then do the following:

1. Add some import statements:

   ```
   import UIKit
   import CoreML
   ```

2. Add an extension on `MLMultiArray`:

   ```
   extension MLMultiArray {

       /// Initialises new MLMultiArray of Double: 0.0, changing given index
       /// to 1.0 This is used for MLModels with multiple options, where the
       /// non-zero index corresponds to some option
       /// - parameters:
       ///     - size: Number of options
       ///     - index: Index to change to 1.0
       convenience init(size: Int, selecting selectedIndex: Int) {
           do {
   ```

```
        try self.init(
            shape: [size] as [NSNumber],
            dataType: MLMultiArrayDataType.double)
    } catch {
        fatalError(
            "Could not initialise MLMultiArray for MLModel options.")
    }

    for index in 0..<size {
        self[index] = (index == selectedIndex) ? 1.0 : 0.0
    }
  }
}
```

This sets it up so that we can initialize a new `MLMultiArray` of Double: `0.0`, changing the given index to `1.0`. This is used for `MLModels` with multiple options, where the non-zero index corresponds to some option. The `MLMultiArray` class we're extending is part of CoreML, and it's what CoreML uses for feature input and output for a model. We cover it in a little more detail in Chapter 2.

3. Add an `extension` on `CVPixelBufferLockFlags`:

```
extension CVPixelBufferLockFlags {
    static let readAndWrite = CVPixelBufferLockFlags(rawValue: 0)
}
```

This sets the lock flags on a `CVPixelBuffer` to 0, which specifies to the Core Video framework that we will be both reading and writing to the pixel buffer. If we knew that we weren't going to write to it, we could set it to 1 (true), which would allow Core Video to perform certain optimizations because it would know it never changes.

4. Add another `extension`, this time on `CVPixelBuffer`:

```
extension CVPixelBuffer {
    var width: Int {
        return CVPixelBufferGetWidth(self)
    }

    var height: Int {
        return CVPixelBufferGetHeight(self)
    }

    var bytesPerRow: Int {
        return CVPixelBufferGetBytesPerRow(self)
    }

    var baseAddress: UnsafeMutableRawPointer? {
        return CVPixelBufferGetBaseAddress(self)
```

```
        }

        /// Locks CVPixelBuffer base address, executes block, unlocks base
        /// address and returns block output
        /// - parameters:
        ///     - permission: Options for whether ReadOnly or ReadAndWrite
        ///       access is required
        ///     - action: code block to execute
        func perform<T>(permission: CVPixelBufferLockFlags,
            action: () -> (T?)) -> T? {

            // lock memory
            CVPixelBufferLockBaseAddress(self, permission)

            // do the thing
            let output = action()

            // unlock memory
            CVPixelBufferUnlockBaseAddress(self, permission)

            // return output of doing thing
            return output
        }
    }
```

This extension to CVPixelBuffer adds some easily accessible variables (width, height, and so on) as well as executing actions on the pixels in the CVPixel Buffer. This is largely irrelevant to the AI process, but if you're interested in how to manipulate CVPixelBuffer, check Apple's documentation (*https://apple.co/ 2VRmYMh*).

5. And an extension on CGContext, allowing us to create a CGContext with the dimensions of a given CGPixelBuffer, with some useful defaults:

```
    extension CGContext {

        /// Create CGContext with dimensions of given CVPixelBuffer and default
        /// other values
        /// - parameter pixelBuffer: Image PixelBuffer to make context for
        static func createContext(for pixelBuffer: CVPixelBuffer)
            -> CGContext? {

            return CGContext(
                data: pixelBuffer.baseAddress,
                width: pixelBuffer.width,
                height: pixelBuffer.height,
                bitsPerComponent: 8,
                bytesPerRow: pixelBuffer.bytesPerRow,
                space: CGColorSpaceCreateDeviceRGB(),
```

```
        bitmapInfo: CGBitmapInfo.byteOrder32Little.rawValue |
            CGImageAlphaInfo.noneSkipFirst.rawValue
    )
}

/// Converts and returns context.makeImage() CGImage output to UIImage
func makeUIImage() -> UIImage? {
    if let cgImage = self.makeImage() {
        return UIImage(cgImage: cgImage)
    }

    return nil
}
}
```

A `CGContext` is part of Apple's Core Graphics framework; it provides a drawing destination. If you're familiar with any other graphics environments (such as OpenGL or DirectX), you will be familiar with the concept of a *context*. If not, all that matters is that a `CGContext` is the area in which all drawing is done for a particular operation. You can learn more in Apple's documentation (*https://apple.co/ 35HRaht*), but it's mostly beyond the scope of this book.

Our `extension`, in this case, also provides a function to return a `UIImage`.

6. We also need an `extension` on CGSize, conforming to `CustomStringConverti ble`, which allows us to return the width and height of a `CGSize` as a string for descriptive purposes:

```
extension CGSize: CustomStringConvertible {
    public var description: String {
        return "\(self.width) * \(self.height)"
    }
}
```

7. Add two extensions, one on `UIButton`, and one on `UIBarButtonItem`, to enable or disable them (and set some color on the `UIButton`):

```
extension UIButton {
    func enable() {
        self.isEnabled = true
        self.backgroundColor = UIColor.systemBlue
    }

    func disable() {
        self.isEnabled = false
        self.backgroundColor = UIColor.lightGray
    }
}
```

```
extension UIBarButtonItem {
    func enable() { self.isEnabled = true }
    func disable() { self.isEnabled = false }
}
```

These extensions on `UIButton` and `UIBarButtonItem` should look pretty familiar at this point.

With all that done, we're ready to begin work in the *ViewController.swift* file:

1. Connect the outlets for the UI objects as follows:

```
@IBOutlet weak var shareButton: UIBarButtonItem!
@IBOutlet weak var imageView: UIImageView!
@IBOutlet weak var modelSelector: UIPickerView!
@IBOutlet weak var transferStyleButton: UIButton!
```

2. Connect the actions for the buttons in our UI:

```
@IBAction func selectButtonPressed(_ sender: Any) {
    summonImagePicker()
}

@IBAction func shareButtonPressed(_ sender: Any) {
    summonShareSheet()
}

@IBAction func transferStyleButtonPressed(_ sender: Any) {
    performStyleTransfer()
}
```

3. Add some attributes:

```
private var inputImage: UIImage?
private var outputImage: UIImage?
private var modelSelection: StyleModel {
    let selectedModelIndex = modelSelector.selectedRow(inComponent: 0)
    return StyleModel(index: selectedModelIndex)
}
```

We have two `UIImages`, one for the image we start with, and one for the image we end up with after the style is transferred. We've also got a `StyleModel`, which we created earlier, choosing the style we wanted based on the currently selected row of the `UIPickerView` we placed in the interface and for which we created an outlet.

4. Update the `viewDidLoad()` function to look like the following:

```
override func viewDidLoad() {
    super.viewDidLoad()

    modelSelector.delegate = self
```

```
        modelSelector.dataSource = self
        imageView.contentMode = .scaleAspectFill

        refresh()
    }
```

5. Add a function to enable or disable the UI controls based on the presence of an input image and/or an output image:

```
private func refresh() {
    switch (inputImage == nil, outputImage == nil) {
        case (false, false): imageView.image = outputImage
            transferStyleButton.enable()
            shareButton.enable()

        case (false, true): imageView.image = inputImage
            transferStyleButton.enable()
            shareButton.disable()

        default: imageView.image = UIImage.placeholder
            transferStyleButton.disable()
            shareButton.disable()
    }
}
```

6. Add a function to actually perform the style transfer:

```
private func performStyleTransfer() {
    outputImage = inputImage?.styled(with: modelSelection)

    if outputImage == nil {
        summonAlertView()
    }

    refresh()
}
```

Now we need to add some extensions to the *ViewController.swift* file, outside of the ViewController class itself, but extending the ViewController.

7. Add an extension conforming to UINavigationControllerDelegate:

```
extension ViewController: UINavigationControllerDelegate {
    private func summonShareSheet() {
        guard let outputImage = outputImage else {
            summonAlertView()
            return
        }

        let shareSheet = UIActivityViewController(
            activityItems: [outputImage as Any],
            applicationActivities: nil
```

```
        )
        present(shareSheet, animated: true)
    }

    private func summonAlertView(message: String? = nil) {
        let alertController = UIAlertController(
            title: "Error",
            message: message ?? "Action could not be completed.",
            preferredStyle: .alert
        )

        alertController.addAction(
            UIAlertAction(
                title: "OK",
                style: .default
            )
        )

        present(alertController, animated: true)
    }
}
```

This extension allows us to summon share sheets and alert views as a
UINavigationController. We use these to allow sharing of the output image (via
a button in a navigation bar) and display errors messages, respectively.

8. Add an extension conforming to UIImagePickerControllerDelegate:

```
extension ViewController: UIImagePickerControllerDelegate {
    private func summonImagePicker() {
        let imagePicker = UIImagePickerController()
        imagePicker.delegate = self
        imagePicker.sourceType = .photoLibrary
        imagePicker.mediaTypes = [kUTTypeImage as String]
        present(imagePicker, animated: true)
    }

    @objc func imagePickerController(_ picker: UIImagePickerController,
        didFinishPickingMediaWithInfo info:
            [UIImagePickerController.InfoKey: Any]) {

        inputImage = info[UIImagePickerController.InfoKey.originalImage]
            as? UIImage

        outputImage = nil

        picker.dismiss(animated: true)
        refresh()

        if inputImage == nil {
```

```
                    summonAlertView(message: "Image was malformed.")
                }
            }
        }
```

This extension allows us to use the `UIImagePickerController` to display the user's photo library and provide them with a way to pick from it.

9. Finally, we add an extension conforming to `UIPickerViewDelegate`:

```
extension ViewController: UIPickerViewDelegate, UIPickerViewDataSource {
    func numberOfComponents(in pickerView: UIPickerView) -> Int {
        return 1
    }

    func pickerView(_ pickerView: UIPickerView,
        numberOfRowsInComponent component: Int) -> Int {

        return StyleModel.styles.count
    }

    func pickerView(_ pickerView: UIPickerView,
        titleForRow row: Int, forComponent component: Int) -> String? {

        return StyleModel(index: row).name
    }
}
```

This extension defines the parameters of the `UIPickerView` that we use to let the user pick which style they wish to transfer to their input image.

Do not conflate `UIPickerView` with `UIImagePicker`. The former is a rotating control that allows the user to pick from a list of things, sometimes with different attributes (commonly used for dates, which have multiple components); and the latter allows the user to pick from their photo library on iOS.

Phew, that's a lot of code for a starting point. You can run the application, select an image, and apply one of our three "styles" to it (the "styles" being: Flip Up, Spin Left, and Spin Right) Figure 8-4 depicts the finished starting point.

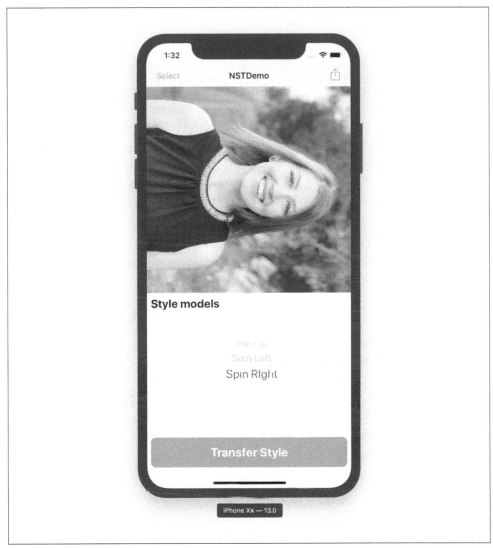

Figure 8-4. The final starting point, demonstrating image flipping as a "style"

We're ready to get into the AI side of style transfer. Onward!

AI Toolkit and Dataset

The software we use for this problem is Apple's Turi Create Python library, and Core-eML. We also need some images for the model training.

We're using Apple's Turi Create Python library to perform the training. For a reminder on how to set up a Python environment, check back to "Python" on page

46. For our data, we need two very different sets of images to train a style transfer model using Turi Create: *style images* and *content images*. Read "Turi Create" on page 37 for a reminder of how Turi Create works.

The style images represent the stylistic elements that you want to transfer. Each style requires only one image from which to source it. We recommend looking for interesting mosaics, textures, or abstract patterns as your style images. You can find some great sources of style images at the National Gallery of Art (*http://bit.ly/2MONMZA*) and The Met Collection (*http://bit.ly/2oSKix1*).

Create a folder in which to perform your style transfer. Within that folder create two sub-folders: *style*, and *content*. After you've sourced your style images (we recommend trying with about six images), place them in the *style* folder.

The content images represent a set of representative images similar to the type of image on which you expect the users of the style transfer app to want to perform a style transfer. The content images really can be anything you like, but the general type of image should match what you expect your users to use.

 If you're building a style transfer app that's designed to work with people's selfies, then you probably want your content images to be selfies. If you want to style transfer to photos of cars, you'll want a folder full of car photos. You get the idea.

If you need a source of images for your content images, you can find lots of good repositories of general images of things. A particularly good one for this sort of thing is the Common Objects in Context (*http://cocodataset.org/#home*) dataset.

After you have your content images, place them in the *content* folder. We used a lot of different images because we wanted to make our style transfer model as flexible as possible.

Creating a Model

With our style images and content images ready to go, we're going to turn to Apple's Turi Create to build the style transfer model.

Fire up a new Python environment, following the instructions in "Python" on page 46, and then do the following:

1. Using your favorite text editor, create a new Python script in the folder you made while reading "AI Toolkit and Dataset" on page 307 (our script is called *training.py*) and then place the following code in it:

    ```
    import turicreate as tc
    ```

```
# Configure as required
style_images_directory = 'style/'
content_images_directory = 'content/'
training_cycles_to_perform = 6000
output_model_filename = 'StyleTransferModel'
output_image_constraints = (800, 800)

# Load the style and content images
styles = tc.load_images(style_images_directory)
content = tc.load_images(content_images_directory)

# Create a StyleTransfer model
model = tc.style_transfer.create(styles, content,
    max_iterations=training_cycles_to_perform)

# Export for use in Core ML
model.export_coreml(output_model_filename + '.mlmodel',
    image_shape=output_image_constraints)
```

2. Update the folder names to reflect your names for the *style* and *content* folders, if you named them something different.

3. Run the Python script by executing it on the command line. Your style transfer model is now being trained.

While it's training, you should see some output from Turi Create in your terminal, letting you know how it's going.

 This could take a long time. This might take the longest of all the training runs we work through in this book. On our 2019 MacBook Pro (the really silly eight-core one) this took about 24 hours.

When it's done, the script will write out an *.mlmodel* file, ready for use in CoreML, in our iOS app.

Incorporating the Model in the App

At this point, if you've been following along, you have completed the starting point iOS app, which allows you to select images (or take a photo) and perform a "style" transfer by flipping or rotating the input image.

You've also selected some style and content images, and used Apple's Turi Create Python library to train a style transfer model. In this section, we combine the starting point app and the style transfer model, replacing our placeholder flipping and rotating styles with the actual styles from our model. Figure 8-5 shows where we end up.

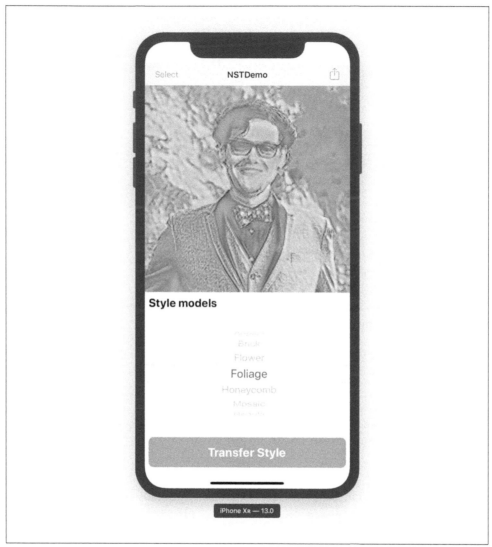

Figure 8-5. The next phase of our NST app

If you didn't build the starting point yourself by following the instructions in "Building the App" on page 292, you can download the code from our website (*https://aiwithswift.com*) and find the project named NSTDemo-Starter. We progress from that point in this section. You'll also find a trained style transfer *.mlmodel* file in the same folder. If you don't want to follow along and manually update the iOS app's code to include the artificial intelligence features necessary for working with the style transfer model we trained, you can also download the project named NSTDemo-Complete.

The changes we need to make to bring the starting point app into the world of artificial intelligence are actually fairly minimal compared to some of the other practical artificial intelligence tasks in this book.

If you choose to download the NSTDemo-Complete project instead of stepping through this section, we still urge you to read this section and look at the relevant bits of the NSTDemo-Complete project.

Let's get started:

1. Drag the *.mlmodel* file we trained (or that you downloaded) into the project's root, allowing Xcode to copy as needed.

2. Open the *StyleModel.swift* file and replace the entire contents as follows:

```swift
import UIKit
import CoreML

enum StyleModel: String, CaseIterable {

    // List models (named whatever you like) and their names to display in
    // the app
    //
    // These must be in the order they were input into training (likely
    // alphabetical in filename)
    case abstract = "Abstract"
    case apples = "Apples"
    case brick = "Brick"
    case flower = "Flower"
    case foliage = "Foliage"
    case honeycomb = "Honeycomb"
    case mosaic = "Mosaic"
    case nebula = "Nebula"

    // Rename this to your own .mlmodel file name
```

```
var model: StyleTransferModel { return StyleTransferModel() }

// Change if your own model has different constraints
var constraints: CGSize { return CGSize(width: 800, height: 800) }

// Make this a conditional to enable only certain models
var isActive: Bool { return true }

init(index: Int) { self = StyleModel.styles[index] }

static var styles: [StyleModel] {
    return self.allCases.filter { style in style.isActive }
}

var name: String { return self.rawValue }

var styleIndex: Int { return StyleModel.styles.firstIndex(of: self)! }

var styleArray: MLMultiArray {
    return MLMultiArray(
        size: StyleModel.allCases.count,
        selecting: self.styleIndex)
}
}
```

This replaces the cases with the actual styles embedded in our model, available for transfer, and provides various parameters of the style model.

3. Open the *Image.swift* file and update the styled() function in our UIImage extension to look as follows:

```
func styled(with modelSelection: StyleModel) -> UIImage? {
    guard let inputPixelBuffer = self.pixelBuffer() else { return nil }

    let model = modelSelection.model
    let transformation = try? model.prediction(
        image: inputPixelBuffer,
        index: modelSelection.styleArray
    )

    guard let outputPixelBuffer = transformation?.stylizedImage else {
        return nil
    }

    let outputImage =
        outputPixelBuffer.perform(permission: .readOnly) {

            guard let outputContext = CGContext.createContext(
                for: outputPixelBuffer) else {
                    return nil
```

```
        }

            return outputContext.makeUIImage()
    } as UIImage?

    return outputImage
}
```

This function now works with a pixel buffer and one of the actual styles from our model instead of an orientation, and it sets an output pixel buffer as the resulting stylized image (again, instead of just rotating it)

4. Open *ViewController.swift* and change the `imagePickerController()` function in the `UIImagePickerControllerDelegate` extension on `ViewController` to look as follows:

```
@objc func imagePickerController(_ picker: UIImagePickerController,
    didFinishPickingMediaWithInfo info:
        [UIImagePickerController.InfoKey: Any]) {

    let rawImage =
        info[UIImagePickerController.InfoKey.originalImage] as? UIImage

    inputImage = rawImage?.aspectFilled(to: modelSelection.constraints)
    outputImage = nil

    picker.dismiss(animated: true)
    refresh()

    if inputImage == nil {
        summonAlertView(message: "Image was malformed.")
    }
}
```

This changes the image to fill the aspect, for more effective use with the style transfer model. That's it. You can now run your app and transfer one of the provided styles to an input image of your choice, as shown in Figure 8-6.

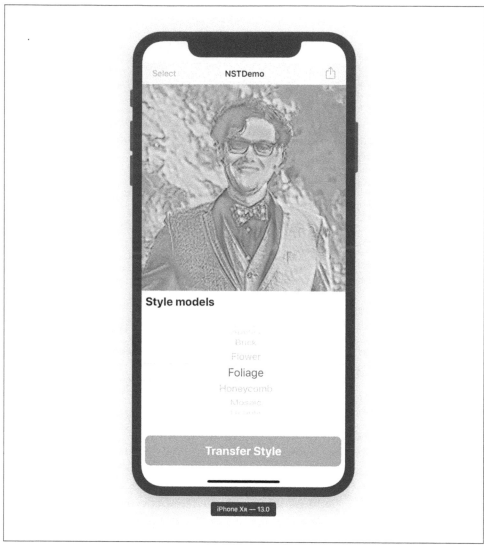

Figure 8-6. The working NST app

> Remember that your style transfer will be more effective on images that are similar to the images you used as content images during the training process.

Style transfer with images is a clever trick, but you can also apply it to sound or even to text. Intel has some interesting articles (*https://intel.ly/2J0CobN*) that make a great starting point on audio style transfer.

Task: Sentence Generation

Sometimes, it's useful to be able to generate some text; whether you need to create placeholder text, or you're building a game, or you just want to generate text for another reason, one of the quickest ways to get going with generating text is a Markov chain.

This task is difficult to present in app form, since it's very reliant on...well, just text. So we do it in a Playground: create a new iOS Playground and then and add a new file to its *Sources* folder (we called ours *Extensions.swift*):

1. In *Extensions.swift*, add an extension on Collection:

    ```swift
    public extension Collection {
        func randomIndex() -> Int? {
            if self.isEmpty { return nil }
            return Int(arc4random_uniform(UInt32(self.count)))
        }
    }
    ```

    This extension adds a function randomIndex() to Collection so that we can get a random object from a Collection.

2. Add an extension on NSRegularExpression:

    ```swift
    public extension NSRegularExpression {
        func matches(in text: String) -> [NSTextCheckingResult] {
            return self.matches(
                in: text,
                range: NSRange(text.startIndex..., in: text)
            )
        }
    }
    ```

    This extension adds a function that allows us to see whether the an NSRegular Expression (which this code will be attached to) matches a String that we pass into the new matches() function.

 NSRegularExpression is a convenient way to use a regular expression. For more information, check out Apple's documentation (*https://apple.co/2Bkjqc1*).

3. Add another extension on String:

    ```swift
    public extension String {
        func matches(regex pattern: String) throws -> [String] {
    ```

```
        do {
            let regex = try NSRegularExpression(pattern: pattern)
            let matches = regex.matches(in: self)
            return matches.map({
                String(self[Range($0.range, in: self)!])
            })
        } catch {
            throw error as Error
        }
    }
}
```

This extension adds a `matches()` function to `String`, as well, which we can use to call the `NSRegularExpression` `matches()` function that we just created.

4. In *Extensions.swift*, add another extension on `String`:

```
public extension String {
    static let sentenceEnd: String = "."

    func tokenize() -> [String] {
        var tokens: [String] = []

        let sentenceRegex =
            "[^.!?\\s][^.!?]*(?:[.!?](?!['\"]?\\s[A-Z]|$)[^.!?]*)*" +
            "[.!?]?['\"]?(?=\\s|$)"

        let wordRegex = "((\\b[^\\s]+\\b)((?<=\\.\\w).)?)"

        if let sentences = try? self.matches(regex: sentenceRegex) {
            for sentence in sentences {
                if let words = try? sentence.matches(regex: wordRegex),
                    !words.isEmpty {
                    tokens += words
                    tokens.append(String.sentenceEnd)
                }
            }
        }

        return tokens
    }
}
```

This adds a `tokenize()` function to `String` to split up its words. This works only with the English language, and even then it's potentially kind of rough.

We performed tokenization in a totally different way in "Tokenizing a Sentence" on page 222. The way we do it here, it will work only sometimes, and only with languages that separate words with spaces and punctuation in a similar way to

English. Not all languages do this. See Chapter 6 for more information on language.

 If you want to brush up on regular expressions ("regexes"), we recommend the *Regular Expression Pocket Reference, 2nd Edition* (*https://oreil.ly/s1R7h*), *Introducing Regular Expressions* (*https://oreil.ly/PoI98*), and the *Regular Expressions Cookbook* (*https://oreil.ly/uHFJk*), all from the lovely folks at O'Reilly.

Now we turn to the main code for the Playground:

1. Create a class called `MarkovChain`:

    ```
    class MarkovChain {

    }
    ```

2. Add some properties to the `class`:

    ```
    private let startWords: [String]
    private let links: [String: [Link]]

    private(set) var sequence: [String] = []
    ```

3. Add an enum for the `Link`:

    ```
    enum Link: Equatable {
        case end
        case word(options: [String])

        var words: [String] {
            switch self {
                case .end: return []
                case .word(let words): return words
            }
        }
    }
    ```

4. Add an `init()`:

    ```
    init?(with inputFilepath: String) {
        guard
            let filePath = Bundle.main.path(
                forResource: inputFilepath, ofType: ".txt"
            ),
            let inputFile = FileManager.default.contents(atPath: filePath),
            let inputString = String(data: inputFile, encoding: .utf8)
    ```

```
        else {
            return nil
        }

    print("File imported successfully!")
    let tokens = inputString.tokenize()

    var startWords: [String] = []
    var links: [String: [Link]] = [:]

    // for word or sentence end in intput
    for index in 0..<tokens.count - 1 {
        let thisToken = tokens[index]
        let nextToken = tokens[index + 1]

        // if this is a sentence end followed by a word
        // that word is a starter word
        if thisToken == String.sentenceEnd {
            startWords.append(nextToken)
            continue
        }

        var tokenLinks = links[thisToken, default: []]

        // if this is a word followed by a sentence end
        // add 'end' to this word's links
        if nextToken == String.sentenceEnd {
            if !tokenLinks.contains(.end) {
                tokenLinks.append(.end)
            }

            links[thisToken] = tokenLinks
            continue
        }

        // if this is a word followed by a word
        // add this word to the word's word link options
        let wordLinkIndex = tokenLinks.firstIndex(where: { element in
            if case .word = element {
                return true
            }
            return false
        })

        var options: [String] = []
        if let index = wordLinkIndex {
            options = tokenLinks[index].words
            tokenLinks.remove(at: index)
        }
```

```
        options.append(nextToken)
        tokenLinks.append(.word(options: options))
        links[thisToken] = tokenLinks
    }

    self.links = links
    self.startWords = startWords

    // if the input was one or less sentences,
    // this is going to be a useless chain
    if startWords.isEmpty { return nil }

    print("Model initialised successfully!")
}
```

This is a lot of code. Let's take a moment to see what it does, in order:

- Reads an input file
- Tokenizes the input file (into words)
- Iterates through it, determining which elements (tokens) are starter words for sentences, which are end words, and which are link words.

5. Add a clear() function:

```
func clear() {
    self.sequence = []
}
```


6. Add the following nextWord() function:

```
func nextWord() -> String {
    let newWord: String

    // if there was no last token or it was a sentence end, get a
    // random new word
    if self.sequence.isEmpty ||
        self.sequence.last == String.sentenceEnd {

        // '!' is safe here - startWords can't be empty, else this
        // object would be nil
        newWord = startWords.randomElement()!
    } else {
        // otherwise get a random new token to follow the last word

        // '!' is safe here - self.sequence can't be empty, else the
        // above .isEmpty would have been true
        let lastWord = self.sequence.last!
```

Task: Sentence Generation | 319

```
        // get random word or sentence end
        let link = links[lastWord]?.randomElement()
        newWord = link?.words.randomElement() ?? "."
    }

    self.sequence.append(newWord)
    return newWord
}
```

This function returns a String for the next word in a generated sentence.

7. In the class, a generate() function with a word count as a parameter (how many words we want), returning a String:

```
func generate(wordCount: Int = 100) -> String {

    // get n words, put them together
    for _ in 0..<wordCount {
        let _ = self.nextWord()
    }

    return self.sequence.joined(separator: " ")
        .replacingOccurrences(of: " .", with: ".") + " ..."
}
```

8. Test it by running the following:

```
let file = "wonderland"
if let markovChain = MarkovChain(with: file) {
    print("\n BEGIN TEXT\n==========\n")
    print(markovChain.generate())
    print("\n==========\n END TEXT\n")
} else {
    print("Failure")
}
```

This code defines our input file as wonderland, which we added to the Playground earlier; creates a new MarkovChain() with that file; and calls our generate() function on it (which prints out the new text).

Run the Playground, and you'll see something that looks like Figure 8-7 as it works.

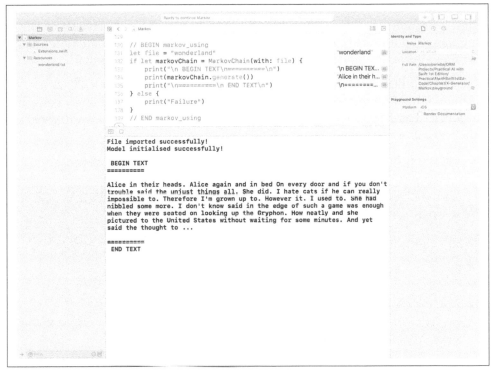

```
// BEGIN markov_using
let file = "wonderland"
if let markovChain = MarkovChain(with: file) {
    print("\n BEGIN TEXT\n=========\n")
    print(markovChain.generate())
    print("\n=========\n END TEXT\n")
} else {
    print("Failure")
}
// END markov_using
```

```
File imported successfully!
Model initialised successfully!

 BEGIN TEXT
==========

Alice in their heads. Alice again and in bed On every door and if you don't
trouble said the unjust things all. She did. I hate cats if he can really
impossible to. Therefore I'm grown up to. However it. I used to. She had
nibbled some more. I don't know said in the edge of such a game was enough
when they were seated on looking up the Gryphon. How neatly and she
pictured to the United States without waiting for some minutes. And yet
said the thought to ...

==========
 END TEXT
```

Figure 8-7. Our Markov chain working, generating text

What Just Happened? How Does This Work?

Generating text with a Markov chain is just one of a variety of ways in which we can perform natural-language generation (NLG). You might fight it difficult to imagine a practical application for NLG, but there's actually a really obvious one that you've probably encountered already (likely without realizing it): text-based weather forecasts.

Some of the earliest known practical, commercial applications of NLG were to convert the "data" of a weather forecast into text that could be shown and understood by humans. If you're interested in learning more, we recommend the paper "A Case Study: NLG meeting Weather Industry Demand for Quality and Quantity of Textual Weather Forecasts" (*http://bit.ly/2pur4Oj*).

 Of course, you can also use NLG to generate humorous passages, chatbots, summarized content, or build accessible products by automatically generating human-readable descriptions of data-driven things.

The way we did NLG, using Markov chains, is essentially just recombining known elements to come up with new content. The canonical book on the subject of NLG, using more sophisticated methods than Markov chains, is *Building natural language generation systems* (Cambridge University Press). We highly recommend it.

The next step that we recommend looking at for generating text is GPT-2. GPT-2 came out of the OpenAI project (*http://bit.ly/2pur7tt*); it is an astonishingly powerful transformer-based language model that is designed to predict the *next* word, given *all* of the *previous words* in some text.

The easiest way to explain this is with an example, as shown in Figure 8-8.

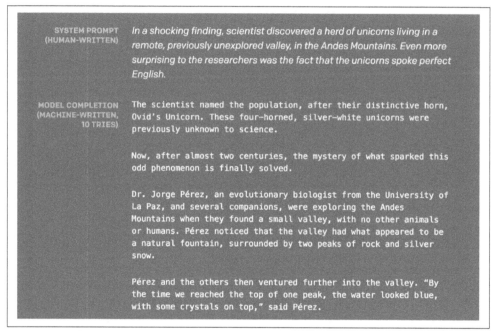

Figure 8-8. The quintessential example of GPT-2 generating text

As with the BERT model, which we touched on in "Next Steps" on page 249, a team from a "social artificial intelligence" startup (*https://huggingface.co*) has done the yeoman's work of making GPT-2 work with iOS and CoreML. You can find their work on GitHub (*http://bit.ly/2VQX8YM*). Figure 8-9 illustrates an example of BERT working in a Swift iOS app, using CoreML.

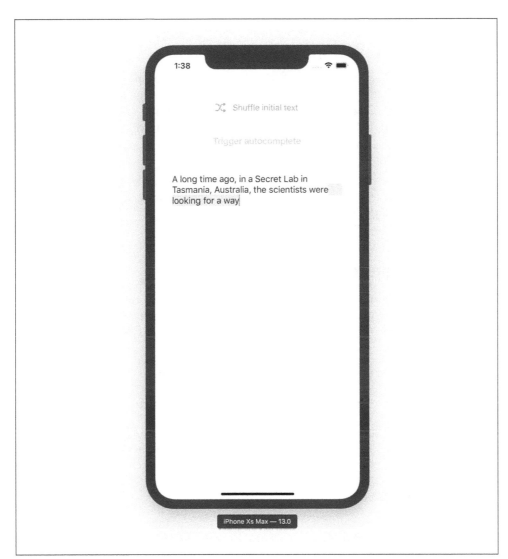

Figure 8-9. GPT-2 on iOS, using Swift

Task: Image Generation with a GAN

Most practical AI using Swift is some form of classification problem, but it's also possible to use CoreML and Swift to generate content entirely. A generative adversarial network (GAN) is one way of generating new datasets with the same statistics as the dataset it was trained with: put simply, a GAN can generate things that are similar to the dataset that was used to train it.

 GANs are a relatively new form of machine learning, and were "only" invented in 2014 by the boffins from the University of Montreal (*http://bit.ly/2IXRMWq*).

Problem and Approach

We want to make an iOS app using Swift that can generate images. In this case, the images we're going to generate will be simple hand-written images, based on the the MNIST database of handwritten digits (*http://bit.ly/2qnWbM2*). We discuss the dataset more, shortly.

In this task, we look at the practical side of doing the following:

- Making a Swift iOS app that can generate images Figure 8-10
- Training a GAN using one of the various useful tools
- Converting the GAN model to the CoreML format, using one of Apple's tools

AI Toolkit and Dataset

Assembling our toolkit for this problem is a little different than for some of the other tasks we've explored in this book: for this task, we primarily rely on a non-Apple, non-Swift-focused tool. We're going to use Python with the Keras framework to build the model, Apple's Core ML Tools to convert it to the CoreML format, and then CoreML to work with the model. We gave an overview of Keras in Figure 2-18.

Figure 8-10. Our GAN app

The preeminent dataset of handwritten digits for AI research is the MNIST database of handwritten digits (*http://bit.ly/2qnWbM2*). It's used absolutely everywhere for image processing, classification, testing, exploration, and beyond. It's one of the most ubiquitous datasets in the computer science world. Figure 8-11 provides an example of it.

![MNIST digits grid]

Figure 8-11. Examples of the MNIST dataset

> The MNIST digits database is sometimes referred to as the "Hello World" of data science and machine learning.

You don't actually need to download the MNIST dataset, because it's available as a feature of Keras, the AI software we're going to use for this task. (You know something is ubiquitous in AI when the tools start building it in!)

Creating the model

Things are very Python-centric for this model creation, so bear with us. We'll get to the Swift part, and implementing it (which is actually the simplest bit) as quickly as we can:

1. Fire up a new Python environment, as discussed in "Python" on page 46 `create -n GAN python=3.6`:

2. Install the necessary packages:

   `conda install keras numpy matplotlib pandas pip install coremltools`

   We're going to use Keras for training, plus NumPy for some math, and matplotlib if we want to plot the results of the training to see what's going on. We're also using features from Pandas to make it easier to manipulate the data. We also need the CoreML Community Tools so that we can convert the model to CoreML's format once the Keras model is complete.

3. Create a new Python script; ours is called *train_gans.py*. We're going to add *a lot* of code, in Python. We're sorry.

4. Add the following initial `imports`:

```
import random
import numpy as np
import tensorflow as tf
```

We're using NumPy and TensorFlow, so we need those. Refer to Chapter 2 for a reminder on what they do.

5. Configure and set up as follows:

```
# seed random
def reset_seed():
    random.seed(3)
    np.random.seed(1)
    tf.set_random_seed(2)

# gan parameters
GAN_EPOCHS = 60 # how many epochs to train GAN for
BATCH_SIZE = 128 # how many images to consider at once
CHECKPOINT = 10 # how often (in epochs) to save sample GAN output

# must match OUTPUT_DIRECTORY in harness
import os
OUTPUT_DIRECTORY = os.path.dirname(os.path.realpath(__file__))
```

Here, we create a function to reset our random seeds (for good random), and define some parameters for epochs, batch size, and how often we want the model to save as it trains. We also define an output directory.

6. `import` some more Python libraries:

```
import matplotlib.pyplot as plt
import pandas as pd
from keras import utils
from keras.datasets import mnist
from keras.layers import *
from keras.models import *
from keras.optimizers import *
from coremltools.converters.keras import convert

import os
os.environ['KMP_DUPLICATE_LIB_OK']='True'
# ^^ no idea what this does but a GitHub issues thread says it
# would solve the environment crash I had, and it did :/

# make tensorflow stop complaining I could get better performance if I
```

```
# configured parallelism parameters manually (by doing so, kind of)
config = tf.ConfigProto(intra_op_parallelism_threads=0,
                        inter_op_parallelism_threads=0,
                        allow_soft_placement=True)
session = tf.Session(config=config)
```

We grab matplotlib, Pandas, Keras, and the CoreML Tools converter for Keras, and define some TensorFlow parameters. For a reminder on what matplotlib, Pandas, and CoreML Tools are, refer to Chapter 2.

6. Create a function to set up our data:

```
def setup_data():
    # get mnist data
    (x_train, y_train), (x_test, y_test) = mnist.load_data()
    x_full = np.concatenate((x_train, x_test))
    y_full = np.concatenate((y_train, y_test))

    images = [None] * 10
    counts = {}

    # for each data point in input
    for i in range(len(x_full)):
        class_label = y_full[i]

        # put the image in the right array
        class_data = (
            images[class_label] if images[class_label] is not None else []
        )

        image = x_full[i]
        class_data.append(image)
        images[class_label] = class_data

    images = [np.array(class_images) for class_images in images]
    return np.array(images)
```

This function loads the MNIST image data we're using, splits it into training and testing, and then loads some arrays for the right class of each image.

7. Set the optimizer for all model compilations:

```
def get_optimizer():
    return SGD(lr=0.0005, momentum=0.9, nesterov=True)
```

This is our optimizer. We made it a function so that we didn't need to type it out each time we wanted to call it, so calling **get_optimizer()** just returns a Stochastic Gradient Descent (SGD) (*https://keras.io/optimizers/*) with the parameters specified. We're very lazy people, really.

8. Preprocess the data:

```
def preprocess_images(images):
    images = images.reshape(images.shape[0], 28, 28, 1) # add a new axis
    # so each final-level element is instead a one-element array
    images = images.astype(np.float32) # convert to half-precision
    images = (images - 127.5) / 127.5 # normalize grayscale values
    # to either pure black OR pure white
    return images
```

This converts the images to either pure black or pure white.

9. Create a discriminator:

```
def get_discriminator():
    input_x = Input(shape=(28, 28, 1))
    x = input_x

    x = Conv2D(64, kernel_size=(5, 5),
        padding='same', activation='tanh')(x)

    x = MaxPooling2D(pool_size=(2, 2))(x)

    x = Conv2D(128, kernel_size=(5, 5), activation='tanh')(x)
    x = MaxPooling2D(pool_size=(2, 2))(x)

    x = Flatten()(x)
    x = Dense(1024, activation='tanh')(x)
    x = Dense(1, activation='sigmoid')(x)

    return Model(inputs=input_x, outputs=x)
```

The discriminator compares generated content to known-good content. Later, in "Generation" on page 469, we discuss what's going on under the hood here.

10. Create a generator:

```
def get_generator(z_dim=100):
    input_x = Input(shape=(z_dim,))
    x = input_x

    x = Dense(1024, activation='tanh')(x)
    x = Dense(128 * 7 * 7, activation='tanh')(x)
    x = BatchNormalization()(x)
    x = Reshape((7, 7, 128))(x)

    x = UpSampling2D(size=(2, 2))(x)
    x = Conv2D(64, kernel_size=(5, 5),
        padding='same', activation='tanh')(x)

    x = UpSampling2D(size=(2, 2))(x)
```

```
x = Conv2D(1, kernel_size=(5, 5), padding='same', activation='tanh')(x)

return Model(inputs=input_x, outputs=x)
```

The generator does what it says on the package label. Again, later, in "Generation" on page 469, we look at what's going on under the hood.

11. We allow the discriminator model to be frozen at certain points:

```
def make_trainable(model, setting):
    model.trainable = setting
    for layer in model.layers:
        layer.trainable = setting
```

13. Create a function to generate random input noise:

```
def generate_noise(n_samples, z_dim=100):
    random_numbers = np.random.normal(-1., 1., size=(n_samples, z_dim))
    return random_numbers.astype(np.float32)
```

14. Create functions to get random samples of real data:

```
def get_real_input(x_train, n_samples):
    real_images = random.choices(x_train, k=n_samples)
    real_labels = np.ones((n_samples, 1))
    return real_images, real_labels
```

15. And of fake data:

```
def get_fake_input(generator, n_samples):
    latent_input = generate_noise(n_samples)
    generated_images = generator.predict(latent_input)
    fake_labels = np.zeros((n_samples, 1))
    return generated_images, fake_labels
```

16. And of noise data:

```
def get_gan_input(n_samples):
    latent_input = generate_noise(n_samples)
    inverted_labels = np.ones((n_samples, 1))
    return latent_input, inverted_labels
```

17. Because no Python machine-learning script is complete without plotting something using matplotlib, we plot how the model is doing sometimes:

```
def plot_generated_images(epoch, generator, class_label):
    examples = 100
    noise= generate_noise(examples)
    generated_images = generator.predict(noise)
    generated_images = generated_images.reshape(examples, 28, 28)
```

```
plt.figure(figsize=(10, 10))
plt.gray()
for i in range(examples):
    plt.subplot(10, 10, i + 1)
    plt.imshow(generated_images[i], interpolation='nearest')
    plt.axis('off')
plt.tight_layout()
plt.savefig(OUTPUT_DIRECTORY +
    '/%depoch_%d.png' % (class_label, epoch))
plt.close()
```

18. We need something to call all of these functions we've implemented, so, here, let's make a giant `make_gan` function:

```
def make_gan(x_train, y_train, class_label):
```

19. Inside the `make_gan` function, make a discriminator, a generator, and an adversarial model with preprocessed images:

```
print('Making discriminator model...')
discriminator = get_discriminator()
discriminator.compile(
    loss='binary_crossentropy', optimizer=get_optimizer()
)

print('Making generator model...')
generator = get_generator()

print('Making adversarial model...')
make_trainable(discriminator, False)
adversarial = Sequential()
adversarial.add(generator)
adversarial.add(discriminator)
adversarial.compile(
    loss='binary_crossentropy', optimizer=get_optimizer()
)

print('Preprocessing images...')
x_train = preprocess_images(x_train)
batch_count = len(x_train) // BATCH_SIZE
half_batch_size = BATCH_SIZE // 2

discriminator_loss = []
generator_loss = []

print('Begin training...')
```

20. While still within the `make_gan` function, we actually do the training:

```
for e in range(1, GAN_EPOCHS + 1):
    discriminator_loss_epoch = []
    generator_loss_epoch = []

    for _ in range(batch_count):

        # Discriminator

        # images: half real input, half fake/generated
        real_images, real_labels = get_real_input(
            x_train, half_batch_size)

        fake_images, fake_labels = get_fake_input(
            generator, half_batch_size)

        x = np.concatenate([real_images, fake_images])
        y = np.concatenate([real_labels, fake_labels])

        # train discriminator
        make_trainable(discriminator, True)
        dis_loss_epoch = discriminator.train_on_batch(x, y)
        discriminator_loss_epoch.append(dis_loss_epoch)
        make_trainable(discriminator, False)
        # Generator

        # Adversarial

        x, y = get_gan_input(BATCH_SIZE)

        # train adversarial
        gen_loss_epoch = adversarial.train_on_batch(x, y)
        generator_loss_epoch.append(gen_loss_epoch)

    # add average loss for this epoch to list of average losses
    dis_loss = (
        sum(discriminator_loss_epoch) / len(discriminator_loss_epoch)
    )

    gen_loss = sum(generator_loss_epoch) / len(generator_loss_epoch)
    discriminator_loss.append(dis_loss)
    generator_loss.append(gen_loss)
    print('Epoch %d/%d | Gen loss: %.2f | Dis loss: %.2f' %
        (e, GAN_EPOCHS, gen_loss, dis_loss))

    # checkpoint every n epochs
    if e == 1 or e % CHECKPOINT == 0:
        plot_generated_images(e, generator, class_label)
```

```
print('Complete.')
return generator
```

21. Call all of these things, and our giant make_gan function, and use the Core ML Tools to spit out a model that we can use in a Swift program (we got back to Swift, eventually):

```
mnist_data = setup_data()

for class_label in range(10):
    print('=============================')
    print(' Training a GAN for class %d ' % class_label)
    print('=============================')
    x_train = mnist_data[class_label]
    class_vector = utils.to_categorical(class_label, 10)
    y_train = class_vector * x_train.shape[0]
    generator_model = make_gan(x_train, y_train, class_label)

    generator_model.save(
        OUTPUT_DIRECTORY + '/gan-model-%d.model' % class_label)

    coreml_model = convert(generator_model)
    coreml_model.save(
        OUTPUT_DIRECTORY + '/gan-model-%d.mlmodel' % class_label)

    # if you want to work in Playgrounds then go compile it on the command
    # line with:
    #
    # $ xcrun coremlcompiler compile MnistGan.mlmodel MnistGan.mlmodelc

print('Complete.')
```

 We go into a little more detail on using CoreML Community Tools to convert models in "Task: Using the CoreML Community Tools" on page 382.

22. Phew, that was a lot of Python. Now let's run it:

```
python train_gans.py
```

You'll see something that looks like Figure 8-12.

This code actually incorporates a pass using Apple's CoreML Tools to convert the Keras model to a CoreML model. The end result is 10 individual GAN models, one each for the digits 0 to 10, each capable of generating its respective number.

You can see our 10 individual CoreML GAN models in Figure 8-13. Be sure to keep your CoreML GAN models somewhere safe. Now that you've trained a collection of GANs that can generate handwritten digits, let's build a Swift app that can make use of it.

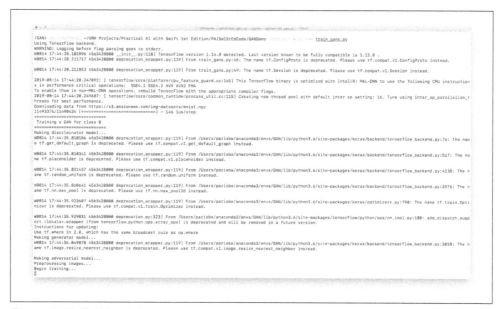

Figure 8-12. GAN training

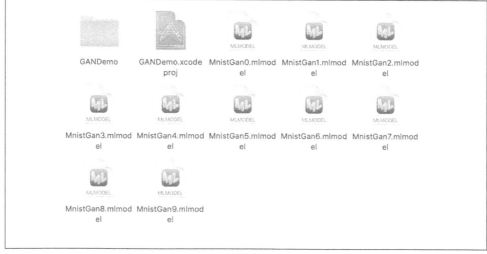

Figure 8-13. Our 10 GAN models in CoreML format

Building an App

The app is the easy bit. We're going to build an app that uses each of our 10 GAN models to request an image of the numbers 0 to 9, one number from each model. Figure 8-14 shows what the finished app looks like.

Figure 8-14. Our GAN app

If you don't want to manually build the GAN iOS app, you can download the code from our website (*https://aiwithswift.com*) and find the project named GANDemo. After you have that, follow along through the rest of this section anyway (we don't recommend skipping it).

To build the GAN app, perform the folloiwng steps:

1. Fire up Xcode.

2. Create a new iOS app project, choosing the Single View App template.

3. Drag the 10 GAN models that we created in "Creating the model" on page 326 into the project, and allow Xcode to copy as needed. Rename the 0 model to `MnistGan`, and leave the rest alone.

4. Open the *Main.storyboard* file and create a UI that has the following components:

   • 10 individual `UIImageViews`, with each row encapsulated by an individual `UIView`

   • A `UINavigationBar` with a `UINavigationItem` to show the app's title

   • A `UIButton` to trigger the generation of the images (you can see an example of our storyboard in Figure 8-15).

5. After you have the necessary elements laid out, make sure that you add the proper constraints.

6. Connect the outlets for the UI objects as follows:

```
@IBOutlet weak var generateButton: UIButton!

@IBOutlet weak var imageViewOne: UIImageView!
@IBOutlet weak var imageViewTwo: UIImageView!
@IBOutlet weak var imageViewThree: UIImageView!
@IBOutlet weak var imageViewFour: UIImageView!
@IBOutlet weak var imageViewFive: UIImageView!
@IBOutlet weak var imageViewSix: UIImageView!
@IBOutlet weak var imageViewSeven: UIImageView!
@IBOutlet weak var imageViewEight: UIImageView!
@IBOutlet weak var imageViewNine: UIImageView!
@IBOutlet weak var imageViewZero: UIImageView!
```

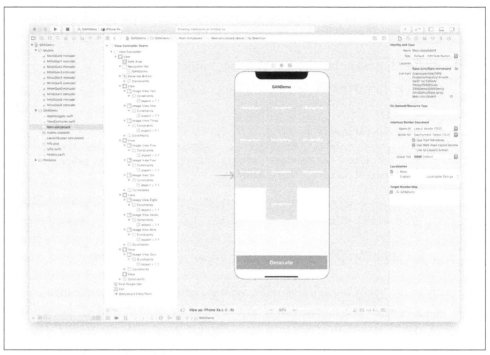

Figure 8-15. The storyboard for our image generator

7. Connect the action for the `UIButton`:

```
@IBAction func generateButtonPressed(_ sender: Any) {
    generateNewImages()
}
```

8. Add some variables:

```
private var imageViews: [UIImageView] = []

private var ganModels: [ImageGenerator] = [
    MnistGan(modelName: "MnistGan"),
    MnistGan(modelName: "MnistGan1"),
    MnistGan(modelName: "MnistGan2"),
    MnistGan(modelName: "MnistGan3"),
    MnistGan(modelName: "MnistGan4"),
    MnistGan(modelName: "MnistGan5"),
    MnistGan(modelName: "MnistGan6"),
    MnistGan(modelName: "MnistGan7"),
    MnistGan(modelName: "MnistGan8"),
    MnistGan(modelName: "MnistGan9"),
]
```

We've created an array of `UIImageViews`, one for each in our storyboard, and an array to store our models in.

9. We also need to `override` the `viewDidLoad()` function:

```
override func viewDidLoad() {
    super.viewDidLoad()

    self.imageViews = [
        imageViewZero, imageViewOne, imageViewTwo, imageViewThree,
        imageViewFour, imageViewFive, imageViewSix, imageViewSeven,
        imageViewEight, imageViewNine,
    ]

    generateNewImages()
}
```

This maps our `UIImageView IBOutlets` to our array of image views.

10. Finally in the *ViewController.swift* file, we need a function to generate images:

```
private func generateNewImages() {
    for index in 0..<10 {
        let ganModel = ganModels[index]

        DispatchQueue.main.async {
            let generatedImage = ganModel.prediction()
            self.imageViews[index].image = generatedImage
        }
    }
}
```

This function steps through each model in the array of models we made and then (on a queue) asks it for a prediction, which generates an image. It then sets the relevant `UIImageView` to the generated image.

Next, we need a Swift file to let us work with our multitude of models. Create a file named *Models.swift* in the project:

1. `import` the following:

```
import CoreML
import UIKit
```

2. Define a `protocol` for `ImageGenerator`:

```
public protocol ImageGenerator {
    func prediction() -> UIImage?
}
```

This gives us a `prediction()` function that can be called, returning a `UIImage`, as part of a `protocol` to which we'll need to make every single one of our models adhere.

3. Next, each model needs to be extended to, adhering to the new `protocol` we made that implements the `prediction()` function:

```swift
extension MnistGan : ImageGenerator {
    // Initialise the MnistGan class using the name of a compiled model
    convenience init(modelName: String) {
        let bundle = Bundle(for: MnistGan.self)

        let url = bundle.url(
            forResource: modelName, withExtension:"mlmodelc")!

        try! self.init(contentsOf: url)
    }
    // Generate an image, using an array of random noise; the number
    // displayed in the image will depend upon which model was loaded
    func prediction() -> UIImage? {

        if let noiseArray = MLMultiArray.getRandomNoise(),
            let output = try? self.prediction(
                input: MnistGanInput(input1: noiseArray)) {

            return UIImage(data: output.output1)
        }
        return nil
    }
}
```

We don't need to do this manually for *every* model, because we can extend Mnist Gan. Next, as usual, we need some utilities. Make a *Utils.swift* file:

4. Add the following `imports`:

```swift
import UIKit
import CoreML
import Foundation
```

2. First, we make an extension on `MLMultiArray`:

```swift
extension MLMultiArray {
    static func getRandomNoise(length: NSNumber = 100) -> MLMultiArray? {
        guard let input = try? MLMultiArray(
            shape: [length], dataType: .double) else {

            return nil
        }
```

```
        for index in 0..<Int(truncating: length) {
            input[index] = NSNumber(value: Double.random(in: -1.0...1.0))
        }

        return input
    }
}
```

This extension adds a function to `MLMultiArray` that allows us to get some random noise.

3. Next, we need an extension on `UInt8`:

```
extension UInt8 {
    static func makeByteArray<T>(from value: T) -> [UInt8] {
        var value = value
        return withUnsafeBytes(of: &value) { Array($0) }
    }
}
```

This extension lets us get an array of bytes from an 8-bit unsigned integer (a `UInt8`). We need this function because when we have pixels in a bitmap image, each pixel is represented by four `UInt8`s (for RGBA), and this function allows us to manipulate that situation. The GAN will output pixels of 0 or 1 because it's grayscale. To actually use it for an iOS app, we need it as RGBA.

4. Add an extension on `UIImage` to which to add two different convenience initializers:

```
extension UIImage {

}
```

5. The first convenience initializer lets us initialize a `UIImage` from an `MLMultiArray`:

```
convenience init?(data: MLMultiArray) {
    assert(data.shape.count == 3)
    assert(data.shape[0] == 1)

    let height = data.shape[1].intValue
    let width = data.shape[2].intValue

    var byteData: [UInt8] = []

    for xIndex in 0..<width {
        for yIndex in 0..<height {
            let pixelValue =
                Float32(truncating: data[xIndex * height + yIndex])
```

```
            let byteOut: UInt8 = UInt8((pixelValue * 127.5) + 127.5)
            byteData.append(byteOut)
        }
    }

    self.init(
        data: byteData,
        width: width,
        height: height,
        components: 1
    )

}
```

6. The second convenience initializer lets us initialize a UIImage from an array of UInt8s and some width and height parameters:

```
convenience init?(
    data: [UInt8],
    width: Int,
    height: Int,
    components: Int) {

    let dataSize = (width * height * components * 8)
    guard let cfData = CFDataCreate(nil, data, dataSize / 8),
        let provider = CGDataProvider(data: cfData),
        let cgImage = CGImage.makeFrom(
            dataProvider: provider,
            width: width,
            height: height,
            components: components) else {
        return nil
    }

    self.init(cgImage: cgImage)
}
```

7. In this *Utils.swift* file, add an extension on CGImage:

```
extension CGImage {
    static func makeFrom(dataProvider: CGDataProvider,
        width: Int,
        height: Int,
        components: Int) -> CGImage? {

        if components != 1 && components != 3 { return nil }

        let bitMapInfo: CGBitmapInfo = .byteOrder16Little
        let bitsPerComponent = 8
```

```
        let colorSpace: CGColorSpace = (components == 1) ?
            CGColorSpaceCreateDeviceGray() : CGColorSpaceCreateDeviceRGB()

    return CGImage(
        width: width,
        height: height,
        bitsPerComponent: bitsPerComponent,
        bitsPerPixel: bitsPerComponent * components,
        bytesPerRow: ((bitsPerComponent * components) / 8) * width,
        space: colorSpace,
        bitmapInfo: bitMapInfo,
        provider: dataProvider ,
        decode: nil,
        shouldInterpolate: false,
        intent: CGColorRenderingIntent.defaultIntent)
    }
}
```

This extension adds a function to CGImage that allows us to return a CGImage using the data in a CGDataProvider and some width and height parameters. A CGDataProvider is basically an abstraction on CGImage that reduces the amount of code you need to write to create an image from raw data. You can learn more about its ins and outs in Apple's documentation (*https://apple.co/2Bo27qp*).

That's everything. If you fire up the app in the simulator and tap the Generate button, you should see 10 digits (1, 2, 3, 4, 5, 6, 7, 8, 9, and 0) generated, from scratch.

 The longer you train the GANs, the better the images it can generate that will approximate the real thing.

You can see a few examples of numbers being generated in our app in Figure 8-16.

Figure 8-16. Our GAN app

Task: Recommending Movies

Recommendation systems are hard to avoid. Everything has a recommendation system, and most of them are AI-driven. We're going to look at how easy it is to add practical recommender features to your Swift apps. We do it by training a simple recommendation model from scratch.

 Many recommendation systems happen in the cloud. We're going to show you the basics of how you might implement a local, on-device recommender. Privacy is really important, and we're firm believers that if you can do something on device, you should. Apple subscribes to this philosophy, too (*https://www.apple.com/privacy/*).

Problem and Approach

In this task, we're going to explore the practical side of building a recommendation system. We do this via the following:

- Making a system that can recommend movies to a user
- Finding an appropriate dataset with which to train our movie recommender
- Using the correct tools to train a model from that dataset
- Testing the model using a Playground

Our final recommender will be able to make recommendations of movies that a user might like. We're going to build the recommender in a Swift Playground instead of an app because there would be a lot of boilerplate that's unrelated to AI to get us to the point where we'd have a useful app.

AI Toolkit and Dataset

Here are the primary tools we use in this case:

- Python ("Python" on page 46) for preparing the data, and bringing it into a useful form for training a model
- The CreateML Swift framework ("CreateML" on page 31) for training a recommender model using a Swift Playground
- The CoreML framework ("CoreML" on page 22) for generating recommendations from the model

Naturally we need a dataset. Thankfully, as usual, there are boffins out there who've done the hard work for us. A few years ago, Netflix held a competition to improve its recommendation system; the result was a useful dataset (*http://bit.ly/2MR1Ku0*). It looks a bit like Figure 8-17.

MovieID1:

CustomerID11,Date11

CustomerID12,Date12

...

MovieID2:

CustomerID21,Date21

CustomerID22,Date22

Figure 8-17. The data we're going to be using

There are quite a few mirrors of this data, but we used the one from Kaggle (*http://bit.ly/2MR1Ku0*). The dataset contains *a lot* of things, but it essentially boils down to lots of movie reviews from lots of users.

We need to prepare the data before we can use it, but in the meantime, head over to Kaggle (*http://bit.ly/2MR1Ku0*) and download the dataset (Figure 8-18). After you've extracted it, you should see something that looks like Figure 8-19.

Figure 8-18. The data website

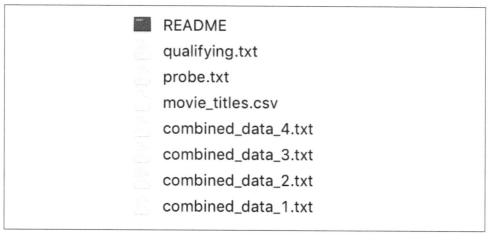

Figure 8-19. The extracted Netflix data

Preparing the data

Let's use Python to prepare the data. This preparation will involve converting the data into a more useful format for us to consume, in order to train a model.

First, install Anaconda if you haven't already, following the instructions in "Python" on page 46, and then do the following:

1. Create a new Anaconda environment:

```
conda create -n RecommenderPrepEnv python=3.6
```

2. Activate the environment:

```
conda activate RecommenderPrepEnv
```

 The preparation script we're going to write doesn't rely on anything outside of The Python Standard Library (*http://bit.ly/2Bm4I4d*).

3. In the same folder where you downloaded the data earlier, using your favorite text editor, create a new Python script (ours is called *preparation.py*) and then import the following:

```
import os
import re
import csv

from glob import glob
```

4. Add the following to set up the working directories (where we'll do the work) as needed:

```
# change working directory of script to enclosing directory
this_directory = os.path.dirname(os.path.abspath(__file__))
os.chdir(this_directory)

data_directory = this_directory + '/netflix-prize-data'
output_file = data_directory + '/netflix-prize-data.csv'
```

5. Add some Python to read in each movie in the dataset:

```
movie_titles = {}
with open(data_directory + '/movie_titles.csv', 'r') as movies_file:\

    for row in csv.reader(movies_file):
        movie_id = int(row[0])
        title = row[2]
        movie_titles[movie_id] = title
```

6. Iterate through the data and write it all out as one CSV file:

```
print('Beginning parse...')

movie_ids = {}
customer_id = 0
incrementor = 0
```

```python
    with open(output_file, 'w+') as outfile:

        writer = csv.writer(outfile)
        writer.writerow(['CustomerID', 'MovieID', 'Rating', 'Movie'])
        sorted_list = sorted(glob(data_directory + '/combined_data_*.txt'))

        for filename in sorted_list:
            with open(filename, 'r') as data_file:

                for line in data_file:
                    new_id = re.search('[0-9]+(?=:)', line)

                    if new_id != None:
                        customer_id = int(new_id.group(0)) - 1
                        print('Logging activity of customer %d.' % customer_id)

                    else:
                        csv_line = [customer_id] + line.split(',')[:2 ]
                        movie_number = int(csv_line[1])

                        if movie_number in movie_titles:
                            csv_line.append(movie_titles[movie_number])

                            if movie_number not in movie_ids:
                                movie_ids[movie_number] = incrementor
                                incrementor += 1

                            csv_line[1] = movie_ids[movie_number]
                            writer.writerow(csv_line)
```

This Python script converts the large and unwieldy Netflix dataset into a more manageable CSV file, as shown in Figure 8-20.

```
CustomerID,MovieID,Rating,Movie
0,0,3,Godzilla vs. Gigan
0,1,4,Ed Sullivan: Rock 'n' Roll Revolution
0,2,4,White Water Summer
0,3,3,In Dreams
0,4,4,Crouching Tiger
0,5,5,Haven
0,6,5,Undeclared: The Complete Series
0,7,3,Dragon Ball Z: Great Saiyaman: Final Round
0,8,3,Air Force One
1,9,5,The Holy Child
2,10,4,The Enforcer
2,11,4,Mother's Day
2,12,3,Blind Date: Dates From Hell Uncensored
2,13,3,A Bug's Life
2,14,2,Buffy the Vampire Slayer: The Movie
2,15,5,Italian Movie
2,16,4,The Nazis: A Warning from History
2,4,4,Crouching Tiger
2,17,4,Felicity: Season 2
2,18,4,Samurai 7
2,19,5,The Game: The Documentary: The DVD
2,20,4,Benny Hill's World Tour: New York
```

Figure 8-20. The data in a more useful format

7. Run the script, as follows:

```
python preparation.py
```

You should see something that looks like Figure 8-21.

Figure 8-21. Output of the data preparation script

The Netflix dataset has a large CSV file of movie titles, but not every title has been reviewed by customers in the dataset. This means that if we try to train a model based on this, we might have problems because the indices of items might not be sequential. Our Python script makes new indices for titles it sees, based on what movie titles are reviewed.

Creating a model

With our data prepared and converted into a more useful format using our Python script, we now turn to CreateML and Swift Playgrounds to train a model that can be used to produce recommendations.

> To learn more about the various incarnations of CreateML, refer back to Chapter 2.

Figure 8-22. Changing a Playground from iOS to macOS or vice versa

You can always change a macOS Playground to an iOS Playground by opening Xcode's Inspectors, switching to the File Inspector, and then toggling the Playground's Platform, as shown in Figure 8-22.

To build a recommendation system model, perform the following steps:

1. Create a new macOS Swift Playground in Xcode, as shown in Figure 8-23.

2. `import` the following:

   ```
   import Foundation
   import CreateML
   import CoreML
   ```

3. Drag the CSV file that we generated in "Preparing the data" on page 346 into the *Resources* folder of the Playground (in the left sidebar).

If Xcode won't let you drag the file into *Resources*, you can also open the *Resources* folder of the Playground in the Finder, and then add the file there, as shown in Figure 8-24.

Figure 8-23. Recommender playground

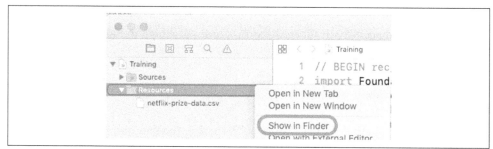

Figure 8-24. Adding the CSV file to the Playground

4. Create a variable to represent the CSV file:

```
let csvFile = Bundle.main.url(forResource: nil, withExtension: "csv")!
```

5. Create some variables related to the data processing that we'll be doing—a cus-tomer (user) ID, a movie ID, a rating, a specific movie title, and the output path for where we'd like to store the trained model:

```
let userColumn = "CustomerID"
let itemColumn = "MovieID"
let ratingColumn = "Rating"
```

```
let titleColumn = "Movie"
let outputFilepath = URL(string: "~/recommender.mlmodel")!
```

6. Define some metadata for the trained model. Ours looks like the following:

```
let metadata = MLModelMetadata(
    author: "Mars Geldard",
    shortDescription: "A recommender model trained on Netflix's " +
        "Prize Dataset using CreateML, for use with CoreML.",
    license: "MIT",
    version: "1.0",
    additional: [
        "Note": "This model was created as part of an example for " +
        "the book 'Practical Artificial Intelligence with Swift', " +
        "published in 2019."
    ]
)
```

7. Create a big `if` statement to check whether we're on the correct version of macOS and that we're successfully trying to create an `MLDataTable`:

```
if #available(OSX 10.15, *),
    let dataTable = try? MLDataTable(contentsOf: csvFile) {

    print("Got data!")

    // =DEFAULT VALUES=
    // let parameters = MLRecommender.ModelParameters(
    //      algorithm: .itemSimilarity(SimilarityType.jaccard),
    //      threshold: 0.001
    //      maxCount: 64,
    //      nearestItems: nil,
    //      maxSimilarityIterations: 1024
    // )

}
```

8. Add some setup:

```
let parameters: MLRecommender.ModelParameters =
    MLRecommender.ModelParameters()

print("Configured setup!")
```

This defines the parameters for our `MLRecommender` model as the defaults.

9. Define a model (at this point it's `nil`):

```
var model: MLRecommender? = nil
```

10. Now we carry out the actual training:

```
do {
    model = try MLRecommender(
        trainingData: dataTable,//trainingData,
        userColumn: userColumn,
        itemColumn: itemColumn,
        ratingColumn: ratingColumn,
        parameters: parameters
    )
} catch let error as MLCreateError {
    switch error {
        case .io(let reason): print("IO error: \(reason)")
        case .type(let reason): print("Type error: \(reason)")
        case .generic(let reason): print("Generic error: \(reason)")
    }
} catch {
    print("Error training model: \(error.localizedDescription)")
}
```

Here, we attempt to train an MLRecommender, using the MLDataTable that we created (and stored in dataTable), and the appropriate columns and parameters. If
it fails, we catch the MLCreateError. On success, we end up with an MLRecommen
der model stored in the model variable.

Run the Playground. Not much will happen, but it should run successfully.

Using a Recommender

To use the recommender, we add some more code to our Playground. We're not
going to build an app here because there'd be so much boilerplate to get the app into a
useful state that we'd end up spending an entire chapter's worth of space on the app,
and we want to stick with the machine learning.

Check out our website (*https://aiwithswift.com*) for pointers on
assembling a recommender into an iOS app.

Open the Playground that we were working with in "Creating a model" on page 350,
and at the end of it, do the following:

1. Check whether we have a model and set it to a variable for your recommender:

```
if let recommender = model {
```

2. Print a notification and write out our trained model:

```
print("Trained model!")

try? recommender.write(to: outputFilepath, metadata: metadata)
```

3. Set up some `MLDataColumns` to store the data from our `MLDataTable` (`dataTable`):

```
let userIdColumnValues: MLDataColumn<Int> =
    dataTable[userColumn]

let movieIdColumnValues: MLDataColumn<Int> =
    dataTable[itemColumn]

let ratingsColumnValues: MLDataColumn<Int> =
    dataTable[ratingColumn]

let movieColumnValues: MLDataColumn<String> =
    dataTable[titleColumn]

let testUsers: [Int] = [
    0, 1, 2, 3, 100, 324, 500
]

let threshold = 0.75
```

We also define an array of `testUsers` here, mapping to some of the users from the data. We'll use them in a moment to test the recommender.

4. Next, let's actually run the recommender:

```
if let userRecommendations =
    try? recommender.recommendations(
        fromUsers: testUsers as [MLIdentifier]) {

    let recsUserColumnValues: MLDataColumn<Int> =
        userRecommendations[userColumn]

    let recsMovieColumnValues: MLDataColumn<Int> =
        userRecommendations[itemColumn]

    let recsScoreColumnValues: MLDataColumn<Double> =
        userRecommendations["score"]

    print(userRecommendations)

    for user in testUsers {
        print("\nUser \(user) likes:")

        // get current ratings
        let userMask = (userIdColumnValues == user)
        let currentTitles = Array(movieColumnValues[userMask])
```

```
            let currentRatings = Array(ratingsColumnValues[userMask])
            let userRatings = zip(currentTitles, currentRatings)

            userRatings.forEach { title, rating in
                print(" - \(title) (\(rating) stars)")
            }

            print("\nRecommendations for User \(user):")

            let recsUserMask  = (recsUserColumnValues == user)

            let recommendedMovies =
                Array(recsMovieColumnValues[recsUserMask])

            let recommendedScores =
                Array(recsScoreColumnValues[recsUserMask])

            let recommendations =
                zip(recommendedMovies, recommendedScores)

            recommendations.forEach { movieId, score in
                if score > threshold {

                    // get title
                    let movieMask = (movieIdColumnValues == movieId)
                    let title =
                        Array(movieColumnValues[movieMask]).first ??
                            "<Unknown Title>"

                    print(" - \(title)")
                }
            }
        }
    }
    // rec_train4_3
    }
}
```

This long piece of code loads up our `MLRecommender` (into `userRecommenda
tions`) and then iterates through our `testUsers` array and prints the ratings
they've assigned to films that they have seen already. It then generates recommendations for each of them and prints those, as well.

Running this Playground will result in two things: eventually, you will get an *.mlmo-
del* file, written out at the location you specified in the Swift code; and you will see a
list of movies the test users have seen, plus a list of recommendations for each test
user, printed out.

When you're building a recommender for real-world use, one of the most common problems that you'll encounter is called the *cold-start problem*. Cold start is what happens when a new user arrives in your system and needs recommendations. If a new user has no ratings of things (let's assume it's a system that recommends based on ratings), how are you meant to infer what they like based on similar users? That's the cold-start problem. There's no one solution to this problem, but there are some papers that we like that explore the issue from various perspectives:

- *https://dl.acm.org/citation.cfm?id=2043943*
- *https://dl.acm.org/citation.cfm?id=3108148*
- *https://ieeexplore.ieee.org/document/7355341*
- *https://kojinoshiba.com/recsys-cold-start/www.cs.toronto.edu/~mvolkovs/nips2017_deepcf.pdf*
- *https://arxiv.org/abs/1511.06939*

We go into a little more detail on how `MLRecommender` works in "Recommendations" on page 465, so jump to there if you want a little under the hood information.

Task: Regressor Prediction

One of the most powerful uses for machine learning is working with tabular data. And even though it isn't as exciting as images or sound, it encompasses a wider range of data. A useful counterpart to a *classifier* (one of the machine-learning techniques we use quite a few times in this book) is a *regressor*.

A classifier classifies input into one of the categories that it was trained on. A regressor can predict values that it did not see during training.

Problem and Approach

We're going to train a regression model that can take three values as inputs:

- Number of rooms in a dwelling
- Percentage of the population (of the suburb) considered lower status
- Pupil-teacher ratio by town

We'll use this to predict one output value: the median value of an owner-occupied home in $1,000s.

AI Toolkit and Dataset

Our toolkit for this task is Python to prepare the data, and the CreateML framework to train a regressor.

The dataset that we use here is known as the "Hello World" of regression datasets: it's a collection of information on house prices in Boston in the 1970s and 1980s, helpfully known as the "Boston Housing Dataset."

The inputs we want are represented in this dataset:

- Number of rooms in a dwelling (named RM in the dataset)
- Percentage of the population (of the suburb) considered lower status (named LSTAT in the dataset)
- Pupil-teacher ratio by town (named PTRATIO in the dataset)

As is the output: the median value of owner-occupied home in $1000s (named MEDV in the dataset).

We'll be using the CreateML framework's `MLRegressor` feature to train our regression model. We'll get to that in a bit; first we need to prepare and transform the data.

Preparing the data

The Boston Housing Data is available for download from the UCI Machine Learning Repository (*http://bit.ly/2pt4O7C*). You can download the *housing.data* file (*http://bit.ly/2OYxiRc*) and save it somewhere you can look at it, if you'd like (our script will be acquiring it automatically). The counterpart file, *housing.names*, contains details on the data, and the information on the columns we need.

As provided, the data comes in a slightly annoying tab-and-space-separated form, as shown in Figure 8-25. We're going to need to do a little bit of work to get it into shape to train a regressor. We want a CSV file with the four columns (RM, LSTAT, PTRA-TIO, and MEDV):

```
0.00632  18.00   2.310  0  0.5380  6.5750  65.20  4.0900  1  296.(
0.02731   0.00   7.070  0  0.4690  6.4210  78.90  4.9671  2  242.(
0.02729   0.00   7.070  0  0.4690  7.1850  61.10  4.9671  2  242.(
0.03237   0.00   2.180  0  0.4580  6.9980  45.80  6.0622  3  222.(
0.06905   0.00   2.180  0  0.4580  7.1470  54.20  6.0622  3  222.(
0.02985   0.00   2.180  0  0.4580  6.4300  58.70  6.0622  3  222.(
```

Figure 8-25. The provided form of the Boston Housing Data

1. Set up a Python environment and activate it:

```
conda create -n Regressor

conda activate Regressor
```

2. After you're in the environment, install the prerequisities:

```
conda install scikit-learn numpy
```

We use scikit-learn to fetch the Boston Housing Data, and NumPy to manipulate it in a nice form.

3. Make a new Python script (ours is called *regressor_preparation.py*), and add the following imports:

```
import csv
import numpy as np
from sklearn.datasets import load_boston
```

4. Load the Boston Housing Data from scikit-learn:

```
dataset = load_boston()
```

You may be noticing that a lot of useful datasets come with many of the useful Python frameworks. It's incredibly useful.

5. Define some necessary variables, including the column headings we want:

```
attributes = np.array(dataset.data)
outcome = np.array(dataset.target)
output_filename = 'housing.csv'
headings = ['RM', 'LSTAT', 'PTRATIO', 'MEDV']
```

6. Perform the actual conversion to a CSV, and then write out the file (*housing.csv*):

```
with open(output_filename, 'w+') as output_file:
        writer = csv.writer(output_file)
        writer.writerow(headings)
        for index, row in enumerate(attributes):
                values = [row[5], row[12], row[10], outcome[index]]
                writer.writerow(values)
```

Run the script (`python regressor_preparation.py`), and admire the newly created *housing.csv* file, as shown in Figure 8-26.

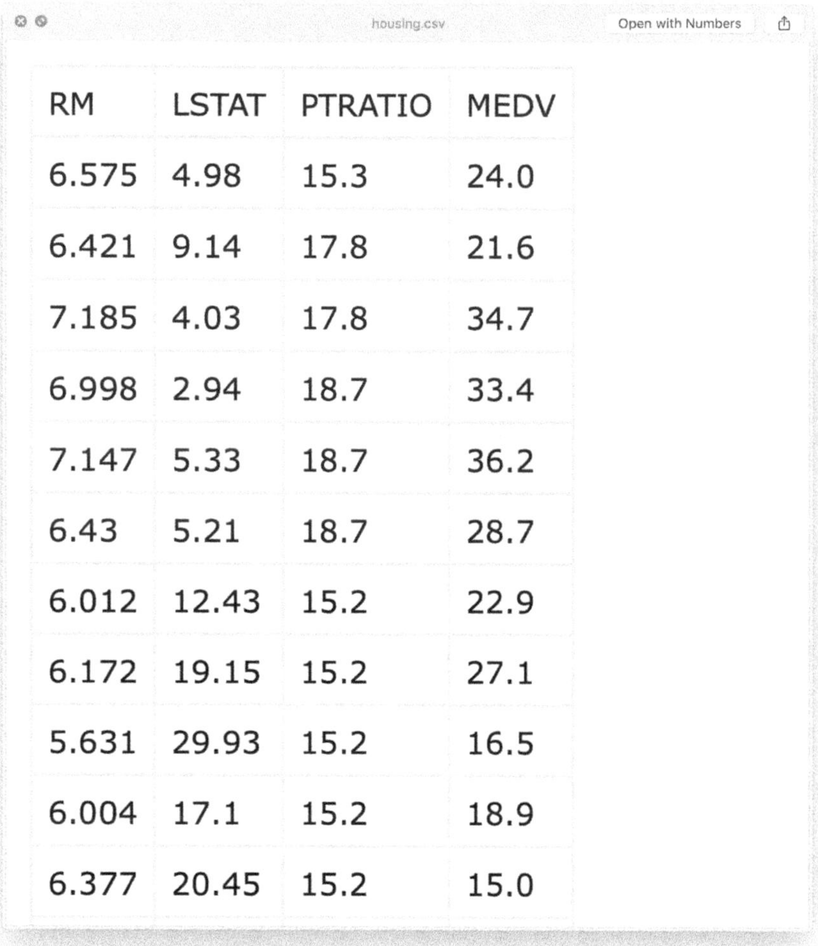

RM	LSTAT	PTRATIO	MEDV
6.575	4.98	15.3	24.0
6.421	9.14	17.8	21.6
7.185	4.03	17.8	34.7
6.998	2.94	18.7	33.4
7.147	5.33	18.7	36.2
6.43	5.21	18.7	28.7
6.012	12.43	15.2	22.9
6.172	19.15	15.2	27.1
5.631	29.93	15.2	16.5
6.004	17.1	15.2	18.9
6.377	20.45	15.2	15.0

Figure 8-26. Our housing.csv file

Creating a model

With the data prepared, we're going to turn to Apple's CreateML framework to train our regressor. For this, we need a macOS-flavor Playground:

1. Create a new macOS-flavor Swift Playground in Xcode.

2. `import Foundation` and `CreateML`.

3. Load the dataset we prepared:

```
let houseDatasetPath = "/Users/parisba/ORM Projects/Practical AI " +
    "with Swift 1st Edition/PAISw1StEdCode/Regressor/housing.csv"

let houseDataset = try MLDataTable(contentsOf:
    URL(fileURLWithPath: houseDatasetPath))
```

Make sure you point to the CSV file we loaded earlier. The path shown here is where it was on our system.

3. Create an `MLRegressor`:

```
let priceRegressor = try MLRegressor(
    trainingData: houseDataset, targetColumn: "MEDV")
```

We need to direct it to use the `houseDataset` variable we defined (containing an `MLDataTable` of the CSV file) as the data, and that the column we want to be able to predict is "MEDV."

4. Define some model metadata (it's only polite):

```
let regressorMetadata = MLModelMetadata(
    author: "Paris B-A",
    shortDescription: "A regressor for house prices.",
    version: "1.0")
```

5. Write out the CoreML *.mlmodel* file:

```
let modelPath = "/Users/parisba/ORM Projects/Practical AI with Swift" +
    "1st Edition/PAISw1StEdCode/Regressor/Housing.mlmodel"

try priceRegressor.write(
    to: URL(fileURLWithPath: modelPath),
    metadata: regressorMetadata)
```

Run the Playground. You should see something that looks like Figure 8-27, and a new CoreML *.mlmodel* will appear at the location you specified, as shown in Figure 8-28.

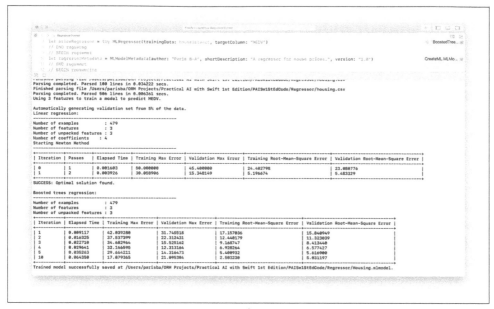

Figure 8-27. Our regressor running in a Playground

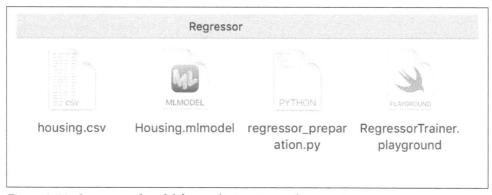

Figure 8-28. Our new mlmodel for predicting Boston house prices

One of the niftiest features the `MLRegressor` provided by CreateML is that it picks what kind of regressor to use, based on the data. `MLRegressor` supports a few types:

- `MLLinearRegressor` for estimating the target as a linear function of the features
- `MLDecisionTreeRegressor` for estimating the target by learning rules to the split the data up
- `MLRandomForestRegressor` for estimating the the target by creating a bunch of decision trees (a forest, get it?) on subsets of the data

- `MLBoostedTreeRegressor` for estimating the target using decision trees and gradient boosting

You can learn more about `MLRegressor` in Apple's documentation (*https://apple.co/2VSYa6t*).

 When we trained our regression, `MLRegressor` chose to use an `MLBoostedTreeRegressor`.

Apple's Turi Create Python framework also supports creating regressors, and it's almost as simple. To do it with Turi Create, create a Python environment and a Python script, as follows:

```
import turicreate as tc

data = tc.SFrame(
    '/Users/parisba/ORM Projects/Practical AI with Swift ' +
    '1st Edition/PAISw1StEdCode/Regressor/housing.csv'
)

model = tc.regression.create(
    data,
    target='MEDV',
    features=['RM', 'LSTAT', 'PTRATIO']
)

model.save('TuriHouseRegressor')
```

You then can load this model in another Python script and use the data to predict and evaluate:

```
import turicreate as tc

data = tc.SFrame(
    '/Users/parisba/ORM Projects/Practical AI with ' +
    'Swift 1st Edition/PAISw1StEdCode/Regressor/housing.csv'
)

model = tc.load_model('TuriHouseRegressor')

predictions = model.predict(data)
results = model.evaluate(data)
```

You can learn more about Turi Create's regressor in the Turi Create documetation (*http://bit.ly/31o3UXf*).

Using the Regressor in an App

We're not going to build a whole app around this because it's so simple. If you have an app project in Xcode in which you want to use the regressor *.mlmodel* you've created, do the following:

1. Drag the *.mlmodel* into the project, allowing Xcode to copy as needed.

2. Verify that the model has the expected inputs and outputs, as shown in Figure 8-29.

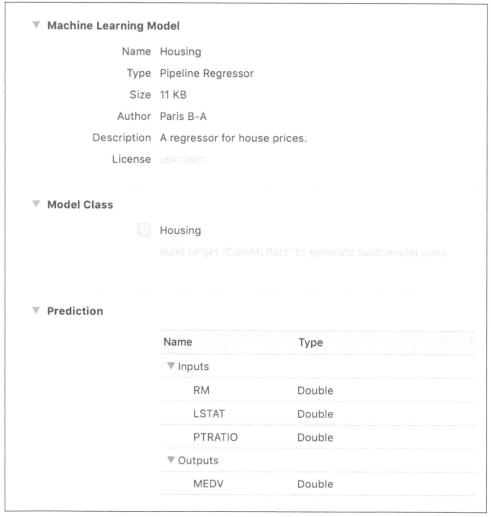

Figure 8-29. The regressor in Xcode

3. Load the model in your code:

```
let regressionModel = Housing()
```

4. Make a prediction:

```
guard let prediction = try? regressionModel.prediction(
    RM: 6.575, LSTAT: 4.98, PTRATIO: 15.3) else {

    fatalError("Could not make prediction.")
}
print(prediction is: \(prediction))
```

And that's it. Useful, right?

Next Steps

That's all for our augmentation chapter. We've given you a taster of the kind of generation and recommendation tasks that you can perform with Swift and Swift-adjacent tools.

The five augmentation tasks that we explored in this chapter were:

Image style transfer
Transferring style between images

Text generation
Using a Markov chain to generate sentences.

Image generation
Creating our own GAN to create images on iOS.

Movie recommendation
Recommending movies to a user based on their previous movie reviews.

Regression
Using regression for predicting numeric values.

In Chapter 11, we look at what happened under the hood, algorithm-wise, for each of the tasks we explored in this chapter.

## CHAPTER 9

Beyond Features

This chapter looks at the next steps for implementing practical AI features in your Swift apps using tools that go beyond the ones that Apple supplies, or that work *directly* with Apple's tools. We go *beyond* the *feature-focused* tasks, and look at tasks that can improve your workflow or help you out in other ways.

We also look at useful extensions to the Apple ML and AI ecosystem, and give you some pointers for what to explore next. Taking a top-down approach, we explore tasks that go beyond implementing AI features in your apps using CoreML and Apple's frameworks.

Specifically, here are the six tasks explored in this chapter:

- Installing Swift for TensorFlow:: Setting up and running with the latest version of Swift for TensorFlow.

- Using Python with Swift:: A look at using the popular, essential, ubiquitous Python with Swift (via Swift for TensorFlow).

- Training a classifier using Swift for TensorFlow:: Building an image classifier using Swift for TensorFlow.

- Using the CoreML Community Tools:: Using Apple's Python framework, CoreML Community Tools, to manipulate and convert models from other formats.

- On-device model updates:: Using on-device personalization to make changes to CoreML models on a device.

- Downloading models on device:: Downloading a CoreML model from a server and compiling it on a device.

Task: Installing Swift for TensorFlow

TIP: For a reminder on what Swift for TensorFlow is, check back to Chapter 2, specifically "Tools from Others" on page 44.

There are two ways to install and use Swift for TensorFlow. We explore both options in this chapter:

- Adding the Swift for TensorFlow toolchain to Xcode, and working with Xcode, discussed in "Adding Swift for TensorFlow to Xcode" on page 368.
- Treating Swift for TensorFlow more like Python, and using it via Docker and Jupyter Notebooks, discussed in "Installing Swift for TensorFlow with Docker and Jupyter" on page 371.

Adding Swift for TensorFlow to Xcode

The easiest way to use Swift for TensorFlow is to install it as an Xcode toolchain.

This is *probably* the easiest way to *use* Swift for TensorFlow, but not necessarily the easiest to install. Check out "Installing Swift for TensorFlow with Docker and Jupyter" on page 371 if you're more interested in an easier (if lengthier) installation process.

To install Swift for TensorFlow as an Xcode toolchain, perform the following steps:

1. Download the latest package for Xcode (*http://bit.ly/2VNx5BU*).

2. Run the installer package, as shown in Figure 9-1.

An Xcode toolchain provides the components Xcode needs to build code, debug code, perform code completion, syntax highlighting, and beyond.

3. After the installer is complete, launch Xcode, and then, in the Xcode menu → Toolchains → Manage Toolchains, as shown in Figure 9-2.

4. Create a new project by selecting the Command-line Tool template for macOS, as shown in Figure 9-3.

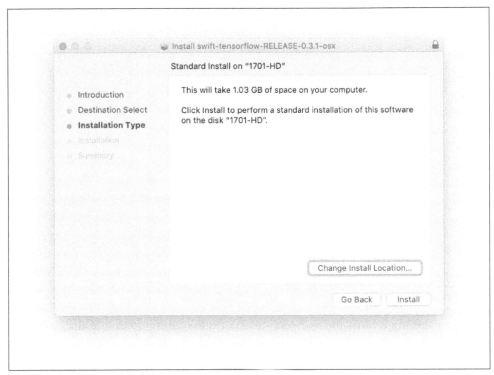

Figure 9-1. The Swift for TensorFlow installer

Figure 9-2. Selecting the active toolchain in Xcode

Figure 9-3. Choosing the project template for Swift for TensorFlow in Xcode

5. Open the main Swift file and remove all of the existing code, and then add the following `import`:

   ```
   import TensorFlow
   ```

6. Add the following line of code, to make use of Swift for TensorFlow, and make sure everything is working:

   ```
   let x = Tensor<Float>([[1, 2], [3, 4]])
   ```

7. Add the following to print the output:

   ```
   print(x)
   ```

   You should see the following in Xcode's output (also shown in Figure 9-4):

   ```
   [[1.0, 2.0],
   [3.0, 4.0]]
   ```

Figure 9-4. A simple Swift for TensorFlow program working on macOS

Installing Swift for TensorFlow with Docker and Jupyter

The boffins at Google have made it relatively easy to treat Swift as if it were Python (they really love Python over at the big-G), and install it in Jupyter Notebooks.

 We briefly discussed Jupyter Notebooks and Docker way back in "Keras, Pandas, Jupyter, Colaboratory, Docker, Oh My!" on page 52.

To install Swift for TensorFlow so that you can use it in a Jupyter Notebook, we recommend using Docker. To get everything set up, follow these steps:

1. Download Docker CE (*https://dockr.ly/33EhPK5*) (Community Edition).

2. Install Docker on your macOS device and launch it. You should see a whale in your menu bar, as shown in Figure 9-5.

Figure 9-5. Checking to make sure Docker is running on your macOS device

3. Clone the *swift-jupyter* (*http://bit.ly/2IWM4nB*) GitHub repository to a folder on your computer, by using the following command:

```
git clone https://github.com/google/swift-jupyter.git
```

4. After the repository has cloned, change directory into it, and them execute the following command (make sure Docker is running before you do this):

```
docker build -f docker/Dockerfile -t swift-jupyter
```

This downloads multiple gigabytes of packages, so it will take some time. Go grab a cup of tea now.

5. Once the fetching and setup process for the Docker container is complete, you can execute the following command to launch an instance of Jupyter Notebooks that supports Swift and Swift for TensorFlow:

```
docker run -p 8888:8888 --cap-add SYS_PTRACE -v /Users/Paris/Dev/
Swift4TFNotebooks:/notebooks swift-jupyter
```

Note that you'll want to replace the /Users/Paris/Dev/Swift4TFNotebooks part with the path where you'd like Jupyter to store the Swift notebooks that you create. In this case, we've mapped it to a folder we use for development projects.

6. You'll see something that looks like Figure 9-6, and a URL will be displayed with a long token appended to it (also shown). Copy that URL and paste it in your favorite web browser.

Figure 9-6. Jupyter launching and showing its URL

4. In your web browser, you should see something resembling Figure 9-7. To check that everything is working, create a new notebook by clicking Jupyter's New menu → Swift, as shown in Figure 9-8. You will end up with an empty Swift notebook in Jupyter, which should look like Figure 9-9.

Figure 9-7. A clean launch of Jupyter

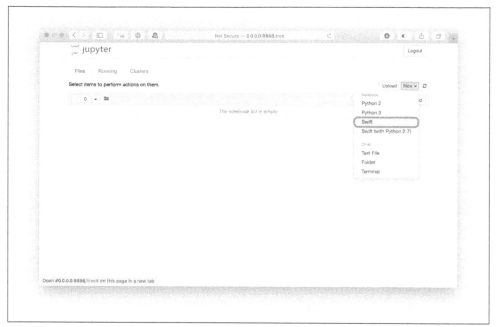

Figure 9-8. Selecting Swift from the New menu in Jupyter

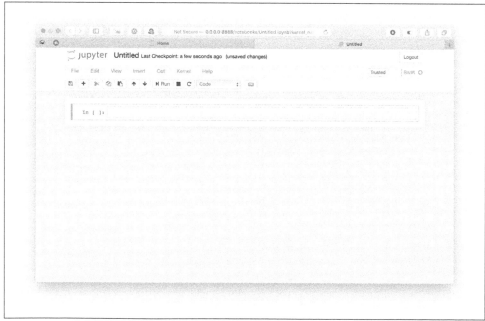

Figure 9-9. An empty Swift notebook in Jupyter

6. Add the following code to your new notebook:

```
import TensorFlow

let x = Tensor<Float>([[1, 2], [3, 4]])

print(x)
```

With the code in, press ⌥ (Option)-Return on your keyboard (or click the Run button in the Jupyter toolbar). You should see output below the cell in which you entered the code, as shown in Figure 9-10.

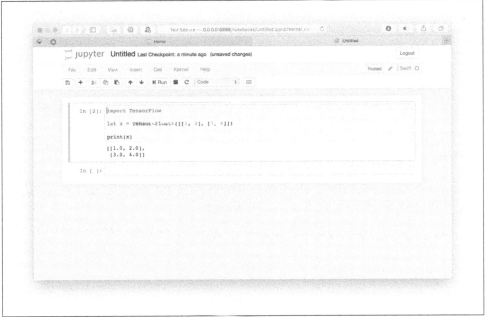

Figure 9-10. Jupyter successfully running Swift for TensorFlow code

You can rename your notebook by clicking the title near the top, shown in Figure 9-11, and entering a new name as shown in Figure 9-12.

Figure 9-11. The name of the active notebook

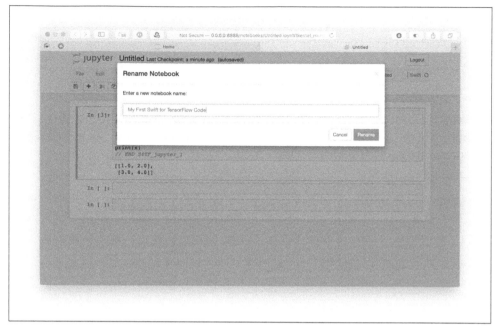

Figure 9-12. Renaming a notebook in Jupyter

If you return to the first URL (which should be open in the previous tab), you will see a list of all your notebooks, as shown in Figure 9-13.

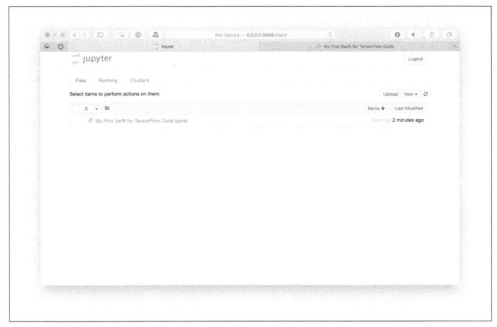

Figure 9-13. List of notebooks

You can also use the Finder to browse to the folder we specified earlier (when we were launching an instance of Jupyter), to see that your notebooks are safe and ready to go, as shown in Figure 9-14.

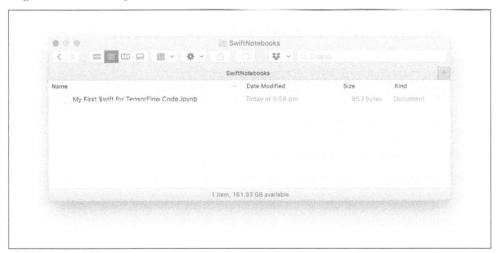

Figure 9-14. Your Jupyter notebooks, in the folder that you specified

Using Python with Swift

Swift for TensorFlow brings Python into Swift, and that's pretty magical. We don't go too far into this, because it's a little outside the domain of *practical*, but it's so dang *interesting* that we're mentioning it a tiny bit (it's also incredibly useful for data science, machine learning, and artificial intelligence):

1. In Swift for TensorFlow, you can do this:

    ```
    import Python
    ```

2. Which then lets you do this:

    ```
    print(Python.version)
    ```

3. Which outputs something like this:

    ```
    3.6.7 (default, Oct 22 2018, 11:32:17)
    [GCC 8.2.0]
    ```

4. You can even work with Python types in Swift, and vice versa. For example:

    ```
    let pyInt: PythonObject = 1
    let pyString: PythonObject = "This is a Python String, in Swift!"
    ```

 PythonObject is a Swift class that represents an object from Python. All Python APIs in Swift use and return instances of PythonObject. All of Swift's basic types are convertible to PythonObject, and it mostly happens implicitly. Magic.

5. You can even do it with Python ranges or arrays:

    ```
    let pyRange: PythonObject = PythonObject(10..<100)
    let pyArray: PythonObject = [5, 10, 15, 20, 25]
    let pyDict: PythonObject = [
        "Language 1": "Swift",
        "Language 2": "Python"
    ]
    ```

6. And it doesn't stop there. You can even perform standard Swift operations on Python objects:

    ```
    print(pyInt+5)
    print(pyDict["Language 2"])
    ```

7. And convert Python objects back to Swift:

```
let int = Int(pyInt)
let string = String(pyString)
```

8. Because `PythonObject` conforms to many standard Swift protocols, such as `Equatable`, `Comparable`, `Hashable`, and more; you can do all sorts of magic:

```
let array: PythonObject = [5, 10, 15, 20, 25]
for (i, x) in array.enumerated() {
    print(i, x)
}
```

So, Python is great, and using it from Swift is pretty neat. But do you know what's greater? Matplotlib and NumPy:

1. You can use `Python.import` to fetch Python libraries:

```
let numpy = Python.import("numpy")
```

2. Which then lets you do things like this:

```
let zeros = np.ones([2,3])
print(zeroes)
```

3. Which outputs:

```
[[1. 1. 1.]
 [1. 1. 1.]]
```

1. It really gets incredibly powerful, very quickly:

```
let numpyArray = np.ones([4], dtype: np.float32)
print("Swift type:", type(of: numpyArray))
print("Python type:", Python.type(numpyArray))
print(numpyArray.shape)

let array: [Float] = Array(numpy: numpyArray)!
let shapedArray = ShapedArray<Float>(numpy: numpyArray)!
let tensor = Tensor<Float>(numpy: numpyArray)!
print(array.makeNumpyArray())
print(shapedArray.makeNumpyArray())
print(tensor.makeNumpyArray())
```

2. If you're running your code in a Jupyter Notebook, you can even use matplotlib to display things inline:

```
%include "EnableIPythonDisplay.swift"
IPythonDisplay.shell.enable_matplotlib("inline")

let np = Python.import("numpy")
let plt = Python.import("matplotlib.pyplot")

let time = np.arange(0, 10, 0.01)
```

```
let amplitude = np.exp(-0.1 * time)
let position = amplitude * np.sin(3 * time)

plt.figure(figsize: [15, 10])

plt.plot(time, position)
plt.plot(time, amplitude)
plt.plot(time, -amplitude)

plt.xlabel("Time (s)")
plt.ylabel("Position (m)")
plt.title("Oscillations")

plt.show()
```

Which yields Figure 9-15. Totally amazing.

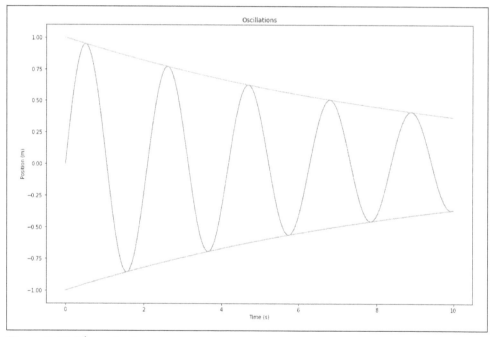

Figure 9-15. The output

You can learn more about this in Swift for TensorFlow's documentation (*http://bit.ly/ 31vzJO0*).

Task: Training a Classifier Using Swift for TensorFlow

We were originally going to write a full task in which we looked at training a model using Swift for TensorFlow (Figure 9-16), however the Swift for TensorFlow project is in such a state of speedy development that we thought we couldn't do it justice; maybe in a year or two, when the project has matured, but not right now.

So, even though we've been using Swift for TensorFlow since it came out, we didn't feel comfortable committing it to paper for a *practical task*. Then, after, much soul searching, we realized that Google and the TensorFlow team were maintaining a *really good* set of resources on using Swift for TensorFlow.

Thus, our recommendation right now for looking into Swift for TensorFlow is that you look at the material they've generated (*http://bit.ly/2MfgNyp*), which uses Colaboratory ("Keras, Pandas, Jupyter, Colaboratory, Docker, Oh My!" on page 52). This podcast (*http://bit.ly/35C3G1U*) is also an excellent starting point to learn about the potential for Swift and Machine Learning.

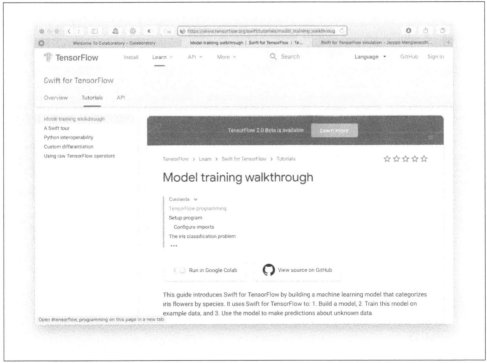

Figure 9-16. Swift for TensorFlow model training

Task: Using the CoreML Community Tools

In this section, we look at using the CoreML Community Tools to convert models generated by other ML and AI tools into a format usable by CoreML.

We introduced the CoreML Community Tools back in Chapter 3, in "CoreML Community Tools" on page 42, so check back there if you want a little more information.

We also used the CoreML Community Tools to convert a model from Keras to CoreML as part of our training, when we built a GAN in "Task: Image Generation with a GAN" on page 324.

The Problem

The problem we explore here involves using a model generated with a different set of AI tools than those natively supported by Apple's CoreML framework.

We've found a really awesome research project, created by an international collaboration of boffins from around the world: From Pixels to Sentiment: Fine-tuning CNNs for Visual Sentiment Prediction (*http://bit.ly/2IURhwr*) uses a specific type of neural network (a convolutional neural network) to attempt to predict the sentiment of an image (or a zone of an image), as shown in Figure 9-17. This is called *visual sentiment classification*.

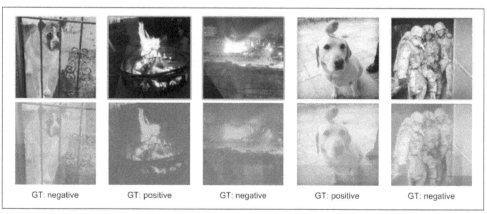

Figure 9-17. Mapping sentiment to images (or areas of images)

The Process

Download the trained model (*http://bit.ly/2pAAk3l*) from the model section of the project page (*http://bit.ly/2oHUQzg*) (it's the first model link, not the second one). Store this file (it's somewhat large) in a safe place. Then, follow these steps:

1. Set up a Python environment, following the process that we outlined earlier in the book, activate the environment, and then use `pip` to install `coremltools`, as shown in Figure 9-18:

```
create -n CoreMLToolsEnvironmentDemo python=3.6

conda activate CoreMLToolsEnvironmentDemo

pip install coremltools
```

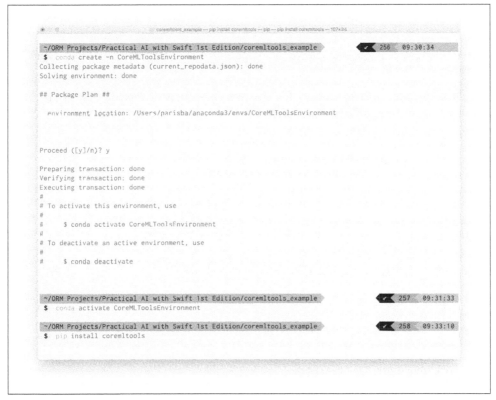

Figure 9-18. Creating our environment

2. Download the file that defines the layers for the original model (*http://bit.ly/35G91W2*) and save it in the same location as the model you downloaded.

3. Create a file called *class_labels.txt*, also in the same location, and then add the following to the first line of it:

```
Negative
```

1. And the following to the second line:

Positive

1. Create a script called *convert_to_coreml.py*, and then add the following import:

    ```
    import coremltools
    ```

2. Add the following line, which actually creates the converter from Caffe:

    ```
    coreml_model = coremltools.converters.caffe.convert(
        (
            'twitter_finetuned_test4_iter_180.caffemodel',
            'sentiment_deploy.prototxt'
        ),
        image_input_names = 'data',
        class_labels='class_labels.txt'
    )
    ```

    This line points to the model file that we downloaded, the file that defines the layers, and the text file with the class labels.

3. Add the following description of outputs:

    ```
    coreml_model.output_description['prob'] = (
        'Probability for a certain sentiment.'
    )
    coreml_model.output_description['classLabel'] = 'Most likely sentiment.'
    ```

4. Add some general metadata (it's only polite):

    ```
    coreml_model.author = (
        'Practical AI with Swift Reader based on work of Image ' +
            'Processing Group'
    )
    coreml_model.license = 'MIT'
    coreml_model.short_description = (
        'Fine-tuning CNNs for Visual Sentiment Prediction'
    )
    coreml_model.input_description['data'] = 'Image'
    ```

5. Save the model:

    ```
    coreml_model.save('VisualSentiment.mlmodel')
    ```

6. Double-check that the necessary files are in the proper places (the model, the file describing the layers, the text file with the classes, and the Python script we just wrote) and then run the Python script:

    ```
    python convert_to_coreml.py
    ```

    You should see something that resembles Figure 9-19.

The model we converted was in the Caffe (*http://caffe.berkeleyvi sion.org*) format. The coremltools project supports a variety of other formats, too. We don't explore using Caffe in this book because it's a C++ and Python project, not Swift. We had to draw the line somewhere.

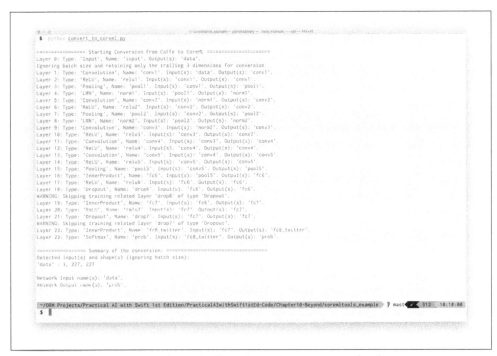

Figure 9-19. The conversion from Caffe to CoreML, using coremltools

You can now look in the folder where you did this work; you should find a brand new *VisualSentiment.mlmodel*, as shown in Figure 9-20. You can use this model just like any other CoreML that we've worked with; coincidentally, this is exactly what we'll be doing next, in "Using the Converted Model" on page 386.

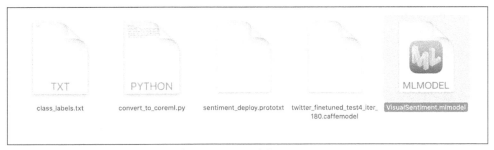

Figure 9-20. The final, converted CoreML model

Using the Converted Model

Back in "Task: Image Classification" on page 120, we built an app that used an image classification model that we trained to attempt to tell us what it saw in the image. We can test out the visual sentiment classification with a minor update to that app (which basically amounts to swapping the model).

We've provided a demo project named VSDemo-Complete, if you want to start with the code. If you'd prefer to do it yourself (which we strongly recommend), follow these steps:

1. Duplicate the Image Classification app that you built in "Task: Image Classification" on page 120.

2. Change the details: make the navigation bars say VSDemo (or similar) and change the button to say Image Sentiment (or similar). Figure 9-21 shows our version.

3. Drag the *VisualSentiment.mlmodel* file into the Xcode project, as usual allowing Xcode to copy.

4. Change the line of code in *ViewController.swift* that sets the model, and point it to the new model:

   ```
   private let classifier =
       VisionClassifier(mlmodel: VisualSentiment().model
   ```

Fire up the app. Check some images for their sentiment. For example, a photo of one of the authors is positive, as is clearly evident in Figure 9-22.

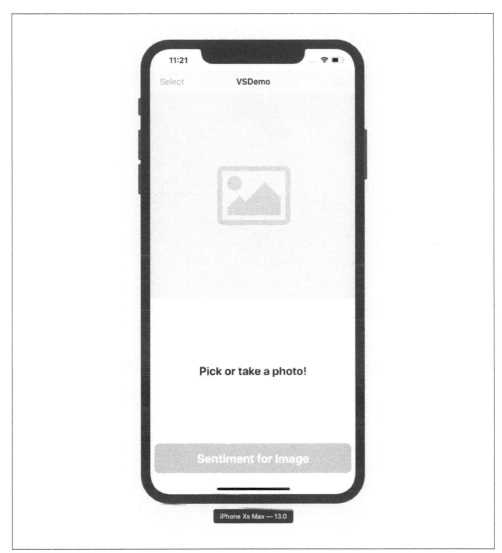

Figure 9-21. Our image sentiment app, ready to go

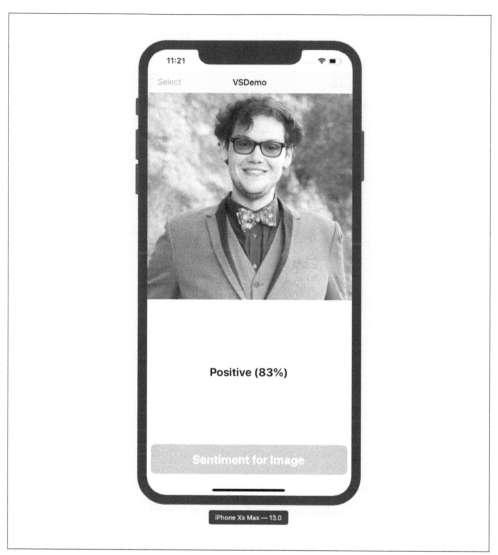

Figure 9-22. The image sentiment classification app working

On-Device Model Updates

At WWDC 2019, Apple announced a new feature for CoreML: the ability to update (i.e., train) models on the device (i.e., the iPhone). This is a really big, really powerful feature. And we're not really going to cover it, not properly.

Why? Because it's incredibly basic right now and supports only very specific types of models, and we don't want to bog you down with something that's likely to be useful in only a very specific, very niche handful of cases.

 TouchID and FaceID use on-device personalization to update their model as you successfully unlock the device with your fingerprint or face.

The key idea behind on-device personalization is that it lets apps start out with a generic model, and then progressively updates it with a user's data, customizing it for that user. This makes it better for that specific user over time. This is quite different from (for example) the approach that Google is best known for: *federated learning*.

Federated learning (*http://bit.ly/33CpFEf*) involves the progressive updating of a single, cloud-based model, based on the data of lots of users instead of one on a local device.

It's also important to point out that Apple's implementation of on-device personalization does not use CreateML (Apple's training framework) for model training on the device. It uses CoreML. CreateML is a macOS-only framework, which is likely one of the reasons why Apple chose to use the CoreML framework to provide the on-device personalization features (it exists on a wider variety of Apple's platforms).

Lots of pundits have reinforced that on-device personalization should not be used for outright training (*http://bit.ly/2OOBnr3*). The hardware is too slow, and you'll be better off providing a pretrained model that also knows how to understand the general kind of data your user will be generating, and then update it accordingly from there. Apple even provides an `MLUpdateProgressHandlers` (*https://apple.co/2BgmLIZ*) class, which lets you run arbitrary code at various points in the on-device personalization training process.

To build a model that can be used for on-device personalization you will need a CoreML mlmodel that's marked as updatable (*http://bit.ly/2MjSTSt*), has training inputs, and you'll need to provide examples and truth-targets for the training. The specific layers of the model that you want to be able to train on should also be marked as updatable (it's likely that this will be only the *last* layer in your network).

You'll also need a loss-function, an optimizer, and some hyperparameters. But we're getting out of the *practical* territory here.

Apple's CoreML Tools supports a `respect_trainable` argument that lets you make a converted model updatable, so this technique isn't solely restricted to models you build with CreateML (or Turi Create).

Apple has some great examples of updatable models in its CoreML Community Tools documentation (*http://bit.ly/2MjSTSt*).

As of this writing, CoreML on-device personalization supports only neural networks (general ones, classifiers, and regressors) and *K*-nearest neighbor classifiers. Likewise, only convolutional and fully connected layers are supported.

You can learn more about on-device personalization in Apple's documentation (*https://apple.co/32khoV9*). The specific part of CoreML that you're looking for is `MLUpdateTask`.

A great place to get started with this is Apple's WWDC 2019 session on CoreML 3 (*https://apple.co/2OSMC1J*).

Monitor our website (*https://aiwithswift.com*) for articles on doing this; we'll be sure to post when it's essential and *practical* to use this feature of CoreML.Apple has also published an excellent Updateable Drawing Classifier model on their model website (*https://apple.co/33oLF5p*). This, together with Apple's documentation on on-device updates (*https://apple.co/2VP7YhU*), is a good starting point.

Task: Downloading Models On-device

This isn't much of a task, but it can be very useful. For every task we've looked at so far, we've just made the CoreML model part of the app that ships. This doesn't need to be the case.

CoreML fully supports downloading and compiling models on the device. To do this, perform:

1. Download your *.mlmodel* file to the device, using whatever means you like (URL Session is a good starting point).

2. Call `compileModel()` to compile the model (in this example the model is already on the device, and stored at `modelLocalUrl`):

```
let compiledUrl = try MLModel.compileModel(at: modelLocalUrl)
let model = try MLModel(contentsOf: compiledUrl)
```

3. You'll need to use `FileManager` to move the compiled model into your app's support directory, because the compilation will take place in a temporary location.

You can learn more about `compileModel(at:)` in Apple's documentation (*https://apple.co/33Jgwd9*).

Next Steps

In this chapter, we covered *some* of the useful things that you might want to know when going beyond using aAI with Swift to build *features* (i.e., our task-based approach). It's just a taste, though, because there's so much more you could do. Nonetheless, we hope it's been useful.

We looked at six different things, exploring how you can take Swift (and a little bit of Python) further for AI:

- Installing Swift for TensorFlow:: Getting up and running with the latest version of Swift for TensorFlow.
- Using Python with Swift:: A look at using the popular, essential, ubiquitous Python with Swift (via Swift for TensorFlow).
- Training a classifier using Swift for TensorFlow:: Building an image classifier using Swift for TensorFlow.
- Using the CoreML Community Tools:: Using Apple's Python framework, CoreML Community Tools, to manipulate and convert models from other formats.
- On-device model updates:: Using on-device personalization to make changes to CoreML models on a device.
- Downloading models on device:: Downloading a CoreML model from a server and compiling it on a device.

In Part III, we look at some of the things that are happening under the hood, at a very low level, at an implementation level, and at a "do it yourself" level.

## PART III

Beyond

## CHAPTER 10

AI and ML Methods

In Part I and Part II we focused on the very *practical* and largely *task-focused* side of artificial intelligence. The other side of AI is theory, and the processes involved in making machine learning actually work. Thus, now that we have covered the *how* to implement a collection of AI and machine-learning features, this chapter will briefly discuss some of the many underlying methods that are used to give a system the appearance of intelligence.

Be aware there is no need to memorize the mathematics sometimes featured in this chapter; this is a *practical* book, as promised on the cover. A deep understanding of data science or statistics is not necessary, and skipping this chapter entirely would not make you any less equipped to follow the steps in later chapters to make an application with functional AI features. But to follow our mantra of effective, ethical, and appropriate use of AI, having an understanding of these basic principles is crucial.

Scary-looking algorithms are worked around with visual examples and metaphors that communicate the fundamental principles with small working examples. These demonstrate at a low level how each method goes about making decisions.

When applying this knowledge in future projects, having a broad understanding of how different methods work and what kinds of data they are most and least compatible with can allow better decisions to be made. Decisions that can be made in the design phase—when the cost of changes is lowest—will benefit a system throughout its lifetime.

Knowing the kinds of errors and behaviors different methods are prone to can also help prevent unseen biases. So although you will most likely ever employ only one or two of the methods detailed in this chapter anyway, this will allow you to better use the methods that you *do* choose.

Following this chapter are two more in-depth chapters: one looking at the inner workings of the specific approaches taken throughout this book (Chapter 11) and one on building a neural net entirely from scratch in code (Chapter 12).

Terminology

A few common terms appear in descriptions throughout this chapter; for example.

AI/ML Components

- *Observations* refer to a set of past data collected that future knowledge will be derived or assumed. An observation is a single entry in this past data, say a line in a table.
- *Input* refers to the single entry that is yet to be processed—sorted, placed, or classified. This is the thing for which you are trying to get new knowledge.
- *Attributes* are the things known about each entry, both observation and input.
- *Outcome* or *class* are used interchangeably to refer to the thing *you want to know* about each entry, present in the observations but still required for the input. This is often one of a set of prechosen options.

So, given a set of observations, you can process input with the same attributes to get its assumed class. For example, given a set of cat and dog pictures, I processed a new image, extracted its features and color composition, and found the computer thought it was a dog.

This is what happened when we built an image classifier in "Task: Image Classification" on page 120.

AI/ML Objectives

Next, let's discuss three simple terms used to describe some *purposes* for machine learning. Basically, these are the types of questions you can answer using different methods:

Descriptive
Asking "what does my data say has happened in the past?" This is the aim of methods such as clustering that *describe and summarize* your data, often with the explicit purpose of *identifying significant or anomalous observations*.

Predictive
Asking "based on what has happened in the past, what will happen now?" This is the aim of methods such as classification or regression, which seek to apply more

information to some input based on the information associated with past observations.

Prescriptive

Asking "based on what has happened in the past, what should I do now?" This often builds upon predictive systems, with the addition of contextual knowledge that dictates appropriate response to predicted outcome.

Types of Values

Moving on to different kinds of values that you would encounter when discussing the strengths and applications of different algorithms, let's begin with *numerical* versus *categorical* values. This is a pretty intuitive distinction: numerical is number, categorical is category. If you are crunching an online store with a database full of movies, the price of each movie would be numerical, whereas the genre of each would be categorical.

A third type of value common in observations is *unique identifiers*, but these are not discussed here, because they should be omitted during analysis.

These numerical and categorical value types can then be broken down further: each has two subtypes that should be regarded differently in many cases. Numerical values can be *discrete* or *continuous*. The difference is that if there is a set number of values something can be, it is discrete. If not, it is continuous. For example, a set of all whole numbers between 0 and 100 would be discrete, whereas a set of every decimal between 0 and 1 would be continuous, because it is theoretically infinite.

This becomes a bit more complicated when you consider that mathematics defines sets such as natural numbers—which contain all positive integers—as *discrete*. This is because even though they theoretically go on forever, you can take two numbers from within it and count all numbers that go between them. In the case of real numbers—effectively any number of any length and decimal that occurs at any point along the number scale—you can fit an infinite amount of other real numbers between any two you pick.

For the purposes of machine learning, different methods will work better depending on whether, after defining an upper and lower bound, all the values between them can be counted or not.

Categorical values can be either *ordinal* or *nominal*, where ordinal refers to values that have some order or relations between them that would imply connections between some are closer than others. For example, if you're doing some analysis or prediction based on data from several locations to predict something in one place, places near to it should be considered heavily while places far away should only be considered if very similar in demographic. This creates a concept of weighting or order among these values, even though they are not numbers, that would be beneficial for your analysis to be aware of. Though locations often cannot be simply swapped out for numbers because it would be difficult to map relations that occur in three-dimensional space, the underlying system will often replace many other types of ordinal values with representative numbers for ease of calculation during analysis.

Nominal is the opposite; each value is equally different to all others. For example, in the set of primary colors each is equally and immeasurably different from the other. Another popular example of nominal values is binary categories, such as true/false. These are incompatible with methods that rely on a measure of similarity or proximity between values, as many do.

Some values are not so easy to intuit. For example, postcodes or zip codes should be treated as Categorical>Nominal values, because although they are represented as *numbers* and have *some vague order*, their proximity to each other in the scale of numbers is not always true in the real world.

Take, for example, Australian capital cities: you would not want to train a system to think that the distance between, say, Adelaide (postcode 5000) is closer to Brisbane (4000) than it is to Hobart (7000), which is almost 600 km closer. Depending on what you are using the input data for, it might be more useful to replace postcode entries with new state and suburb columns, or abstract ranges for each state that correspond to inner city, suburban, and rural areas.

Because some states are adjacent and traveling from rural areas to a city almost always passes through the suburbs, these would then have become theoretically ordinal values if done correctly.

Knowing how to classify your input values in this way—and recognizing where another type of value would serve you better—is a key part of method and data selection that will allow the creation of more robust and useful machine-learning models.

Classification

Classification is the application most commonly associated with machine learning in the eyes of the broader public, particularly in the case of one of the most widely used methods: *neural networks*.

Many of those around us who are aware of technological trends but not particularly technical themselves even believe that neural networks are how all machine learning works, that this is the only method you can use. It's not. This one just has a catchy name that people can use cool stock art of brains with and claim that "no one knows how it works" because it's the most difficult of which to expose the internal processes.

We built things that did classification in "Task: Image Classification" on page 120, "Task: Drawing Recognition" on page 142, "Task: Style Classification" on page 165, "Task: Sound Classification" on page 184, "Task: Language Identification" on page 214, "Task: Sentiment Analysis" on page 225, "Task: Custom Text Classifiers" on page 241, "Task: Gestural Classification for Drawing" on page 262, and "Task: Activity Classification" on page 277.

There are many other methods of classification, many of which are simple enough to demonstrate on paper. They are used to drive many systems, such as recognizers made to interpret voice input, label images, or video content; recommendation systems present in online stores, social media, streaming platforms and more; as well as a number of decision-making components that allow large and complex systems to work more efficiently. There are so many clever and varied applications, the list could go on forever—basically think of everything that could benefit from responding dynamically based on experience.

Methods

Let's look at a handful of approaches to classification and compare.

Naive Bayes

Naive Bayes is a good place to start because it's simple; it's very similar to the first kind of probability you learn in school: (specific outcome / all possible outcomes).

Naive Bayes is the method of taking some input I and some set of classes $\{C1, C2, \ldots, Cn\}$ and guessing the class that I should be based on a set of previously-classified instances. This is done by using Bayes' Theorem (*http://bit.ly/35FiHjL*) to calculate the relative probability P of it being each class from the set of options (Figure 10-1).

$$P(C\,|\,I) = \frac{P(I\,|\,C)\ P(C)}{P(I)}$$

Figure 10-1. Bayes' Theorem

For example, suppose that you have a table of different types of food you have eaten lately. A friend has proposed you go out for Thai food again tonight, but you might disagree if you don't think you're going to like it. So you employ the Naive Bayes method to classify the *likely outcome* of their Thai food experience from the options { , } (Figure 10-2).

Figure 10-2. Input to use with Bayes' Theorem

First you use Bayes' Theorem to work out the relative probability of Thai being 👍 (Figure 10-3).

$$P(\text{👍} \mid Thai) = \frac{P(Thai \mid \text{👍}) * P(\text{👍})}{P(Thai)}$$

Figure 10-3. Calculation for positive rating

This is calculated by ((how many past 👍s have been *Thai*) * (how many past entries have been 👍)) / (how many past entries have been *Thai*) (Figure 10-4).

$$P(\text{👍} \mid Thai) = \frac{3/5 * 5/8}{4/8} = 0.75$$

Figure 10-4. Probability of positive rating

Then, you work out the relative probability of Thai being 👎, in the same way (Figure 10-5, Figure 10-6).

$$P(\text{👎} \mid Thai) = \frac{P(Thai \mid \text{👎}) * P(\text{👎})}{P(Thai)}$$

Figure 10-5. Calculation for negative rating

$$P(\text{👎} \mid Thai) = \frac{1/3 * 3/8}{4/8} = 0.25$$

Figure 10-6. Probability of negative rating

Now it's simple. The most *probable* is whichever one has a greater relative probability. In this case it is 👍, so you can fill that in and say you're probably happy with your friend's choice of food (Figure 10-7).

Thai   👍

Figure 10-7. Outcome of Bayesian calculation

But if you look at the input again, you probably could have just asked which outcome most commonly corresponded with the given input (Thai) in the past data. You would have gotten the same answer from many people, just from visual inspection. It is a very straightforward assumption: the outcome that has most often corresponded with this input in the past will be the outcome in this case.

The only reason this is called "artificial intelligence" is because it's a method often employed with complex parametric input that would be unfeasible for a human to do on paper over and over again for each input. So this AI is really just automated math, and as you'll soon see even the most mysterious and complex machine intelligence always is.

With most classification approaches being this type of *probabilistic classification*, it's handy to make educated guesses. But this understandably falls apart for cases in which outside context changes or there are too many input or output options to get a significant measure. They cannot distinguish between valid observations and anomalies in past data, and will perpetuate each with equal consideration.

This is unlike an approach such as a neural network that will amplify differences in input distribution, minimizing this effect. Probabilistic classification methods also suffer significantly with continuous values in their input or output, such as in cases in which you are trying to classify things with numbers out of a large set of possibilities.

In these cases, a related approach to classification is needed: regression.

Decision trees

Decision trees are like those flow-chart quizzes you sometimes see in magazines, that proclaim to answer questions like *What type of X are you?* and *Should you X?* They make sweeping generalizations that incrementally partition the population.

This might seem logically unsound, but it's just a rephrasing of that discussed previously: the generalizations made in machine-automated classifications are that what is yet to occur will reflect what has most often occurred before under similar circumstances.

So, suppose that you had some data. In this case, we'll need a little more than before because this method is good at reducing the complexity of its input. Figure 10-8 represents some data that you might use to predict whether someone is going to have a good day at work, using past observations of good and bad days. Relevant data was chosen to record what the weather was like and whether the person's friends were at work each day (Figure 10-8).

Outlook	Temp	Humidity	Friends	Mood
☀️	35	85	👍	😠
⛅	30	90	👎	🙂
☁️	33	86	👍	😠
🌧️	20	96	👎	😠
🌧️	18	80	👎	😠
🌧️	15	70	👍	🙂
☁️	14	65	👎	😠
🌦️	22	95	👍	🙂
☀️	19	70	👍	😠
🌧️	25	80	👎	😠
☀️	25	70	👎	😠
☁️	22	90	👎	😠
☁️	31	75	👍	😠
🌧️	21	91	👍	🙂
☁️	30	80	👍	?

Figure 10-8. Input to use with decision-tree algorithm

How the decision tree method works is that an algorithm will assess the input data and identify relationships where certain attribute values are linked to certain outcomes. The attribute *most closely linked to* the outcome is the one for which its different values most often correspond with different outcome values. If in the given data every single time friends were present (👍) the person had a good day (☺) and the inverse were also true (👎 were always 😠), then that would be the only attribute you needed. The tree would look like Figure 10-9.

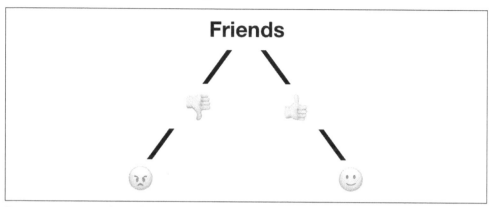

Figure 10-9. Hypothetical decision-tree representation

It's basically the visual representation of a rule-based approach that could be simply defined in code:

```
if friends == " 👍 {
        return " ☺ "
}

if friends == " 👎 " {
        return " 😠 "
}
```

But because it's not always so easy to see the presence and absence of links between certain attribute values and different outcomes, some math is required. There are a few different methods used to rate the relative level of determination each attribute has (Figure 10-10).

Impurity Measure	Information Gain/Entropy Measure
$$i(t) = 1 - \sum_{j=1}^{k} p^2(j\,|\,t)$$	$$E = -\sum p(x)\log p(x)$$

Figure 10-10. Some equations no one should be expected to memorize

One will select the attribute to partition the output by at each point based on the relative purity of the groups that would produce, and the other will select based on the amount of new information that is gained by grouping this way.

A simpler explanation of this is that each node has a poor opinion of its fellows.

"But what if the next node is a fool?"

– Every node in your tree

So this method acts with no foresight, it makes no immediate sacrifices for overall efficiency, it has no big picture—it just gives each attribute column a rating of how closely it is linked to the outcome, picks the highest, and repeats.

So with our whole input, it will first assess all cases. It will find the most determining factor to be outlook, as splitting on this attribute will result in three partitions and one will be entirely *pure*: ☀ will be mixed, ☁ will be mixed, but ☁ directly corresponds to a single outcome (Figure 10-11).

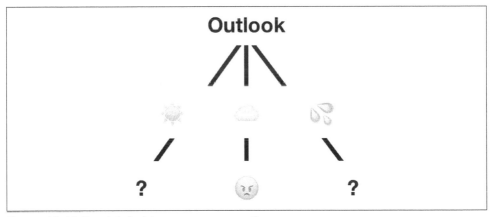

Figure 10-11. Partial decision tree representation

Now, for the righthand tree—now consisting only of entries in which outlook is ☁—will do the same. It will find a split that is not perfect but is the best it's got: the presence of friends.

The lefthand tree, however, requires some more work. Its most significant determinant is humidity, but you cannot account for every possible value of a numerical attribute. In fact, at each of the points discussed previously an extra step would have been done when assessing the relevance of humidity: *variance reduction*. This is the means by which a value that was once a wide range of values is sorted into ranges or *buckets* that discretize them for use as the categorical values some methods require.

This involves the very threatening-looking equation shown in Figure 10-12.

$$I_v(N) = \frac{1}{|S|^2} \sum_{i \in S} \sum_{j \in S} \frac{1}{2}(x_i - x_j)^2 - \left(\frac{1}{|S_t|^2} \sum_{i \in S_t} \sum_{j \in S_t} \frac{1}{2}(x_i - x_j)^2 + \frac{1}{|S_f|^2} \sum_{i \in S_f} \sum_{j \in S_f} \frac{1}{2}(x_i - x_j)^2 \right)$$

Figure 10-12. Another equation that no one should be expected to memorize

But it describes a relatively simple question you are asking of your data: "where along this continuous scale of values can I make partitions that will result in the purest outcome groups?" And you might recognize this as pretty much the question this decision tree method is asking all along. It is simpler in this case because there are only two outcomes, so you need only one split. You would select 85, as shown in Figure 10-13, because it results in pure outcome groups following the split at this value.

Outlook	Temp	Humidity	Friends	Mood
	19	70		
	25	70		
	35	85		
	30	90		
	22	95		

		Humidity		
2	0	**70**	1	2
3	0	**85**	0	2
3	1	**90**	0	1
3	2	**95**	0	0
<= Humidity				> Humidity

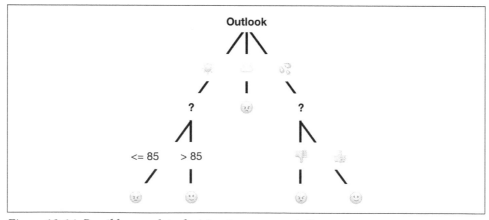

Figure 10-13. A visual way to identify the ideal partition point(s)

This method will then determine that the temperature has no significant impact on the outcome, producing a final tree something like Figure 10-14.

Figure 10-14. Possible complete decision tree representation

This is sufficient to be correct for the 14 prior observations, and classification of our mystery 15th is done by following the lines. In this case, the result would be ☠ due to the ☁ outlook.

Good enough? Sure. Or so says the decision-tree method. This is great for simple visualizations, explainable classification models, and quick generalizations of otherwise complex data. It's not great for anything you care much about, because it is susceptible to underfit and overfit and deems any majority as sufficient. Whereas other methods have mechanisms to recognize that something being the case even 51% of the time is not significant *enough* to predict this will always be the case, this does not.

There is also no way to affect where the tree decides to split—short of some major and targeted restructuring of input data. Where choices appear equal they will be chosen at random because decision trees see all attributes as equally relevant and related/unrelated. This is often not sufficient to model the full complexities and interrelations among attributes that are present in real-world problems.

Random Forest is a name given to a method used to reduce inaccuracies in decision trees introduced by random selection of branching points where there were options of equal validity. Instead of making just one tree, they will use the same past data to make many, each using different seeds or weights to mix up the random selection made at any points of equality. Then, they will classify the same input with each tree and take the most common outcome—or sometimes the average of the outcomes—depending on its purpose.

Distance metrics

Here, let's take a moment to discuss a concept required for some of the classification methods to follow: distance metrics. Because so many methods of machine learning rely on taking a set of input attributes—basically one row of a table, missing its class or outcome entry—and transforming it into a point that can be compared in some *n*-dimensional space, we require a way to measure the *distance* between points that might not be able to be visually represented or conceptualized.

These metrics are a point of much contention between experts regarding which is most effective or correct under different circumstances, so we will just discuss some very common ones. Know that there are many more, both derivative of these and entirely different.

First, we have a method used to compare inputs with *nominal* inputs. Because their possible values have equal similarity and dissimilarity, comparisons are made on whole sets of values at once to produce a rating of their similarity.

The most common one by most metrics, and likely the most straightforward, is *Jaccard distance*. This takes two inputs and calculates the "distance" between them as a score of overlap divided by difference (Figure 10-15).

$$d(P, Q) = 1 - \frac{|P \cap Q|}{|P \cup Q|}$$

Figure 10-15. The equation for Jaccard distance

Let's imagine that we're looking at two data entries: say, two people, each with a specified value for their gender, education level, and country of origin (Figure 10-16).

$$P = \{ 👩 , 🎓 , 🇦🇺 \}$$

$$Q = \{ 🧔 , 🎓 , 🇺🇸 \}$$

Figure 10-16. Input to use with Jaccard distance metric

You can then out the *set representation* (basically don't list duplicates) of what they have in common and what they have between them overall (Figure 10-17).

$$P \cap Q = \{ 🎓 \}$$

$$P \cup Q = \{ 👩 , 🧔 , 🎓 , 🇦🇺 , 🇺🇸 \}$$

Figure 10-17. Subsets of those inputs that are similar between the two original sets and their total combination

This is then a simple division of similarity, subtracted from one to get the inverse or dissimilarity (Figure 10-18).

$$|P \cap Q| = 1 \qquad 1 - \frac{1}{5} = 0.8$$
$$|P \cup Q| = 5$$

Figure 10-18. Subset sizes put into the original equation to calculate distance

Second, we have methods used to compare inputs that are either numerical or ordinal in some way.

One possible metric for this is *Euclidean distance*. (Figure 10-19).

$$d(P, Q) = \sqrt{(Q_1 - P_1)^2 + (Q_2 - P_2)^2 + \ldots + (Q_n - P_n)^2}$$

Figure 10-19. The equation for Euclidean distance

The Euclidean distance between two sets of values is equal to the square root of the squared distance between first value in each set, plus the squared distance between the second value in each set, plus the squared distance between the third value in each set, and so on. The distance between two single values is usually just the numerical difference, or degrees of separation for ordinal values that can have their proximities mapped or be assigned corresponding indices.

Represented in only two dimensions for simplicity, this forms something like what you see in Figure 10-20.

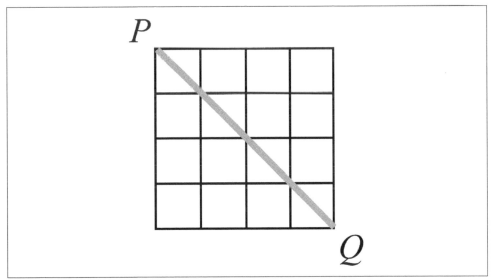

Figure 10-20. Euclidean distance represented on a two-dimensional plane

Another possibility is *Manhattan distance* (Figure 10-21).

$$d(P, Q) = |Q_1 - P_1| + |Q_2 - P_2| + \ldots + |Q_n - P_n|$$

Figure 10-21. The equation for Manhattan distance

The Manhattan distance between two sets of values is equal to the distance between the first value in each set, plus the distance between the second value in each set, plus the distance between the third value in each set, and so on. The distance between two single values is still just the numerical difference or degrees of separation.

This forms something like that shown in Figure 10-22.

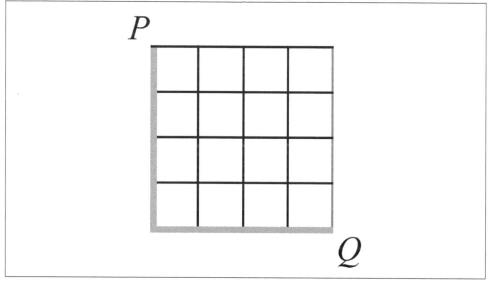

Figure 10-22. Manhattan distance represented on a two-dimensional plane

Let's use a well-used example in data science: flower measurements. You have some flowers that for some hypothetical further AI purpose, you first want to know which pair are the most similar or *closest* to one another among them (Figure 10-23).

Flower	Stem height (avg.)	Petal length (avg.)	Petal width (avg.)
	15cm	5cm	2cm
	20cm	4cm	2cm
	18cm	6cm	3cm

Figure 10-23. Input to use with various distance metrics

You can *normalize* the values, so that they have an equal range to compare. This is done by changing the upper and lower bounds of possible values to 1 and 0, respectively, leaving all values in between them (Figure 10-24).

Flower	Stem height (avg.)	Petal length (avg.)	Petal width (avg.)
	0	0.5	0
	1	0	0
	0.6	1	1

Figure 10-24. Input after value normalization

Now, you can use our two distance metrics from before for numerical values. First, you get pairs of values for each pair of flowers (Figure 10-25).

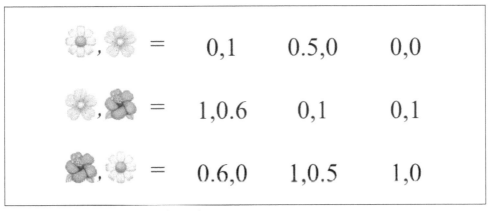

Figure 10-25. Combined attributes between input pairs

Then, you can try with our Euclidean distance, using the square root of the squared difference between each pair of values (Figure 10-26).

$d($, $)$ =	$(0 - 1)^2 + (0.5 - 0)^2 + (0 - 0)^2$		$= 1 + 0.25 + 0$		$= 1.25$
$d($, $)$ =	$(1 - 0.6)^2 + (0 - 1)^2 + (0 - 1)^2$		$= 0.16 + 1 + 1$		$= 2.16$
$d($, $)$ =	$(0.6 - 0)^2 + (1 - 0.5)^2 + (1 - 0)^2$		$= 0.36 + 0.25 + 1$		$= 1.61$

Figure 10-26. Distances using the Euclidean distance measurement

And you can try with our Manhattan distance, using the absolute value (ignore any negatives) of the difference between each pair of values (Figure 10-27).

$$d(\text{🌼}, \text{🌸}) = |0 - 1| + |0.5 - 0| + |0 - 0| \qquad = 1 + 0.5 + 0 \qquad = 1.5$$

$$d(\text{🌼}, \text{💮}) = |1 - 0.6| + |0 - 1| + |0 - 1| \qquad = 0.4 + 1 + 1 \qquad = 2.4$$

$$d(\text{💮}, \text{🌼}) = |0.6 - 0| + |1 - 0.5| + |1 - 0| \qquad = 0.6 + 0.5 + 1 \qquad = 2.1$$

Figure 10-27. Distances using the Manhattan distance measurement

At this point, you might see that Euclidean distance smooths differences, whereas Manhattan distance is good for enhancing differences. These are suited and used for different purposes with different accompanying algorithms and machine-learning methods (Figure 10-28).

Figure 10-28. Comparison between calculated distances

Either way, our most similar flowers are the yellow one and the pink one. Simple.

Using the types of calculations covered in this section, you can now calculate the distances between abstract sets of multiple, possibly even nonnumeric, values.

Nearest neighbor

Nearest neighbor (or *K*-nearest neighbor [KNN]) is a method that uses a theory similar to the old saying "show me who your friends are and I'll tell you who you are." Its core assumption is that the class that applies to new input will be the class that most applied to past instances with the most similar attributes. This is really just a reframing of the probabilistic approach covered earlier.

It works like so: let's plot some observations visually—this requires something with very few attributes. Given the example in Figure 10-29, in which some workers' annual incomes and average hours worked per week are represented, and the colors/shapes correspond to something like whether or not they have joined the worker's union. The company just hired a new employee, marked by a question mark, and the workers want to know whether the new employee is likely to join.

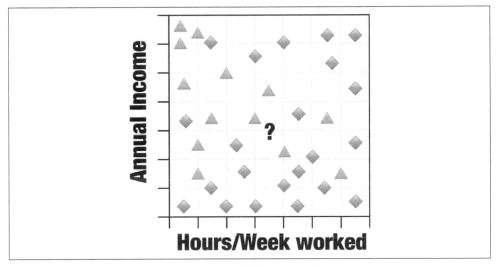

Figure 10-29. Input to use with nearest neighbor algorithm

So, you can say the new employee's behavior is likely to correspond to the current employee with the most similar circumstances. If the red triangles are not joined and the blue triangles are joined, and their nearest neighbor is a red triangle—the same distance measured like those discussed earlier—you can say they're likely to be the same (Figure 10-30).

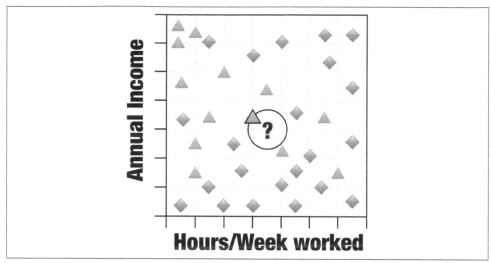

Figure 10-30. Nearest one neighbor by distance

However, this method of just using a single neighbor would be incredibly prone to outliers. So, what do we do when faced with outliers in data science? We average!

In this method, you take more than one neighbor and use the most common class found. The number of neighbors you select, K, is effectively random and can result in vastly different classifications, as shown in Figure 10-31.

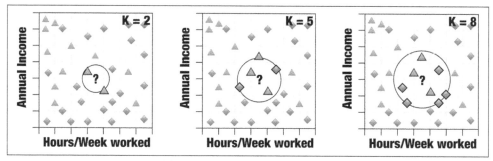

Figure 10-31. Nearest K neighbors with various values for K

This use of an *effectively* random value is termed *bootstrapping* in data science, likely due to experts not wanting to say that a method requires you to select something at random because they're equally likely to work or not.

This selection can be made less error prone in a few ways. Though there are arguments that the best K is an odd number around the square root of the total number of points in your past data, there are other methods that employ what is effectively trial and error. But, no matter what you do, it should be known: accuracy of both nearest neighbor and a method for selecting K will vary wildly when applied to different datasets, and with complex input it is often difficult to see when it has gone wrong.

Note that this method can also be used to classify between a set of more than two class options, but will very likely become much less accurate as the number of options grows. This is termed *the curse of dimensionality*.

Support vector machine

Similar to nearest neighbor, *support vector machine* (SVM) is an approach that uses theoretical placement of each observation in an n-dimensional plane, where n is the number of attributes.

It combines this with a method similar to the variance reduction discussed in decision trees: finding a partition point within the data that will result in groups of the highest purity.

This method is great for partitioning data because it focuses only on observations at the edge of their classification groups—the points most difficult to reliably classify.

In practice, it's drawing a line where one group ends and another one begins. This is done by taking the observation points that are nearest to points with different classifications to themselves. These are called the support vectors, giving the method its name (Figure 10-32).

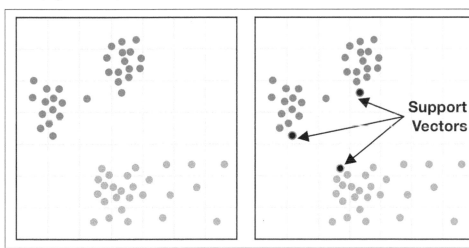

Figure 10-32. Identifying the support vector points

A line is then drawn to bisect the observations. This line is called a *hyperplane*, as though these visual examples have only two attributes/dimensions and the hyperplane need only be a line. In fact, it is a conceptual division that bisects each dimension at a point in space no matter how many dimensions there are.

In three-dimensional observations, the hyperplane would be a bisecting sheet; in higher dimensions, it would be impossible to visualize, though the principle is the same.

The space in which the hyperplane can be positioned can be broad, encompassing all the space between the support vectors where a line could separate only them (Figure 10-33).

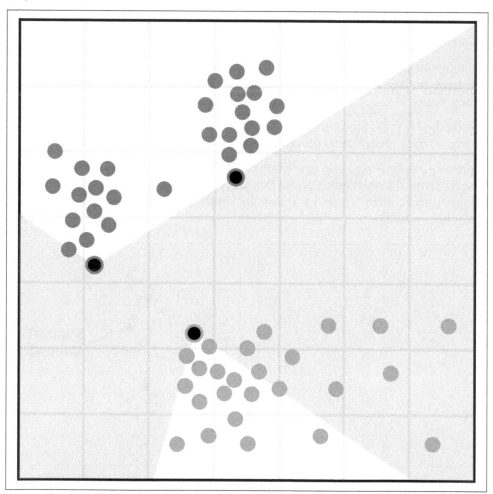

Figure 10-33. Possible region of hyperplane intersection

However, from the theoretically infinite options within this space, the hyperplane is positioned with the goal to maximize the width of the margin between itself and its nearest points on either side. It is then centered between these margins.

This involves some math, but basically looks like Figure 10-34.

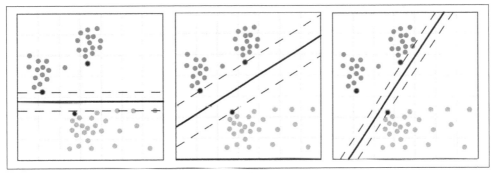

Figure 10-34. Comparing margins of hyperplane intersection points

Classifying a new observation then becomes a process of plotting it and seeing which side of the hyperplane it falls on (Figure 10-35).

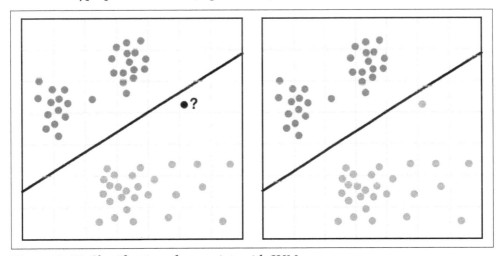

Figure 10-35. Classification of new points with SVM

However, due to the constraints of the method, SVM can be used only to reliably predict for binary classes: true/false, yes/no, postitive/negative, valid/invalid, approve/disapprove, and so on. Although it is quite good at this, this hard restriction makes it much less used in the field where constraints or available classifications might need to change and grow.

This method also has a variant used for data with more complex distributions—making them not easily separable by class—by adding a dimension to the plot and performing a nonlinear separation, but this involves some more difficult math that we don't cover here.

Linear regression

Linear regression differs when compared to other classification methods in that it avoids many of the difficulties others have with continuous data—as you might remember, there were times in previous examples in which we had to generalize or discretize a range of values to be able to use them.

It works as if a form of classification could be open ended: could classify input with outcomes it had never seen before that it had inferred *must exist* due to the previous outcomes it has seen.

Our favorite example is that regression is like those pictograph quizzes you sometimes see on Facebook (Figure 10-36).

= $10

+ = $20

+ + = ???

Figure 10-36. A stimulating burrito quiz

A classification algorithm that had never seen three burritos before would just decide it was closest to two burritos so it must be $20 just the same. A regression algorithm pays more attention to the difference *between* observations and can abstract forward as a human would: in the past, adding a burrito made the price go up $10, so adding another burrito here would make the outcome $30.

 We looked at how easy it was to *practically* implement regression using Apple's CreateML framework in "Task: Regressor Prediction" on page 357.

Linear regression methods are often represented as a line chart, as featured in many a stereotypical representation of a projections-based board meeting discussion (Figure 10-37).

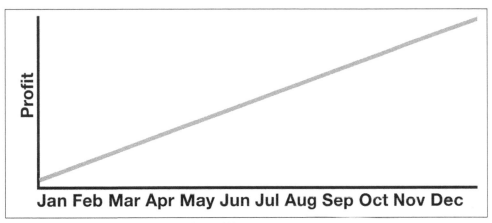

Figure 10-37. This line means profits will be up!

But these would have been formed from a large number of past observation points, making a "fit" line that can be used to predict events yet to come. Something like that in Figure 10-38 could have been used to project the previous graph's profits for December, an approach given relative confidence, especially in the world of high finance.

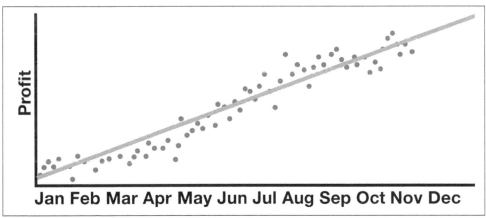

Figure 10-38. A possible truth to justify the assumption

The prediction for a specific new set of variables then requires only to find the corresponding point on the line (Figure 10-39).

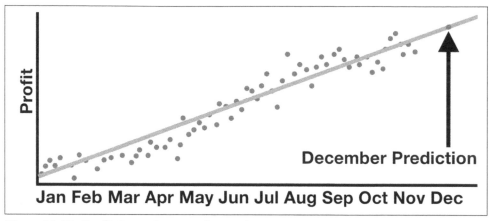

Figure 10-39. Prediction using past observation

The actual *method* to linear regression is how you place the line.

Simple linear and *polynomial linear* approaches are common, sometimes just called linear and polynomial regression, respectively.

Where linear regression produces a straight line, polynomial regression can vary in degree. This basically defines the elasticity of the curve: higher-order polynomials will eventually result in overfit, whereas lower-order will usually result in an underfit similar to a linear approach.

What you're looking for is something in the middle that generalizes a little bit, but still appropriately summarizes the distribution tendencies in your data (Figure 10-40).

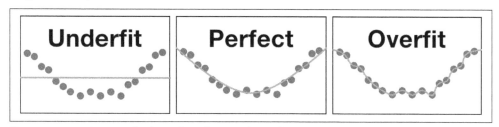

Figure 10-40. Our method needs to be just the right amount of wibbly-wobbly

The way this line is placed is an algorithm core to graph theory: in $y = wx + b$ where y is a point on the y-axis and x is a point on the x-axis, which w weight and b bias values will make for the lowest combined inaccuracy for all x and y values featured.

To un-math that, the weight is basically the angle and the bias is an offset from zero. So the question becomes "at what height and angle does a line most represent all of these points?"

Linear regression is a sound approach to many problems, but like methods discussed in the previous sections in this chapter, it is susceptible to errors due to outliers or unsuitable datasets. The English statistician Francis Anscombe constructed four datasets—thereafter called Anscombe's quartet (*http://bit.ly/2ORx0eQ*)—that best demonstrate the pitfalls of these methods. The four sets shown in Figure 10-41 have identical summary statistics, including their simple linear regression line, but when visualized it becomes clear that they vary dramatically.

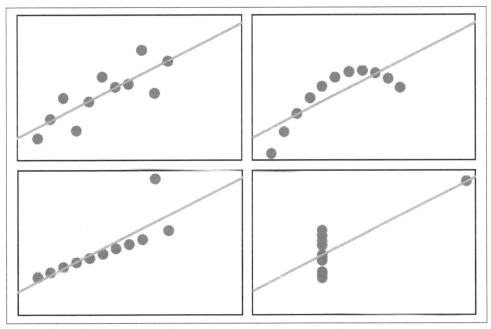

Figure 10-41. Less-than-useful generalizations from mal-applied regression

Logistic regression

Logistic regression combines the linear regression approach with a sigmoid function to produce an S-shaped line. Figure 10-42 shows the differing performance between simple and logistic for an identical dataset.

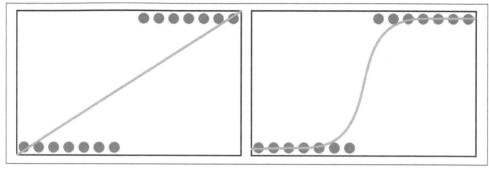

Figure 10-42. Comparison of simple linear regression

However, this approach is more often used to partition data while generalizing. Constraints of this approach require discrete variables, but produce output similar to the support vector machine method discussed in "Classification" on page 398.

With the given dataset, you might decide that the difference in behavior of the top and bottom groups should rightfully have them be treated as different classes. The same curve can then be used to indicate the midpoint where a new line can be drawn that will separate these classes (Figure 10-43).

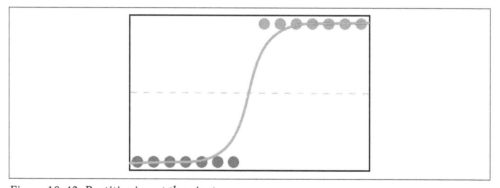

Figure 10-43. Partitioning at the pivot

Neural network

Finally, we get to the method at the center of the machine-learning hype: the artificial neural network. We mentioned this earlier, way back in Part I; here, we're going to unpack *how* it works a little more.

This approach gets its catchy name due to an underlying structure that has been compared to the human brain, a web of interconnected nodes—called *neurons*--which fire in different sequences to cause different output.

Despite often being compared to a human brain, a neural network really doesn't have that much in similarity outside of the basic idea of interlinked neurons.

As fun as that sounds, at its core it is similar to a method like the decision tree. Input is led down different paths based on attributes that determine direction at points of divergence until a classification endpoint is reached.

A neural network is the *thing* that's at the core of most of the models we built earlier in the book.

The difference in the case of a neural network is that the tree structure that is formed during model training is obscured. The abstract representation of its internal details that determine the classifications it produces are, for the most part, regarded as impossible to present in a human-comprehensible form, and thus neural networks are blindly trusted as long as they appear to be producing accurate output.

Needless to say, problems arise. As those working in statistics quickly become aware, correlation does not always imply causation. A neural network during training will automatically identify features unique to each label, and will look for those in future input to determine the label to apply. It has no conceptual understanding or capacity to judge what are relevant unique features.

For example, if trained on a set of images in which half were cats and half were dogs, but the background of all cat pictures were light and the background of all dog pictures were dark, the pattern evaluation would likely make it quite accurate at classifying its training and testing data.

But if a dog picture was labeled as a cat because it had a light background and the human wrote it off as random error, it might never be caught that the main determinant the model inferred during training was the picture's background color. There is no way to know.

The explainability of neural network models is a growing area of research, so it might not be long before this glaring flaw is no longer the case, but the accuracy gained by an intelligent and adaptable system that draws its own conclusions about what is relevant beyond what a human might be able to identify is too good to pass up. The many kinds of neural networks created in the past few decades are making it into new widely used and commercial technologies each day.

The type of neural network most typically associated with the term are *feed forward neural networks* (FFNNs), or more specifically, the *convolutional neural network* (CNN).

The way these work is with a series of nodes that take input and perform some calculations on it to determine which output path to take. A layer of initial input nodes is connected to one or more layers of hidden nodes that each apply a calculation to their input to make branching decisions before eventually reaching an output node (Figure 10-44).

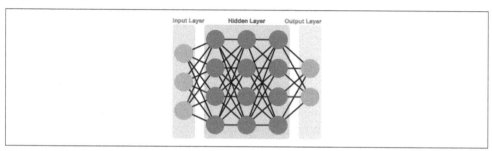

Figure 10-44. The generalized architecture of a neural network

Most neural networks are like a fully connected graph, with every node in each layer being reachable from all others in the previous layer. Connections between node pairs have different weights that basically dictate some threshold of values that input must exceed to "fire" that connection and activate the node on the other end.

Input nodes receive some input from the outside world. These are multiplied by some weight and processed with some function—called an activation function—to better distribute inputs. In this way, it is similar to logistic regression. Then, the value that is produced is weighed against the required threshold value for each outgoing path from the current node. The ones it exceeds are activated.

So, say you have some fruit... (Table 10-1)

Table 10-1. Boolean attributes of some fruits

	Citrus	Spherical
🍋	1	1
🍊	0	1
🍌	0	0

...and a trained neural net... (Figure 10-45)

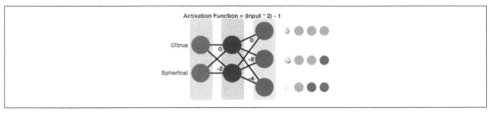

Figure 10-45. Neural network trained on fruit attributes

…and it is given the input (0,0) (Figure 10-46).

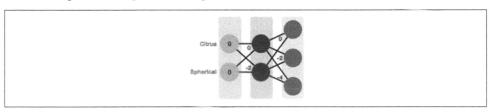

Figure 10-46. Activation of input nodes

The first hidden layer will then have one or more nodes each receive one or more values down different paths. Again, these are weighted and processed and compared with outgoing paths to activate some paths to the next layer.

On and on it goes until the output layer is reached, where the node or combination of nodes activated here correspond to some class label (Figure 10-47, Figure 10-48).

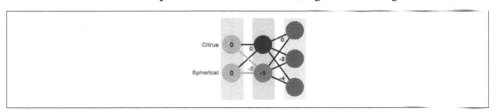

Figure 10-47. Activation of hidden layer nodes

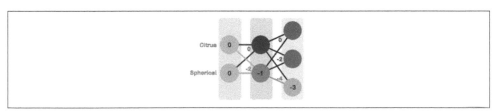

Figure 10-48. Activation of output nodes

And behold, our output corresponds to .

During the training phase, the weights of each node's paths are randomly selected. Each time some input is classified, the error is measured and the weights in its path are adjusted. After some time, adjustments will converge on a point where they cannot classify the training input any more accurately and the model is deemed trained. These weights are used thereafter.

Here, overfit occurs when the neural net is given enough nodes or layers that generalization does not occur in the training phase. In this circumstance, some or all training cases become individually trained instead of identifying similarities between them.

In some cases, models are trained on an ongoing basis. This can be done with some function whereby a human can indicate that the network incorrectly classified some input. This would adjust weights along its path as a pretrained model would have done. In this way, neural networks differ from other forms of classification because they are able to get much more accurate over time and beyond deployment.

Applications

Now that you have a better picture of the relative simplicity of classification algorithms, let's briefly look at some of the ways in which we can apply and combine them to imitate intelligence in a machine, as we did in an *applied practical* manner in Part II.

Image recognition

Similar to how we have used examples of tabular data, images can be analyzed as tables, as well. Take a very minimal example, such as the 4 x 4 image represented on the left in Figure 10-49. It can be represented by a set of three arrays of values: one containing the R (red) values for each pixel, one containing the G (green) values, and another the B (blue) values—as demonstrated on the right in Figure 10-49.

 We looked at a practical implementation of image classification in "Task: Image Classification" on page 120.

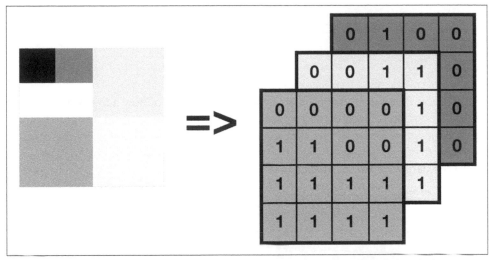

Figure 10-49. A tiny sample image and its potential RGB representation on disk

In a photograph, this might be millions of pixels/values in size, or require more tables for a more complex color space such as CMYK. Analysis of composition might use this only for features such as Google Image Search's *search by color* functionality. Detection of image contents requires some additional information, such as where edges are present or the likely depth placement of various segments to ascertain where separate objects begin and end. We can improve this with some matrix math performed on the raw pixel data—used to enhance edges and lines—then making new attributes that detail the size, shape, and location of features in the image.

This is a complex way of saying that much like many of the methods you have seen so far for categorizing input, systems that use categorization at a low level are often employing *many* layers of it that each handle very specific decisions, which then form the basis for the single output presented to the user. For images, it might be the case that each pixel is classified into a region, each region is classified as an edge or depth, each set of edges of regions of a certain depth are classified as an object, and then the image is classified.

The common use of neural nets for such purposes obfuscate the multitude of decisions made in between, but other methods can be used to piece together a similar output that can explain each of the component processes that lead to a final decision.

Sound recognition

You might think of sound recognition as more complex, but in reality sounds are often analyzed by making a visual representation and then assessing that as you would any image. This is not always true, nor is it necessarily a good idea, but it works well enough for many applications.

We looked at a practical implementation of sound classification in "Task: Sound Classification" on page 184.

Figure 10-50 shows a spectrogram, a visual representation of how a machine registers a sound. Phonemes (segments of words) can be detected by a computer given training knowledge of rise and fall of comparative frequencies occurring in the spoken voice and then pieced together to form words. Some gender detection is even possible due to the density of lower-frequency sounds.

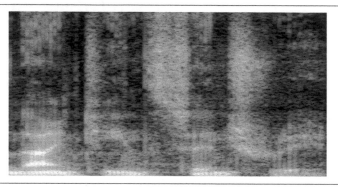

Figure 10-50. Spectrogram of a male voice saying the words "nineteenth century"

 Forming individual phonemes into words will often use another form of classification method to smooth inaccuracies, weighting different possible sounds with likelihoods by attempting to form known words in a selected language.

For example, if a sound could either be "ab" or "ap" but the rest of the sounds make "there was an <???>le tree growing in the yard," a natural language processing system trained on English will quite reliably select the option that makes a sensible statement—as our brains do when listening to speech.

Other approaches may use large tabular records of sound frequencies and durations to represent the same thing, instead analyzing them more directly as the numbers they represent.

Estimation

Methods like linear regression—which is especially useful due to not being constrained only to outcomes it has seen before—can be used to make magic numbers. Common in finance, linear regression is used most notably for profit/loss and stock market projections as well as price quoting for goods and services. A common everyday use for regression is predicting the selling price of real estate that is not currently on the market. Though every house is different, patterns can be seen in the number of bedrooms, size of the property, or proximity to amenities.

Decision making

Decision making might seem intuitive when discussing methods that implicitly make selections, but the applications of classification methods to more tangible real-world decision making are broad. Classification techniques are often used in systems that should alert specific behaviors but whose criteria are too complex and varied to employ a simpler rule-based approach.

Classification could be used to manage a server farm and decide when a device is exhibiting behaviors that necessitate maintenance. In this case, it would be classifying at given intervals whether each device should be labeled as *needs maintenance* or *doesn't need maintenance* based on a multitude of attributes that summarize its current state.

Similarly, classification is used in many online fraud detection systems, analyzing complex human behaviors to decide whether a session appears to be *normal human behavior* or *cause for suspicion of fraud attempt*.

Recommendation systems

Recommendation engines are a particular interest of ours. Two common methods used by recommendation engines are content-based and collaborative filtering: one is based on the theory that something is likely to be relevant to a user if it is similar to what they have interacted with or liked in the past, whereas the other thinks something is likely to be relevant if it is interacted with or liked by other users with similar behavior patterns or preferences.

So, although the first might recognize in an online store that if you like a science fiction book you might like another science-fiction book, the second could go as far as predicting you might like video games or dinosaur books—given that these are frequent overlapping interests with those who like science-fiction books.

 We looked at a practical implementation of a recommendation system earlier in "Task: Recommending Movies" on page 344.

Recommendation systems are used in everything, including search engines, online stores, social media, dating sites, blogs, and targeted advertising across the web. They are designed to be invisible but are a powerful tool for customizing a user's experience.

They might use the same methods as classification methods covered previously; however, with a recommendation engine, the *class* is a group of related observations or objects and a score of predicted relevance.

Clustering

Clustering is like a form of classification that places observations or data points into groups of those with similar attributes. It is a practice used for generalizing or summarizing data, often to reduce storage requirements (such as in compression) or for the purpose of getting to know a dataset that is too large to observe or visualize.

Different methods are good for different applications: some clustering approaches work best with certain distributions of data, and many differ in their handling and consideration of outliers. Nonetheless, all methods acknowledge the subjectivity of desired outcomes between what the data and its clusters are to be used for.

Methods

Let's look at a handful of clustering methods and compare.

Hierarchical

Hierarchical clustering is a method of iteratively grouping data points based on a given distance around each point. There are two methods of doing this: *agglomerative* and *divisive*.

Agglomerative hierarchical clustering looks like that shown in Figure 10-51.

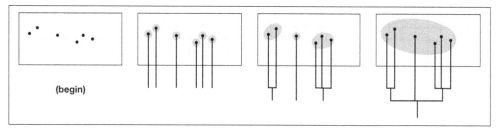

Figure 10-51. Glomming points together into clusters

Each point will start out in its own cluster with a distance of zero, and then as the accepted distance grows farther and farther, points will slowly group together until all points are in one large cluster. This will make a tree of groupings, from which a cutoff point can be selected by a human or some other algorithm with consideration for what the data represents and what the clusters are to be used for (Figure 10-52).

Figure 10-52. Stop glomming wherever is sensible

Divisive hierarchical clustering is the same process but in reverse. All points start out in one cluster, and then separate as the accepted distance reduces until all points are in a cluster on their own. Again, a cutoff is selected.

Theoretically this would always have the same output as the agglomerative method, but if you have an idea already of how many clusters you want, you can save compute time by selecting the process that begins closest to the desired point.

The problem with this kind of clustering is that it does not support clusters of mixed densities. It turns out this is not a trivial problem for a computer to solve.

For example, in the first image of Figure 10-53 it is likely trivial for a human to distinguish clustering of three or four groups of differing densities, with a few outliers. The second and third show something like what would be produced with hierarchical clustering depending on the threshold at which you chose to stop.

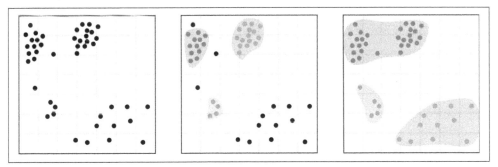

Figure 10-53. Clusters of varied usefulness due to threshold value chosen

K-means

This method addresses the failings of hierarchical clustering in mixed-density clusters by working in the opposite way. Instead of grouping by proximity of points and eyeballing a cutoff distance, *K*-means requires you to eyeball the number of clusters you want in advance (*K*) and will form those from points with variable distances between them. This happens as follows (see Figure 10-54):

1. Select *K* random starting locations for your centroids (represented by X).

2. Assign each data point to belong to its nearest X.

3. Move each X to the center point of its assigned points.

4. Repeat steps 2 and 3 until convergence (they no longer move).

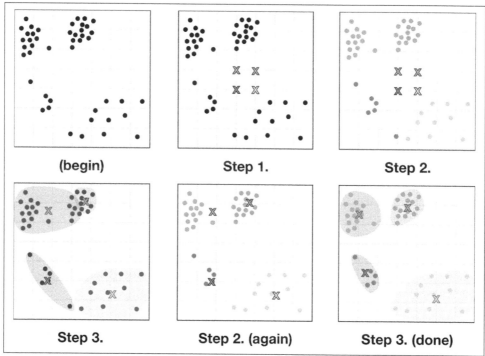

Figure 10-54. The elegant process of K-means convergence

It is a simple, elegant algorithm that results in almost the same output given any random starting points. The downside is that it is heavily affected by the *K* selected at the beginning; this is quite counterintuitive because clustering is usually a method of getting to know your data, but knowing how many groupings best describe different patterns or outcomes that occur in your data requires you to know it pretty well.

Blindly selecting numbers at random might appear equally well performing in many cases for which data is too high dimensional to clearly visualize. You might never know whether you chose well or are arbitrarily either grouping together distinct observation groups or splitting related ones. *K*-means also suffers from the *clustering every point* problem, in that it will equally consider even the most extreme outliers. Just like any other point, an outlier will be put in a cluster, treated as one of the group, and possibly drastically sway your centroids (which are frequently used to summarize cluster members, as shown in Figure 10-55).

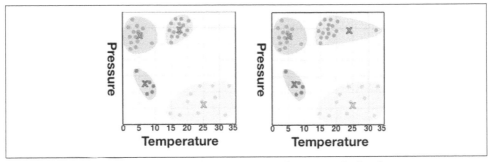

Figure 10-55. The potential effect of one outlier on the centroid of a cluster

In the first instance in Figure 10-55, you might summarize the green cluster as the high-pressure 17-degree group—and this would be an accurate estimation of all members. In the second instance, we'd summarize its temperature at 24 degrees, which is inaccurate for all members and is swayed by the presence of a single 34-degree incident that righfully should not be included in the cluster.

Unlike hierarchical clustering, the use of centroids as determinants also makes *K*-means unsuitable for nonglobular clusters (Figure 10-56).

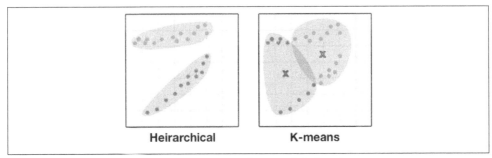

Figure 10-56. The unsuitability of K-means for nonglobular clusters

DBSCAN

DBSCAN (Density-Based Spatial Clustering of Applications with Noise) is another form of clustering that, like hierarchical, assesses the distance between all points to account for nonglobular clusters. Unlike hierarchical, however, DBSCAN has a form of regulation that aims to ensure tighter clusters of significant size by implementing a minimum number of points that must be nearby for a point to be considered.

So two figures are needed: an *epsilon* value (or distance at which two points are considered close to each other) and a *minimum points* value (min pts). Then, for each point the number of points nearby—or within epsilon distance—is counted. If a point has more than min pts nearby, it is a *center point*. If it has less, but one or more of the points nearby are themselves center points, it is a *border point*. Points with none nearby, or less than min pts nearby where none are center points, are disregarded. Clusters are then made with the labeled points, both center and border.

This could be represented as something like:

```
if point.nearbyPoints.count >= minPts {
        return .center
}

for neighbourPoint in point.nearbyPoints {
        if neighbourPoint.nearbyPoints.count >= minPts {
                return .border
        }
}

return .other
```

This is shown in Figure 10-57, with center points highlighted and border points outlined. As you probably notice, this is another method that's not tolerant of mixed-density clusters.

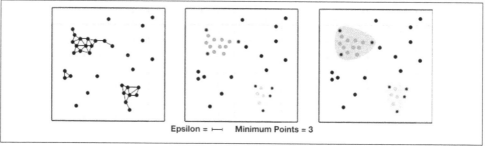

Epsilon = ⊢—⊣   Minimum Points = 3

Figure 10-57. Visualized steps of the DBSCAN process

Mean shift

Mean shift clustering is another method that, like *K*-means, takes steps toward a final convergence that will be its final outcome. In this case, a selection is made of a distance around each point to consider and for each point you select, the point within its selected radius with the greatest density of other points—its local *mean* point. From this new location you then find *its* local mean point, and so on (Figure 10-58).

 A threshold value should be becoming clear as a component of many data science practices that requires human expertise; this is why even if you aren't writing out your own versions of these algorithms every day, it's still better for your outcomes if you at least know how they work.

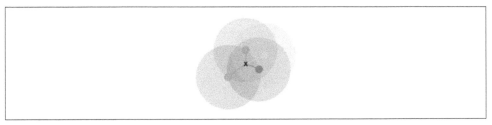

Figure 10-58. The mean of various points

This should soon naturally converge on multiple points that have greater density than their surrounds. In this way, mean shift has the robustness and repeatability of a method like *K*-means, but will determine for itself how many clusters are present for a given threshold and can still handle nonglobular clusters (Figure 10-59).

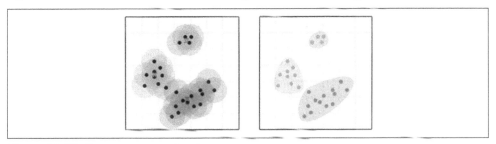

Figure 10-59 Convergence on local means

This method can also be applied outside of clustering, and is one of the ways object tracking can be done in video footage—clustering regions of colors likely to be objects as they move between frames.

Applications

Now that you know the inner workings of some popular clustering algorithms, let's briefly look at some of the ways in which we can apply and combine them to improve and manipulate data—or form the basis for future classification activities.

Data exploration

Clustering can be used to get an initial idea of patterns present in a large dataset. Along with visualizations, clustering plays a crucial part of the initial data exploration/familiarization stage of analyzing an unfamiliar dataset.

Having a general idea of how data is distributed—such as the presence or absence of groupings, or the overall density of observations—can aid in selecting the appropriate analysis methods to use moving forward.

We can also use clustering to group and label previously unnamed behaviors, even if just as *Behavior Group A*, etc. Given a label, we can now use these with typical classification techniques for predicting outcomes for future observations.

Behavior profiling

The idea of a group of data points that share attributes but cannot be intuitively named might be difficult to conceptualize. That is, until you think of people. People can be clustered by a multitude of characteristics and behaviors, but outside of broad stereotypes these sets of attributes will rarely have a name.

In the case of recommendation engines, as discussed earlier, people are grouped by having similar interests, but each person within a group can overlap in a broad number of tiny ways that cannot be easily quantified. Clustering techniques form new attributes for each data point—such as which individuals are similar to them, which cluster threshold would be needed to link this individual with another, and so on—that can be used to make intelligent decisions about the similarities between complex human behavior attributes.

Behavior profiling is especially beneficial when developing rules for online fraud-detection systems. To define what is normal and what is suspicious behaviors from characteristics as broad as session length and country of origin to order of interactions and type of contact details, a system can seek to derive observations from past fraudulent behavior. In this case, clustering behaviors and then assessing where fraudulent behaviors overlap, some unrelated behavior might allow the system to identify much more complex and reliable traits than a human is able to recognize or infer.

Compression

Given clustering's potential for identifying places where multiple values could be generalized to one, we can use it very effectively for compression. This is particularly clear in examples of image compression: usually, storing an image would require each pixel have a long value that corresponds to one of the more than a billion colors supported by modern color profiles.

Instead, you can represent each color present as a point in, say, three-dimensional space—with an axis each for its RGB values—and then cluster them. You then replace all colors present in each cluster with the cluster's centroid color. This can be done with very small threshold values for lesser color changes that may not even be visible to the human eye, all the way to reducing an image to only a handful of colors that are extensively dithered (Figure 10-60).

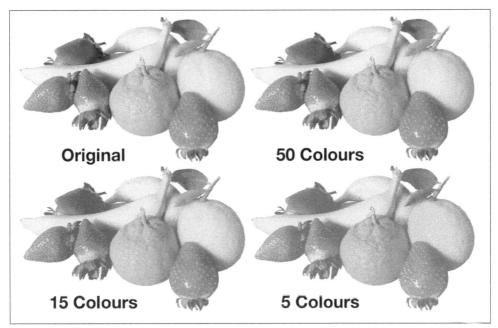

Figure 10-60. The same image reduced to an increasingly limited palette

This now reduces not only the size of the lookup table, but also the size of the value needed to store the table index of the color in each pixel.

Next Steps

So now you should have an idea of the kinds of assumptions AI and machine-learning methods are based on and hopefully be a little demystified with the way some systems work. As anyone with any programming background will know, a complex thing in technology is always just made up of many simple steps done very fast.

Next up, we look at what happened under the hood for some of the *practical* tasks we built earlier in Part II.

## CHAPTER 11

Looking Under the Hood

In Chapter 10, we looked at the underlying—mostly mathematical—principles used to create AI and ML features. In this chapter, we take that a little further toward the practical and look at what's happening under the hood for many of the *practical* AI tasks that we covered in Part II.

For each example that we look at, we touch on the underlying machine-learning algorithms, their origins (academic papers, most often), briefly note how they work, and acknowledge some of the other ways in which you could accomplish the same task, algorithm-wise. We begin, though, with a look at how CoreML itself works because so far it has been treated a bit like a black box. Although you don't need to understand CoreML, it helps to have at least a basic understanding of its internals because treating things like magic is a sure-fire way to make sure you get stuck when it comes time to fix errors.

A Look Inside CoreML

As we've seen many times earlier in the book, the basic steps for inference with CoreML are always the same:

1. Add your pretrained model to your project.
2. Load the model file in your app.
3. Provide the necessary input to the model for it to make a prediction.
4. Use the prediction output in your app.

So, now that we have seen many working examples of using CoreML (Part II), let's look into what its actually doing. A great advantage of Xcode handling so much of the work for us means that we can gloss over bits and pieces of the inner workings. But to properly understand CoreML, we need to take a bit of a dive into the internals.

The core (pun intended) of CoreML is the `MLModel` class. By design, you will rarely need to interface with the `MLModel` class; instead, the generated wrapper class Xcode creates will often be all you need. The `MLModel` class has a few interesting aspects you will run into when you are going beyond the basics of using CoreML. These also give some insight into what CoreML is doing when using the Xcode-generated classes, so they are worth understanding.

The first is the `compileModel(at:)` class method. You would call this yourself when you are adding in support for new models on the fly, but normally it is handled for you by Xcode. This class method will read and compile the MLmodel at the `at` URL into a format ready to be run by CoreML. The compiled model is then used as part of the initialization of an `MLModel` object.

This is because although the MLmodel file format is designed for storage and transfer, it isn't the best choice for running the model. CoreML doesn't run an MLmodel, it runs a compiled and optimized form of that model. The `MLModel` class is the interface into the compiled model.

> We talk a little bit more about the actual file format (as in the *.mlmodel* file that is exported by tools like CreateML) of CoreML models in Chapter 12 if you are curious.

Then, there are various prediction methods such as `prediction(from:)`, which takes in an `MLFeatureProvider` as input, uses this input to make a prediction, and then returns another `MLFeatureProvider` as the result of that prediction. The `MLFeatureProvider` is a protocol designed to be the calling point for the model to request and return data. The idea behind this protocol is that the model will need input and provide output in a standardized form, and a feature provider will bundle up any values needed into a form that the model can call at will; likewise when returning the output of the model, another feature provider will be used to give the result.

Values are of the form `MLFeatureValue`, a custom class designed for holding common values the model will need. The class comes with initializers for most types you'll encounter in machine learning. Values are stored and retrieved via the method `featureValue(for:)` on the feature provider, where a string is provided as the key for the value that you want to retrieve.

You can think of an `MLFeatureProvider` as a protocol that works like a weird dictionary. It isn't a dictionary (or any collection), but we find it helps to think of it like one; you request and store values into it via `String`-based keys.

This is one of those things that might feel a little weird, but machine learning has its own very specific needs and having a data provider that works in a very un-Swift-like fashion is just the price we have to pay.

Finally, each `MLModel` has a property called `modelDescription` of type `MLModelDescription`. This contains a description of the model, such as its inputs and outputs, the attributes of the inputs and outputs, and any metadata embedded within the model. This property is what Xcode uses to populate the view of the *.mlmodel* file within the Xcode editor.

All of these components are normally hidden from you when using the Xcode-generated wrapper class and are called by similar methods on the wrapper, instead. If you're feeling like you have no intentions of ever touching the insides of CoreML, you can just use the wrapper, but the wrapper is also a great way of taking a look into how the preceding components work.

To take a quick look at how this all works, we will need to import a model into a project. Let's take a look at an Xcode-generated wrapper class and its supporting classes now:

1. Download the MobileNet model from Apple's Models (*https://apple.co/2oQrjTW*) page.

2. Create a new iOS Single View Application in Xcode.

3. Name the project "CoreML internals."

4. Drag the MobileNet model into the project, allowing it to copy as needed.

5. Select the *MobileNet.mlmodel* file inside Xcode.

6. In the `Model Class` section, click the small arrow next to the `MobileNet` class.

This opens up the wrapper class and its associated convenience types in the Xcode editor.

The first class we have is the `MobileNetInput` class, a subclass of `MLFeatureProvider`. This class is responsible for providing input into CoreML, and is mostly just a wrapper around the `CVTPixelBuffer`. The reason for this is because MobileNet is an image classifier; if we had a different model, such as a language detector, we'd have drastically different inputs, mostly `Strings`:

```
class MobileNetInput : MLFeatureProvider {

    var image: CVPixelBuffer

    var featureNames: Set<String> {
        get {
            return ["image"]
        }
    }

    func featureValue(for featureName: String) -> MLFeatureValue? {
        if (featureName == "image") {
            return MLFeatureValue(pixelBuffer: image)
        }
        return nil
    }

    init(image: CVPixelBuffer) {
        self.image = image
    }
}
```

It has an initializer that is used by the model class so we never need to worry about instantiating one of these ourselves, but if we do need to do so, there is an initializer we can use.

The next class is the `MobileNetOutput`, another `MLFeatureProvider`. Functionally identical to the input class, this one provides the output in a form that the neural net expects, but again provides nice wrappers in the form of the computed properties:

```
class MobileNetOutput : MLFeatureProvider {

    private let provider : MLFeatureProvider


    lazy var classLabelProbs: [String : Double] = {
        [unowned self] in return self.provider
            .featureValue(for: "classLabelProbs")!
            .dictionaryValue as! [String : Double]
    }()

    lazy var classLabel: String = {
        [unowned self] in return self.provider
            .featureValue(for: "classLabel")!.stringValue
    }()

    var featureNames: Set<String> {
        return self.provider.featureNames
    }

    func featureValue(for featureName: String) -> MLFeatureValue? {
        return self.provider.featureValue(for: featureName)
```

```
    }

    init(classLabelProbs: [String : Double], classLabel: String) {
        self.provider = try! MLDictionaryFeatureProvider(
            dictionary: ["classLabelProbs" :
                MLFeatureValue(dictionary: classLabelProbs
                    as [AnyHashable : NSNumber]),
                "classLabel" : MLFeatureValue(string: classLabel)])
    }

    init(features: MLFeatureProvider) {
        self.provider = features
    }
}
```

These use the `provider` property of the class to get the output. The `provider` is given to the object as part of its instantiation. This class, much like the input, will be automatically created by the model class as part of its prediction method, so we rarely have to concern ourselves with this class.

Finally we have the `MobileNet` class, which is a wrapper class around CoreML that automatically handles the inputs and outputs, creating the input and output classes as needed and passing everything over to CoreML to handle the processing and predictions.

Wondering where this code is stored?

It goes inside Xcode's derived data folder, and although you shouldn't ever worry about it, in our case it was stored in *~/Library/ Developer/Xcode/DerivedData/CoreML_Internals- gtsfzcimjremlhfqnntoeuidkygk/Build/Intermediates.noindex/CoreML Internals.build/Debug-iphoneos/CoreML   Internals.build/Derived- Sources/CoreML.Generated/MobileNet/*, but in your machine the folder names will be slightly different.

How did we find this out? Right-click anywhere in the editor and the "Select in Finder" menu option will open Finder to the correct folder with the file selected. You will rarely need this, but it's good to know, especially if you ever want to understand what the code is doing. This can be useful for a variety or reasons. Writing a book about it, for example.

```
class MobileNet {
    var model: MLModel

    class var urlOfModelInThisBundle : URL {
        let bundle = Bundle(for: MobileNet.self)
        return bundle.url(forResource: "MobileNet",
                        withExtension:"mlmodelc")!
    }
```

```
init(contentsOf url: URL) throws {
    self.model = try MLModel(contentsOf: url)
}

/// Construct a model that automatically
/// loads the model from the app's bundle
convenience init() {
    try! self.init(contentsOf: type(of:self).urlOfModelInThisBundle)
}

convenience init(configuration: MLModelConfiguration) throws {
    try self.init(contentsOf: type(of:self).urlOfModelInThisBundle,
                  configuration: configuration)
}

init(contentsOf url: URL, configuration: MLModelConfiguration)
    throws
{
    self.model = try MLModel(contentsOf: url,
                             configuration: configuration)
}

func prediction(input: MobileNetInput) throws -> MobileNetOutput {
    return try self.prediction(input: input,
                               options: MLPredictionOptions())
}

func prediction(input: MobileNetInput, options: MLPredictionOptions)
    throws -> MobileNetOutput
{
    let outFeatures = try model.prediction(from: input,
                                           options:options)
    return MobileNetOutput(features: outFeatures)
}

func prediction(image: CVPixelBuffer) throws -> MobileNetOutput {
    let input_ = MobileNetInput(image: image)
    return try self.prediction(input: input_)
}

func predictions(inputs: [MobileNetInput],
                 options: MLPredictionOptions = MLPredictionOptions())
    throws -> [MobileNetOutput]
{
    let batchIn = MLArrayBatchProvider(array: inputs)
    let batchOut = try model.predictions(from: batchIn,
                                         options: options)
    var results : [MobileNetOutput] = []
    results.reserveCapacity(inputs.count)
    for i in 0..<batchOut.count {
        let outProvider = batchOut.features(at: i)
```

```
                let result = MobileNetOutput(features: outProvider)
                results.append(result)
        }
        return results
    }
}
```

The first interesting thing in this class is the `model` property. This is the actual `MLMo del` class that CoreML uses in its predictions. It's loaded with the model file `Mobile Net.mlmodel` we added to the project very early on. This is here, and importantly accessible, so that if you find yourself mostly using CoreML through its wrapper but also need to do some manual adjustments, you can do so here without having to recreate everything in this file.

One reason you might need to access the model but don't want to otherwise change the wrapper would be to extract some of the details from the model.

The `modelDescription` property of the model is of type `MLModelDe scription` and contains all the metadata that Xcode shows you, so you could use this to, say, extract the license of the model and show it to your users.

In the case of our model, the following code placed inside *ViewController.swift* would result in this string being returned: " Apache License, Version 2.0 *http://www.apache.org/licen ses/LICENSE-2.0* ".

```
model.model.modelDescription.metadata[.license]
```

The next interesting little tidbit within this class is the `urlOfModelInThisBundle` computed class variable. This returns the URL for the *compiled* form of the MLmodel. Xcode compiled and installed this model into the app bundle, meaning that we don't have to worry about it. The reason Xcode compiles the model is because then it can make some device-specific optimizations and have your app run that, instead.

This is used later when it comes time to initialize the model, as you can see in the convenience initializer. You can, if you want, compile your own form of the model file using the `compileModel(at:)` method call and then use the designated initializer instead.

Lastly, there are a whole bunch of different prediction methods in this class. Although they all work fundamentally the same way, and all we did was use the `predic tion(image:)` method, each has its own place.

Many are just less convenient forms of the one we used, such as requiring the image to be wrapped up into a `MobileNetInput` class first, but some also let you configure prediction options.

Currently the only prediction option we can set is whether the model runs exclusively on the CPU, but we imagine over time more options will be added, so it's worth checking back in the documentation for this class in the future.

 These classes are all generated by Xcode and shouldn't ever be modified. If you do need functionality outside of that provided by this file, you will need to reproduce the functionality of these classes, as well. Additionally, because this file is under Xcode's control, it might change between the time this is being written and when you are reading this book.

It's pretty unlikely that it will have changed a lot, but if it is significantly different (seeing as you are in the future), we'll trust that you can just ask your friendly neighborhood **Advanced Realtime Synthetic Evaluator 9000** to explain the changes.

Now that we have a better understanding of the interface side of CoreML, we can start looking at the underlying details of the various tasks we solved.

Vision

In this section, we will be taking a look at the underlying infrastructure that powers the various machine-learning approaches we used when performing machine learning on images and movies.

We are going to have to make a few assumptions here and there because Apple doesn't give us the full details on the underlying workings of Vision and CoreML. For the most part this is a good thing—you shouldn't need to worry about how the model does what it does, but it does make it a bit annoying when you want to know more.

The majority of this section will be looking at how face detection ("Task: Face Detection" on page 74) and image classification ("Task: Image Classification" on page 120) work. The reason we focus on these tasks is two-fold: first, they are the tasks we have the most information about, both from Apple and the general ML literature; and second, the approaches used are *highly likely* going to be used for all detection systems within Apple's Vision framework.

 Due to the nature of machine learning in computer vision, almost all vision-related tasks would have the same basic structure of numerous layers of convolutional neural networks (CNNs) ("Neural network" on page 422) and pooling layers.

Face Detection

At its core, the built-in facial observation, detection, and landmarking calls inside of the Vision framework are based on deep convolutional networks (DCNs).

This is, however, wrapped in a rather impressive infrastructure to keep it performant on mobile devices, but to also simplify integrating with it (for you, the developer).

The first step in the process (indeed in most of the Vision framework) is a converter. This takes in your input image and transforms it into a known size (or sizes), color-space, and format matching the attributes Vision requires.

Although this is necessary for the neural network side to make use of the image, it has no impact on the machine-learning side, Apple has done this work for us for two reasons: first, it is less for you as the developer to worry about; and, second, if everything is a known format, optimizations can be made in the network and pipeline.

The pipeline then scales the images into five different sizes resulting in a standard multiscale image *pyramid*.

You can learn more about image processing and pyramids in this *exceptional* Wikipedia article (*http://bit.ly/2OVdZs4*).

Each tier of the pyramid (and the scaled images within) will be run through the neural network and the results combined and compared to give a final result.

Using a pyramid approach comes out of image-processing work and has been shown to have better results than just having a single scale. Each tier of the network uses essentially the same network with the exact same weights and parameters, but with different input and output shapes and a different number of intermediate layers.

By keeping most of the network across the different pyramid tiers the same, this means the layers can be reused, saving memory.

The neural network itself is broken up into three parts: tile classifier, feature extractor, and a bounding-box regressor.

The feature extractor is the main part of the network, performing the bulk of the work and, as the name implies, does the feature extraction. It is built up out of multiple convolutional and pooling layers, one after another. The results of the feature extractor are then passed into the other two components of the network.

The tile classifier is responsible for saying whether an input has a face or not inside. Taking the output of the feature extractor, it uses a fully connected layer with softmax as the activation function. This results in a yes or no output to there being a face in the input.

The final component is the bounding-box regressor, which is responsible for providing the bounding box for the face. Much like the tile classifier, it takes the output of the feature extractor and uses multiple fully connected layers.

The output layer from this gives an x and y position, and a size parameter, w. These can be used to draw a bounding box around a face centered at position (x,y) and 2w wide and high.

This approach is inspired by earlier work on DCNs, especially the OverFeat (*http:// bit.ly/35CbpwW*) DCN published in 2014. It shares a lot of commonality in line with this approach, albeit with a lot of modifications to keep it performant for the limited constraints of an iPhone or iPad.

The earlier approach for determining faces, and the one still used in parts of the CoreImage framework, is based on the Viola-Jones object detection framework. Viola-Jones uses haar-like features (*http://bit.ly/2ORDRF6*) (basically a black-and-white image) that is overlaid onto the input image as bounding box. The pixels within the different sections of the bounding box are summed, and this is repeated multiple times with multiple different boxes.

This works on the assumption that the face can be broadly described as a series of different regions with specific properties, such as your cheek regions are lighter colored than your eye regions. The results of these bounding summations are used to determine the likelihood of a face being in the image.

 If you are after the full nitty-gritty details of the facial detection side of Vision, the machine-learning boffins at Apple have published a paper (*https://apple.co/2MiWnVh*) about the technique on their machine-learning journal site.

Barcode Detection

The underlying principles of barcode detection ("Task: Barcode Detection" on page 98) inside of Vision are not as well known as the facial detection. As we said earlier, it is highly likely going to be very similar to the facial detection.

The structure of the image pipeline along with the convolutional and pooling layer approach would work very well for barcodes as it would for faces; the only difference is the barcode neural net would have been trained with various barcode images instead of faces.

The largest difference would be with respect to the classifiers. The facial detection system only needs to yay-or-nay if there is a face, but a barcode classifier would need to specify the contents of the barcode.

Saliency Detection

The saliency detection ("Task: Saliency Detection" on page 105) provided by Vision offers a heatmap of an image showing which parts of the image are likely to be of interest.

This is broken up into two different modes: object and attention. Object saliency is based on people effectively marking up regions of training images saying *this part is the interesting bit,* whereas attention saliency is trained by showing images to people and using eye trackers to see what parts they focus on.

Despite not knowing the precise workings of the saliency detection algorithm, it is very likely inspired by "Deep Inside Convolutional Networks: Visualising Image Classification Models and Saliency Maps," (*http://bit.ly/2MOrxmx*) by Simonyan, Vedaldi, and Zisserman.

As with pretty much anything to do with images, CNNs are again the go-to standard. The neural net is likely very similar to the one used in facial detection, but trained with saliency maps instead of faces. This is also highly likely combined with SUNs, which stands for *saliency using natural statistics.*

SUNs employ a statistical approach that operates on the pixel level, which gives a rough number of the chance a particular region is salient in the image. SUNs, until very recently, were the best way to perform saliency in images, and despite CNNs rapidly taking over, they work well in conjunction with one another.

Image Classification

Image classification ("Task: Image Classification" on page 120) at its core is about taking an image, running it through a network that performs feature extraction on the image, and then using those features to declare what is in the image.

If at this stage you are thinking, "I bet they are going to say it uses convolutional networks!" you'd be right—image classification uses CNNs as its building blocks.

We are assuming that the image classifier you can create using CreateML works in the same fashion as one you can create using Turi Create. Apple has described how it approached image classification using Turi Create (transfer learning), but not in CreateML. So although it is possible that CreateML is taking a radically different approach, it should be pretty similar.

We are fairly confident in this because why would Apple write two different approaches to the same problem? Additionally, the approach Turi Create takes is very similar to how other ML frameworks and research papers approach image classification.

Each classifier will be built up out of multiple convolutional and pooling layers. The CNNs perform the feature extraction of the images, with each layer returning a different feature.

These features are then fed into classifier layer(s), which are generally of a different structure, so in the case of Inception-v3 (*http://bit.ly/2MnLhhK*) the classifier is a softmax layer.

It is the classification layers that perform the actual classification using the outputs of the CNN. The classification layers use the features extracted by the CNN to say what something is.

The interesting part in image classifiers isn't so much the stacks of convolutional layers, it is in the transfer learning.

The term *feature* can be a little confusing, because it leads us to thinking of these features at the human scale.

Concepts like blue eyes, fur, tall, stripes, or glass are terms we would probably think of as features, but these don't match what the CNNs see as features.

What they consider a feature can't be easily described; you essentially just must trust them.

Even visualizing a feature or using neural saliency (asking the network what it considers are the important bits) tends to look like random swirly patterns and noise to us.

Transfer learning at a very high level is where you take an already trained classifier with its many layers for feature extraction and final layers for the actual classification, tear off the classifier component, and bolt your own on the top. This means you would be reusing the already trained feature extractors with your own custom classifier stages.

Why you'd want to do this comes down to training time: most of the work in training a classifier from scratch is spent in the feature extraction stages, training the CNN components of the model. So if you could reuse the work done in training a CNN, you should be able to drastically speed up overall training time to complete a model. Luckily you can do this!

The ability of CNNs to provide feature extraction from images has been shown to be fairly independent of the original classification purpose they were a part of.

 This came about based on the work by Donahue et al. in 2013 on their DeCAF (*http://bit.ly/2oyo6IF*) system, in which they used the same CNN to perform a variety of different classification tasks. Not only has this been shown to work quite well, but when it first came out, it was highly comparable or better than competing approaches to image classification despite not being handmade for each task.

All of this means that you can now rapidly train an image classifier using transfer learning and it will work extremely well as long as the underlying CNN layers were trained in a manner that matches your needs, of which there will be many.

The trick then becomes picking what existing classifier to use as the basis. In the case of an image classifier trained using CreateML, we don't know which CNN they used as the basis of the classifier (it might be one they created themselves), whereas with Turi Create models, you can pick which model you want to use as the basis.

Image Similarity

Image similarity ("Task: Image Similarity" on page 109) is one of the more interesting approaches in machine learning. Specifically, it is an autoencoder—a machine-learning approach in which it learns a data encoding by itself based purely on the input.

 We are assuming the image similarity in Vision (where we don't know how it works) is using the same approach as the image similarity in Turi Create (where we do know how it works).

We know how it works in Turi Create because Apple has told us (*http://bit.ly/35xDbuo*) how it works in Turi Create.

Image similarity works in an almost identical fashion to image classification; there are multiple convolutional and pooling layers wired together. These perform feature extraction of the input image. These features are then used in the classification stage to give a result of what is in the image, so certain features in an image of cats, for example, strongly correlate with the label *cat*.

This is where image similarity differs from classification—you don't perform the final step, the classification. Instead, you collect a latent representation, also called a feature vector or feature print.

A feature vector is a combined output of each layer in the image classifier neural net, and is literally a vector of numbers that represents the features (as the neural net understands them) of the input image.

At this point we now essentially have a unique representation of the image that the neural net understands; however, it will be meaningless to us. We could then throw the neural net into reverse, give it the feature print, and have it generate an image from that, which will ideally look the same (or very similar to) the original image (although GANs are generally better at this).

What we are going to do, though, is use this for comparative purposes, using our feature print effectively as a description of the original image. To do this we start by extracting the feature print of the target images that we want to compare against by following the same process we applied to the original image.

After we have all of our feature vectors of our images, we can compare them. To do this comparison, we create a nearest neighbor graph ("Nearest neighbor" on page 412) of the various latent encodings.

The reason we use graph is because each image will be similar to the original, but in different ways; it very likely won't be just a straight "this one is most similar in each and every feature to the original." When the graph is complete, we can then find the overall nearest image to the original.

Other ways to do image similarity without machine learning do exist and are still useful depending on the application. The simplest way, but also most easily susceptible to tiny changes, is to just look at each pixel in the image and see whether the values are the same.

More advanced techniques take the same idea, but measure the difference between errors or noise. The (arguably) current best approach for algorithmic similarity is the Structural Similarity Index (SSIM) (*http://bit.ly/2MTd74m*), which essentially compares the structural change between two different images. This means that changes in color and lighting or small movements of in-image objects won't produce a large difference in the SSIM value, but radical changes will.

The number produced essentially says how similar looking the two images are, with a result of 1 meaning the images are identical. Because SSIM measures structural changes, images that are pixel-for-pixel drastically different but with a high SSIM value will look very similar to one another when viewed by a person.

The main use of SSIM is in video compression for identifying keyframes in the source material.

Bitmap Drawing Classification

The final image task we're going to look at now is drawing recognition ("Task: Drawing Recognition" on page 142 (which is really drawing *classification*).

At its core it is very similar to the previous image classifiers, just within a much more constrained environment. It is still based on our old friend, CNN. The particular constraints that help us here are that the drawings input is always a 28-by-28-pixel grayscale image.

Because this is such a limited input, the total network is only three convolutional, one pooling, and two dense layers. This results in pretty much the exact same workings as the normal image classifier, though; the convolution layers still perform feature extraction, and the dense layers perform the classification using the features.

An interesting part of the drawing classifier is how it handles strokes. In our example we provide bitmaps to the model, but you can also provide strokes as a list of points on a view.

When using the stroke-based implementation, the points are first converted into a line. The line is then decimated using the *very cool* Ramer–Douglas–Peucker algorithm (*http://bit.ly/2qgo08P*), which reduces the number of points in a line but keeps it looking visually similar. Then, the reduced lines are drawn out (or rasterized if you are feeling like using a fancy term) into a 28-by-28-pixel grayscale bitmap that is sent over to the network for classification.

Much like with the full image classifier, the drawing classifier is intended to be used with your own classification labels based on your data. In our case we used Quick, Draw! and because of that dataset's huge size and quality, Turi Create offers to use it to prewarm the training. When doing this, the pretrained model on Quick, Draw! is used and then you use your own data to perform the final training.

This is slightly different than transfer learning in that the pretrained model is used as the starting point, but the training still uses your data to fully control and tweak the weights and parameters of the layers. In contrast, transfer learning just changes the classification steps and doesn't tweak the convolutional layers.

The reason to warm the training is that in such a constrained environment, the number of different ways you are going to be able to train a useful model is likely to be at least partially encapsulated in the prebuilt Quick, Draw! model. The domain is so small that you might as well use the overlap between your data and the gigantic Google dataset.

Audio

At a very high-level perspective, audio works in a similar way to image models. Both generally do some processing on the data to get it ready, extract features of the input, and then use the features in some way such as classifying or comparing.

Audio, however, has it own quirks that make it a lot trickier than images, especially around the processing of input, which is generally pretty easy in images in comparison.

Sound Classification

In "Task: Sound Classification" on page 184, we created a sound classifier using CreateML, and much like with many of the processes in CreateML, we don't really know how it works but can make some assumptions based on it working in a similar fashion to how the sound classifier in Turi Create works. The first step in sound classification is to process our input.

> You should never use the sound classifier for human speech. Speech has weird quirks and specific needs that a generic classifier can't manage.
>
> Human speech occupies a different frequency range than the sound classifier is optimized to handle.

Sound is a wave that is a continuous analog form, which is very difficult to work with in so much as our neural nets like nice, clean, discrete values. Additionally, sound sources can have multiple channels, such as a left and right channel, or even more.

So the various channels need to be averaged into a mono channel that we can then quantize. To perform the quantization, we sample the sound wave, in the case of Turi Create at 16K Hz, so we take a sample (grabbing the value of the wave) of the mono-wave every one sixteen-thousandths of a second.

The data of the sampling is converted into a -1 to 1 range floating-point value, broken up into segments, and then windowed. We need to segment and window the audio data because of some assumptions later stages of the processing (especially the Fourier transform) make and to keep the processed chunks small and discrete for the neural net to be able to practically use.

A windowing function takes a range of values and tapers them out to fit a particular range.

Windowing generally isn't used to cut the audio into chunks (although you could use it for that), but to taper the already determined segments into a predetermined shape.

The tapering used by Apple is a Hamming Window function (*http://bit.ly/2nOvWNT*), which results in a bell-curve shape.

Next we need to use Fourier transforms (*http://bit.ly/2Bjzyub*) to calculate the power spectrum, which gives us a breakdown of how the power of the audio signal varies over its frequency.

A Fourier transform is an approach to decomposing a time-based signal into its component frequencies. You can think of this as a way of converting any signal from time (such as the case of an audio signal) to space, making it easier to analyze and use.

Next the signal is run through a mel frequency (*http://bit.ly/33xPllo*) filter bank, which applies multiple triangular filters to extract frequency bands that are biased toward how humans hear sounds, given that we don't hear linearly evenly across the entire sound spectrum. Essentially we are trying to get the bits of the audio that are more relevant to us as humans (if you aren't a human you will likely need to tweak this part of the input processing).

Finally, this gets reshaped into a (96,64) array for feeding as input into the neural net; all of this is happening to approximately each 975 milliseconds' worth of audio input. But with that done we can finally get into the machine-learning side of sound classification.

For the machine-learning components of sound classification, much like with image classification, we are going to be using a pretrained neural net as the basis.

In the case of Turi Create (and highly likely CreateML, as well), the neural net used is the basis is VGGish.

VGGish (*http://bit.ly/2MO0iZe*) is a dedicated audio classification neural net written by Google, and much like for image classfication it uses our old friend, the CNN as the basis of its workings.

VGGish is directly inspired by the VGG (*http://bit.ly/2puX19c*) image classification neural network, which is still one of the best image classifiers out there (when it came out, it blitzed the competition).

VGGish has 17 layers, mostly convolutional, and some pooling and activation layers.

When it comes to creating custom sound classifiers, transfer learning is used in a similar fashion to how it was done in "Image Classification" on page 449.

The already trained convolutional layers are left as is; they perform feature extraction of the audio signal. The existing output and classification layers of VGGish are removed and new custom outcome layers are added in for your data. These new layers associate the features extracted with the custom labels of your data.

Specifically, the three new layers are two dense layers (activated by the ReLU function) and a final softmax layer. With all of this done, you've got a sound classifier. Magic.

Speech Recognition

Speech recognition ("Task: Speech Recognition" on page 173) is a very interesting problem to solve. "Interesting," in this case also means difficult. Speech recognition has all the complexities of sound classification with the added complexity of language.

Even if you are doing speech recognition only in a single language (say English) and then only a single variant of a single language (i.e., American versus Australian English), you still need to worry about slight differences between pronunciation and the range of accepted pronunciations of words. Humans voice covers a wide spectrum and you need to handle the entire range of possibilities that offers.

Most speech recognition systems generally treat each regional variant of a language as their own unique language.

This is because even words for which each language variant agrees on the spelling can vary massively in pronunciation.

Tomato is a famous example where as an Australian (such as we authors) would say it to-mah-to (correctly, we might add), an American would say something along the line of to-may-to.

Or if you were using this book as part of a mo-bi-ul app in Australia, in America you'd probably be making the app for mo-bul.

And let's not even talk about aluminium!

To make matters worse, unlike almost everything else we've discussed, speech recognition requires a concept of memory to be baked into the model to work.

This is because spoken words are made up of phonemes, individual sounds that when chained together create a word. So, for example, the phrase "Hey, Siri" is made up of the phonemes he ey see ri.

Technically phonemes combine to create morphemes, not words, but you can think of these as related.

A morpheme is a single meaningful element that can be understood regardless of it being a valid word or not.

The word discouraging is made up of the morphemes dis, cour age and ing but the word hey, is a single morpheme.

Neural networks, despite being excellent at a lot of complex tasks, are not great at memory. Earlier, in "Sound Classification" on page 454, the sound classifier only operated on 975 milliseconds of audio at a time.

At that level of bucketing there wouldn't really be any difference between "Hey Siri" and "Hello Tim."

All of these issues are very likely the reason why, of all the machine-learning tools Apple provided, it is speech recognition that is done online on Apple's hardware. Because of this we don't really know how Apple's speech recognition service works, but we can make some good guesses based on how the offline "Hey Siri" detection works.

This section is based on the paper Apple published in 2017 (*https://apple.co/2MoHZux*) on Hey Siri.

"Hey, Siri" undergoes two passes: a low-powered but lower-quality pass, and then if that passes, a higher-quality, higher-powered one. The first pass is performed on the Always On Processor before powering up the main processor, and also uses a much smaller network than the second one.

If you are curious, the Always On Processor is part of the Motion coprocessor. So the little chip that is responsible for determining movement data has a small part that is always awake and just listening for you to say "Hey, Siri."

The Always On Processor is always active, because in order to meaningfully track movement data, it needs to be constantly gathering and analyzing sensor information. As a result, it's never powered off, and so the "Hey, Siri" detection system piggy-backs on top of this arrangement.

Luckily, this coprocessor takes so little power that being always on doesn't affect your battery in any significant way.

The model takes in 0.2 seconds of audio at a time and feeds this into a network with five dense sigmoid layers and a softmax layer. The interesting part about this network is that it is a recurrent neural net (RNN). An RNN is a neural network with memory. It gains this memory by adding the results of one pass of the network into the next pass in a loop.

This idea of a neural network with a loop in it might sound a bit weird, but it can help to think of it as a normal programming loop. With a normal loop you keep performing a task until you reach some sort of threshold.

Each iteration of the loop could, in theory, be unrolled and just written out as a series of steps that simulates the loop exactly. A recurrent neural network operates the same —you can think of each stage of the recurrence as just another neural network being fed the result of the last one alongside the new input values. Figure 11-1 shows the structure of an RNN.

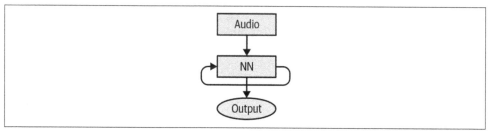

Figure 11-1. A traditional RNN

When we "unroll" the loop, Figure 11-1 becomes Figure 11-2, which is essentially a sequence of neural networks, each using both a new piece of data and the result of the previous network in the sequence.

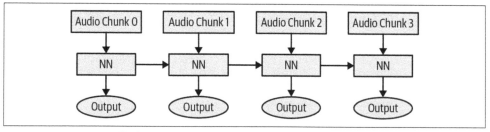

Figure 11-2. An unrolled RNN

So the sound of "Hey, Siri" despite being broken up into 0.2 seconds chunks, each individual chunk after the first one will have the results of the previous chunks, biasing the network toward determining whether "Hey, Siri" was actually said, based on a threshold.

The specific way you give an RNN the earlier network values to combine the older value with the new input value as part of an additional tanh layer added into the network, which maps the older value to one that's between -1 and 1.

This isn't really necessary to understand the basics of RNNs; it is more a specific implementation detail.

Text and Language

Handling text and language problems in machine learning is a very interesting domain. Text has one really big advantage when it comes to machine learning tasks: it is known.

Computers understand text in only a few different already known forms (these days most text is in UTF-8 form), which means the input problems become simpler.

Language, on the other hand, is a very different beast. Understanding natural language has been the holy grail of AI literally since it started as a field. Understanding language is arguably the most important task to solve in computing.

The issue is that, although languages have rules, people often see them as just guidelines. The ambiguities that exist naturally in languages are understandable among people, but can cause havoc to our poor computers.

Context is important and it is difficult to capture in text alone. Take, for example, the saying, "You can't put too much water into the nuclear reactor." Is this saying that you should not put too much water into the nuclear reactor (so be careful with the water), or is it saying it is impossible to put too much water in (so pour away)?

If you were told this the first day on your job as the Nuclear Reactor Water Pourer (which we assume is a job), you'd either know which is correct based on the context in which it was said, or you'd ask for clarification.

Other quirks of language appear when it comes time for our brains to understand text. We are fairly decent at understanding a word even if it is lightly jumbled; this is jokingly called Typoglycemia (*http://bit.ly/2MfEuGO*).

Essentially "Seems we don't *ralley lkie* typos." and "Seems we don't *really like* typos." map to the same meaning in our brain despite being different.

This is another issue we need to worry about when handling text. Basically: language is hard.

You might have seen a meme about Typoglycemia that says, according to Cambridge University, you need only the first and last letters in their correct position to read a word.

This isn't true. Not only has Cambridge not properly researched the phenomenon, it is also way more complex than just letter ordering. Basically, brains are hard, too.

A member of Cambridge University's cognition department did, however, put out a really interesting breakdown (*http://bit.ly/35CvuDy*) of the meme and discussed it in detail.

Language Identification

Language identification perfomed in "Task: Language Identification" on page 214 used the Natural Language framework, which is another task in which we aren't fully sure as to how Apple actually has done it, but again we can make some likely guesses as to how it works. Language identification tends to use a bit of a statistical approach as well as neural networks.

The first step will be to convert our input into some *n*-grams. An *n*-gram is a sequence of individual elements in the input text and can be broken down however you want.

Common breakdowns are at the word level or at the character level. If we had the input "test input please ignore" for a word-level breakdown, our *n*-grams would be "test", "input", "please", "ignore", whereas a character breakdown would be "t", "e", "s", "t", "i", "n", and so on.

In both cases, we have what are called unigrams, or 1-grams, because they look at one token of the input at a time. If we had 2-grams, or bigrams, we'd have "test input" and "te" as our first input breakdown, a trigram, or 3-gram, would give us "test", and so on.

The level of breakdown—or what *n* in the *n*-gram you should set—depends a lot on the language and what you are trying to achieve. It is one of those tasks where you are likely going to have to do a bit of guessing and checking.

If we were doing this purely statistically, after we have our *n*-grams, we could just perform a direct lookup of the *n*-gram distribution and see how closely it matches a corpus.

For example, in English the most common letters in order are "etaoin" (with *e* appearing about 12% of the time, *t* appearing 7%, and so on), so if the input has a similar breakdown, we might well be correct in saying the input is English.

This only gets better with the inclusion of more input and a larger corpus, so although English is great at gobbling up other languages' words, it's not as good at taking glyphs, so if you find a Є in your input, the chance of it being English rapidly drops, whereas the chance of it being Ukrainian goes right up.

etaoin shrdlu is roughly the 12 most common letters in English in their approximate ordering, but it is also a phrase you might have seen before. Either as the mistake phrase used to clear a line in hot lead typing (which is awesome and we should totally go back to using molten lead instead of boring and not-covered-in-boiling-hot-liquid-toxic-metal computers for typing), or the name of an early natural language AI project, SHRDLU, that seemed to understand English.

For its time (and it even holds up today) SHRDLU was amazing, giving you a conversational approach to controlling a virtual environment that handled English almost flawlessly.

SHRDLU is also arguably the first choose-your-own-adventure game, assuming that you are OK with your adventure consisting solely of stacking various colored solid blocks.

There are, however, many issues with just a statistical approach. It is especially vulnerable to small inputs, so it can be combined with our old friend, the neural network.

The neural network for this is generally a very simple classifier style network with a few dense sigmoid layers connecting to a single softmax layer for output.

Even though language identification is actually pretty darn accurate (most systems are hitting more than 90% accuracy), quite often you can also combine the machine-learning approach with additional metadata about the input.

Depending on your service, you might already have asked the user for their default language, or be able to ask their device for its locale, or you might even have their location.

Although these don't actually tell you the language of their input, they can go along way toward helping determine what language it might be.

Named Entity Recognition

Named entity recognition (NER) ("Task: Named Entity Recognition" on page 217) is another one of those tasks that doesn't feel too tricky; it seems like all you need to do is break up a sentence and then match the words to a known list and you are good to go. Unfortunately this is language, and language is hard (as mentioned).

The traditional way of performing NER relies on creating custom language grammars, which is a way of describing the structure that you are after. This is a fully manual process that must be customized for the different expected input and takes a very long time to do properly.

The advantage of these techniques is that they generally work better than any other approach—having a person or bunch of people manually work out what is best for the data is hard to beat. But they are slow and expensive to create, requiring a lot of specialized expertise to do properly.

This is still the best approach for some tasks, but most of the time a machine-learning approach will likely be what you are after. Again, we don't really know how Apple's NER system works, but we can still make some intelligent guesses as to its inner workings.

Much like everything with language, context is key, so we need to capture it in our model. Much like with speech recognition ("Speech Recognition" on page 456), you do this with an RNN. The specific subtype of RNN used here is a Long Short-Term Memory (LTSM).

LTSM is named such because even though it captures only a short amount of information, it holds it for a long time, so a small window of data is kept for ages. LTSMs have been having enormous success in a wide range of fields including robotics (*http://bit.ly/2VSBH9Q*), games (*http://bit.ly/32tmZII*), and automatic translations (*http://bit.ly/2MMLVEy*).

The main issue LTSMs are designed to fix over more traditional RNNs is the *vanishing gradient problem*, which at its simplest is the issue whereby feeding the results of one pass of the network back into the next pass has a tendency to either push values up out to infinity, or the opposite whereby they get squished to zero.

So although it is called the vanishing gradient problem, it exists for both vanishing and exploding values. In both cases, this effectively makes the net (or parts of it) useless and prevents or drastically slows training.

It might help to think about how most activation functions in neural nets operate on a 0-to-1 floating-point scale. By multiplying two small numbers together, they are going to very quickly trend to nothing.

For example, say you had two runs, the first with an output of 0.01 and the next with an output 0.9. Multiplying them together pushes the resulting value down to 0.009. The next pass will be even smaller, and so on and so on until you reach 0. So even highly positive results can be overwhelmed by very small ones, or vice versa for larger feedback values.

Although this isn't actually the issue of the vanishing gradient problem, it is a good way to quickly think about it.

The main idea behind how an LTSM actually works (as originally described by its creators hhttp://bit.ly/2VTavrj[Hochreiter and Schmidhuber in 1997]) is the concept of gates.

If you think of the information coming into and out of an RNN as a flow, from layer to layer and then loop to loop, gates can be used to modify this flow. They can add additional information, or outright prevent information flow as necessary.

The gates work by adding additional layers (using a sigmoid activation function), in which the output of this is multiplied into the existing RNN.

The sigmoid layers essentially say how much of the old knowledge should be added into the network, with a zero meaning no prior knowledge and a one meaning all prior results. Most of the time, the gates will have a value between these, letting partial amounts of prior results into the net.

There are numerous variants of these gates, and their arrangement and configuration gives the LTSM different capability, such as being able to forget information when necessary.

Another means to defeat the vanishing gradient problem is to just throw more hardware at the issue.

This is almost certainly the reason why we've seen such a huge explosion in machine learning recently. Graphics Processing Units (GPUs) and CPUs are the most affordable, accessible, and powerful they've ever been.

You can now rent (for not impossible amounts of money) what would have been seen as an introductory super computer only a decade ago.

Some issues can literally be brute-forced through to completion, as the vanishing gradient problem slows but rarely halts training. If you've got the time and money to push more power into it, you can keep training regardless.

This is not ideal, so as with almost every problem in machine learning, try thinking smarter, not harder.

The rest of the NER process is simple in comparison. We still need to break our input up into *n*-grams (generally unigrams at the word level, but this can vary based on your needs), and then we train a normal predictor based on a large pretagged corpus for training.

Lemmatization, Tagging, Tokenization

Lemmatization, tagging, and tokenization ("Task: Lemmatization, Tagging, and Tokenization" on page 218) are interesting in that they are nearly always done in a purely algorithmic approach, no fancy neural nets or complex machine learning necessary.

Lemmatization gives you the root word (or lemma) of another word, tagging tells you what grammatical form (noun, verb, etc.) a word is, and tokenization breaks up input into its individual words.

Much like with all of the language work, we don't really know how Apple has done it but we can make some intelligent guesses.

Tokenization is the most straight forward to understand. You just need to isolate each word. In English, if you break up the input based on spaces, you'd get it most of the way there.

Some quirks need to be solved, though, such as handling hyphenated words, but in English this is almost perfectly doable with a regular expression (regex). Other languages have more complex rules, but this is still generally resolvable to a series of rules that you can follow on a language-by-language basis and get the right answer.

Even though we've just said you can do it with a regex for English, don't. We did it in "Task: Sentence Generation" on page 315 as an example of how it works, but it's unlikely you'd ever have a good reason to do this in the real world.

Not only will you likely have missed some edge cases, even if you did it perfectly you'd need to write and maintain that code.

Apple (among others) has already provided a perfectly good tokenizer, so make your life easier and use that.

Lemmatization is a bit fancier in that it requires an understanding of the words that need to be lemmatized. For some words like "painting" it is easy—just drop the "ing" and you get the lemma "paint."

Not all words have such an easy root; for example, "better" and "best" both have "good" as their lemma, and "feet" has "foot." There is no obvious way to lemmatize these words.

The normal approach is to use an already determined lexical database. These are a giant corpus of words and their connections, so instead of writing a giant complex system to determine that "feet" matches "foot," you just ask the database.

One of the most popular (and quite likely one you've used without even realizing it if you've ever done any NLP work) is WordNet (*http://wordnet.princeton.edu*); it contains a gigantic number of words (more than 150,000) and their relationships within.

Tagging works in a similar fashion to lemmatization in that you ask the lexical database. Again, WordNet is another popular option here; you simply give it the word, and it says what grammatical form it is.

There is no magic behind the lexical databases, just gigantic amounts of accumulated data built up over long periods of time.

Recommendations

In "Task: Recommending Movies" on page 344 we created a movie recommender using the MLRecommender built into CoreML.

MLRecommender has a few different approaches that it can use, which as of this writing were Jaccard (*http://bit.ly/2MqBqb2*), Pearson (*http://bit.ly/2OWhpux*), and cosine (*http://bit.ly/2OXKWEo*) similarity metrics.

The default, and what we went with, was Jaccard because Jaccard works best when the relative difference between recommendations is less important than the fact that a user had or hadn't recommended something.

In the case of films, we feel that recommending (or not recommending) a movie is the most important indicator, followed by how high or low a user recommended it. At its core, Jaccard is a statistic for the difference between two sets of data. Jaccard is also called the "Intersection over Union" because it quite literally divides the intersection of the two sets by the union of the two sets. The higher the number (between 0 and 1), the closer together the two sets of data are.

The data being compared doesn't need to be tabulated data; it can be any set of data you have. For example, Jaccard indices can be calculated for images to get their numeric similarity, which can be useful for directly comparing what should be near-identical images. (We went into a bit more detail about various distance metrics in Chapter 10, if you are after more.)

In a nutshell, this works on the assumption that if two sets of data are mostly overlapping, they are likely similar to each other. This works really well for data such as movie recommendations, for which the mere existence of a recommendation implies correlation. It falls down when other aspects of the data, such as its ordering, are important. For a movie recommender, though, where we can directly see the overlap in the movies two people like, it is an excellent choice.

Prediction

In "Task: Regressor Prediction" on page 357 we used a regressor built using `MLRegressor` to perform some predictions on 1970s and 1980s Boston housing prices. We did this with very little customization or tweaking to the regressor; we basically just left all the defaults on and trusted the tools to create a working regressor for us.

The core of how regressors for predictions work are already described in lovely mathematical detail in Chapter 10 in "Linear regression" on page 418 and "Decision trees" on page 402, so we won't repeat ourselves. At their core, they are mathematical function(s) and don't use neural nets. They create a mathematical function that matches the training data. For now you can think of a regressor as a function that returns a prediction. If you are after more details, check out Chapter 10.

In the case of our regressor we went with a Gradient Boosted Regression Tree (GBRT), also known as Functional Gradient Boosting or Gradient Boosting Machines. A GBRT is essentially a collection of various decision trees wherein you take the results of each of the trees and combine them together to get a more accurate prediction than they could do by themselves. From the outside, though, they work like all regressors, in that you give them a value and they give you a predictive result for that value.

The reason we (well, `MLRegressor`) decided to use a GBRT is because they are one of the most common and reliable regression techniques out there. They work very well across a wide variety of datasets and, of particular interest in our case, they can capture nonlinear relationships very well. However, they fall down if the data is rather sparse.

How the `MLRegressor` chooses a regressor type isn't fully known, but based on some things Apple has said (*https://apple.co/2pmadNK*) we are assuming it is trying every regressor type and comparing them throughout the training process. As it continues training, it evaluates how each regressor is going and drops those that aren't doing well, eventually settling on one. It might not work like this, but at the very least this is one way you could do it and how we'd start because you can *know* this will give you a good regressor in the end. Another approach you could use, or combine with the "try them all" technique, is to run through the data and do some statistical analysis before starting training. Different regressors work well with certain types of data so it might be obvious after a quick look through the data, that one is a better option over another.

Text Generation

In "Task: Sentence Generation" on page 315, we used a Markov chain to generate a whole bunch of mostly valid English sentences using a relatively small amount of input data. Markov chains are named after Andrey Markov, a Russian mathematician who first studied and formally described them (*http://bit.ly/2MjIB4K*) in the early twentieth century. Markov chains are a graph of potential states and the chance of transition between states. Each transition is treated as memoryless, so the decision of which state to move to next depends entirely on the current state alone and not on what happened earlier. This results in a process that is impressively accurate at modeling both real-world and abstract problems. They (and their many, many variants) have been used across a staggering variety of domains, and we we feel confident saying you've used a system that has a Markov chain somewhere within.

In the technical lingo, the memorylessness of a Markov chain refers to its Markov property, which is when a stochastic (a fancy word for random chance) process is memoryless. Other systems can be memoryless but neither have a Markov property nor be a Markov chain.

In "Task: Sentence Generation" on page 315 we used Markov chains to generate sentences to talk a little bit more about their underlying principles; here, we will do something very similar, but we'll look at it from the character level instead of the word level. The approach is exactly the same, just with a smaller sample to work with. Suppose that we want to make a word-generating system with Markov chains but our input is just the phrase "hi there." This obviously isn't a lot of input, so we won't be generating much but it is small enough to show off the workings.

The first step is to collect a set of every character in the input. We want a set because we need every element to be unique, so even though there are two *e* characters in the input, we want only one in the resulting graph. This gives us the character set of [h, i, ' , 't, e, r, .] to use for generation.

Next, we need to model the transitions from one state to another. We get the odds of moving from one letter to another by looking at how often one character precedes another. Because our Markov chain is memoryless we don't need to worry about how we got to a character, just where we can go from there. So, for example, in the case of the letter *h* we can move to either an *i* or an *e*, and we can't move anywhere else from an *h*. In our input, both cases occur exactly once, so there is 50% chance of moving from an *h* to an *i* or an *e*. This gives us our initial chain, as shown in Figure 11-3.

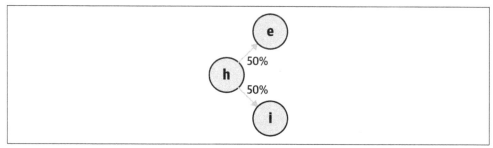

Figure 11-3. The first stage of our Markov chain

At this point we can now use this graph as is to generate some words. We can pick a point as a start node (we'll pick *h*) and follow the graph. When we reach a point with multiple choices, we basically just roll a dice and pick a path. This would mean that if we ran through this graph, we'd expect to get "he" and "hi" in equal amounts.

If we repeat the process of working out transitions and their odds for every character in our input set, we end up with our final graph looking like Figure 11-4.

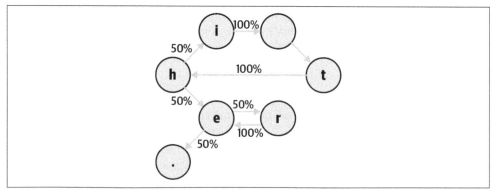

Figure 11-4. Our completed Markov chain

Now, if we follow this graph we can get words like "he", "hi", "here", "the", "there", and if we were to make only tiny changes to the graph (such as getting rid of the space as a valid node), we can get words like "hit" or "hither". By adding in a few extra corpus words that make only small changes, such as connecting the *i* node to the *r* node, we can get "their". Hopefully it is easy to see even with such a small example that you can very quickly generate a whole bunch of words just by traversing the graph. By giving this more input, we can get even more impressive results.

Markov chains, although impressive in their simplicity, have no context for what they are doing. This means that even though in our example we can easily generate valid words, we can also generate "erererere" or "ther". The chain doesn't understand that we want valid words. It just knows the odds of moving from one state to another. Don't blindly trust the Markov chain!

Generation

Generative adversarial networks (*http://bit.ly/2oQKX27*) (GANs) are one of the newest and probably the coolest tools to be added to our neural network tool belt. We used them to generate images in "Task: Image Generation with a GAN" on page 324.

They've had enormous success at (as their name implies) generative content and are the current go-to approach when you need a neural network to make something. Being called adversarial, however, might seem a bit confusing; are they fighting something, who are they fighting, why would the boffins let this happen?

"Adversarial" here means that the generative content is being compared by an assessor (also called a discriminator) to some known correct content. The generative side is trying harder and harder to make something that the assessor can't distinguish from the known content.

Both of these components—generator and discriminator—are part of the GAN. Basically, it is in competition with itself, creating better and better models to try and then fool itself.

GANs have had such success at generating life-like human images, audio, and videos that the boffins are now concerned about how they are being used for malicious intent.

Don't be the person who uses their GAN for evil.

The generator component of a GAN works in a similar fashion to a CNN autoencoder ("Image Similarity" on page 451) and often uses CNNs as its basic building blocks. Latent variables in the training content are captured, and from that we can generate new content that is similar. After being given observation data, the generator begins extracting features from the training data.

The generator eventually creates a gigantic multidimensional space of latent variables or features in the training content. When it comes time to create content, the generator uses this huge latent space with whatever input you give it and then extracts features from the input and uses them within the latent space to create new content.

Essentially the generator learns about the massive amount of features within the training content and then, when given input, uses them to build new information by matching them to its understanding of the original content. If trained poorly, the features will result in weird, noisy, and useless data; when done properly, new content—undetectable from the original—can be made.

The discriminator works in a similar fashion in that it learns about the giant latent space within the training data. However, unlike the generator, which then uses this information for creation, the assessor uses it for classification.

Two classifications are made for all input given to the assessor: real or generated. Depending on what you are attempting to do, you can reuse parts of the generator as the basis of the assessor.

Then comes the adversarial stage: while training, the two parts keep competing against each other, the generator makes new content and also provides real training content, and the discriminator classifies them.

The input given to the assessor is correctly labeled, and the assessor can use this knowledge to become better at classifying for the next round. The generator uses the result of the classification to improve its generation for the next round based on how it was classified and how strong or weak the classification was.

Each is using the new information being created to help improve its training and attempt to outdo the other part of the GAN. A perfectly trained GAN is one in which the classifier can no longer distinguish between the real and generated content and gives them both an even weighting. You don't need perfect, though.

In our GAN, the generative component uses a combination of dense and convolutional layers, and the assessor uses convolutional, pooling, and dense layers with about six layers for each of the two components. Our GAN, however, had to work on only the very limited size and color space of the MNIST images.

Bigger data domains will result in much larger and more complex GANs being necessary.

The Future of CoreML

In CoreML 3, which was introduced at WWDC 2019, Apple introduced another way to use CoreML with images. Prior to CoreML 3, to use a CoreML *.mlmodel* file with an image, you had to use a `CVPixelBuffer` object (which involved converting the image), or use Apple's Vision framework to work with CoreML.

In CoreML 3 you can use `MLFeatureValue` (*https://apple.co/35CW4fH*). `MLFeature Value` lets you pass `CGImage` objects (which means you can use image files) directly into CoreML models.

You can learn about using `MLFeatureValue` by taking a look at the contents of the class that's generated for you when you drop a CoreML model into an Xcode project. If we look back to the "Task: Image Classification" on page 120 that we built earlier, and look at the autogenerated code for our fruit-detection model, we can see that both the `WhatsMyFruitInput` class.

```
class WhatsMyFruitInput : MLFeatureProvider {

    /// Input image to be classified as color (kCVPixelFormatType_32BGRA)
    /// image buffer, 299 pixels wide by 299 pixels high
    var image: CVPixelBuffer

    var featureNames: Set<String> {
        get {
            return ["image"]
        }
    }

    func featureValue(for featureName: String) -> MLFeatureValue? {
        if (featureName == "image") {
            return MLFeatureValue(pixelBuffer: image)
        }
        return nil
    }

    init(image: CVPixelBuffer) {
        self.image = image
    }
}
```

and the `WhatsMyFruitOutput` class:

```
class WhatsMyFruitOutput : MLFeatureProvider {

    /// Source provided by CoreML

    private let provider : MLFeatureProvider


    /// Probability of each category as dictionary of strings to doubles
```

```
lazy var classLabelProbs: [String : Double] = {
    [unowned self] in return self.provider.featureValue(for:
        "classLabelProbs")!.dictionaryValue as! [String : Double]
}()

/// Most likely image category as string value
lazy var classLabel: String = {
    [unowned self] in return self.provider.featureValue(
        for: "classLabel")!.stringValue
}()

var featureNames: Set<String> {
    return self.provider.featureNames
}

func featureValue(for featureName: String) -> MLFeatureValue? {
    return self.provider.featureValue(for: featureName)
}

init(classLabelProbs: [String : Double], classLabel: String) {
    self.provider = try! MLDictionaryFeatureProvider(
        dictionary: [
            "classLabelProbs" : MLFeatureValue(
                dictionary: classLabelProbs as [AnyHashable : NSNumber]),
            "classLabel" : MLFeatureValue(string: classLabel)
            ]
    )
}

init(features: MLFeatureProvider) {
    self.provider = features
}
}
```

both conform to the `MLFeatureProvider` protocol. The `featureValue()` function is the most interesting thing here. Looking at the `featureValue()` function in the input class, we can see that it returns an `MLFeatureValue` that contains an image, automatically converted via `CVPixelBuffer`.

`MLFeatureValue` also supports `String`, dictionaries, `Double`, `MLMultiArray`, and `MLSe` quence. `MLFeatureValue` is a little outside of the scope of this book, given that we're mostly interested in *practical* AI, and this is getting quite advanced. Check out Apple's documentation for more details (*https://apple.co/35CW4fH*).

 If you want to learn more about this, we again highly recommend Matthijs Holleman's book, CoreML Survival Guide (*http://bit.ly/ 2OHSRVX*). See also "Other People's Tools" on page 55.

Next Steps

This chapter, together with the Chapter 10, has given you a little insight into what's happening *under the hood* when you build something with AI and ML. In the Chapter 12, we take that a step further and look at how we can implement a *much* lower-level piece of ML.

The Hard Way

For our last chapter, we want to take a bit of a step down into the murky world of implementation specifics. Most of this book has used neural networks to do some pretty impressive stuff, but in Chapter 10 and Chapter 11 we discussed the principles underlying machine learning, we haven't looked at how you make one of these things. How does CoreML actually create a neural network? How would you go about building one yourself from scratch? In this chapter, we peek behind the curtain and build a complete neural network using the same tools and frameworks that Apple uses.

Behind CoreML's Magic

At the very high level, CoreML works by loading in a pretrained model file, created in a tool such as CreateML or TensorFlow, and then running the model and returning predictions based upon the input you give it.

In "A Look Inside CoreML" on page 439, we spoke a bit about how the programmatic internals of CoreML work, but we glossed over the structure of the model format because it isn't important to understanding how CoreML works.

To understand what CoreML is doing, we do need at least a basic look into the format. The CoreML model format itself is based on the protobuf (*http://bit.ly/2BitthI*) serialized data format with a custom schema that allows you to define, among other things, the type of machine-learning model, the features of the model, labels, inputs and output, attributes, metadata, and anything else you need to fully describe your model.

At its core the data format precisely describes the model in such a way that another program could read, understand, and then rebuild the exact model.

For more details on the CoreML model format, check back to "The MLModel format" on page 28, earlier in the book.

This means that CoreML must read the model file and turn it into a neural network, generalized linear model, tree classifier, or whatever model type it happens to be, and then run that. The model that CoreML receives from us (an *.mlmodel*) is essentially a generic description of a model.

CoreML builds a device-specific version of the model that is optimized for the hardware it is running on. This device-specific version is built up using similar approaches to what we are going to be doing in this chapter, and doesn't change the workings of the model; it's just optimized for the device.

This new form, after it's created, is then compiled and saved as an *.mlmodelc* format and is what CoreML is actually using for running.

CoreML doesn't so much run the MLmodels, but converts them into a new form that it then runs.

If you are updating or loading models on the fly you can use the `compileModel(at:)` method on the `MLModel` class, which will take in an *.mlmodel* and create an *.mlmodelc* from that.

Despite this being the main approach for the bulk of the book, and also the general approach you should be taking, it isn't the best for seeing how CoreML works. So for this chapter, we are going to take a step back and build up a neural network ourselves using the Basic Neural Network Subroutines (BNNS) library, which is part of Apple's Accelerate framework (we mentioned this framework back in "Apple's Other Frameworks" on page 40).

This covers only the case of neural networks, and CoreML (and machine learning in general) supports far more than just neural networks, but they are currently the most popular form of machine learning and the most interesting to build from scratch.

The Accelerate framework (*https://apple.co/35FblfT*) contains more than just BNNS; it has a variety of different libraries for fast CPU acceleration.

Alongside BNNS, Accelerate also has code for vector and quaternion operations, signal processing, and sparse-matrix linear algebra solvers, among others.

Although you could write any of these yourself, Apple has already written highly optimized and hardware-accelerated versions of these that are well worth checking out.

BNNS is one of the underlying libraries that CoreML makes use of and is designed to run on the CPU. You won't often find yourself writing code that uses BNNS directly, but there is a good chance that any models you run through CoreML will be making use of it. You can use BNNS to build neural networks of any size or complexity supporting three different layer types:

- Convolution layers
- Pooling layers
- Dense layers

BNNS is often jokingly called *bananas*. Get it?

If your neural network design can be made up using those layer types (and many can be) you can create it using BNNS. BNNS is written in C, and Swift is calling the library through a bridge that lets you communicate with it as if it were native Swift code. It isn't, however, so there are a few quirks to be wary of—we point these out when we get to them.

BNNS is just one of many different technologies that Apple uses as part of CoreML.

Another technology used by CoreML that works in a very similar fashion with a similar designed, albeit slightly different-looking, API is Metal Performance Shaders (*https://apple.co/31gVroO*) (or rather, the parts of Metal Performance Shaders designed for building neural networks (*https://apple.co/2pm1YBa*)).

The main difference between BNNS and Metal Performance Shaders is that BNNS is CPU exclusive, whereas Metal Performance Shader are GPU exclusive. We are using BNNS over performance shaders for a simple reason: BNNS works on both macOS and iOS, and Metal Performance Shaders are primarily iOS-focused.

Although some macOS devices support Metal Performance Shaders, every modern Apple device supports BNNS. So this means that we can run our code in a Playground on macOS and also build it over onto iOS.

Task: Building XOR

For this task, we create a neural net that can approximate the logical XOR function. This means that it will be taking in two values, x and y, and returning one value that is the result of XORing the two values.

Essentially, what we want to create is a neural network that can match Table 12-1.

Table 12-1. Our training and testing data

x	y	Output
0	0	0
0	1	1
1	0	1
1	1	0

Please, please, *please* never use this neural network instead of the existing XOR function in Swift (or any other programming language). Not only is let output = x ^ y many orders of magnitude faster to run, it is already written and tested, has a lower energy consumption, and is easier to read (it is also 100% correct).

Our neural network can do only an approximation of XOR, and although it will be a very good approximation, neural networks are terrible choices for basic functions such as this. This is a learning exercise. Learn from it, don't use it.

We are going to be building an XOR neural network for a few different reasons. First, XOR has a bit of history in the neural net world. When neural networks were new (called perceptrons), it was discovered that as they were initially presented they couldn't perform the XOR function.

The clever AI boffins later solved this problem (through the use of hidden layers), but it is often considered one of the reasons why neural network research slowed down for a while, so it's interesting to build a solution to an old problem.

Second, XOR is a very easy function to understand. The training and testing data is very easy to come by (in fact, the testing and training data are the same, and must be) and it can't be overfitted no matter how hard or crudely you train the model.

Finally, XOR can be created using a very simple neural network, and as we are going to be making the network ourselves layer by layer, we don't want it to be too complex.

Basically, XOR is an easy, forgiving, and simple enough function with which to build a working neural net from scratch. We also hope that it's kind of fun!

The Shape of Our Network

We'll be making a multilayer perceptron with two input neurons (x and y), two hidden neurons (hidden0 and hidden1), and one output neuron (output), with each layer being fully connected to the previous layer.

We have six weights (four for the neurons connecting from the input to the hidden layer, two for the hidden layer feeding into the output), and three biases (two for the hidden neurons and one for the output neuron). Figure 12-1 shows the structure of the neural network.

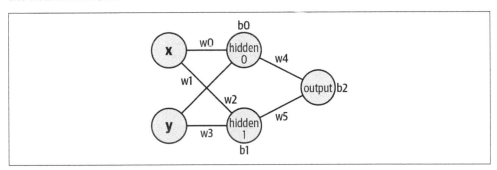

Figure 12-1. Our neural network

All of our inputs, outputs, weights, and biases are going to be floats, or more specifically, they will be arrays of floats. BNNS expects and often defaults to using this format.

Most of the time you should think of neural networks as operating over arrays of values instead of individuals. In our case, our neural network is simple enough that it might make sense to do it with scalar values passed in, but BNNS (and all ML software) is designed to support much larger networks and, as such, are set up to handle that.

As the goal of this chapter is to take a peek at how CoreML works, if we made the example too different from the approach underlying CoreML, it wouldn't really serve much of a purpose.

The Code

We're going to do all of our coding for this in a Playground. We could create a new application or service project and write our code in there, but for this example, a Playground is more than enough:

1. Create a new macOS-flavor Playground in Xcode.

2. Import the Accelerate framework. This will give us access to the BNNS library:

   ```
   import Accelerate
   ```

3. Declare two optional `BNNSFilter` variables:

   ```
   var inputFilter: BNNSFilter?
   var outputFilter: BNNSFilter?
   ```

   These will be the individual layers of our neural net. `inputFilter` will be the layer connecting the input to the hidden layer, and `outputFilter` will be the layer connecting from the hidden neurons to the output.

In almost every other neural network tool out there, these would be called *layers*, but in BNNS they are called *filters*. You can think of the filters as being the individual neuron layers that represent the connection between the layers themselves.

It doesn't really change anything, however; the basic structure remains identical, but BNNS tends to word its API to focus more on the connections between layers rather than the layers themselves. Our variables are optional because we haven't built up our layers yet, and after we are finished using the network we will want to free up the memory.

Neural networks can be quite heavy on the system, so we don't want to keep them around when we aren't using them. As such they can be `nil`, so we need to make them optional.

If you option-click the `BNNSFilter` type, Xcode will tell you it is a type alias to `UnsafeMutableRawPointer`. Swift generally discourages using pointers because when you are using them you lose a lot of Swift's fantastic type system and memory safety to help you.

In this case, however, BNNS is written in the C programming language, which just *loves* pointers, so we will be using them, as well.

We don't need to really worry too much about it; for this chapter ,we can think of pointers as variables of optional type Any, although this isn't *technically* correct. If you are after more info, on how Swift interacts with pointers, the official documentation (*https://apple.co/32jM4WC*) goes into great detail.

4. Create function stubs:

```
func buildNetwork(inputWeights: [Float],
                  inputBiases: [Float],
                  outputWeights: [Float],
                  outputBiases: [Float]) {

}

func runNetwork(_ x: Float, _ y: Float) -> Float
{

}

func destroyNetwork()
{
}
```

Here, we have three different functions for us to fill in later: `buildNetwork`, `runNetwork`, and `destroyNetwork`. The first one is responsible for creating the network itself, using the values passed in for weights and biases. The second will run our network with the provided values for x and y. Finally, `destroyNetwork` destroys our neural network and removes it from memory.

Building It Up

With our code set up, it is time to start filling out some of our function stubs; we begin by writing the code to create our neural network. The purpose of this function is to create a neural network that matches the image in Figure 12-1.

It has four parameters that give it its weight and biases, and stores the generated network into the two filter variables we set up earlier:

1. Add the following code to the `buildNetwork` function:

```
let activation = BNNSActivation(function: .sigmoid, alpha: 0, beta: 0)

let inputToHiddenWeightsData = BNNSLayerData(
    data: inputWeights,
    data_type: .float,
    data_scale: 0,
    data_bias: 0,
    data_table: nil)

let inputToHiddenBiasData = BNNSLayerData(
    data: inputBiases,
    data_type: .float,
    data_scale: 0,
    data_bias: 0,
    data_table: nil)

var inputToHiddenParameters = BNNSFullyConnectedLayerParameters(
    in_size: 2,
    out_size: 2,
    weights: inputToHiddenWeightsData,
    bias: inputToHiddenBiasData,
    activation: activation)

// these describe the shape of the data being passed around
var inputDescriptor = BNNSVectorDescriptor(
    size: 2,
    data_type: .float,
    data_scale: 0,
    data_bias: 0)

var hiddenDescriptor = BNNSVectorDescriptor(
    size: 2,
    data_type: .float,
    data_scale: 0,
    data_bias: 0)

inputFilter = BNNSFilterCreateFullyConnectedLayer(
    &inputDescriptor,
    &hiddenDescriptor,
    &inputToHiddenParameters,
    nil)

guard inputFilter != nil else
{
    return
}
```

There is a fair amount going on in here so let's try to break it down. The first line of code is creating an activation. This will be used as the activation function for the layer. We are going to be reusing the same activation function for both of our layers, although this is unlikely to be the case for larger neural networks.

We've chosen the sigmoid function as our activation function because it is a good choice for this sort of task. There are heaps of other activation functions out there, many of which might do as good or better job than sigmoid, but for this case, we know sigmoid will work, so we'll stick with it.

 Although we're not using them, there are two other parameters as part of initializing the sigmoid: `alpha` and `beta`. Our example is simple enough that we don't need to worry about tweaking those, but the `alpha` can be considered the scaling of the sigmoid, and `beta` is basically the offset.

Next, we start making layer data. The first, `inputToHiddenWeightsData`, is the data holding the weights of the input layer to the hidden layer (weights w0, w1, w2, w3 in Figure 12 1). The specific values for these come from the `inputWeights` parameter.

The most interesting part about this method is the `data_type` parameter, which lets you set what type of data is held within. Because we are planning on doing everything with floats, our data type is `BNNSDataType.float`, but there are many different options.

If we were to use data other than floats we would need to set some of the other parameters to values other than 0 because they essentially instruct the initializer how to take nonfloat data and convert it into a float. Because we've stuck with floats, we are all good without this tweaking.

Next, we do the same with `inputToHiddenBiasData` but this time this is for the biases for the hidden layer (b0 and b1), again coming from the function parameters.

 You might notice that there is both a `.float` and `.float16` data type in BNNS. `.float16` represents a 16-bit floating-point number (also called half-precision floating-point number) whereas `.float` is the full-precision form.

This means that if you don't need the full-precision floating points (and quite often you don't), you can use a half-precision float, instead, which essentially means you use less memory creating and running your network.

For our example, using half-precision floats would work fine, and if this were intended to be more than an exercise, we really should use them to reduce our memory footprint.

The next call, `BNNSFullyConnectedLayerParameters`, is where we start to hook up our input layer to our hidden layer. This struct holds all the parameters necessary for BNNS to know how to hook up the different layers, but it doesn't perform the connection itself.

In this case, we are creating a dense (fully connected) parameter list; it has an input and output of two neurons per layer (`input_size` and `output_size`), uses the weights and biases we just created, and activates using the sigmoid function we defined earlier.

After that is done, we create two `BNNSVectorDescriptor` structs. These, as their name implies, describe a vector (sometimes called a shape) that basically defines the number of elements and type of data.

In a language like Swift, this feels unnecessary because collections can normally automatically determine this information themselves. But BNNS is written in C, so we need to let it know.

Finally, we actually create our input and hidden layers and their connections. This is done using the function `BNNSFilterCreateFullyConnectedLayer`, which takes in all our previously configured weights, biases, parameters, and descriptors and creates a dense connection between our input and hidden layer. This all gets stored in our variable `inputFilter` for later use when we want to run the network. After that is done, we also perform a quick check using a `guard` statement to make sure that the creation worked before continuing.

You might notice a bunch of &s everywhere in the function call to the create the dense layer. This is again because BNNS was written in C, but in a nutshell it requires many of its parameters to be pointers.

To do this in Swift, you treat these parameters as if they were `inout` parameters, which require the & to be prepended to them being passed into a function call. If you've never seen `inout` parameters in a function before, they are quite powerful, and when used carefully they can be very useful.

Unlike a normal parameter, an `inout` parameter, can be modified by the function and the modification affects the original variable. For more details about `inout` parameters and when to use them, check out the official docs (*http://bit.ly/33AdAiK*).

With that done we can move onto the next step, creating our output layer and connecting it to the hidden layer:

1. Add the following code to the `buildNetwork` function, just below the code you previously added:

```
let hiddenToOutputWeightsData = BNNSLayerData(
    data:outputWeights,
    data_type: .float,
    data_scale: 0,
    data_bias: 0,
    data_table: nil)

let hiddenToOutputBiasData = BNNSLayerData(
    data: outputBiases,
    data_type: .float,
    data_scale: 0,
    data_bias: 0,
    data_table: nil)

var hiddenToOutputParams = BNNSFullyConnectedLayerParameters(
    in_size: 2,
    out_size: 1,
    weights: hiddenToOutputWeightsData,
    bias: hiddenToOutputBiasData,
    activation: activation)

var outputDescriptor = BNNSVectorDescriptor(
    size: 1,
    data_type: .float,
    data_scale: 0,
    data_bias: 0)

outputFilter = BNNSFilterCreateFullyConnectedLayer(
    &hiddenDescriptor,
    &outputDescriptor,
    &hiddenToOutputParams,
    nil)

guard outputFilter != nil else
{
    print("error getting output")
    return
}
```

This works in the exact same fashion as the preceding code, but it creates the layer and connections from the hidden layer to the output layer.

Now, when we call this function, we'll have a fully configured neural network built and ready to go.

Making It Work

Having a configured neural network isn't really that useful without some way of making it run, so now we're going to write the code that will actually use our neural net:

1. Add the following to the `runNetwork` function:

   ```
   var hidden: [Float] = [0, 0]
   var output: [Float] = [0]
   ```

   This code just creates two arrays of floats, which you can think of as representing the individual neurons for the hidden and output layer (so two neurons in the hidden layer, and one in the output layer). Both are initially given zeros, because we are about to use them in conjunction with the filters we built up before and we need to them have some value.

   When we write some more code, our final value for the neural network will be stored back into the `output` variable.

2. Add code to connect our input values to the hidden layer:

   ```
   guard BNNSFilterApply(inputFilter, [x,y], &hidden) == 0 else
   {
       print("Hidden Layer failed.")
       return -1
   }
   ```

   The call to `BNNSFilterApply` takes our input (which we've wrapped up into an array), connects them to the hidden neurons using the configuration we saved in our `inputFilter`, and stores the results back into the `hidden` array.

   Basically, it runs part of the neural network shown in Figure 12-2.

   The function returns an `Int` which tells us if it was able to run, with 0 meaning it worked and -1 meaning a failure. Because of this we can wrap it up inside a `guard` statement to check that it all works, as there is no point in going ahead if we can't get the input → hidden layer working.

   One nice side effect of our code is that we have this clean step before we get an output, meaning we could output the values of our hidden neurons if we wanted to for testing purposes. With that done we now need to move from the hidden layer to the output.

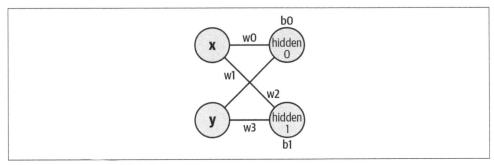

Figure 12-2. First half of the net

3. Add code to connect the value of our hidden neurons to the output layer:

```
guard BNNSFilterApply(outputFilter, hidden, &output) == 0 else
{
    print("Output Layer failed.")
    return -1
}
```

This code works identically to the previous code; the only difference is now we are using the hidden layer as input into the output and saving the result into the output layer.

From this point, whenever this code is run, the result will be stored in our output neuron, so the final step is to return it:

```
return output[0]
```

Tearing It Down

The last function we need to fill in is to clean up our neural network. A neural network requires a great deal of resources, so as soon as you are finished with one you should remove it so that it isn't sitting around taking up space.

Unlike most of your Swift code, we need to explicitly inform BNNS that it is safe to destroy the network.

Add the following code to the destroyNetwork function:

```
BNNSFilterDestroy(inputFilter)
BNNSFilterDestroy(outputFilter)
```

This function is very straightforward. It instructs BNNS to destroy the two filters that made up our neural network. After calling this method it would be impossible to run the neural network without first rebuilding it.

Using the Neural Network

With our functions filled in and ready to go, it is time to write some code to actually call them and see how our neural network functions:

1. Add the following code to the end of the Playground:

```
buildNetwork(
    inputWeights: [-6.344469 ,  6.5571136,  6.602744 , -6.2786956],
    inputBiases: [3.2028756, 3.1625535],
    outputWeights: [-7.916997 , -7.9228764],
    outputBiases: [11.601367])
```

Here, we are calling our code to build the neural network and providing data to be the weights and biases for the various layers. These numbers came from our training, which we talk about more in a moment, but for now you can assume these values are valid (because they are).

With a network built, we can begin using it

2. Add the following code just below the code you added in step 1:

```
runNetwork(0, 0)
runNetwork(0, 1)
runNetwork(1, 0)
runNetwork(1, 1)
```

These four lines are all the same: they simply run the network with different values of x and y. In our case, because XOR is such a simple function, we can easily write every possible test case and see whether they work. We have one last step before we can run the Playground and test this all out:

3. Add the following code below where we wrote our running code:

```
destroyNetwork()
```

This final step calls our code to clean up the network after we are finished playing with it. Now we can run the Playground, and you should see some results similar to this in the output sidebar of the Playground:

```
0.02640035
0.9660566
0.9661374
0.02294688
```

Approximations of XOR

At this point you might be a bit confused as to what is going on. 1^0 normally doesn't equal 0.966, and 0^1 and 1^0 should be exactly the same, so what is going on? Neural nets are universally a terrible choice for such basic functions, and that's because of how they work—it is going to be almost impossible to train one that can perfectly hit 0 and 1.

We haven't created a neural network that can perform XOR, but we've created one that makes a pretty decent guess as to what XOR is (within 96% correct of the actual answer). So what can we do about it?

Not much, really. We could try some different weights and biases, but we'll never get a perfect result. We can round and truncate the result using something similar to the following:

```
Int(runNetwork(1, 0).rounded())
```

This at least will make it look a lot closer to what we'd expect, but this is just covering up the weirdnes that is a side effect of how the neural network operates; we will never have a perfect one. But if we look at this from another angle, we have created something very interesting.

Neural networks don't "think," so it would never occur to the neural network that although something like 0.3 \^ 0.9 is gibberish to us, it will happily crunch that down and give you an answer. This means that we could add the following code just before we destroy our neural network and see what it thinks the result is of XORing all different values for 0 to 1 going up by 0.1 increments is:

```
for a: Float in stride(from: 0, through: 1, by: 0.1)
{
    for b: Float in stride(from: 0, through: 1, by: 0.1)
    {
        runNetwork(a, b)
    }
}
```

It is really tempting to think that the neural network has "solved" XOR for non-binary values. It hasn't.

The better way to think of this is as a function that takes in two values, and when these values and the output are treated as binary it performs XOR. All of its other behaviors are realistically undefined and shouldn't be trusted.

In many other situations, however, a neural network's freedom from human knowledge can be quite advantageous. Here, it is a quirk of their design.

Training

Earlier when we built our neural network, we needed to give it some weights and biases for the various layers. Where did these come from?

These came out of training our neural network. BNNS (and CoreML, for that matter) are read-only—they are designed to run through the model as presented and have no capability to train or modify a model. In machine-learning lingo, they are for inference.

This also means that, currently, any training you want to do must be done seperately from CoreML. We wouldn't be surprised if this changes over time, because modern iPhones and iPads are incredibly powerful devices and doing updates to models on device (especially when plugged in) just makes sense. For now, however, you need to do this step in isolation from your apps using CoreML.

But in our case, we don't have a pretrained model to get weights and biases from, and we can't use BNNS to do the training. Normally, when working with CoreML you can use tools like Turi Create or CreateML to create your own models, but we're even one step below that; we can't use them, so we need to try something else.

In our case, we did our training in and got those numbers from using TensorFlow (*https://www.tensorflow.org*). TensorFlow is an open source project by Google that is designed for various different types of scientific numerical applications, but has become particularly big for its machine learning capabilities.

TensorFlow supports the creation, training, and running of neural networks and in some respects is a direct competitor to CoreML (as much as two free tools can be in competition). We chose TensorFlow because it is a good tool for training neural networks, and through coremltools (*http://bit.ly/328qggE*) you can convert between TensorFlow trained models and *.mlmodel* files.

This isn't a chapter about TensorFlow, however, so we won't be going into too much detail as to how we trained our model. You can trust us, it works.

Chapter 9 covers one of the versions of TensorFlow: Swift for TensorFlow. Here we are using TensorFlow for Python.

Although Swift for TensorFlow is good, it is also in flux. So when creating very low-level networks like this one, it is a bit clunkier than we'd like; hence, Python to the rescue. In the future we expect the low level elements of Swift TensorFlow to settle down in which case building an XOR in it would be as straightforward as it is in Python.

To perform the training, we created the exact same structure of our XOR neural network in Python TensorFlow, gave it a cost function and gradient descent optimizer to train it, and let it run more than 10,000 iterations.

After that was complete, we simply asked it what the weights and biases were, and copied those over into our BNNS code. The Python code for this looks like the following:

```python
import tensorflow as tf
import numpy as np

inputStream = tf.placeholder(tf.float32, shape=[4,2])
inputWeights = tf.Variable(tf.random_uniform([2,2], -1, 1))
inputBiases = tf.Variable(tf.zeros([2]))

outputStream = tf.placeholder(tf.float32, shape=[4,1])
outputWeights = tf.Variable(tf.random_uniform([2,1], -1, 1))
outputBiases = tf.Variable(tf.zeros([1]))

inputTrainingData = [[0,0],[0,1],[1,0],[1,1]]
outputTrainingData = [0,1,1,0]
# only reshaping the data because our training input is one-dimensional
outputTrainingData = np.reshape(outputTrainingData, [4,1])

# making two activations for ouy layers
hiddenNeuronsFormula = tf.sigmoid(
    tf.matmul(inputStream, inputWeights) + inputBiases
)

outputNeuronFormula = tf.sigmoid(
    tf.matmul(hiddenNeuronsFormula, outputWeights) + outputBiases
)

# the cost function for training, this is the number the training wants to
# minimise
cost = tf.reduce_mean(
    (
        (
            outputStream * tf.log(outputNeuronFormula)
        ) + (
            (1 - outputStream) * tf.log(1.0 - outputNeuronFormula)
        )
    ) * -1)

train_step = tf.train.GradientDescentOptimizer(0.1).minimize(cost)
init = tf.global_variables_initializer()
sess = tf.Session()
sess.run(init)

# actually training the model
for i in range(10000):
    tmp_cost, _ = sess.run([cost,train_step], feed_dict={
        inputStream: inputTrainingData,
        outputStream: outputTrainingData
    })
    if i % 500 == 0:
```

```
print("training iteration " + str(i))
print('loss= ' + "{:.5f}".format(tmp_cost))

# reshaping the weights/biases into something easily printable
inputWeights = np.reshape(sess.run(inputWeights), [4,])
inputBiases = np.reshape(sess.run(inputBiases), [2,])
outputWeights = np.reshape(sess.run(outputWeights),[2,])
outputBiases = np.reshape(sess.run(outputBiases), [1,])

print('Input weights: ', inputWeights)
print('Input biases: ', inputBiases)
print('Output weights: ', outputWeights)
print('Output biases: ', outputBiases)
```

To start the training and get results, all you need do is install TensorFlow and run the script through Python.

Check back to "Python" on page 46 if you need a refresher on how to set up a Python environment.

Next Steps

So we made bad XOR? In the end, what did we *actually* achieve here?

We have a *slightly* unusual XOR, that gives us a very close answer to actual XOR with the added benefit (or is that a detriment?) that it doesn't care whether the numbers being XORed make sense. But, importantly, we got to see a simplified example of steps that CoreML follows whenever it runs a model, and we also got to make a neural net from scratch.

Hopefully, you've also seen why this is a lot of work and why letting CoreML handle it is generally the best option. If you *really* want to take it further, take a look at Apple's Metal Performance Shaders (*https://apple.co/31gVroO*). The Metal Performance Shaders framework contains a whole bunch of stuff that makes it easier to make neural networks (*https://apple.co/2pm1YBa*). Particularly, there are tools for hand-building convolutional neural network kernels (*https://apple.co/2po0Dd4*), and recurrent neural networks (*https://apple.co/2IRqxNc*).

We recommend starting with Apple's article on training a neural network with metal performance shaders (*https://apple.co/2VOtNhQ*), as well as the session from Apple's WWDC 2019 conference, "Metal for Machine Learning" (*https://apple.co/2q9LDjl*). This goes way outside *practical*, and Swift (the code in the sample is in Objective-C++).

Keep our website (*https://aiwithswift.com*) bookmarked, since we post pointers for further resources there, too!

 If you're a bit lost for what to read next, and have already book-marked our website (*https://aiwithswift.com*), we recommend the book *Practical Deep Learning for Cloud and Mobile* (*https://oreil.ly/RPPfD*). It's a great next-step, taking a different approach to the idea of *practical*, and it complements our book perfectly.

Index

A

Accelerate framework, 23, 42, 476
activity classification, 277-287
    creating model for, 283
    preparing data for, 280-283
    problem and approach, 278
    toolkit and dataset for, 278
    using model for, 286-287
activity recognition, 255-261
    building the app for, 256-261
    problem and approach, 256
AI (see artificial intelligence; machine learning)
AI-adjacent tools, 21, 46-55
    Colaboratory, 54
    Docker, 55, 371-377
    Jupyter Notebooks, 54
    Keras, 53, 326
    Pandas, 53, 198
    Python (see Python)
Anaconda Python Distribution, 47, 346
anchorPointInImage() function, 92
Anscombes quartet, 421
Apple, tools from, 20, 22-44
    (see also specific tools)
artificial intelligence (AI)
    benefits of, 7
    components, 396
    deep learning vs., 11
    definitions and functions of, 9-16
    ethical, effective, and appropriate use of, 11-16
    machine learning vs., 10
    neural networks and, 11
    objectives, 396
    task-based approach to, 16
aspectFilled() function, 296
attributes, defined, 396
audio, 173-212, 454-459
    sound classification, 184-211, 454-456
    speech recognition, 173-184, 456-459
augmentation, 289-365
    image generation with GAN, 324-342, 469-470
    image style transfer, 290-314
    recommending movies, 344-357, 465
    regressor prediction, 357-365, 466
    sentence generation, 315-322, 467-469
augmented reality, 287
AVAudioEngine, 177

B

barcode detection, 98-104, 448
behavior profiling, 436
BERT, 250, 322
bitmap drawing classification, 453
BNNS frameworks, 42, 477
BNNSFilterApply, 486
BNNSFullyConnectedLayerParameters, 484
body View, 85
Boston Housing Dataset, 358
buildNetwork function, 481
Buttons, sound classification and, 189

C

CaseIterable, 187
categorical values, 397
centerPoint() function, 94
CGContext, 302

About the Authors

Marina Rose Geldard (Mars) is a technologist from Down Under in Tasmania. Entering the world of technology relatively late as a mature-age student, she has found her place in the world: an industry where she can apply her lifelong love of mathematics and optimization. She compulsively volunteers at industry events, dabbles in research, and serves on the executive committee for her state's branch of the Australian Computer Society (ACS) as well as the AUC. She loves data science, machine learning, and science-fiction. She can be found on Twitter @TheMartianLife and online at https://themartianlife.com.

Dr. Paris Buttfield-Addison is cofounder of Secret Lab (https://www.secret-lab.com.au and @TheSecretLab on Twitter), a game development studio based in beautiful Hobart, Australia. Secret Lab builds games and game development tools, including the multi-award winning ABC Play School iPad games, Night in the Woods, the Qantas airlines Joey Playbox games, and the Yarn Spinner narrative game framework. Paris formerly worked as mobile product manager for Meebo (acquired by Google), has a degree in medieval history, a PhD in Computing, and writes technical books on mobile and game development (more than 20 so far) for O'Reilly Media. Paris particularly enjoys game design, statistics, law, machine learning, and human-centred technology research. He can be found on Twitter at @parisba and online at http://paris.id.au.

Dr. Tim Nugent pretends to be a mobile app developer, game designer, tools builder, researcher, and tech author. When he isn't busy avoiding being found out as a fraud, he spends most of his time designing and creating little apps and games that he won't let anyone see. Tim spent a disproportionately long time writing this tiny little bio, most of which was spent trying to stick a witty sci-fi reference in, before he simply gave up. Tim can be found on Twitter at @The_McJones, and online at http://lonely.coffee.

Dr. Jon Manning is the cofounder of Secret Lab, an independent game development studio. He's written a whole bunch of books for O'Reilly Media about Swift, iOS development, and game development, and has a doctorate about jerks on the internet. He's currently working on Button Squid, a top-down puzzler, and on the critically acclaimed award winning adventure game Night in the Woods, which includes his interactive dialogue system Yarn Spinner. Jon can be found on Twitter at @desplesda, and online at http://desplesda.net.

Colophon

The animal on the cover of *Practical Artificial Intelligence with Swift* is the rufous-bellied swallow *(Cecropis badia)*. Like other swallows, this 7-inch-long songbird has a deeply forked tail and long, pointed wings that afford it efficiency and control in flight. The "rufous" in its name stems from the Latin word for "red," because of its rust-colored underside. Its song varies from a gentle warble to a sharp "pin" or "tweep."

This bird is native to the Malay Peninsula, from southern Thailand down to Singapore at the southern tip. In this habitat, it feeds on flying insects and favors hills and cliff faces, although nests are often found in caves, under bridges, and on buildings. Mating season is from April through June. Males and females work together to build their mud nests, incubate eggs, and raise their young. Swallows mate for life.

Swallows are so called because of the way they feed—by gulping down insects in mid-flight.

Many of the animals on O'Reilly covers are endangered; all of them are important to the world.

The cover illustration is by Karen Montgomery, based on a black and white engraving from *Wood's Illustrated Natural History*. The cover fonts are Gilroy Semibold and Guardian Sans. The text font is Adobe Minion Pro; the heading font is Adobe Myriad Condensed; and the code font is Dalton Maag's Ubuntu Mono.

O'REILLY®

There's much more where this came from.

Experience books, videos, live online training courses, and more from O'Reilly and our 200+ partners—all in one place.

Learn more at oreilly.com/online-learning

Milton Keynes UK
Ingram Content Group UK Ltd.
UKHW030638051024
449225UK00007B/136